MW01059213

Environment, subsistence and system

Themes in the Social Sciences

Editors: *Jack Goody & Geoffrey Hawthorn*

The aim of this series is to publish books which will focus on topics of general and interdisciplinary interest in the social sciences. They will be concerned with non-European cultures and with developing countries, as well as with industrial societies. The emphasis will be on comparative sociology and, initially, on sociological, anthropological and demographic topics. These books are intended for undergraduate teaching, but not as basic introductions to the subjects they cover. Authors have been asked to write on central aspects of current interest which have a wide appeal to teachers and research students, as well as to undergraduates.

First books in the series

Edmund Leach: *Culture and Communication: the logic by which symbols are connected: an introduction to the use of structuralist analysis in social anthropology*

Anthony Heath: *Rational Choice and Social Exchange: a critique of exchange theory*

P. Abrams & A. McCulloch: *Communes, Sociology and Society*

Jack Goody: *The Domestication of the Savage Mind*

Jean-Louis Flandrin: *Families in Former Times: kinship, household and sexuality*

John Dunn: *Western Political Theory in the Face of the Future*

David Thomas: *Naturalism and Social Science: a post-empiricist philosophy of social science*

Environment, subsistence and system

The ecology of small-scale social formations

ROY ELLEN

University of Kent at Canterbury

CAMBRIDGE UNIVERSITY PRESS

Cambridge
London   New York   New Rochelle
Melbourne   Sydney

Published by the Press Syndicate of the University of Cambridge
The Pitt Building, Trumpington Street, Cambridge CB2 1RP
32 East 57th Street, New York, NY 10022, USA
296 Beaconsfield Parade, Middle Park, Melbourne 3206, Australia

First published 1982

Printed in the United States of America

Library of Congress catalogue card number: 81-18035

British Library Cataloguing in Publication Data
Ellen, Roy
Environment, subsistence and system: the
ecology of small-scale social formations.
– (Themes in the social sciences)
1. Anthropo-geography
I. Title   II. Series
304.2   GF41

ISBN 0 521 24458 7 hard covers
ISBN 0 521 28703 0 paperback

For Nikki

Contents

vwvwvwvwvwvwvwvwvwvwvwvwvwvwvwvwvwvwvwvwvwvwvwvwvwvwvwvwvwvwvwvwvwvwvwvwvwvwvw

Preface   *page* xi
Acknowledgements   xv

1   ENVIRONMENTAL DETERMINISM AND CAUSAL   1
    CORRELATION
    Environmentalism – some inadequacies of environmental-
    ism – a question of scale – the culture-area concept – types of
    environmental correlation – natural and humanly modified
    environments – behavioural and environmental factualism –
    correlation and causation

2   POSSIBILISM AND LIMITING FACTORS   21
    Possibilism – human interference and the modification of
    pristine ecosystems – particularism, functionalism and the
    neglect of ecology – correlative studies in the possibilist
    tradition – limiting factors – swidden cultivation and settle-
    ment – carrying capacity – environmental limits on the selec-
    tion of cultivation sites – key variables and prime movers –
    conclusion

3   CULTURAL ECOLOGY AND THE EXPLANATORY   52
    IMPERATIVE
    Julian Steward – 'hunter-gatherer' societies and the patrilocal
    band – monographic cultural ecology cultural material-
    ism and vulgar Marxism – the critique of cultural ecology

4   HUMAN ECOLOGY AND THE BIOLOGICAL   66
    MODEL
    Biological and human ecology – the idea of ecosystem –
    defining the boundaries of the ecosystem – micro-
    environments – ecological niche and symbiosis – generalized
    and specialized ecosystems – objections and limitations to
    biological concepts – conclusion

Contents

5 THE FLOW OF ENERGY AND MATERIALS 95
Introduction – the character of human energy relations – material cycles and nutrient flow – ethnography and human energetics – the flow of energy in a Maring population – describing energy and nutrient flow – energy yield, consumption and dietary studies – energy expenditure – problems and technical difficulties in the collection of ecological data – energy, materials and adaptation – the argument for hard data

6 ECOSYSTEMS AND SUBSISTENCE PATTERNS I 123
Variation in human ecological systems – modes of subsistence and subsistence techniques – total ecological production – total ecological effort – ecological efficiency – patterned output and techniques – patterned ecological effort according to activity – the patterned character of energetic efficiency

7 ECOSYSTEMS AND SUBSISTENCE PATTERNS II 154
Yield, effort and efficiency over time – spatial distribution – fraction of population – problems in describing subsistence

8 SYSTEMS AND THEIR REGULATION 177
Systems theory and the analysis of ecosystems – complexity, closure and process – negative feedback and homeostasis – the cultural regulation of ecological relations – canons of proof, ethnographic omission and sociological explanation – the problem of closure – equilibrium models – ecological functionalism – open systems and purposive behaviour – cause and effect – group adaptation – change and positive feedback – systems language, concepts and representations – systems as frameworks and explanation

9 INFORMATION AND THE MANIPULATION OF THE ENVIRONMENT 204
Introduction – interpretative and cognitive models – the analysis of classifications and its critique – the range and relevance of ethnoecological data – indigenous classifications of land and vegetational surfaces – information and decision making, the impact of information and scheduling – generative analysis of ecological end-states – reassessment

10 ADAPTATION: A SUMMARY AND RECONSIDERATION 236
Introduction – mechanisms of cultural adaptation – defini-

Contents

tion and measurement – levels of adaptation – temporal
context – context and contradictions – conclusion

11   THE REPRODUCTION AND EVOLUTION OF SOCIAL AND   252
     ECOLOGICAL SYSTEMS
Material flow and the flow of value – ecological systems and
social formations – system and generation – conceptualizing
evolution and history – the relationship between phylogenetic and cultural evolution – the problem of transition –
population, subsistence change and energy output – the
evolution of open systems

12   ECOLOGY IN ANTHROPOLOGICAL METHOD AND   274
     THEORY
On empirical contributions and techniques – of frameworks
and theory – resisting a discourse of oppositions and imma-
nence

Notes   280
Bibliography   287
Name Index   313
Subject Index   319

Preface

ʊʍʊ

During the last hundred years an enormous amount has been written, under various guises and for differing purposes, on what might be described as human ecology. It is not the aim of this work to reproduce it. Nor do I intend to present broad programmatic statements or make any claims for the possibility of developing some integrated subject-area and approach stemming from biology, as proposed by some writers. Such claims are theoretically naive and call for impossible programmes of empirical research. Instead, my aim is to tackle certain ecological issues which have a bearing on ethnographic description and analysis, contemporary social theory and the general anthropology of environmental relations.

This area of interests cannot be isolated satisfactorily in either a substantive or a formal sense. To do so would either give the impression that all analyses of culture and social relations dissolve into an all-embracing ecology, or that this area represents an autonomous sub-discipline. Both extremes are mistaken. Without necessarily elevating the ecology of human subsistence to the status of theory, domain or discipline, the area can be taken to represent a field – a problematic – that historically has acquired some degree of autonomy, but which contributes only partially (though critically) to a more general anthropology. It is *ecological* in the sense that it is broadly concerned with the interplay between human population behaviour and environmental variables, in terms of spatial and temporal relations involving the exchange of energy, material and information.[1] It is *anthropological* (rather than narrowly *cultural* or *social*) in contrast to an ecology focussed on physiological and genetic relations. The separation does not imply that behavioural, physiological and genetic aspects of ecology are unrelated. This is demonstrably not the case. The separation is practical, though not so arbitrary that it is impossible to find some phenomenological legitimacy.

The present work consists of two overlapping parts. As the concerns of the first part diminish, so those of the second increase; there is no clear dividing line.

The first part is a series of discussions of models proposed within the last hundred years to explain and examine certain facets of the relationship between human behaviour and environment in an anthropological idiom: determinism, possibilism, cultural ecology, ideas derived from modern biology, energetics and systems theory, and a critique of such work. Each model is discussed in terms of both its usefulness and the problems revealed in the light of more recent developments. Although the approach adopted is broadly a historical one, it is not intended to be a history of the study of human–environment relations as such. There have been some attempts to accomplish this end, but they have been swash-buckling, ideological and trivializing (e.g. M. Harris 1968, Feldman 1975). My aim is to look at the theoretical essentials of each model and its substantive contribution to description and explanation; I am not concerned with personalities. It is assumed that overall scientific progress is cumulative and that in order to understand the dimensions of an ecological problematic it is necessary to consider various attempts to wrestle with the environmental equation in relation to contemporary theory and analysis in this field. For each case I present a broad outline of the structure of the model, an indication of the theoretical, methodological and practical difficulties it raises, and an account of the applicability of those propositions or aspects of the model which are still of analytic value. There is also an attempt to show how each model has tried to overcome the inadequacies of earlier approaches and the extent to which it has been successful. In the perspective of the history of scientific ideas no model is ever a complete waste of time; most contain an elemental idea of fundamental importance, though this is often masked by extreme formulations or caricatures of the positions held up by critics as exemplars for parody and rejection. Each set of ideas is conditioned by its contemporaneous intellectual, ideological, and social milieu, and each has contributed, if only temporarily and in a minor way, to an overall understanding. With each shift in the paradigm it is characteristic of the structure of science that the rejected model leaves certain ideas which carry over and may be subsequently built on and incorporated into new models. It is these ideas I wish to salvage. This is the familiar process of the dialectics of critical reasoning. If there were no continuity of this kind science would not be possible.

Recent research on small-scale populations has involved the application of ecological models for explanatory and descriptive purposes, and, where appropriate, methods and data drawn from biological ecology and bioenergetics. This has had significant effects in terms of tangible results, explanatory hypotheses and general theory. It has demonstrated the ecological context and implications of various behaviour patterns; it has influenced speculation on the evolution of social behaviour by seeing it in terms of the progressive modification of human ecosystems; in some cases it has altered entrenched assumptions about the structure of subsistence economies and patterns of settlement. It has also furnished new and detailed data for the analysis of productive processes. The employment of a systems approach has helped focus on the integration of particular ecological variables, rather than on the earlier attempts to obtain broad correlations between social organization and environment.

The second part of this book, which begins to develop largely from Chapter 5 onwards, is an outline review and introduction to this recent research, and a reaffirmation of the usefulness of certain methods and analytical procedures. It introduces problems involved in the use of ecological concepts and models, to enable the reader to sort out fact from fantasy in the considerable and still-growing body of writing which employs such approaches. It is primarily about small-scale human systems, although it would be impossible and unproductive to draw a clear distinction between these and larger industrial and trading systems. Certainly, no attempt has been made to examine the environmental relations of all existing or possible human systems. As this is a work of social and anthropological theory, as well as a guide to methods and literature, I have avoided detailed discussion of the concepts and data of biological ecology, nutrition, mathematics, epidemiology and demography, unless directly relevant to the topic at hand. Such discussions are, on the whole, not a useful part of a book concerned with human cultural behaviour and social relations, and can sometimes be misleading. These matters are discussed adequately elsewhere, and can be located through consulting the bibliography. Equally, I have avoided repetitious coverage of conventional non-ecological analyses of social formations, *so far as this is possible*, for environmental relations cannot be fully understood except in conjunction with an analysis of social relations in general. To this end, Chapter 11 (which is unashamedly general in character) tries to bring together the social theory most pertinent to an examination of environmental interactions. My focus is therefore on what is fashionably described as the 'interface' between social organization and ecological relations. In doing this I am attending to an area traditionally neglected in most presentations of British social anthropology.

This book was conceived in 1975. Even before that date, a large body of work (much of it exemplary) was available in the area of the ecology of small-scale populations. For this reason citations, of recent studies in particular, are perforce selective and illustrative. Sometimes references are to general and bibliographic sources rather than the specific cases. On the other hand, it has sometimes been expedient to refer to my own ethnographic research. Its obvious accessibility has made it a convenient source of simple and suitable illustrations, but I hope it is not too obtrusive.

A book of this kind is neither intended nor able to be exhaustive, and I have tried to strive for coherence rather than present an unwieldy synthesis. Since I began my research much more work has become available, including several general textbooks. As developments are so rapid in this area – subject as it is to the combined intelligences and resources of a variety of disciplines – there would be little need to justify a further general work. But, as I have indicated, my aims are in some important respects different, as are some of the theoretical considerations to which I attach particular significance. A kind reviewer (Taylor 1979:180) has described an earlier brief introduction by me on the same subject as 'a much-needed guide for the perplexed in search of what constitutes the discipline'. Perhaps this book might best be regarded as an extension of that less ambitious piece.

Acknowledgements

vvvvvvvvvvvvvvvvvvvvvvvvvvvvvvvvvvvvvvvvvvvvvvvvvvvvvvvvvvvvvvvvvvvvvvvvvvvvvvvvvvvvvvvvvvvvvv

Some of the material incorporated into this book has already appeared elsewhere, in the same or in a slightly different form. Parts of Chapter 2 have appeared as 'Anthropology, the environment and ecological systems', an introduction to *Social and Ecological Systems*, edited by Philip Burnham and myself (1979, Association of Social Anthropologists Monograph 18). Part of Chapter 8 has been published in the same volume as 'Sago subsistence and the trade in spices: a provisional model of ecological succession and imbalance in Moluccan history'. Parts of Chapters 5, 7 and 12 have appeared in 'Problems and progress in the ethnographic analysis of small-scale human ecosystems' in *Man* (N.S.), 1978 (vol. 13, pp. 290–303). I would like to thank the editor of *Man*, Academic Press and the Association of Social Anthropologists for permission to use this material. An earlier version of Chapter 7 was first presented to a British Ecological Society Tropical Group meeting in October 1978; it is published here for the first time.

I am grateful to the following publishers and learned journals for permission to reproduce short passages, tables and diagrams from the work of authors whose names are acknowledged in the text: Academic Press, Addison-Wesley, Allen and Unwin, *The American Journal of Sociology*, *American Naturalist*, *Annual Review of Ecology and Systematics*, Antropologica (Sociedad de Ciencias Naturales la Salle), *Behavioural Science*, Bernice P. Bishop Museum, Cambridge University Press, Clarendon Press, *Current Anthropology*, Duckworth, Edward Arnold, Greenwood Press, Harvester Press, *Human Ecology* (Plenum), Martinus Nijhoff, Methuen, Oxford University Press, Pergamon Press, *Progress in Geography*, Rand McNally, Ronald Press, *Scientific American* (W. H. Freeman), Seminar Press, *Social Science Information*, Tokyo University Press, *Transactions of the Connecticut Academy of Sciences*, University of California Press, University of Illinois Press, Wiley–Interscience, William Brown and Yale University Press.

Hilary Callan, Professor G. Ainsworth Harrison and Professor J. S. Weiner have been helpful in clarifying various matters, while David

Acknowledgements

Reason will recognize the effects of some justifiably stiff criticism in Chapter 1. The original figures were drawn by Barbara Glover and Jane Shepherd. Nikki Goward has read the entire draft manuscript with great care, and with no less insight.

ROY ELLEN
University of Kent at Canterbury

1

vv

Environmental determinism and causal correlation

Huntington explained the Mongol migrations by the fluctuations in rainfall and barometric pressure in the arid zones of central Asia. Brooks carried on the good work by basing a graph of rainfall in central Asia on the migrations of the Mongols! The first extrapolated from the barometer to the Mongols, and the second, with even less justification, from the Mongols to the barometer. What better example of a serpent biting its own tail?   Emmanuel le Roy Ladurie 1972:17

ENVIRONMENTALISM

Ecology could no more have existed as a science in the early nineteenth century than could biology one hundred years earlier (Foucault 1970: 125–65). Although both had precursors (geography on the one hand, and natural history on the other), the material and intellectual conditions just did not exist. While the ideas associated with this shift (those we associate with Charles Darwin and Ernst Haeckel) have been very important in shaping the development of ecological studies in anthropology, the investigation of man–environment relations in general has a far longer history. It has been subject to a wide spectrum of influences, principally emanating from the philosophies of evolutionism (in its widest sense), materialism and environmentalism. Although these labels are by no means mutually exclusive, I am here principally concerned with the last of them.

The term 'environmentalism' is generally applied to explanatory schemes which maintain that human social and cultural behaviour is to a large extent determined, in a mechanistic fashion, by the natural habitat. Philosophically, it corresponds to what the Russian historian Lev Mechnikov called 'geographical fatalism' (Matley 1972:109–10). It is a point of view which has a lengthy and sometimes ridiculous pedigree, traceable – like all good things – to the ancients: Aristotle,

1

WP

Herodotus, Polybius, Hippocrates[1] and Marcus Vitruvius Pollio. It has
been brought down to us via Ibn Kaldun, Isidore of Seville and such
Enlightenment thinkers as Jean Bodin and Montesquieu in France,
Helvetius and d'Holbach in Switzerland and John Arbuthnot in England (F. Thomas 1925). For Marvin Harris (1968:10–12, 55–6) it is in
John Locke's *An essay concerning human understanding* that we find the
formal rationale and stimulus for the idea that environment conditions
thought and social action. However, historical evidence seems to suggest that ethnographic environmentalism owes more to geography
and geographical determinism than to an abstract concern with epistemological issues.

There is little to be gained here by rehearsing the arguments of
these writers, particularly since they have already received extensive
treatment elsewhere (F. Thomas 1925, M. Harris 1968). The basic
contention of environmentalism is that much (if not all) human social
behaviour, physical form and psychological make-up is attributable to
climate, although there are differences of opinion as to what traits
different climatic conditions give rise to. Plato and Aristotle viewed
Greece as providing the ideal climate for government; for Montesquieu
progress was stimulated in regions of strong winds and great storms.
Such crude attempts at explaining social activity have continued into
the present century in a modified form, as allegedly scientific writing
as well as popular tracts. Ellsworth Huntington (1924:301), for example, could still claim that the 'highest' forms of religion were to be
found in temperate zones.

That environmentalist work most relevant to the purposes of this
book is the nineteenth-century tradition of geographical determinism,
embodied in the work of the German, Friedrich Ratzel. The work of
Ratzel (1889, 1896) involved the first systematic attempt to relate extant
ethnographic literature to geographical causation. In so doing it
formed the root of what has been called the anthropogeographical
school. The dominant concept of this approach was that of 'habitat',
differences in which were often regarded as sufficient to explain cultural diversity.

Although the environmentalism of Ratzel has considerable failings,
it seems positively mild compared with the extreme positions adopted
by Victor Cousin and Ratzel's own student, Ellen Churchill Semple.
For Cousin social structure could be read from a map in much the same
way as we interpret contours (Spate 1968:93); and in not allowing
cultural factors a role in human evolution Semple (1911) adopted a
similar position (Sauer 1934:661). Both 'out-Ratzeled Ratzel'. Ratzel
had qualified his doctrine in various ways by making some allowance
for the independent influence of cultural and historical factors, and by

employing the judicious language of trends and tendencies where appropriate (Wanklyn 1961). The same is true of the work of Otis Mason (1895) and G. Holmes (1919:47) in the United States. However, whatever the differences between these writers, and notwithstanding the fact that this is still an area of debate, their general disposition is clear.

At about the same time G. V. Plekhanov was exploring environmentalist theory in the context of Marxist analysis. The main difference between the anthropogeographers and the Russian environmental Marxists seem to have been that for the former the environment could, in principle, affect any aspect of culture; while for the latter it was above all the productive forces which were determined in this way. The doctrinal basis of this view is not altogether clear. Indeed, Marx has often been directly criticized for having transferred the determining forces to the economy and neglecting the role of nature (Matley 1972:113). One possible source of this misconception is the section in *The German ideology* where Marx notes that the writing of history must ultimately begin from natural events (McLellan 1971:34), while there are several passages in Engels's *Dialectics of nature* which might be given an environmentalist interpretation (Matley 1972:113–15). But, in general, it must be said that the relationship between environment and economy in the writings of both Marx and Engels is much more complex and subtle (e.g. Marx 1964:82, 86–7; Schmidt 1971, Parsons 1977). Neither insisted on the infinite capacity of humanity confronted with nature, nor on the inescapable determination of the same by its conditions of existence.

SOME INADEQUACIES OF ENVIRONMENTALISM

The shortcomings of the environmentalist position – whether Ratzelian or vulgar Marxist – have become clear in the light of subsequent geographical, anthropological and ecological research. In its paradigmatic form, the approach was basically mechanistic, concerned with simple unidirectional causation and admitting little (if any) scope for a dialectical relationship between historical and material factors. It provided an idealist formal theory and a classification into which static societies could conveniently be slotted. Its methodology and popularity were rooted in a positivistic and statistical empiricism, that inductivist view of science which begins with careful unprejudiced observation of facts and ends with their correlation: a vision of science as simple cause and effect. This crude scientism ignores the possibility that it is only because of the simplicity of the grounds for prediction of objects and events studied in physical science that it is possible to test

3

hypotheses to a relatively high degree of probability. The grounds for predicting social phenomena and events are infinitely more complex, and because of this hypotheses are generally only confirmed to a low probability.[2] Moreover, empiricist approaches specify (amongst other things) what can be correlated without always making the underlying model explicit.

This gives rise to a further difficulty: that the problematic of environmentalism is conceived in such polar Aristotelian terms as 'environment' versus 'culture'. It is inevitable that problems specified in such gross terms should elicit gross and unhelpful answers (Geertz 1963:1, Vayda 1965:3). At the ideological level this is linked to such notions as 'man against nature', the 'conquest' of nature, nature existing for the provisioning of society, and that key nineteenth-century idea of the emergence of *Homo sapiens* from environmental dependency (Abbott 1970, Anderson 1973:201). In this view progressive improvement through humanization of the earth rests with the development of the arts and sciences, although (paradoxically) the treatment of the environment as a reified whole becomes increasingly difficult as humans gain increasing mastery over it. Such assumptions and propositions are evident both at the level of global generalization and in specific ethnographic cases. Generally speaking, however, the more specific the case, the more modification is necessary to the pure environmentalist explanation; the more exceptional the instances, the more intricate the argument and the less convincing the explanation.

There is now an increasing number of empirical studies showing that what was previously regarded as environmentally determined behaviour is more likely to be a function of social factors well within the limits imposed by the environment. For example, environment has previously been held to be an adequate explanation for the nomadic movement of food-collecting communities. Intensive ethnographic research in recent decades has shown that this is very often wishful-thinking. Among the reasons Woodburn (1972:201–6) lists for group movement among the Hadza of the Lake Eyasi region of Tanzania are nightmares, plagues of insects, game killed at a distance from the settlement, fouling of the camp with debris and excreta, death, illness, and fission due to social conflict. Adequacy of food resources is only one of many variables involved.[3]

It is also important not to confuse environmentalism as a paradigm with environmental determinism as an explanation of specific empirical observations, just as it is necessary to distinguish philosophically between ideological empiricism and empirical data. That in certain instances human behaviour is determined by environmental variables is not only a testable hypothesis, but one which is demonstrably true in common-sense terms. It is an entirely different matter to claim that whole economies, even subsistence patterns, are determined by the environment. What is both theoretically sterile and misleading is to see man–environment correlations as legitimate ends in themselves and to reduce investigation and analysis to the mechanical attainment of this end.

The methodological difficulties of environmentalism are in part engendered and compounded by *post hoc* historical and literary analysis. In saying this I am not suggesting that secondary materials cannot be used to advantage in other ways, but rather that their use is particularly conducive to the kind of inductivist approach I have outlined. Correlations are often made on the basis of flimsy and incomplete records, or even casual observations. How is it possible to demonstrate convincingly an environmentalist hypothesis given such evidence, especially when we know of the difficulties of testing them under contemporary fieldwork conditions?

It is important to remember that environmental variables usually interact with social phenomena with great subtlety and at a micro-ecological level (Vayda 1965:3), where the key processes can seldom be satisfactorily understood except for situations where fresh data are continually available (Leach 1961:304–6). Thus, while it is impossible to establish a correlation between wind systems and the arrangement of camps among the nomadic Hadza, it *is* possible to show that the direction of the prevailing wind and the presence of trees combine to influence the dispersion of huts and the orientation of their entrances (Woodburn 1972:195). Social formations or their constituent analytical components – settlement patterns, modes of production, institutional structures, economies or whatever – are rarely simply the product of specific environmental conditions.[4] One thing is certain: whatever remains of value in the environmentalist position is not to be found in programmatic statements or rhetorical assertions, but in the application of models and hypotheses to concrete ethnographic cases.

A QUESTION OF SCALE

The problem of drawing correlations between environmental and social phenomena is very much a question of magnitude – the geographical (or demographic) scale of the correlations postulated. It is scale which determines the number of dependent and independent variables that may be involved in a single correlation. There is no particular level below which the problem of the influence of multiple variables is entirely overcome but, in a statistical sense and for most practical ethnographic purposes, the more specific the correlation the

5

greater the possibility of there being a single determining relationship and the greater the accuracy in predicting future events under specified conditions. Thus Huntington's proposition (1924:314) that stimulating climates give rise to higher civilizations involves a whole range of untested and untestable assumptions at too great a level of generality. The much more limited proposition that among the Nuaulu of eastern Indonesia seasonal variability in rainfall affects garden output is stated in sufficiently precise terms to be testable, subject to the limitations involved in testing any proposition. It might be considered that such a correlation is of so low an order as not to be worth testing empirically, other than on the basis of casual observation. This, however, relates to the question of value accorded to precision in scientific work. It is quite another matter, and one which tends to vary from one subject-area or discipline to the next. The point is that by fragmenting gross environmental categories ('the environment', 'the climate', and so on) into constituent variables there is a greater probability of arriving at scientifically valid statements. This is not to say, however, that we can automatically assume that there is a *direct* causal relationship between the variables specified.

Figure 1.1 provides an example of how gross environmental categories can be reduced to manageable proportions in terms of ethnographically relevant variation within the area appropriated by a single population, in this case swidden agriculturalists. Swidden cultivation is a subsistence technique whereby plots are created in forest or bush clearings by cutting, drying and burning or mulching. Such plots are usually cultivated for only a few years before they return to fallow. The first point to be made with regard to Figure 1.1 is the extensiveness of possible sources of environmental variation. However, the diagram is by no means exhaustive, each of the categories being capable of further subdivision depending on the problem being investigated. In some cases it may be necessary to partition available sources of water and moisture (1.1) into, say, daily precipitation (1.1.1), proportion of rain–days (1.1.2), soil moisture (1.1.3) and dispersion of water-courses (1.1.4).

The second point to note is the interconnectedness of variables. For example, subsurface macro- and microbiology (2.2.6) may be highly dependent on local temperature (1.3). In fact, some variables can appear equally legitimately under different headings, as with soil moisture classified as both 1.1.3 and 2.2.5. This only goes to show the inadequacies of any simple classification of variables in this way. The taxonomy depicted in Figure 1.1 by no means reflects the objective relations between these things. It is only a construct for ordering data for the purposes of analysis. Such classifications are necessary in any systematic treatment of the subject. They indicate the possible extent

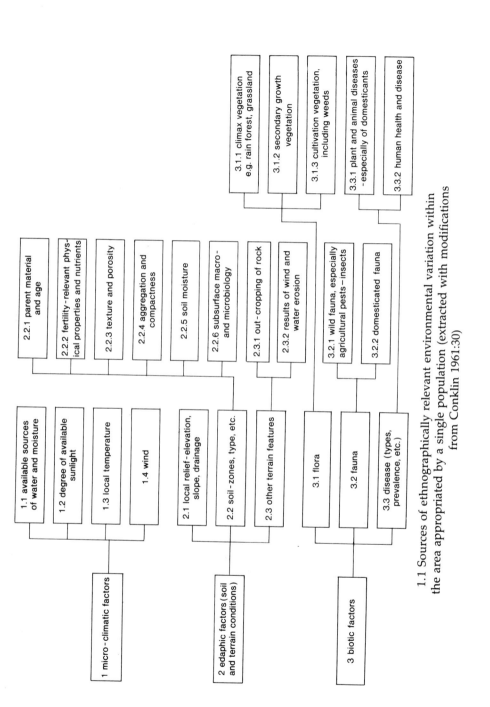

1.1 Sources of ethnographically relevant environmental variation within the area appropriated by a single population (extracted with modifications from Conklin 1961:30)

7

of relevant variables, so ensuring completeness of description, fore-stalling the exclusion of critical factors and widening understanding. In short, such *aides-mémoires* promote rigour in analysis.

A third and final point to make in this connection is that it has been necessary to include man-modified elements of the environment (altered topographies, artifacts, domesticated flora and fauna) along-side 'natural' components (3.1.1.–3.3.2), clearly indicating the diffi-culty of separating these two kinds of variables analytically.

All three points made above – the complexity of environmental variation, the interconnectedness of variables and the relationship between natural and artificial factors – anticipate matters to be de-veloped below and in subsequent chapters.

THE CULTURE-AREA CONCEPT

The question of geographical scale is inevitably linked to the culture-area concept. In its most elementary form, this is the spatial or geo-graphical delineation of entire social formations, or associations of linked cultural particularities. It has been used as a classificatory de-vice, a descriptive and comparative tool and a method for the tran-scription of culture history. More important, it is a test of the validity of a particular kind of environmentalist approach. If environment does, indeed, determine culture then it must be expected that comparison will reveal geographical regularities.

The culture-area concept has its immediate scientific origins in the work of Ratzel and was further developed by Mason. The latter deline-ated, though imprecisely (Vayda and Rappaport 1968:481), twelve 'ethnic environments' for the North American region (O. Mason 1895). This schema, as modified by W. H. Holmes (1914), formed the basis for Wissler's later frameworks (e.g. 1917). It was Wissler who first recog-nized that the natural areas of North America corresponded closely with culture areas, and attempted to account for this in a simple determinist pattern. But while Ratzel and Mason saw the essential determinant as the habitat or physical environment, Wissler (1926:216–217; 1929:79) referred to the dominant food source or mode of subsis-tence. This gave the effects of food production (which were regarded as being relatively resistant to change) a mediating role between habi-tat and culture not dissimilar to the role of the means of production in Plekhanov's Marxist formulation (Matley 1972:112). While, for Wissler, food areas could be tied to physical environments, it was inevitable that they would not be completely identical and that the centres of distribution for constituent traits would not necessarily match the cen-tre of an environmental zone (1926:216–17). The work of Mason and

Wissler was developed further by Alfred Kroeber (1939), who systematically examined the relationship between environmental and cultural variables for the same region, plotting the limits of biogeographic areas against cultigen distribution and working out estimates for the pre-Columbian population levels of various groups. Kroeber's environmentalist work, however, was constrained by his particularism and a belief that culture was primarily to be understood in terms of other cultural factors – views inherited from his teacher Franz Boas. The issues raised by particularism and cultural determinism as they relate to ecology are discussed further in the next chapter.

In my observations on scale in man–environment relationships I have already pointed to reasons why the enterprise of demarcating culture areas linked to environmental zones might be an extremely difficult one. Increase in scale inevitably means greater complexity in environmental variation within an area, greater complexity in terms of the interconnectedness between variables and in terms of the relationships between natural and man-modified elements. The critique can be much more specific than this.

Not only have the units selected been too gross spatially, some of subcontinental proportions, but those of widely divergent size have frequently been lumped together indiscriminately as culture areas. Investigations of environmental correlations on a subcontinental scale present formidable methodological problems. On *a priori* grounds alone there are good reasons to believe that cultural and environmental diversity within such an area defies its systematic examination as a unity (Vayda and Rappaport 1968:481). Furthermore, the criteria for designating a particular culture area are usually derived from the application of a small number of distinctive features. However, selection has tended to be intrinsically arbitrary and therefore of inconsequential validity. The arbitrariness of the factors employed to designate culture areas has resulted in conflicting typologies for different regions, the degree of conflict being related to the geographical scale of the isolates. Such disparities arise partly from the fact that cultural configurations and social formations often overlap and sometimes coincide. This has been demonstrated in detail for northern Pakistan by Barth (1956:1087) and for northern Arabia by Sweet (1969:168). Notwithstanding these problems, Wissler was attracted by the apparent consistency in relations between generalized culture and environmental areas for the material he examined, and was tempted to impute a determining effect. But a partial correlation between a cultural trait and environmental variable is not a sufficient condition for establishing a causal relationship.

Finally, the culture-area concept projects, and is dependent upon,

9

extreme stasis in the relations between human behaviour and the environment. Social formations (unlike the epiphenomenal cultural configurations which are even more an artifact of analysis) are observably systems with an internal dynamic of their own. This is not easily conveyed by plotting distributions on maps. Centres and peripheries change over time. Indeed, cultural content and social form may change so rapidly in successive periods as to resemble more closely forms and patterns of areas other than those of immediate predecessors of successors in the same area. This situation was recognized by Julian Steward (1955) who also pointed out the different analytical and empirical status of the concepts of 'cultural configuration' and 'social formation'. However, in their confusing terminological guise as simply 'culture' and 'social structure', he failed to appreciate the abstract quality of the first and the contrasting possibility for objective reality encompassed in the second. Despite this it was clear that areas with a common cultural content might have very different social forms, and similar social forms dissimilar cultural content (Steward 1955:82).

The problems created by drawing static boundaries on maps were also recognized by Kroeber, who was anxious to portray both sequential and spatial variation within culture areas (1939:6). It is possible that Kroeber saw Wissler's 'age-area' hypothesis as a means of developing a more dynamic culture-area concept. The problem of stasis, however, is intrinsic to the method, and, despite recent attempts to take account of temporality and variation (Schwartz 1959), has not been adequately resolved.

Now these difficulties involve reducing statistically continuous data to rigid two-dimensional spatial representations. In this respect, they are comparable to the delineation of biogeographical zones – that is the so-called 'natural regions' (Darlington 1957:419–23) – or even ecosystems in the strict contemporary use of this term. It is important to recognize in all three cases that we are concerned with concepts for ordering data, which only secondarily may be means for demonstrating statistical probabilities in correlations between grouped data. Only in the third case are we concerned with an entity which is also definitionally a system of empirical relations. If the culture area becomes reified, considered as some concrete entity *sui generis*, rather than simply an analytical construct, problems of the kind indicated are bound to arise. There is no need to reject *a priori* the idea of areas in which environmental and behavioural variables combine to give distinctive patterns, or reject the use of such features for the purpose of classification. This is both legitimate and necessary. It is important, though, to recognize the limitations of the term 'culture area' as an ordering device and the arbitrariness of the classificatory factors employed, and to avoid transforming a category into an integrated system.

TYPES OF ENVIRONMENTAL CORRELATION

Environmental correlations are not all of the same order. The question of the scale of variables has already been mentioned, but another important set of factors are the qualitative differences between different kinds of environmental phenomena. A basic list must at least distinguish the following categories: climatic; geological, geomorphological and edaphic; vegetational; and faunal.

Climatic factors provide the most convenient illustrations for didactic purposes, and often involve the most dramatic relationships between environment and social behaviour. Thus, Lee (1972) has shown a clear relationship between flexibility in !Kung San band composition in Botswana and seasonal and longer-term water availability. At a greater level of generalization, earlier work by Birdsell (1953) had demonstrated a relationship between mean annual rainfall and the population density of aboriginal Australian groups. For a population of around 500 persons he claimed that the density could be predicted from the exponential equation featured in Figure 1.2, where Y = size of tribal territory and X = mean annual rainfall. The equation was derived from a 'J'-shaped curve on a scattergram where group area was plotted in hundreds of square miles against mean annual rainfall in inches, for 123 groups (see Figure 1.2).

It is possible to criticize Birdsell on the unreliability of his data (Hiatt 1962), on the grounds that his categories of variables affecting the density equation – physical environment, biotic resources and socially determined 'extractive-efficiency' – are all dependent upon one another, and on his use of rainfall as a proxy for all available water. It is also possible to doubt his corollary hypotheses: that advanced political organization seems to result in increased size of group population, while recent acquisition of circumcision and/or subincision ceremonies is associated with a transient decrease in group size. What is incontestable is that mean annual rainfall can be shown empirically to be a factor systematically related to changes in group size and density, and that correlations between environmental variables such as rainfall and demography are commensurable.

These are useful illustrations for several reasons. To begin with meteorological phenomena are among those least likely to be directly affected by local human activity. They can be treated as independent variables and thus clearly identify themselves either directly or

11

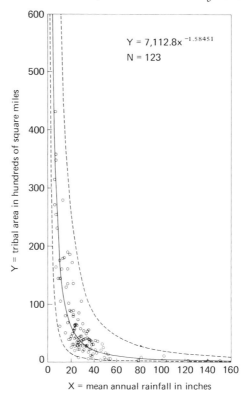

1.2 Correlation between rainfall and size of group area for 123 aboriginal Australian tribes (after Birdsell 1953: fig. 4)

indirectly. Secondly, meteorological data can be readily measured and accumulated in large quantities with relative ease, whether they concern wind-direction, rainfall, sunlight, cloud-cover, humidity, temperature or whatever.

One point, however, which may constitute an obstacle in analysis is that climatic variation of ecological significance is often local. Unless good records are available at a district level, meteorological recording has to be undertaken in connection with ethnographic fieldwork. Failure to appreciate this, and reliance on regional or even national information, has occasionally resulted in useless documentation and conclusions. The importance of *local* records, of course, applies to geological, edaphic, geomorphological, vegetational and faunal information as well. This is not to say that regional data are invalid and sometimes region-wide correlations of ecological significance occur. In such cases, however, there is a far greater possibility of error and the intervention of extraneous variables, as discussion of the culture-area concept has already indicated.

Plausible correlations between climatic variables and human behaviour have been demonstrated in an extensive body of literature. Most of these, as one might expect, relate to climatic effects on subsistence behaviour, but correlations have also been reported between such things as seasonality and incidence of birth (Cowgill 1966) and temperature, sleeping arrangements and genital mutilation (Whiting 1964).

In turning to correlations between geomorphological factors and social behaviour we must distinguish between those that are straightforward and readily quantifiable (such as the climatic factors discussed above), and a less easily quantifiable type. The former includes such correlations as matching the nitrogenous content of soils to the location of gardens, soil acidity to choice of settlement sites and so on. The second type involves correlations between different kinds of topographies, soil and rock types to settlement patterns. It is, of course, possible to devise means of quantifying such relationships, but it requires complicated manipulation of the data. Such relationships are often best illustrated through the use of maps or aerial photographs.

Among the most frequent correlations to appear in anthropological and geographical literature are those between vegetation types and social forms. The terms 'habitat', 'niche' and 'ecosystem' are often incorrectly used when what is really being described is the pattern of vegetation. Such correlations are usually of the broad unquantified type, but as with geomorphological variation the only obstacles to quantification are the resources and resourcefulness of the investigator. The types of correlations involved include everything from entire habitats and patterns of subsistence (sometimes erroneously described as 'economies': Weiner 1964:411), to narrower correlations, say, between the distribution of a particular culturally valued plant species and types of social behaviour. Thus associations can be shown between the distribution of hallucinogenic fungi and the social use of a particular kind of transcendental state which it gives rise to, or between the distribution of the *Metroxylon* palm and the presence of a particular type of technique to appropriate the sago contained in its trunk.

Of those environmental correlations so far considered those involving animals have perhaps attracted most attention in the ethnographic literature. The kinds of correlations which have been discussed include such diverse subjects as the relationships between the limits of tolerance of zebu cattle to tsetse fly and Fulani patterns of transhumance (Stenning 1957), and camel pastoralism in north Arabia and the minimal camping unit (Sweet 1969). In fact, most work on nomadic pastoralists has at some point or another sought to make correlations of this kind (e.g. Leeds and Vayda 1965).

In listing types of environmental variables a fifth category is sometimes added, namely demographic factors. In the sense that the previous categories may contain modified elements and are therefore products of human social activity, one might envisage population structures in much the same light. However, because it is possible to treat population statistics in a rather abstract way, apart from a consideration of social organization, I believe certain writers (e.g. Feldman 1975:68) have confused demography with environment, and demographic determinism with environmental determinism. Demographic pressure has certainly been effective in the evolution and maintenance of social structures, this much has been evident since the writings of Rousseau and Turgot (Harner 1970:70, 86), but it is most definitely a characteristic of social groups and not of their environment. It can have no independent existence as a factor other than this. Consequently, such factors are generally considered here either as a response to environmental factors, or as an intermediate part of a causal chain (e.g. malarial mosquito – population depletion – social response).

NATURAL AND HUMANLY MODIFIED ENVIRONMENTS

It is self-evident that human activities may alter natural environments, and geographical and ecological studies have shown in detail the mechanisms by which this has taken place, and extent to which it has occurred (W. L. Thomas *et al.* 1956). Here the term 'natural' is being used to mean unmodified by *Homo sapiens*, but, of course, this does not mean that environments are not being constantly modified by other organisms. In fact, 'pure nature' does not exist, and from an anthropological point of view the environment, must logically include humans and the results of their activities. The 'natural regions' distinguished by biogeographers commonly correspond to regions extensively transformed through human manipulation, and are only 'natural' in a rather general sense. Similarly, what are often described as environmental correlations are, in fact, correlations between behaviour and products of that behaviour, in the form of a modified landscape. What are often described as determining relationships between environment and behaviour are, in fact, determining relationships between modes of subsistence and other aspects of social behaviour. The portable and minimal dwellings of food-collectors are the result not of arid environments but of a mobile means of subsistence and the absence of a complex social organization of technology, neither of

14

which is necessarily determined by the differential availability of food resources. The same is true of pastoral nomads, such as the Kazak and other horse and sheep herders of the south Siberian steppes. Among those cultivators who have more permanent and elaborate dwellings this is not solely because of more favourable environmental conditions, but because the mode of subsistence specifies this as a possibility.

Some idea of the semantic complexities surrounding the issue of what constitutes the environment in the first place can be seen by comparing two parallel distinctions central to anthropological explanation – *culture:nature* and *nature:nurture*. The concepts of *nature* employed in these oppositions are not identical. In the first sense it includes both the genetic component of an individual and the environment. In the second sense the environment is quite clearly part of *nurture, nature* being essentially physiological and genetic in its effects. *Nurture* is, of course, the means by which *culture* is transmitted, and in human terms *culture* and the *social* environment is therefore the proximate context of development. The scientific usefulness of concepts of *nature* and *environment* is highly questionable. Both are very much social categories (Boulding 1978:31, Lukacs 1971:234, Douglas 1972). Human social formations have progressively incorporated nature, such that abstract and formal distinctions between culture and environment are generally unhelpful.[5]

Altered environments, as much as unaltered ones, may determine certain patterns in social organization. Thus environmental determinism cannot simply be represented as ENVIRONMENT→SOCIETY, but must be represented as ENVIRONMENT ⇄ SOCIETY. All environmental factors listed in the previous section may be so modified. Populations of plant and animal species may be selectively husbanded, soils may be artificially enriched, climates altered through the removal of tracts of vegetation and entire topographies transformed through the creation of irrigated rice terraces. These are all obvious examples, but often the interrelationship between the modified and unmodified aspects of the environment can be extremely subtle. Leach (1961) and Conklin (1968), in particular, have drawn attention to the importance of studying culturally transformed micro-environments where these interrelationships are to be observed. Thus the subtle interrelationships between natural and modified environments only serve to re-affirm that humanity and nature are not the two independent entities that are so often reflected in ideologies; society is not the negation of nature. The problem is, as Marx pointed out (Schmidt 1971:63–93; Moscovici 1976:145–6), that *Homo sapiens* is both part of nature, appropriating from it, and yet also capable of controlling it.

15

BEHAVIOURAL AND ENVIRONMENTAL FACTUALISM

One underlying assumption of environmentalism, some other anthropological 'ecologies' and sociological positivism, is that the units of information that are correlated are treated as though they (a) have some independent existence of their own, and (b) are irreducible to smaller parts which might affect their testability or the validity of the correlation. It is easy to see how the social side of the equation has been influenced by the physical. On the one hand there is rainfall in millimetres, altitude in metres, soil nitrogen in milligrams and so on, while on the other the incidence of cultural and social phenomena is treated as if they too had the same kind of objective existence. It becomes clear that we are concerned with a version of Durkheimian social facts, with the added complication of environmental facts which are intrinsically neither social nor cultural but which may well be equally arbitrarily selected. In this respect the critiques of this aspect of Durkheimianism are also relevant here (e.g. Marshall 1974–5). However, it is a matter of normal scientific practice that units involved in specific correlations are initially treated as though they were autonomous. Otherwise we would be forever lost in an endless maze of ramifying correlations. The result of testing a hypothesis may lead to modification in the conceptualization of the original units involved. Behavioural phenomena tend to be more arbitrary, without a physically observable existence easily subject to re-analysis under laboratory conditions. The problems involved are understandably of a far greater magnitude, requiring increased caution in the selection of units for comparison and correlation. While it is inescapable that certain units used are treated as 'facts', some of the implications of the cult of factualism are to be avoided.

An example of a correlation from the non-behavioural sciences that may subsequently be modified on further investigation is the following: 'the presence of lateritic soils leads to rapid growth of Leguminosae'. The correlation can be confirmed by simply measuring the growth rates for legumes on lateritic and non-lateritic soils. However, a more detailed examination may indicate that in effect it is only one component of the soil, namely a higher lime content, that encourages legume growth. A comparable ethnographic example might be: 'output of sago among Nuaulu producers is reduced during the southwest monsoon'. It may well be that the season itself, that is calendricity or temporal rhythm, is not the causal agent at all but the rain pattern which is part of the total microclimatic complex. To bring the examples completely within a sociological frame of reference: while there may well be a causal correlation between capitalism and the increase of inequality as measured by the ownership of wealth, it is not capitalism at a phenomenological level which is the causal agent but the process of capital accumulation among a minority leading to class-formation with all its self-amplifying consequences. Thus, in these examples, the problem of analysis revolves around the scale of correlation and, necessarily, also the character of causal chains and whether these are direct or indirect.

CORRELATION AND CAUSATION

As the difference between testable and untestable correlations is relative and perhaps in the last instance dependent on the laws of probability, so the difference between direct and indirect correlation is somewhat arbitrary and depends on the problem under investigation and the scale of analysis that is methodologically appropriate. In drawing a specific correlation it is not always clear whether the relationship is direct or indirect, or whether the environmental factor is itself determined by some other factor. For example, to what extent is a correlation between climate and human patterns of settlement better expressed as one between vegetation types and settlement? Such a difficulty highlights the analytical inadequacy of these various categories. In the tropical rain forest vegetation, soil structure and microclimate are intricately interrelated and mutually dependent on one another. What justification is there for selecting one variable of the complex and typing it with any one feature of human behaviour?

It is almost always possible to introduce an intermediate factor in a causal chain. We can explore some of the problems by taking the following simple proposition: 'among the Nuaulu there is an inverse causal relationship between amount of rainfall and output of *Metroxylon* sago'. This proposition is testable in a statistical sense from information provided, but there is no way of knowing whether the correlation is direct or indirect. Common sense would indicate that the causal chain must specify a minimum of one intermediary link for it to make sociological sense. If we were dealing with genetic responses we might be justified in assuming that there is a direct behavioural relationship. The presence of rain might be a sufficient stimulus in itself to trigger a decrease in output, as in the reflex between increased sunlight and pupil dilation. Increasing sunlight falling on the human eye causes sensory perceptors to communicate that information to the cerebral hemispheres where motor neurons are triggered to contract the pupil, so avoiding damaging the light-sensitive tissues of the retina. But in our first proposition increased rainfall does not act directly in this physiological sense; a decrease in the output of sago is not a genetically

17

programmed response. Additionally, there may be more than one link:

Make

$$a \longrightarrow b \longrightarrow c \longrightarrow d$$

a	b	c	d
rainfall	slippery, muddy and flooded paths	inhibition of rapid transport	decrease in output of sago

Here, for each permutable correlation (*a b, b c, c d*), the greatest correlation would be expected to exist between adjacent sets in the series (*a b, b c* and *c d*, rather than *a c, a d* and *b d*). Thus indirect causation may be considered in terms of the concept of causal chain.

Multiple causation in this context occurs where a social event is determined by more than one causal agent. Multiplicity may logically be of a serial or parallel (simultaneous) kind. Serial causation is, in effect, the indirect causation and causal chains of the last section. It is understood, that each new step in serial causation introduces a new element which affects the final outcome. If this were not so (that is, if, say $a-b-c=a-c$) there would be no reason to emphasize the intermediate stages, since they contribute nothing to the outcome; $a-c$ would be as statistically efficient an explanation as $a-b-c$. However, in ecological ethnographic work it is often crucial to introduce the variable of historical time, and, since an intermediate stage *b* may have effects other than in terms of the chain $a-b-c$, it may be important to demonstrate its existence. For example in the chain $a-b-c$, *b* may be unnecessary in explaining the relationship between *a* and *c*, but may determine a fourth variable, *d*. It is therefore important to separate final from efficient causes; actual historical causation from logical devices such as Occam's razor.

Multiple causation in parallel may be due to causative agents that are related or unrelated. In most empirical ecological situations, however, the causative agents are usually related, although the links connecting the factors may be complex. A rather general example of this is illustrated in Figure 1.3. Here, a decrease in the availability of migratory herd ungulates is hypothesized as resulting in a shift to a broader pattern of resource appropriation for a small, mobile band of hunters. This is effected by two possible pathways which mutually reinforce each other: reduction in size of subsistence territory and increase in population. The more distant the various factors involved in determining a single condition, the greater the number of variables that are likely to be related.

Much ethnographic data can only be satisfactorily analysed by introducing both parallel and serial causal sequences. Thus, Stauder in his work on the Majangir of southern Ethiopia (1971:124) has argued that

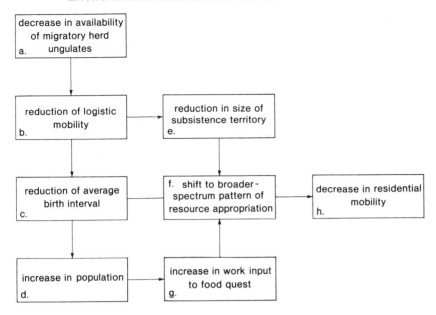

1.3 Closed system diagram indicating one processual sequence by which a small, mobile band of hunters of migratory herd ungulates might evolve into a larger, more localized, but still residentially mobile population (adapted from Harris 1977 fig. 2)

the fission and re-arrangement of settlements may involve a combination of environmental factors – edaphic, topographic and vegetational – in varying proportions at different times. But it is highly probable that edaphic factors other than those determined by the soil conditions may be involved. This is also true for those factors affecting Nuaulu selection of garden sites (Ellen 1978:108–60), and those affecting Birdsell's rainfall–population-density equation for aboriginal Australian groups. That is, dependent variables are being represented as if they were independent.

For Wissler (1926:212) 'the method usually followed in ecological studies is to seek correlations between the characters of life forms and the specific characters of the environment and, if it is found that these usually happen together, it is assumed that some causal relation exists between them'. Now this assumption is a common one and underlies much of the discussion so far. But while it is possible to demonstrate direct and indirect, single and multiple causation, a demonstrable correlation does not necessarily indicate a causal relationship. Thus if it can be shown that sago output among the Nuaulu is positively correlated with output of animal protein this does not mean that protein appropriation is directly causally related to sago appropriation, although the ethnography does indicate that sago-processing over long periods provides opportunities for hunting. Rather, both animal protein and sago output are inversely – but largely independently – proportional to increase in rainfall.

It is necessary to be properly sceptical of converting statistical correlations into multi-levelled sequences of causation (Vayda and Rappaport 1968:485). Simple uni-directional causal processes seldom occur in human environmental relations. The kinds of causes entertained by the environmentalists were, for the most part, far too simple and naive to account for the complexities between variables which we now know to exist. Not the least of these is that environmental variables are themselves a product of the interaction between human and non-human activities. The crucial correlations are rarely those gross, observable relationships between totalities but rather the subtle and hidden connections between particularities.

2

vwvwvwvwvwvwvwvwvwvwvwvwvwvwvwvwvwvwvwvwvwvwvwvwvwvwvwvwvwvwvwvwvwvwvwvwvw

Possibilism and limiting factors

POSSIBILISM

In the United States, Germany and Russia environmentalism had a deep impact on the study of human ecological relations. But, as is somehow inevitable with grand theoretical generalizations, later students (while acknowledging the source of their inspiration) came to be suspicious of the all-embracing claims it made. Wissler, despite his work on cultural areas and admitted debt to Ratzel, could not be persuaded to accept wholeheartedly the positive formative effect of the environment. For him, the environment was a passive limiting agency rather than a causal factor (Wissler 1929:339). The environment set limits but did not determine. It was this negative formulation of geographical determinism, *possibilism*, which was to influence much future work.

It is fruitless to locate the precise intellectual origins of possibilism since it must have existed for as long as speculation on human interaction with the environment. An early geographical version is found in the work of Vidal de la Blache (1902); and in Soviet writings of the Stalinist period we find the supreme example of ideological and scientific expression of anti-environmentalism (Matley 1972:114, 119). The response among anthropologists came a little later. In part it reflected theoretical weaknesses within the environmentalist tradition, but was also the product of historical particularism, sociological functionalism, the conduct of ethnographic fieldwork, and an increasing appreciation of the degree to which the environment had been modified by *Homo sapiens*.

Environment, subsistence and system

HUMAN INTERFERENCE AND THE MODIFICATION OF PRISTINE ECOSYSTEMS

One of the most important reasons for the demise of environmentalism was the recognition that so much of nature is modified by human activities. Although many plants and animals also alter their surroundings, either purposely or incidentally, only *Homo sapiens* does so completely and with such various, such rapid and such consciously planned adaptations to changing conditions. During the course of the nineteenth century this idea was being supported by increasing evidence from the description of actual societies. Theoretically it was encouraged by a Baconian philosophical tradition, notions of progress and a liberal humanism which saw man as essentially rational. Such views were reflected in the political economy of both Marx (Schmidt 1971) and Engels (1954),[1] and the natural history of individuals as diverse as Buffon (Glacken 1967:658–9) and George Perkins Marsh (1965). Indeed, many modern geographers (e.g. Sauer 1925), following Marsh, have seen their enterprise largely in terms of the analysis of the human transformation of nature. Ironically, the diametrically opposed ideology of the contemporary 'ecological movement' – owing more to Rousseau than to Bacon – has also encouraged this focus, but by emphasizing in particular those changes which result in unwelcome pollution and despoilation.

Few environments are uninfluenced by humans and almost all landscapes are culturally modified to some extent. Partly because of this, the character and structure of local ecosystems are everywhere relatively recent. Although most plants and animals predate human entry to specific ecosystems, some are more recent than the human migrants, for example parasites and micro-organisms. The activities of human populations themselves provide new niches. Consequently, the stable and apparently conservationist strategies of many small-scale societies are largely an illusion. Even the most rudimentary technologies and those subsistence patterns which apparently leave the natural ecosystem unaltered can have a significant impact on the environment. Wells (1970) reports on the possibility that deforestation in central North America was caused by plains Amerindians. It has also been suggested (Krantz 1970) that humans were responsible for the extinction of Pleistocene megafauna in Europe, and that grassland was repeatedly fired during the British Mesolithic to initiate cycles of occupancy by desired game, sometimes with permanent effects (Simmons 1969). In New Guinea, deliberately caused fires have been discovered at an altitude of 3,000 metres which have destroyed forest, and thus dramatically simplified the ecosystem. Forest edges have been

22

damaged by grass fires, and much grassland owes its origin and maintenance to fires. Natural fires are either absent or rare, fires are often started to trap small game deliberately or incidentally, or to provide warmth or for pure pleasure. Even above the limit of gardening, the environment has been altered by high-altitude trading paths and for hunting and gathering (Manner 1977:215)

Cultivated land now occupies 10 per cent of the surface of the earth, and a considerably larger percentage of those parts capable of supporting vegetation (Brown 1970:95). The process of plant cultivation has led to enormous changes in the structure of biotic associations; field clearance alone has destroyed forests, native grasslands and many other types of natural community. The kinds of crops grown and the techniques used have affected the quality of the soil (Clarke and Street 1967). The impact of agriculture on the native flora of northern Europe and elsewhere is well known (e.g. Clark 1954, Day 1953). Swiddening has also greatly altered the ecology of montane New Guinea, and many introduced plants have established themselves wild, including the noxious weeds of cultivation and edible plants (Manner 1977:215). *Homo sapiens* has increased the productivity of domesticated species genetically and through nurture. Agriculture has been intensified through techniques for altering the energy, water, nitrogen and mineral cycles of the biosphere; through mechanization, irrigation, fertilization and chemical control of weeds and insects. Re-shaping the hydraulic cycle through the diversion of river water on to land has raised the water table. By draining swamps and building irrigation schemes the landscape is re-worked: new kinds of habitat are created, either beneficial, as in the case of wet rice terraces; or destructive, as in the case of *Imperata* grasslands formed through extensive forest clearance in New Guinea, or in the increase of *Schistosomiasis* vectors following deliberate flooding (Brown 1970:100). Waste products, pollution, technical practices and induced erosion have destroyed local environments. In many places, domesticated animal species have replaced wild dominants, and food production has altered not only the relative abundance of species but also their global distribution and the ecology of the plant matter upon which they feed. Animal domestication has resulted in an increase in predators, parasites and other types of association. All of these changes have affected terrestrial and freshwater ecosystems, and, to a lesser extent, marine ones; while the character of such changes, their variety and extent are now well documented by biologists, ethnographers and ecologists, in both professional and popular publications (Sangster 1971, Thomas *et al.* 1956, Ucko and Dimbleby 1969).

Environment, subsistence and system

PARTICULARISM, FUNCTIONALISM AND THE NEGLECT OF ECOLOGY

Some of the objections to environmental determinism have been re-viewed in Chapter 1. Within anthropology these have most often been associated with what has become known as 'cultural' (or 'historical') 'particularism', and the work of Franz Boas, Alfred Kroeber and Robert Lowie in the United States. There is a certain irony in the link between the adjective 'Boasian' and possibilism. Although Boas asserted that the environment only had a certain limiting effect (1896:906), he was responsible for noting one of the first convincing culture–environment correlations: the relationship between the location of Eskimo settle-ments, the formation of sea ice and the movements of inshore seals (1888:417). A comparable enduring paradox is found in the essay by Mauss and Beuchat (1906) on Eskimo seasonal variations. This has been interpreted as a vindication of historical materialism on the one hand and as an attack on geographical determinism on the other (J. J. Fox 1979:11, Douglas 1972a:20).

The basic particularist position is that cultures, environments and histories are so variable that any generalization is hazardous. If so, then to describe environmental variables as constraints gives them recognition without assigning status. Raised to the level of abstract theory, culture was a thing *sui generis* (the superorganic), while biology (the organic) was constant. The immediate causes of cultural phe-nomena were held to be primarily other cultural phenomena, while social change proceeded independently of environmental conditions (Kroeber 1917, 1939:1). However, for Kroeber (1939:205):

no culture is wholly intelligible without reference to the non-cultural or so-called environmental factors with which it is in relation and which condition it . . . the interactions of the culture and environment become exceedingly complex when followed out. And this complexity makes generalization un-profitable, on the whole. In each situation or area different natural factors are likely to be impinging on culture with different intensity.

He also acknowledged that the environment might inhibit new variation, since once adaptations have occurred they are difficult to change, and that therefore adaptation to a specific environment makes it difficult to adapt to another (Alland and McCay 1973:161). Kroeber was drawn to this emphasis on the limiting effects of resources rather than on opportunities through conceptualizing culture as a unitary system (1939:4). His concern for simplistic correlation and holistic generalization concealed the possibility of valuable empirical gener-alizations between cultural and environmental variables.

Possibilism and limiting factors

Kroeber (e.g. 1923) noted that different kinds of societies – like the Hopi Pueblos and nomadic stock-raising Navaho in the American southwest – may occupy similar environments. He argued that environment could not explain culture because identical environments are consistent with distinct cultures, because cultural traits persist in areas where it would be advantageous for them to disappear, because they do not develop where they would be useful, and because they may disappear where one would least expect it.

Despite his particular position, empirically Kroeber did much to isolate limiting factors of great ethnographic interest and was more prepared than most of his predecessors to use precise information drawn from natural science, ethnohistory and archaeology to this end. In his careful documentation of the correspondence between cultural and natural areas in pre-Columbian North America (1939), he compared culture areas modified from the original scheme published by Wissler (1917) with natural areas based on vegetation zones reflecting climate and soil, and supporting a specific fauna. These are related in turn to data on demography and subsistence techniques. A pattern emerges from this which links 'cultural climax' and increased density to coastal residence, though not agriculture itself. Climate is held to limit the development of culture through the constraining effects of available water on subsistence possibilities and thereby population increase. Kroeber was able to show that reliable maize-growing among Amerindians was restricted to places where there was at least a summer season of one month, with adequate precipitation and no killing frosts. He maintained that the seasonal distribution of rainfall permitted the diffusion of maize cultivation from Mexico to the Pueblo area, but prevented its spreading to California. But his acknowledgement that concordances are often incomplete, with partial relationships and overlap between boundaries, suggests that he saw cultural and environmental areas as temporary accommodations, giving a subtler meaning to the concept of possibilism. For Kroeber, the absence of static and fixed culture areas contradicted the implication of possibilism, that humans are not capable of innovative decisions and choices (Bennett 1976:211). It is ironic that although Kroeber furnished possibilism with much of its theoretical justification, he also did most to cast doubts upon its suitability. He did not, however, perceive the theoretical implications of his work.

The possibilist implications of Kroeber's work are developed more explicitly in that of Betty Meggers (e.g. 1954). Meggers divides environments into four types according to their potential for agriculture, suggesting that the level to which a culture can develop depends upon this. For Meggers, an increase in energy output produces a decline in

25

cultural complexity and a change in the general cultural product. She illustrates her ideas with the example of the growth and decline of Maya civilization and uses other Amerindian material to show how cultural development is prevented by limited food resources. She also asserts that low soil fertility due to high humidity and rainfall decisively limits agricultural potential in certain areas, such as the swidden cultivation zone of South American tropical forests.

Because the examination of the connections between environment and social behaviour has always been closely associated with geographical determinism, what is now described as *ecology* has had an ambiguous position in British anthropology. In so much as the work of its Victorian predecessors was evolutionist, racialist, sociological, historical, influenced by Hume and the romanticists or the Benthamite school, so it was implacably opposed to geograpical determinism. But as a product of the Enlightenment it was also residually environmentalist. Comte, who was so influential in shaping a later social anthropology, though critical of the environmentalism of Montesquieu, was himself prone to exaggerate the efficiency of physical agencies. Although Ferguson strenuously upheld that the passionate ingenuity of man enabled him to overcome the disadvantages of any climate or situation, he was still of the opinion that temperate zones facilitated the growth of civilization. For Herbert Spencer, history was the steady progression from warmer to more productive habits demanded by the feebler stages of social evolution to the colder, less productive and more difficult regions away from the tropics. Morgan held that the cultural differences of peoples at the same 'level' were to be explained environmentally. Over and above this was always (a sometimes implicit) folk-environmentalism affecting the often slipshod and untutored judgements of travellers, missionaries, colonial officers and other early ethnographers. So perhaps environmentalism was not as incompatible with then-current racist and evolutionary theories as is popularly thought (Thomas 1925, Lowie 1937:58, Stocking 1968:251).

But at the level of theoretical and ideological generalization, the cards were stacked against environmentalist interpretations. The theories of Le Play, Ratzel and Demolins were, by general consent, 'far too pretty to be true' (Marett 1912:97–100). Such suspicion was reinforced by theoretical developments in the first half of the twentieth century. Neither diffusionists nor functionalists could tolerate the environment as an element in causal processes if their theories were to remain elegant and free of embarrassing contradictions.

Moreover, the extent to which a society was able to modify its surroundings was becoming increasingly clear: a matter no longer of philosophical assertion but of ethnographic confirmation. In such circumstances empiricism was a safe doctrine. Detailed evidence was thus marshalled against the various versions of environmentalism and materialism, including a caricature of Marxism. It hardly helped matters that determination by the environment was sometimes confused with that by the technical means of subsistence and production.

That an emerging British school of social anthropology should have adopted so apparently intransigent a position is no doubt partly due to the necessity of establishing a set of distinctive intellectual credentials. It was also a result of internalizing the circular explanations fashionable in French sociology, particularly via the influential writings of A. R. Radcliffe-Brown (Gray 1964:6). It is noteworthy that Durkheim's principle of explaining the social only in terms of the social paralleled the Boasian notion of 'superorganic' in its epistemological and polemical function; society, like culture, was a thing *sui generis*. Furthermore, the Durkheimian slogan underpinned the subsequent claim that the discipline be treated as an autonomous source of explanations (Gluckman 1964).

Theoretical developments, then, discouraged the treatment of environmental relations, and they rarely featured at the level of generalization, occupying a peripheral and passive role. Radcliffe-Brown, in the words of Netting (1974:21), 'consigned studies of subsistence adaptation to an "external realm" where labored archeologists and ethnological historians of diffusion. The topic could safely be left with museum catalogers of material culture or such contemporary experts as the geographer, the agronomist, and the rural sociologist.' The same attitude is reflected in later textbooks. Theoretically, ecology remained residual; the dominant paradigm was one that ruled out a central place for environmental interactions. This was so despite a sustaining myth which might reasonably have allowed some role for such forces, and which held that explanation must necessarily move from the particular analysis to the general statement.

The British anthropologist Daryll Forde occupies a position on environmental relations very similar to that of Kroeber. Among the first two generations of British social anthropologists it was Forde who maintained, virtually single-handed, a theoretical interest in this area, while at the same time articulating the case against geographical determinism.

Forde had been trained first as a geographer and then as an archaeologist before turning to social anthropology. As a geographer he was aware of the crude environmentalist assumptions still current in that discipline but had been particularly influenced by the works of L. Febvre (1925), P. Vidal de la Blache (1902, 1911) and R. Ahrens (1927). As an archaeologist and anthropologist who had received part of his training in America, he had been affected in part by the historical particularist approach of Boas, Kroeber and Lowie, but equally by the empiricist British ethnographic tradition. He rejected the culture-area concept on the grounds that general classifications are inadequate for the analysis of cultural possibilities and because local histories often showed it to be of little applicability (Vayda and Rappaport 1968:482). Unlike the Boasians though, who were largely concerned with texts obtained from informants, Forde concentrated more on material culture and environmental data. His first and most important book, *Habitat, economy and society*, first published in 1934, was a general treatise with comparative ethnographic sketches which are ecologically orientated. In it he is consistently concerned with functional relations, both internal and external to the particular society being discussed. He shows continual awareness of alterations in the significance of environmental variables due to technological innovation and social change and the complex interweaving of synchronic connections and historical developments (Alfred Harris in Fortes 1976:473). Perhaps the key passage in understanding his general position is the following (1934:464–5)

Physical conditions enter intimately into every cultural development and pattern, not excluding the most abstract and non-material; they enter not as determinants, however, but as one category of the raw material of cultural elaboration. The study of the relations between cultural patterns and physical conditions is of the greatest importance for an understanding of human society, but it cannot be undertaken in terms of simple geographical controls alleged to be identifiable on sight. It must proceed inductively from the minute analysis of each society. The culture must in the first place be studied as an entity and as an historical development; there can be no other effective approach to interrelations of such complexity.[2]

Thirty-six years later Forde was still able to plead for more attention to be directed 'to the detailed and effective analysis of ecological relations as an integral part of any ethnographic study' (1970:18). Among British anthropologists of the period 1930–60 (apart from Forde) only V. G. Childe (e.g. 1951) vigorously promoted the idea of material causation. One of Childe's students, J. G. D. Clark (1954), combined the concerns of his teacher with those of the prevailing functionalism of his day in a more overtly 'systems' approach.

The position of Forde on environmental issues was essentially a product of his eclectic theoretical socialization, but for those more firmly entrenched in particularism and social anthropology the experience of fieldwork was to play a key role in determining attitudes and shaping theory. The beginnings of anthropological fieldwork in the United States had the effect of stressing the causal role of non-

environmental factors in culture, the difficulty of making generalizations which would account for every ethnographic case and the
variability of environmental factors within an area being examined.
Boas was converted to possibilism from being a Ratzelian on the basis
of his Eskimo fieldwork (Harris 1968:266, but see Stocking 1968).

Among British anthropologists the internalization of possibilist
assumptions was a more gradual and less visible process. The environment could not be ignored, for it was the first thing which confronted
the fieldworker. It was widely regarded that 'no sociological study of a
community [could] be undertaken without an understanding of the
natural environment within which it exists and from which it draws its
subsistence' (Royal Anthropological Institute 1951:35). And yet it was
obvious that environment alone never determined social organization.
It was therefore easy to resort to generalizations claiming that the
environment simply acted to limit what was possible.

Accordingly, given a certain *a priori* theoretical disposition, the treatment of ecology (generally meaning 'environment') was also seen as
obligatory, but in the event something of a ritual exercise. It became a
discrete section in monographs, often the first chapter: a few background facts on the distribution of vegetation, rainful records and
topographical features were presented *in vacuo* before proceeding to
the main focus, the analytically autonomous domain of social organization. The concept of *subsistence* was treated narrowly, as if mere
techniques bore little relation to social organization. If discussed at all
(Gray 1964:6), descriptions of environmental variables were naive and
inadequate, something which has occasioned justifiable criticism from
geographers (Mikesell 1967). The most important and virtually the
only exception to this picture until the mid-fifties was the work of
Audrey Richards on the Zambian Bemba (1932, 1939).

Nevertheless, fieldwork experience and the analysis of ethnographic data compelled a softening of empirical attitudes. As is often
the case, individual analyses tended to push the ethnographer into a
more moderate position, towards a stress on the substantive uniqueness of his or her own data. If this was the general case, then on
occasions the specific conditions of fieldwork demanded a particularly
close attention to environmental factors. For example, ecological
models appear much more successful in explaining hunter-gatherer
behaviour (Steward 1936, Baumhoff 1963, Oliver 1962). Such societies
are often small, dispersed, self-sufficient, modify their environment to
a limited extent only, but, perhaps more important, exhibit social differentiation such that group behaviour tends to express the cumulative
and consensual adaptations of individuals to environmental factors. It
is no coincidence that the greatest successes of ecological analysis have

29

been with peoples of simple technology. Among the first populations to be subjected to empirical investigation of this kind were the Eskimo. As I have already mentioned, it was Boas (1888) who first drew the correlation between sea ice, the distribution of food and human population dispersion; and Mauss and Beuchat (1906) went on to demonstrate a general twofold morphology based on seasonal variations. Revealingly, when ecology does at last get a mention in a widely used textbook (Mair 1972), it is in relation to a discussion of hunting and gathering. In different ways, fieldwork in societies with other subsistence bases has had similar results; among pastoralists, for example, and expansionist swidden cultivators. In such cases environmental relations are superficially represented as being clearer – they appear more direct.

CORRELATIVE STUDIES IN THE POSSIBILIST TRADITION

Partly as a result of the influence already mentioned, but also in part as a response to the explanatory sterility of pre-war functionalism, the fifties and sixties gave rise to a series of studies which, while broadly phrased in the language of 'possibilism', made some attempt to explain patterns of structural variation in terms of key environmental variables. Of those British analyses which did concern themselves with ecology during the phase of functionalist supremacy, most attempted to show links between environmental variables and particular social institutions, to show a correlation between social organizations and environment, but not necessarily to assign the environment causal status. We find a prototype of this kind of approach in the work by Mauss and Beuchat (1906) on Eskimo seasonal variations. Mauss (1906:54) shared Kroeber's view on environmental determinism, namely that social morphology (even material structures such as dwellings) was not the simple function of environment espoused by Ratzel (Durkheim 1900, J. J. Fox 1979). On the other hand, Mauss acknowledged that there were certain general correspondences between a social morphology closely linked to environment and subsistence and the institutions of social life (1979:76). Lienhardt (1964:38–40) and Fox (1979) have seen in the essay by Mauss and Beuchat the model upon which Evans-Pritchard's analysis of the Nuer is based.

To begin with, such studies either reflected this general Maussian approach, or – as we have seen – were an outcome of particular fieldwork conditions. Increasingly, however, they were tied to theoretical critiques of functionalist analysis, such as Worsley's critique of the Fortes analysis of Tallensi kinship (1956) and Leach's *Political systems of highland Burma* (1954) on the cyclical oscillation of Kachin political structure between socio-ecological extremes.

Among the more important of these studies were a series undertaken on East African pastoralist societies. It is interesting and significant that Forde singled out a number of these for discussion in his 1970 Huxley Memorial Lecture. He examined two examples, based in the first place on Evans-Pritchard's Nuer data (1940), and in the second place on the analyses of Gulliver (1955) and Dyson-Hudson (1966) on the Jie, Turkana and Karimojong of nothern Uganda and Kenya. It is useful to summarize briefly the main arguments here to illustrate the dominant character of ethnographic analyses concerned with environmental relations in the British tradition. Their plausibility is consequently only of secondary interest.

In his analysis of Nuer political relations, Forde argues that relations between larger Nuer tribes reflect not only the process of territorial expansion and demographic growth but also the underlying differences in environmental conditions. He is able to do this by observing the different form of political relations in two separate environmental zones. In the earlier Nuer homeland, west of the upper Nile, the topography offered only small and isolated areas of high ground for seasonal occupation. Seasonal movements tended, therefore, to be confined. Tribal units were correspondingly small, around 10,000 persons. On the other hand eastern Nuer land was characterized by more extensive areas of higher ground. The wet-season settlement area was therefore correspondingly larger and water supplies were more restricted. This lead to a much wider dispersal of the population and larger political groups of between 50,000 and 60,000 persons (see Bonte 1979).

The second example is concerned with the interpretation of the different kinds of local and formal groups found in the Karimojong cluster, composed of the Jie, Karimojong and Turkana. During the dry season the Jie and Karimojong camp around river-bed water holes: all that is available. Population density is around 5.79 persons per square kilometre. Homesteads are built permanently at reliable water points by agnatically related kin, usually groups of brothers. Some cultivation is practised. Among the Karimojong, agriculture is rather more marginal and there is less stress on agnatic ties. The country occupied by the Turkana is much more arid with a population density of around 1.35 persons per square kilometre. The uncertain climatic conditions are allied to the absence of concentrated or permanent settlements. Cultivation is absolutely minimal depending on irregular rainfall. The herd-owning unit is correspondingly smaller and is never more than two generations deep. Here there is a greater reliance on an extensive and dispersed set of social relationships. So, as we move from the Jie to the Karimojong to the Turkana, there is increasingly earlier fission of agnatically related groups correlated with an increasingly uncertain and arid environment.

These summary discussions of the literature may be misleading in that they are, necessarily, contractions of extended and often intricate analyses. But they do neatly show the pervading character of such studies – broadly possibilist and correlative, expressing environmental variables as limiting factors. In many ways they are the sociological analogue of twin studies, 'the exposure of the same or similar cultural materials to different environmental influences' (Vayda and Rappaport 1968:487).

LIMITING FACTORS

The notion of 'limiting factor' is central to the possibilist conception of human ecological relations, and it is clearly necessary to scrutinize its use in a little more detail.

There are, of course, *absolute* limits to human survival: at specific barometric pressures, altitudes, temperatures, rates of evaporation of body water relative to wind movement and pressure, optimal and minimal levels of food intake and energy manufacture (Reynolds 1976:11). All these have a direct effect on physiological fitness, and affect the rate of reproduction. They all limit the environments – artificial or natural – in which human populations can live without the aid of special technological assistance.

It is also possible to demonstrate broad correlations between types of habitat, mode of subsistence and population density from which we might infer the presence of limiting conditions (Table 2.1). Such general tabulations were a prominent feature of early human geography and cross-cultural comparison, sometimes implying deterministic links. Interpreted through the conceptual apparatus of possibilism, these schemes indicate *indirect* limits to survival. They do not affect human bodies directly, but rather the possible techniques for supporting those bodies with food and protection. Dry lands and deserts, for example, support only simple food collectors and hunters, such as the !Kung of the Kalahari and aboriginal Australians, or nomadic herdsmen such as the Saharan Tuareg and Bedouin. Only in oases and riverine areas can cultivation be practised. If irrigation were to be introduced into hitherto arid zones, they would, by definition, cease to be deserts. Equally, arctic, tundra and boreal environments tend to support only hunting, food-collecting and nomadic modes of subsistence. This is explained by the presence of permafrost and climatic

Table 2.1 *Some major types of ecological system in relation to forms of human subsistence*

Ecological system	Example	Major characteristics	Food collectors, hunters, fishers	Animal husbanders	Simple cultivators	Advanced cultivators
Tundra	Melville peninsula (Canada)	permafrost	Eskimo	Lapps		
Northern coniferous forest	Siberia	heavy snow, cool summer	Tungus, Naskapi			
Deciduous hardwoods	Atlantic Europe	cold winter, hot summer; cool winter, warm summer	Mesolithic Europeans		Virginia Amerindians	contemporary Western Europe
Short grass prairie	Patagonia	limited rain, fire	Tehuelche, Argentina	Mongols	Pawnee	Ukrainians
Mediterranean scrub	Aegean islands	dry summer, mild winter	Californian Amerindians	(none for long)	Mapuche (Chile)	Italians
Subtropical desert Savannah	Kalahari East Africa	erratic rain seasonal rain, deep roots	!Kung (Botswana) Hadza (Tanzania)	Tuareg, Bedouin Fulani (Nigeria)	Tuareg Bemba (Zambia)	Egyptians northern India
Tropical rain forest	New Guinea	even rain	Tasaday (Philippines), Mbuti (Zaire)		Kuikuru (Brazil)	parts of Sulawesi (Indonesia)
Arctic iced seas	Bering Sea	mainly ice-covered, sharp seasonal distinctions	Eskimo			
Temperate plankton–herring seas	North Sea	temperate climate	European fisheries			
Blue water tropical seas	Caribbean, Sargasso Sea	low nutrients	Miskito turtling			

conditions which fluctuate violently between various maxima and minima. In hot deserts the operational factor is simply the absence of water; in cold deserts it is the absence of water, trapped in ice or a frozen subsoil, and temperatures which no cultigens are known to tolerate. Apart, though, from these rather obvious exceptions, the major subsistence strategies are found in all major human habitats.

While generalizations of this kind tell us something about the extreme conditions to which *Homo sapiens* can adapt under given social and technical conditions, they advance our knowledge of the interaction of social relations, culture and environmental variables very little. For the most part, they are peripheral to an understanding of social organization and its variations. Despite theoretical rhetoric, explicitly possibilist ethnographic analyses are rare. No doubt this has something to do with the fact that, when put to the test, it is difficult to be precise about how *specific* conditions do limit. In such circumstances generalizations are a safe option, encouraged by a theory which is anyway disinclined to focus on ecological relations.

Because food-collecting populations have for so long been regarded as the classic example of limitation on social development through the presence of environmental extremes, it is not surprising that it should be here that we find the clearest empirical specification of possibilist ideas. The study by Birdsell (1953) discussed in Chapter 1 is a good case in point. Birdsell's approach uses the 'law of the minimum' first published by the plant physiologist Justus Liebig in 1840. This principle, following Odum (1953:88), states that the occurrence and success of an organism in a given situation are limited by certain materials essential for growth and reproduction, and that those materials available in amounts most closely approaching the critical minimum (that is, in shortest supply) will tend to be the limiting ones. As we have seen, Birdsell was able to show that the density of a number of aboriginal Australian tribes correlated with rainfall, and that the greater the variability the greater the tendency for correlation. This he saw as an illustration of the Liebig effect. There are, however, several difficulties with this explanation. For example, he uses rainfall as the best available measure of limitations on plant growth, although it is the properties of local soils which will actually determine how much rain is available to plants. Different soils may produce radically different vegetation in areas of identical average rainfall. Consequently, *effective* water is likely to be a better measure. Furthermore, Birdsell reduces a number of complex phenomena subject to many influences – population size and density, patterns of mobility and breeding habits – to a single explanation, assuming the factors to be in equilibrium and the food habits controlling the selection of nutritive resources to be relatively fixed (Bennett 1976:176–7; but see Birdsell 1973:355–6). The time when observations are made is important: groups tend to have wide ranges and band composition is in a constant state of flux. This is not to say that the Liebig effect does not operate in human populations. It has been suggested (Bennett 1976:177) that it may possibly occur in agricultural populations where specialized food production depends on highly specific and marginal resources, such as where marginal moisture has a critical effect on the success of grain farming. The grain-producing areas of the North American and central Asian plains are an example of this. The difference between the small-scale tribal case and industrialized agriculture is the extent to which the technology has been created to cope with marginality. In both cases the Liebig principle is really equivalent to strategies available for coping with resource factors; if limited, then the marginal resources may be seen as an environmental minimum beyond which the agricultural regime cannot adjust.

SWIDDEN CULTIVATION AND SETTLEMENT

Swidden, or long-term-fallowing horticultural regimes are to be found in many diverse habitats and have incorporated a great variety of techniques of cultivation and domesticated plants. They characteristically involve the partial or complete clearance of bush by cutting, and often burning; short-term cultivation in the area cleared; and abandonment to fallow for a longer period of time than the preceding phase of cultivation.

Although it is difficult and potentially misleading to generalize about such a widespread form of cultivation, it is useful to isolate a number of general attributes of swiddening, following D. R. Harris (1972: 246–51):

1. It is essentially small-scale, with cleared plots seldom larger than a hectare.

2. Plots may be planted with single crops, such as maize, rice, manioc, taro, yam, millet or sweet potato, depending on the region; or planted with a mixture of different crops, often including trees and shrubs as well as herbs.

3. Swiddening is land-intensive and labour-intensive. As plots are cultivated only for short periods there are usually large areas of fallow land unused surrounding a settlement. Technology is generally limited to axes, knives of various kinds, digging sticks and the use of fire. Between 500 and 1,000 man-hours per year are spent in cultivation activities, no less time than some food collectors spend on their entire

subsistence. Though intensive, labour does not require much cooperation, and is usually handled on a household basis.

4. Contrary to popular belief, swidden techniques can be highly
productive compared with fixed-field cultivation.

5. It is characteristically associated with low population densities,
because of the large amounts of land always in fallow. It is this which
limits population rather than productivity. Gross densities seldom
exceed 58 per square kilometre, and may be as low as 1.5 in parts of the
Amazon basin.

6. High densities are usually associated with root-crop cultivation
under tropical forest conditions. For example, certain Chimbu tribes in
the New Guinea highlands exist at densities between 162 and 201 per
square kilometre, largely on the basis of the propagation of sweet
potato (Brookfield and Brown 1963:119–22).

7. Settlements are generally dispersed and composed of fewer than
200–250 individuals.

Swiddening – sometimes misleadingly called 'shifting' cultivation –
has repeatedly been characterized as a limiting technique. It has been
claimed that: *specifically*, it limits the period (a) that a particular plot
may be used and (b) that a settlement may be occupied; and that
generally, it has prevented the development of complex social formations.

There is no doubt that swidden techniques reduce crop yield over
time: through the increase of pests, diseases and weeds, a deterioration in the physical and nutrient condition of the soil, topsoil erosion,
and changes in the number and composition of soil organisms (Netting
1974:26). The organic matter in many tropical soils is low, and nutrients released by burning woody vegetation (phosphorus, nitrogen
and potassium) decline with leaching and crop removal (Nye and
Greenland 1960:40–5, 118–20). Although declining yield may often be
due to insect pests and competing weeds (Janzen 1973), there is now
considerable evidence to suggest that swiddening may be highly destructive under population pressure: through a rapid draining of nutrients, increasing cutting of younger forest and re-use of old plots.
The reaching of critical limits may be apparent from the stripping of
topsoil, sheetwash erosion and gullying, as in parts of nothern Ghana;
while there may be a precarious nutritional level, seasonal hunger,
weight loss and substantial population emigration (Netting 1974:26–7).
Where re-location of settlements is caused by environmental degradation through the progressive siting of plots at increasing distances from
the village, land exhaustion may be a permanent recurrent condition of
the system, or it may be an exceptional occurrence due to a steep rise in
population density. Cases of recurrent shifting have been reported for

central African seed cultivators, such as the Mambwe on the weak, leached soils of the woodland savannah (Allan 1965). However, provided population increase does not lead to a shortening of the fallow period to the point where it is impossible for the soil to recover its fertility, periodic settlement re-siting is not inevitable (D. R. Harris 1972:249).

Often plots may return to fallow before they are effectively exhausted of nutrients. Weed growth, economic and social (even supernatural) considerations may be more important in shifting the location of gardens than environmental degradation (Ellen 1978:177–80, Carneiro 1964:15–17). Likewise, actual re-location of settlements is as likely to be linked to availability of protein sources in animal populations or security, as among the Peruvian Amahuaca (Carneiro 1964:16); or to migratory pioneering, as among the Iban in large areas of pre-colonial Borneo (Freeman 1970), and many other peoples on cultivation frontiers.

The relationship between the length of cultivated period and length of fallow is shown in Table 2.2. It might seem reasonable to expect an increase in the land-use factor to reflect growing impermanence of settlement location and system instability. However, the Kompiai and Nduimba peoples of New Guinea with factors of 6.4 and 12 respectively are not only sedentary, but moving through phases to more intensive appropriation of existing resources without appreciable ill-effects (W. C. Clarke 1966). Similarly, the Kuikuru of central Brazil, with a land-use factor of 8.3, have maintained settlements in the same place for up to 90 years, while only reluctantly cultivating old plots (Carneiro 1960). The cultivation–fallow ratio is not the same as the ratio between the length of time the soil will sustain cultivation with satisfactory results and the period required for the restoration of fertility, and therefore does not necessarily reflect critical density or degree of shifting. Neither can a typology based on the degree of permanence – such as Allan's (1965) 'permanent', 'semi-permanent', 'recurrent', 'shifting' – necessarily reflect progressive environmental degradation.

But there are other factors which affect the population and settlement potential of swiddening: local surface topography, soil fertility, microclimate, the presence or absence of weed grasses and insect pests. More generally, there is zonal variation in climate, soils and vegetation which must be taken into account. One key factor of this kind is the length of the growing season which the ecosystem permits, for swiddening has its greatest potential where this can be maximized. This might suggest the humid tropics, but most humid tropical soils are not very fertile below the surface horizon, restoration of soil fertility is a slow process, and there is a short and not always dependable

Table 2.2 *Relationship between length of cultivated period and length of fallow for selected populations*

Population	Years cultivated (y)	Years fallow (r)	Approximate land-use factor (r/y)	Source
1. Central Africa, various semi-permanent groups	5–8	5–8	0	Allan (1965)
2. Central Africa, various permanent groups			2	Allan (1965)
3. Hanunoo, Philippines	3	8	2.6	Conklin (1957)
4. Batainabura, New Guinea highlands	2	5–10	3.75	Clarke (1966)
5. Central Africa, various groups displaying recurrent occupancy	2–6	6–30	4.5	Allan (1965)
6. Upper Kaironk, New Guinea highlands	1.25–2.5	10	5.3	Clarke (1966)
7. Northern Thailand	1	5–6	5.5	Judd (1964)
8. Kompiai, New Guinea highlands	1.25–2.5	12	6.4	Clarke (1966)
9. Nuaulu, eastern Indonesia	1–3	2–25	7	Ellen (1978)
10. Central Africa, various permanently shifting groups	2–3	20–30	7.2	Allan (1965)
11. Kuikuru, central Brazil	3	25	8.3	Carneiro (1960)
12. Nduimba, New Guinea highlands	1.25–1.5	16	12	Clarke (1966)
13. Tsembaga, New Guinea	1	14	14	Rappaport (1968)

dry season for burning cleared vegetation. As ash is a crucial source of nutrients this results in less fertile soil. Burning is particularly important where grains, such as maize, are grown. Root crops may be more dependent on a mulch-like litter of organic debris than ash. In colder and temperate zones of the high and mid-latitudes, on the other hand, natural regeneration is checked by low temperatures and, in continental areas, low and irregular rainfall. Seasonal drought and long dry seasons may be an inhibiting factor between the temperate zones and the humid tropics, but in intermediate tropical zones with a short but regular dry season, conditions for swiddening are optimal. Vegetation type may also affect productive potential, and swidden is best adapted to forest ecosystems, both technically and ecologically. Forest clearance provides more nutrients per hectare than shrub or herbaceous vegetation, and herbaceous vegetation (such as *Imperata* grassland) is often a mark of overworking the system. Techniques used by swidden cultivators are also unsuitable for properly clearing and managing grasslands.

Crop complex may also affect settlement potential. Protein-rich seed crops absorb more nutrients than starchy root crops. Seed-crop swiddening is therefore, on the whole, less stable than vegecultural swiddening because it requires a longer fallow period to restore fertility and is therefore less capable of supporting sustained population growth. There is evidence for the instability of maize and rice-dominated swidden systems from both South America and Southeast Asia, and of their progressive invasion of vegecultural areas (D. R. Harris 1969:13, Spencer 1966). Grain-based swiddening is likely to be even more unstable in temperate zones, where regeneration is slower. In general the high land demands of swiddening ensure that, unless the system is intensified, settlements are usually dispersed and population low; and that high densities are only possible with root-crop polyculture (D. R. Harris 1972:258).

Early accounts of swidden cultivation characterize it as unplanned, aimless, nomadic and unproductive, uneconomic in terms of land and labour and destructive of the environment (Whittlesey 1937). That this is in many cases inaccurate has been shown by recent work. Nevertheless, the tendency of some investigators to become completely enamoured of their object of scrutiny, presumably sustained by a Rousseauesque primitivism or functionalism, has not been very helpful. In this view swiddeners seem so harmoniously integrated into their resource base that it is hard to believe that they might be damaging it at all (Street 1969:106).

Swiddening is unproductive per unit area of land cultivated, but in terms of yields per unit of labour its productivity is high, sometimes exceeding fixed-field cultivation. For example, Leach (1959) has demonstrated that tribal peoples in upland Burma recognize that swiddening in forest areas produces higher yields for less work than continuous cultivation in terraced fields (see also Harris 1972:247). Yields can be even higher where cultivators engage in polycultural planting, as the harvesting of different cultigens is staggered throughout the year. Conklin (1954) reports 40 different types of crop in a single Hanunoo swidden in the Philippines, and similar data are now available from elsewhere. Because productivity in a forest-fallow system may be high, more than meeting essential calorific requirements, it is capable of producing surpluses with ease (Carneiro 1964:17–18). In many cases populations are not appropriating their environments to the full.

The productivity of plots may be maintained over long periods by varying the cropping pattern from year to year, by introducing silviculture after the first year, and so on. In this way forest-fallow systems may be transformed into permanent cultivation, even under tropical conditions. In parts of the New Guinea highlands, fallow periods have become increasingly shorter, though plots no less productive, under population and social pressure, altering completely the character of the subsistence pattern. Clarke (1966) has identified five phases, which can be applied more widely: (1) forest-fallow (2) bush-fallow (3) short-fallow (4) annual cropping (5) multi-cropping. That this represents a succession is shown by evidence of preceding phases and initial signs of succeeding phases at each site, and from archaeological data.

Such evidence shows swiddening to be a dynamic system of land use with a quite elastic productive capacity, allowing for an increase in population through agricultural intensification and the shortening of fallow (Boserup 1965). It suggests that swiddening need not necessarily inhibit the development of complex social formations, contrary to the expressed view of writers such as Meggers (1954). For example, classic lowland Maya civilization in Yucatan between 900 B.C and A.D. 900 was almost certainly based on swidden cultivation and man-powered transportation. It was also able to support ceremonial and population centres with elite groups and specialists, some existing continuously for 250 years (Dumond 1961). However, it now seems feasible that this was made possible through the cultivation of root crops such as manioc and sweet potato, and perhaps limited silviculture, rather than on the less stable high-input-demanding maize regime (Bronson 1966). Elsewhere, for example in parts of Southeast Asia, Ceylon and West Africa, root-crop swiddening may also have permitted the development of centralized polities, although in each case the situation is complicated by the factor of trade in food and critical resources, dependency on other non-domesticated foods and the movement of surplus food from periphery to centre. Where swiddening is practised without the development of complex polities, this cannot simply be the reason, though it may be a contributory factor. In reviewing Meggers's hypothesis for South America, recent work has supported the existence of Amazon chiefdoms (e.g. Carneiro 1970), emphasized more specific environmental factors (precise ratings of temperature, rainfall, soils and landforms) and recognized that technical, economic and political factors may often be more crucial than environmental ones in determining productive potential (Denevan 1966). The availability of protein and fat-rich fish resources may be more crucial in restricting population concentration than swiddening (Lathrap 1968); while the disappearance of permanent high-density, stratified populations of swiddeners in the riverine areas of the Amazon basin was probably due as much to European penetration as to environmental degradation (Netting 1974:23–4).

CARRYING CAPACITY

Arguments of the above kind clearly rest on the ability to determine the critical population which can be permanently supported under a given set of conditions. Where they have been criticized it has been for failing to accurately gauge these limits. In particular, there has frequently been an assumption that one variable – energy, or the amount of land necessary for the collection or domestication of sufficient calories and other materials – is always the key limiting one. I shall examine the issues involved in relation to swidden cultivation, as this has occasioned a lively interest in the literature.

Carrying capacity, or the maximum population that a particular environment can support indefinitely without leading to degradation, has long been of interest. It has been employed to estimate the size of aboriginal populations, their growth potential, the limits of the system of which they are part, and the point at which various factors become critical (Brush 1975). It has been used to explain why certain societies have maintained a particular population level, not developed specified organizational forms, shift repeatedly from one locality to another, or are exceedingly poor. The first person to develop a means of measuring carrying capacity for populations of cultivators was Allan (1949), but the formula most widely used in ethnographic work has been that of Carneiro (1960). As Feachem (1973) has shown, the various formulae suggested are all basically the same, and all assume that the ratio of cultivated land to available land equals the ratio of current population to carrying capacity. The computation involves calculating five variables from field data: population (P), total arable land (T), length of fallow (R), area of cultivated land necessary to support a hypothetically average individual with food for one year (A), and the number of years before a productive plot is abandoned (Y). Their relationship can be expressed in the following equation:

$$P = \frac{T}{\left(\frac{R + Y}{A}\right) Y}$$

Unfortunately, there are immense difficulties in determining carrying capacity. The total amount of available land may vary

considerably between different areas, and Allan (1965) has estimated that
this ranges from 5 to 50 per cent of the total land in tropical Africa,
averaging around 25 per cent. Length of necessary fallow also varies
(Table 2.2), according to crop, altitude, soil quality and intensity of
cultivation. Moreover, what land is available and the length of fallow
in any particular locality is not simply an environmental and technical
question, but a social one as well. For reasons such as these it may
make sense in any specific analysis to distinguish between several
different fallow periods, and between cultivated land, all land *potentially* cultivable, and land cultivated at different intensities. Clearly,
what is cultivable and what is adequate fallow are not easily standardized cross-culturally.

Estimates of land required per person are equally difficult to compute. These are usually based on individual food consumption or
experimentally derived values. Both approaches are hazardous.
Actual consumption may not be a good guide to what is required in the
long run. One method of calculating the land required to feed one
person adequately is to estimate the calories consumed by the entire
population and divide this by the annual calorific yield of each unit-
area of cultivated land (Rappaport 1968:288–92). In swiddening the
actual land required is that in use *plus* fallow. Leeds (1961:18) explains
it in the following manner:

The proportion of land held in reserve for future cultivation must be several
times greater than that under cultivation at any given moment, the proportion
varying with such factors as the rate of fertility recovery, the type of weed and
grass invasion, the rate of growth of the secondary forest, the rate of mechanical reconstruction of the soil, and so on. Thus of the total amount of land
potentially available in a given expanse of territory, only a part can be horticul-
turally exploited at any one time. Where the total potentially arable land in a
given expanse is itself only a small proportion of the total area, the amount of
land available for cultivation at any one moment is, of course, minute.

Spatial variation within the system under examination may be underestimated but crucial. There may often be a wide range of carrying
capacities over a small area, say, within the confines of a single society.
This is especially so where soils are variable (Allan 1965). Techniques
of cultivation are not always uniform within a single population, and
many peoples practise combinations of extensive and intensive techniques simultaneously. Plots at different stages of development or
regression to fallow have different outputs, and even plots at the same
stage of development may vary widely in their composition. In grain-
growing areas the ratio of seed grain to that available for consumption
may vary, and thus affect the productive efficiency of the system
(Table 2.3). Population size, population mobility and carrying capacity

Table 2.3 *Carrying capacities and other related data for selected pre-industrial populations*[a]

Location	Date	Subsistence	Population per km² (total population)	Carrying capacity per km²	Population as percentage of carrying capacity	Crop yield per hectare in kcal	Area (ha) required to feed one person	Seed: harvest ratio	Source
1. Kuikuru, central Brazil	1956	manioc swiddens	0.01 per acre	395 per acre – infinite			0.262		Carneiro 1960
2. Lamet, highland Vietnam	1951	rice swiddens	2.9 (total area)	16–20		2,670	0.3		Izikowitz 1951
3. Tambon Baw, north Thailand	1958–9	rice swiddens	13	40		4,000		1:31	Judd 1964
4. Mru, Vietnam	1950–60	rice swiddens	23	23	1.00		0.3–0.5	1:50	Löffler 1960
5. Hanunoo, south Philippines	1952–4	rice and mixed swiddens	30	48		4,000	0.2	1:48	Conklin 1957
6. Yaruro, Venezuela	1950–60	manioc swiddens	41.4	115			0.2	1:100	Leeds 1961
7. Iban, east Malaysia	1949–51	rice swiddens					0.3		Freeman 1970
8. Tsembaga Maring, New Guinea highlands	1962	yam swiddens; domesticated pigs	42.43 (204)	284–457 (total area)	0.45–0.72	1,360			Rappaport 1968
9. Nuaulu, eastern Indonesia	1969–71	mixed-root swiddens; sago collecting	(180)	40–200 (3,829 total area)					Ellen 1978
10. Miskito, Nicaragua	1968–9	swiddens; hunting, fishing	(997)	(4,693 total area)					Nietschmann 1973:241
11. Oaxaca valley, Mexico	1300B.C.	irrigated maize	(550)	(1,200 total area)	0.05				Kirkby in Bayliss-Smith 1978
12. Ontong Java, Solomon Islands	1910	taro, coconut, fishing	(1,350)	(2,045 total area)	0.66				Bayliss-Smith 1978
13. Tongatapu Island, Tonga Group	1773	yam and taro swiddens	(8,650–19,000)	(27,700–34,600 total area)	0.25–0.69				Green, in Bayliss-Smith, 1978
14. Kachin, highland Burma	–1954	rice swiddens				1,360–3,630	0.25		Leach 1954

a Virtually all figures given here require some qualification, because of the peculiar characteristics of the situation or techniques employed by the researcher. The comparative usefulness of the table is therefore restricted, and is meant to be illustrative rather than definitive.

are influenced not only by cultivation potential or usable land area, but by factors such as the availability of protein-rich fish, game (Nietschmann 1973:239–40), and other non-domesticated resources (Ellen 1978:181–3).

Calculations are usually based on certain other-things-being-equal assumptions which take little account of deterioration. Street (1969:106) points out that deterioration is a cumulative process and that technology, cropping pattern, and *per capita* food consumption are never qualitatively or quantitatively constant in a given subsistence system. Resources and inputs fluctuate over time (Hayden 1975), as do outputs. There may be seasonal or annual fluctuations, or ones over longer time periods, in the relative intensity of particular limiting or tolerance factors. Relatively minor technological changes may alter the capacity of the ecosystem to support a given population, while the critical level depends on the equilibrium struck between humans and other species. Losses in crop productivity due to weeds, pests and diseases do not necessarily remain constant and have to be considered in calculating carrying capacity. Local rates of erosion, leaching, retrogression of vegetation and changing yields have also been overlooked by anthropologists, while the usefulness of chemical analysis as a comparative measure of soil fertility is limited due to difficulties in interpretation (Nye and Greenland 1960:98).

Most formulae for calculating carrying capacity tend to be mechanistic and do not allow for critical local variation, although some attempts have been made to improve upon the pioneer approaches (Brookfield and Brown 1963). Unqualified indices may be quite misleading and the variables required seldom known accurately. But by varying the formulae and attaching qualifying conditions to ensure appropriateness to specific cases, the comparative value of the calculations is diminished (Brush 1975:806–7). Moreover, indices seldom indicate the population which could *survive* in a given area, and other environmental limiting factors may operate below this level (Rappaport 1968:88). Because of this, some (e.g. Lea 1964:12) have dismissed such attempts entirely, but such a drastic measure is not really necessary. It is sufficient to interpret the 'critical limits' determined by the formulae with the scepticism they deserve, and view carrying capacity in general as much more of a gradient (W. C. Clarke 1971:190).

Such technical and environmental factors, variable as they are, are only part of the information required to determine the population capacity of pre-industrial cultivation systems. Carrying capacities within a region may vary with the efficiency of political and administrative control, while land-tenure rules, by influencing the spatial distribution of landholdings, can create differences in carrying capacity where environmental and technical conditions are otherwise identical. Beyond environment, local social relations of production and mode of subsistence must be taken into account. For example, the quantity and variability of surplus production and surplus time required; the extent of variability in seasonal conditions, and therefore labour requirements; and whether variability in harvest between different seasons is perceived as providing the necessary insurance against famine. Finally, estimates of carrying capacity have generally assumed a subsistence economy, and ignored the integration of local economies into regional, national and international systems (Clark and Haswell 1971).

In any improved model of carrying capacity it is necessary to take into account *variable* levels of output and labour input,[3] in addition to the factors already mentioned. While food production may dominate an economy, production for exchange stimulated socially or through trade may be crucial. Terms of trade often mean that marketed surpluses reduce the population level a region can support. Moreover carrying-capacity calculations should take into account labour input (as a reasonable measure of perceived welfare) and quantity of production. All output for a given soil or crop type is relative to the intensity of input, which is itself socially constrained. On the basis of such observations, Bayliss-Smith (1978:131–3) has suggested that carrying capacity be re-defined as 'the population supportable by the *maximum* level of yield compatible with an *acceptable minimum* level of return'. A 10:1 output:input ratio is about the minimum acceptable (M. Harris 1971:217, Leach 1976:11, Bayliss-Smith 1978, Rappaport 1968:262). Determined empirically this minimum is 1,750 kcal per hour of labour for major economic activities in subsistence societies. It is also necessary to take into account nutritional and cultural constraints affecting the production of certain foods, all the forms of appropriation and the proportion of the total energy needs of a population that each product should supply, as well as the energy yields for each major land use at various levels of labour intensity, including the maximum.

Once the carrying capacity has been determined, the average labour input per productive person required for the population to be supported is calculated, and the mean labour inputs at lower population densities. The aggregate energy yields of the economy may be portrayed graphically, and the impact of labour inputs on increasing output per person above the level needed for subsistence estimated. From this a matrix may be formulated giving, for different levels of leisure and surplus, the populations supportable by a specified economy. Bayliss-Smith terms these 'standard populations' and they represent the maximum supportable at different levels of welfare.

Given what is now generally agreed to be the under-production of most kinship-based economies (Sahlins 1972:41–99), this seems a much more useful approach.

ENVIRONMENTAL LIMITS ON THE SELECTION OF CULTIVATION SITES

Carrying-capacity computations concern environmental resources at the level of population. Even so, we have seen how necessary it is to consider variability of different factors in the local system, and the subtle and often crucial ways in which social relations and values may affect their expression. The limiting elements of the environment are mediated through social relations and must be much more specifically defined, and their interaction with social variables carefully discerned. This is clear from two recent studies of the upper and lower altitudinal limits for settlement: with respect to frost in the New Guinea highlands and malaria among the Kenyan Meru (Waddell 1975, Netting 1974:243). What in one analysis may be regarded as independent limiting factors may in another be divisible into yet finer ones, providing yet further scope for the interaction of social factors. The *level* at which we determine limiting factors is itself problematic. The issue is well illustrated in the way the Nuaulu of eastern Indonesia select sites for cultivation.

Within the area appropriated by the Nuaulu (Ellen 1978:108–60) particular localities are chosen for intense cultivation. In narrowly environmental terms land is mainly rejected for any of the following reasons: poor drainage (including swamp land), limiting surface conditions such as eroded terrain, topography (including slope), soil conditions, limiting vegetation (e.g. *Imperata* grassland), exposure to sun and wind and previous use of land.

Nuaulu gardens are generally situated on valley walls, though not to avoid drainage problems. Flooding is of little concern and gardens on valley floors may occasionally be waterlogged. Where flooding is likely certain crops are avoided and others with high-water tolerance, such as taro, are planted. Rapid drainage on steep slopes is offset by almost daily rainfall to retain soil moisture. Rock outcrops are avoided, and in places are used as cemeteries. The occurrence of coralline limestone in certain areas requires selective placing of plots, but this is generally in areas that are also avoided because of their distance from settlements and are only cultivated by some clans because of shortages in land nearer to the village. Occasional erosion may sometimes block paths but thick vegetation cover prevents most erosion. There is no erosion due to overcultivation. Differential planting of species is practised to secure optimum sunlight and temperature conditions. Local relief is such that the greatest surface area for gardens is on steep valley slopes. Over 70 per cent of the plots are on slopes which may be as steep as 35°. In addition to relief factors, the fact that flat areas, coastal margins, valley floors and alluvial plains are claimed by non-Nuaulu makes them inaccessible. Such land may also be avoided because it is already occupied by groves of cash crops or because residual areas may be too small. Difficulties due to soil variation are coped with by differential planting of species responsive to such variation. Gardens on very poor soils are abandoned prematurely. The light and workable topsoils of the valley sides are preferred to the difficult soils of the valley bottoms. Soils in areas of coralline limestone are recognized as fertile but are unworkable in other respects. Limiting vegetation is of little consequence, and *Imperata* grassland in particular is rare. Mature forest may occasionally present technical and labour difficulties in clearing, and for this reason may sometimes be avoided, but otherwise is regularly cut. Particular trees and sections of forest may be left standing if they pose insuperable technical problems, or if they contain species valued for their products. Most land is cut from secondary forest, of which medium growth and bamboo thicket is preferred for technical reasons.

In the process of selection, social factors enter at every stage. Land may be unavailable for religious reasons, because it is already under cultivation, because an individual may have no clan right of clearance, or because the rights are of a different kind. Clans with less land cannot therefore afford to be as discriminating with regard to environmental impediments as those with plenty. Additionally, whether a particular portion of bush is cut may be affected by anticipated labour requirements, time considerations, long-term planning, conflict of individual interests, distance and accessibility from village, relationship to garden house, and other gardens (particularly those of different stages of development in a garden complex). In short, the environmental limiting factors are there but they are locked into a constantly altering web of social factors which determine their material effect on the dispersion of plots.

KEY VARIABLES AND PRIME MOVERS

The concept of carrying capacity was originally based on the assumption that it is energy, available in the bulk of food produced in a given area, which is limiting. Such a preoccupation with energy in anthropology carries through from the early work of White (1949) to that of more recent writers (e.g. Rappaport 1968). In addition to energy, humans require water, vitamins, minerals and nutrients derived from protein, fat and carbohydrates in order to survive, function and maintain optimal health (Little and Morren 1977:35). Recent fieldwork among the Gadio Enga and Maring (Morren 1977:282, 308) suggests that energy is not limiting for these New Guinea highland populations. Only in extreme cases does energy appear to be limiting in human populations, and it is only so in certain special circumstances among the Maring (Vayda and McCay 1977:414). It therefore cannot form the basis of evolutionary arguments which see energy maximization as a primary determinant, as, for example, in the work of Brookfield and Hart (1971; see Morren 1977:308).

To counter this problem certain writers (e.g. Dornstreich 1977:260) have emphasized the limiting character of protein availability and of the amount and distribution of foods in tropical diets primarily composed of vegetable matter. However, Vayda and McCay (1977:414) note that there is no evidence to suggest that protein is an important limiting factor for any New Guinea people, and are concerned that an obsession with calories may be replaced by one with protein. All current empirical evidence points to the possibility that both energy and protein may be limiting under certain conditions, but also that more often neither is limiting in itself. We now know that the availability of certain vitamins or trace elements may – in some cases – ultimately determine the survival of an animal population.

What is clear is that the concept of a 'limiting factor' cannot *a priori* be allotted to any one thing, whether expressed in the form of Liebig's principle, or in some other way. The difficulties presented by the Liebig principle were recognized in 1913 by Shelford, who suggested that organisms can only survive under conditions they can tolerate and that the availability of critical materials is only *one* of these conditions. But while looking at the environment as a set of limits is practical, the impression given by both Liebig's and Shelford's approach is misleading, since single factors are by no means consistently limiting. The real limits are much more complex and can only be determined on the basis of careful empirical analysis which includes investigating the effects of reaching such limits. Other factors may be more abundant, but nevertheless moderate the effects of potential limiting factors. Limiting factors must be determined on the basis of substantive empirical analysis, and the effect of their non-implementation. They will rarely determine the survival of a population, but their removal may allow for population growth, surplus accumulation and so on. Also, Liebig's principle clearly cannot be expected to operate in an unstable ecological system, or one undergoing change. In these circumstances it is not the least abundant element which is limiting but the interaction of many elements. Furthermore, single critical factors may fluctuate such that a population can tolerate shortages for certain periods. What is critical is *duration*.

CONCLUSION

Analyses in the possibilist tradition have contributed in a number of important respects to our understanding of human environmental relations. Possibilism is rightly associated with a recognition that physical conditions enter intimately into social and cultural patterns. It has resulted in increasing attention to variation, the extent to which *Homo sapiens* has modified his environments, and how subsistence patterns themselves were shaped by social organization and belief (e.g. Richards 1932, 1939). It has fostered exploration of the concept of 'limiting factor'. It has warned against simple geographical controls and advocated the detailed analysis of each society. The focus on empirical fieldwork, however, has been the most important legacy of the possibilist viewpoint, and it has been fieldwork which has encouraged and sustained its general theoretical stance.

Where possibilism succeeded was in its stress on the importance of empirical investigation; where it was inadequate was in its methodology and theory. Because it was linked in part to anti-Marxist and anti-materialist ideology and the rejection of evolutionary holism, it was compelled to adopt a sometimes crude inductionism and a logically vacuous circularity in argument (Baker 1962, Gellner 1963). Its empirical strength was reduced to empiricist weakness. Anthropologists were increasingly bewildered by the variety of cultural experience. Possibilism addressed itself, therefore, to limited problems posed in an idiom which claimed to be scientific but which avoided questions of causality and origin.

The theoretical thrust of possibilism is therefore negative. Accepting that humans can control and change nature should not lead us to believe that this ability is infinite and Promethean. Industrial societies are often said to have overcome the imperatives of physical environment, but this is true only in a relative technological sense, and in the sense that the more complex the social organization the more easily a greater surplus product and connected geographical spread can mitigate environmental hazards in particular areas (Watson and Watson 1969:113). No matter how 'advanced' a society, there are always environmental factors to which it must adjust. Cultural evolution increases not only the possible range of techniques for transforming nature, but also the requirements of a population in the form of energy and materials. With technological progress, the links between human populations and the environment become more complex. It is not a

49

freeing from nature, but its wider utilization. Such arguments do not invalidate the notion of the determinate character of particular environmental variables, simply the mechanical way in which they are sometimes applied. Possibilism has had to adapt itself to an increasingly local field of specification in the search for limiting factors. Rather than dealing with broad cultural regions, the emphasis has shifted to local topographies and micro-environments (e.g. Leach 1961).

In using the safe phraseology of 'constraints' and 'limiting factors' to indicate notions of vaguely permissive and restrictive parameters, the practitioners of possibilism believed they had solved (or avoided) the problem of determinism. They had not. It is simply that the determinism to which they unconsciously appealed was indirect and negative. Describing a factor as a determinant rather than a constraint might be seen as a device for attributing primacy to certain factors rather than others. Water both determines the location of settlements (in that it prevents them in other areas) and constrains their dispersion. Also, if the condition of existence of a form is a single factor then we are more likely to describe it as a determinant than if there are several conditional factors. For example, the distribution of the tsetse fly (a vector in human sleeping sickness and bovine *Trypanosomiasis*) *limits* the localities habitable by cattle-keeping Fulani in northern Nigeria at certain times of the year, and results in a movement during the wet months to areas north of the forest (Stenning 1957). If we accept that pastoralist subsistence is a constant then it makes perfect logical sense to say that the movement to drier zones is *determined* by tsetse distribution, under given conditions. Similarly, to say that seed-based swiddening is a limiting factor in the development of high-density stratified polities is the same as saying that seed-based swiddening, along with other unspecified factors, determines the existing social formations of this kind.

So possibilism is logically an inverted determinism in which phrases such as 'the environment limits but does not determine' are nonsense. In any empirical analysis the one must *functionally* dissolve into the other. It is precisely this which has enabled me to use Birdsell's analysis of aboriginal Australian territorial groupings in both Chapter 1 and Chapter 2. To view determinism and possibilism as mutually contradictory simply perpetuates a logical tautology. The environment does indeed set limits on what is socially possible under a given set of conditions. It sets outer limits for the evolution of particular systems and the character of their reproduction; and its sets technical limits to interior processes and developmental cycles, such as the selection of garden sites. But in restricting the options it is also helping to determine the final outcome. Throughout, the effects of the environment are mediated by social relations which bear a particular cultural load; both are products of an immediately contingent historical sequence. This appears to have been what Forde meant by the 'middle term' (1934:463), and it is this which determines the variety of possible responses to changing conditions. The problem for the anthropologist is often not to discover whether a variable constrains or determines, but to assess the degree and character of its flexibility. And the extent to which a variable constrains or determines is itself dependent on the cultural configuration resulting from those historically prior environmental relations through which it is mediated.

3

Cultural ecology and the explanatory imperative

In Britain during the thirties environmental possibilism had been no more than a footnote to an empirical and functionalist sociology which was rapidly gaining in confidence and authority. In the United States it was largely an apology for cultural particularism. But dissatisfaction with the intellectual sterility of an empiricism which sought neither explanation nor generalization was to crystallize into a vigorous, if not always coherent, opposition. A regard for the tradition of Wissler and Kroeber, close disciplinary links with prehistoric archaeology (which tended to accentuate material culture and environmental relations), the absence of a dominant theoretical focus (such as existed in Britain) and a new interest in developments in biology all led to a renewed interest in the more positive treatment of relations between culture and environment. These developments conveniently focus on what has been labelled *cultural ecology*,[1] and which is indissolubly associated with the name of Julian Steward.

JULIAN STEWARD

The work of Steward has been the greatest single influence on ethnographic ecology to have come from *within* anthropology. Although Steward had been influenced by Wissler and Kroeber, the differences between the respective approaches are crucial:

1. Kroeber and Wissler (and also Forde) had worked in an essentially geographical idiom. Steward, by contrast, was much more interested in the subtle interrelationships between environment and culture. His work was therefore much more *ecological* in the sense in which we would use this term today.

2. Although Kroeber had attempted to demonstrate correlations beween environment and culture – as between natural areas, cultural areas and population levels in pre-1500 North America – he did not

52

suggest, as did Steward, that similar combinations of environments and technologies tend to be *functionally* and *causally* related to similar social organizations (M. Harris 1968:339–40). Steward was concerned with *explanation* rather than *correlation*, with an *active* rather than a *passive* causal role for the environment, and hence with process rather than classification for its own sake.

3. Whereas Wissler and Kroeber had set their culture–environment equations within an overall particularist framework, linked to a study of culture history and diffusion, Steward was more overtly materialist, in an attempt to break loose from the 'culture from culture' tautology.

4. While earlier writers had sought to establish *general* relationships between environment and culture, phrased in the broad determinist or possibilist language of evolutionary stages and culture areas, Steward was concerned with the application of his ideas to the solution of particular concrete ethnographic problems and the establishment of particular *culture types*. His emphasis on the *local* rather than the *regional* environment assisted in the demolition of the concepts 'environment' and 'culture' as independent wholes.

5. Finally, Steward's ideas were linked to an explicit notion of cultural evolution in which ecological relationships were seen as part of a network of cultural adjustments and adaptations. A specifically evolutionary orientation had been neglected by his immediate intellectual forerunners. But the notion of evolution employed was not of fixed stages through which all societies passed, but of a multilinear process involving a number of possible pathways incorporating different patterns of environmental, social and technical features, while his concept of environmental adaptation was clear, specific, linked to empirical examples and always of a theoretically specified character. Cultural ecology was therefore the study of the adaptive processes by which human societies and cultures adjust through subsistence patterns to a given environment.

In 1936 Steward published his essay, 'The economic and social basis of primitive bands'. This was his first coherent statement of how the interaction between culture and environment might be analysed in causal terms, without lapsing into particularism (M. Harris 1968:666). His method remained broadly unchanged when in 1955 he set out three fundamental procedures in *The theory of culture change*. These were to examine: (1) the relations between environment and exploitative or productive technology (2) the patterns of behaviour involved in appropriation through a specific technology in a particular area and (3) the extent to which behaviour patterns involved in appropriation influence other aspects of culture (Steward 1955:40).

For Steward the interaction between culture and environment

was an incremental process. His analyses focussed attention not on explaining why similar social structures should arise in different environments, but on the similarities found in populations experiencing comparable environmental conditions. Rather than suggest simple correlations between social form and habitat, he attempted to demonstrate the functional relationship between such things as population density, agricultural output, technology, settlement patterns and social organization (Harris 1968:337,666).

Steward attempted to surmount the problem of which variables to select by paying primary attention to those features which empirical analysis showed to be most closely connected to the use of the environment. This constellation of variables he called the 'cultural core'. The number of variables was further reduced by concentrating on those which were significant for particular populations: the spacing of water holes for desert nomads, the distribution of game among hunters, and so on. Steward (1955:37) explains that:

The core includes such social, political and religious patterns as are empirically determined to be closely connected with these arrangements. Innumerable other features may have great potential variability because they are less strongly tied to the core. These latter, or secondary features, are determined to a greater extent by purely cultural–historical factors – by random innovations or by diffusion – and they give the appearance of outward distinctiveness to cultures with similar cores.

Moreover (1955:93):

The diagnostic features . . . will depend in part on particular research interests, upon what is considered important . . . It should be noted, however, that functionally interrelated economic, social, political, religious and military patterns as well as technological and esthetic features have become the basis for developmental taxonomies. These features do not constitute total cultures. They form cultural cores, which are defined according to the empirical facts of cross-cultural type and level.

Steward was concerned with how different cultural cores created similar or different institutions, a concern inevitably leading to the espousal of a concept of multilinear evolution. Both were typological enterprises. For example, in a celebrated paper with Murphy (Murphy and Steward 1956), he compares Canadian Montagnais Algonkian with Mundurucu rubber tappers in Brazil. Both participate in marginal extractive economies which have been subjected to similar forms of exploitation by, and dependence upon, a dominant intrusive culture. This has led to ethnocide and the collapse of traditional social relations, culminating in an atomistic social order where individual families are dependent on traders who buy raw materials. 'Core' adaptations are seen as causal and the analysis as elucidating yet another 'type', in this case, resource extractive marginals (cf. Gould, Fowler and Fowler 1972).

'HUNTER-GATHERER' SOCIETIES AND THE PATRILOCAL BAND

One of Steward's best-known studies is of the formation of patrilineal patrilocal landowning bands under conditions of hunting and gathering subsistence. It is also a good extended example to use in exploring the strengths and weaknesses of his approach.

Steward argued that patrilineal patrilocal landowning bands are formed under conditions of low population density (0.39 persons or less per square kilometre), where non-migratory and scattered game are the main food resource, and where transport is restricted to human carriers. He describes the operation of these factors in the following way (1955:135):

The scattered distribution of the game, the poor transportation, and the general sparsity of the population made it impossible for groups that average over 50 or 60 persons and that have a maximum of about 100 to 150 persons to associate with one another frequently enough and to carry out sufficient joint activities to maintain social cohesion. The band consists of persons who habitually exploit a certain territory over which its members can conveniently range. Customary land use leads to the concept of ownership. Were individual families to wander at will, hunting the game in neighbouring areas, competition would lead to conflict. Conflict would call for alliance with other families, allies being found in related families. As the men tend to remain more or less in the territory in which they have been reared and with which they are familiar, patrilineally related families would tend to band together to protect their game resources. The territory would therefore become divided among these patrilineal bands.

Where game permitted, larger, *composite*, bands were possible, as among the Algonkian of Canada.

Steward claimed that his model should be ideally approximated in such groups as aboriginal Australians and Kalahari Bushmen, and Service (1971) has since modified the Stewardian argument somewhat and seen the former as displaying a prototypical foraging organization. However, recent studies have cast some doubt on the existence of patrilocal bands of this type in both groups, while undermining the model more generally (e.g. Hiatt 1962, 1968). The Stewardian position has been challenged on three main counts:

1. The model assumes that hunter-gatherer societies exist under harsh environmental conditions. This view is based on a stereotype

55

encouraged by early studies on the Eskimo, and the evolutionist assumption that peoples with such a limited technology and who are manifestly unable to modify their environment must necessarily be the least emancipated from the brutal forces of nature. Field research in the last decade has demolished this image (e.g. Lee and DeVore 1968). It is now clear that, with minor exceptions, most hunting and gathering populations have an adequate and reliable food base, that little effort (compared with calories consumed) is necessary to provide for their physical requirements, and that life-spans are surprisingly long with few signs of anxiety and insecurity. For example, Lee (1969) has reported that !Kung San in the Dobe area of the Kalahari spend between 12 and 18 hours per week in food-getting, and that while the very young and very old are equally unproductive they seem to constitute about 40 per cent of the population of most camps. Woodburn (1968) has similarly emphasized the relative absence of subsistence effort in Hadza groups of western Tanzania. Much of the evidence is collected together by Sahlins (1972) in his celebrated but over-argued essay on 'The original affluent society'.

2. The model assumes that hunting is always the most important and determinant strategy in those populations which are – perhaps erroneously – labelled 'hunter-gatherer'. In fact, outside the arctic region, hunting is always unpredictable. Even in the Kalahari, nuts, fruits, roots and berries constitute 60–80 per cent of annual diet by weight, *Ricinodendron* nuts providing the !Kung with an adequate supply of calories and protein and 50 per cent of all their food. Including meat, their diet yields 2,100 calories per head per day (Lee 1969). Hunting and gathering populations have a wide and detailed knowledge of their environment, and groups such as the !Kung and Hadza have a more secure subsistence buffer against famine than their sedentary neighbours. Only the Eskimo, in an environment where extreme weather conditions prevail, run the risk of chronic starvation.

3. Steward based his original model on the Ute, western Shoshoni and other peoples of the interior of the American northwest, for which the ethnographic data are poor. We now know that hunter-gatherer bands are highly flexible, responding to fluctuating resources. The personnel of !Kung bands is constantly changing, with about half of the adult men always living in the groups of their wives (L. Marshall 1960). In particular, there are marked fluctuations in the size and dispersal of bands, expanding in the dry season and contracting in the wet (Lee 1972). A comparable pattern of summer aggregation for hunting and winter dispersal for the appropriation of non-herding animals is reported for nineteenth-century Amerindians of the Great Plains (Oliver 1962).

Cultural ecology and the explanatory imperative

In the light of recent research, Lee and DeVore (1968) set out the main sociological features of hunting and gathering populations as follows: (1) small local groups of about 50 individuals in broad geographical regions; (2) non-isolated local groups linked extensively through social relations of marriage, kinship, visitation and work-organization; (3) egalitarian relations with accumulation of food or personal possessions; (4) land and resources not considered the exclusive right of particular groups, permitting mobility to take advantage of shifting resources; (5) local groups tending towards bilateral affiliation rather than a unilineal pattern; (6) size fluctuation in response to food availability. Local groups are therefore non-corporate and non-territorial. In his later writings, Steward (1968:343) acknowledged that a band size of 25 is more common for aboriginal Australians, San and the western Shoshoni, and that seasonal variability in composition is widespread. B. J. Williams (1974) has suggested a compromise with the Stewardian position. He does not believe that composite bands and bilateral affiliation are common, and follows Service (1971) in claiming that the patrilocal band was more common in the past. More recently, Peterson (1979) has argued that the obsession with band flexibility has led to the neglect of ideologies of landownership which really do exist. The difficulty with all such generalizations is that hunting and gathering populations now occupy only marginal zones, whereas prehistorically they had a far wider distribution where ecological and social conditions must have varied more considerably.

MONOGRAPHIC CULTURAL ECOLOGY

The cultural ecological approach to ethnographic analysis did not really begin until the decade following publication of *The theory of culture change*. But by the late fifties and early sixties there was a growing dissatisfaction with vague culture-typing and functionalist approaches which could not be subjected to Popperian canons of scientific testability, or were too rigid to accommodate change and individual variation. The clearly specified steps in the Stewardian formula, and its stress on adaptation, proved attractive, particularly as the data (some of them quantifiable) existed to test it. Many cases could be cited; a few will have to suffice.[2] For example, Louise Sweet (1965) has argued that among the Bedouin an adaptive core can be identified in a 'minimal camping unit', and that camels grazing on arid pastures and small mobile social units necessary for rapid and frequent movement determine basic social organization. Similarly, Sahlins (1958) illustrates how differences in the social and political organization of closely related Polynesian peoples are a response to islands with

57

varying topographies, areas and resource patterns. Robert Netting (1968), in his work on Kofyar cultivation in central Nigeria, provides a good example of the same approach applied to a population with a swiddening subsistence base. Goldschmidt (e.g. 1965) has used similar techniques in his studies of east African pastoralism. But what all these cases have in common is that in each of them concrete analysis involves some modification of the basic Stewardian formula: the sharpening of vague categories (Netting 1968), the introduction of probabilities, the recognition that causal hypotheses hold true under certain specific conditions and not others (Sweet 1965). Some of the problems, as well as the appeal of the Stewardian approach, are demonstrated in the literary analysis undertaken by Sahlins (1961) on segmentary lineage societies.

The principal strength of cultural ecology for Sahlins is that it avoids circular functionalism (Baker 1962). This kind of tautologous reasoning is particularly evident in Evans-Pritchard's analysis of the segmentary patrilineal kinship relations of the Nuer, where segmentary lineage structures are 'explained' with reference to a 'segmentary principle'. In re-examining the Nuer ethnography and comparing it with that of the Tiv of central Nigeria, Sahlins concludes that segmentary lineage organization can be seen much more profitably as a social means of achieving territorial expansion, triggered by increasing population pressure. Predatory expansion begins at the lowest segmental level and works its way upwards, involving increasingly larger units recruited on the basis of segmentary opposition. In this way it relieves internal pressure through outward expansion. Segmentary lineage societies are therefore organized not so much for internal cohesion as for external opposition, as an adaptation to intertribal competition.[3] The emphasis is on simple causation, and on explaining segmentary organizations as a cross-cultural *type* which is invariably the result of parallel developments.

Such an elegant explanation, however, presents several difficulties. Empirically, there are ethnographic records suggesting that groups with quite different kinship relations may equally facilitate outward expansion. The Iban of Sarawak (Freeman 1970), for example, are well-known for their extensive territorial expansion during the nineteenth century. The Iban local group appears ideally suited to such expansion, to the formation of temporary alliances, and – like the Tiv and Nuer – Iban society was not permanently integrated at the village level. Here the unit of predatory expansion was a local group consisting of cognatically affiliated groups. By contrast, the intrusive movements of Galla warriors across northeast Africa do not appear to have been linked in any special way to kinship arrangements, though they do appear to have been facilitated through an age-set organization (I. Lewis 1965). At a more general level, Sahlins's argument is naive in its simple linear determinism, its distortion of subtle and complex ecological interactions, and in its neglect of the influence of distinctive local histories. For example, Bonte (1979) has recently argued that among the Nuer variable environmental conditions and differential access to land favourable to pastoral production have led to the unequal accumulation of cattle by individuals. The unequal status of individuals leads to differential lineage status, and internal political and economic competition. This encourages a dynamic of expansion, which tends to restore the possibility of equality. Bonte suggests that the structural form of kinship – segmentary patrilineages – obscures the role of kinship in production, and that the segmentary dynamic prevents the development of permanent inequalities. Thus segmentation is linked to expansion but not to predation.

It is now clear that no simple and invariable correlations can be drawn between kinship patterns and ecological conditions in an adaptive sense. But this does not mean that in the cases of the Tiv and Nuer segmentary lineage organization does not act as an effective means of expansion. While we cannot automatically assume that because something so functions it is necessarily a specific adaptation, it is quite possible that its very effectiveness has encouraged its persistence and explicit use for this purpose. In this sense it is an adaptation, forged by individuals through an existing social organization. That other organizations can be similarly employed, or that segmentary organizations do not always serve this purpose, then becomes beside the point.

CULTURAL MATERIALISM AND VULGAR MARXISM

Of those anthropologists who would directly acknowledge the influence of Steward, few are completely uncritical of him, and – as we have seen – some of his basic analytical concepts have only been used after some modification. Among the most effective and enthusiastic of his propagandists, as well as critics, is Marvin Harris. Several of the monographical studies of cultural ecology are methodologically closer to the views of Harris than Steward (e.g. Netting 1968) and it has been Harris who has articulated the revised Stewardian position most effectively and held to it with greatest tenacity.

For Harris, both cultural ecology and cultural evolution rest on the philosophical foundation of a cultural materialism derived from Marx and Engels. Above everything else Harris seeks causes and origins and abhors an anthropology which is reduced to the discussion of 'limited problems cast in an ostensibly scientific idiom' (Harris 1968:530). But

59

Environment, subsistence and system

Harris's Marxism is singularly un-Marxist, though not necessarily wrong for that. He divides social and cultural structures according to ideology, social organization and 'techno-economic' base, the first two being seen as adaptive responses to conditions created by the third. This forms the basis for his materialist theory of history, while predictability of social responses to the same environment under similar technical conditions identifies him with Steward and establishes a legitimacy for wide-ranging cross-cultural comparison through time and space (Harris 1968:4, 658). But Harris rejects the Marxism of *Das Kapital* on the grounds of its contamination with Hegelian dialectics (*ibid.*:230) in favour of the early Marx of the 1845 manuscripts and *The critique of political economy*: 'Social life is essentially *practical*. All mysteries which mislead theory to mysticism find their rational solution in human practice and in the comprehension of practice' (Marx 1971:82). In its rejection of crude economic and environmental determinism, and in the distinction between base and superstructure, Harris sees a parallel between Marx and the causal theory of Steward.[4] He might also have noted (although he did not) a similarity between the Stewardian cultural core and the *morphologie sociale* of Mauss.[5] But Harris is operating at a high level of generalization. He characterizes his approach as nomothetic in contrast to idiographic, meaning that he is concerned with broad generalization about types of social formation over long time periods rather than descriptions of particular cases at any one moment.

But there are difficulties with both Harris's overall theoretical stance and his interpretation of Marx (cf. Llobera 1979). At one level Harris's brand of 'techno-environmental' determinism involves an obvious truism, but in any concrete analysis of the short term becomes absurd. Given a sufficiently long time span and degree of generalization, technological, economic and environmental factors can 'explain' almost all trends of survival and decline, but the nomothetic rhetoric of similarities, tendencies and relativities, and broad classifications of types of social formation has somehow to be translated into the language of ethnographic analysis. Is it really possible to reduce, as techno-environmental determinism requires, intensive agriculture to the ownership of land and continuous occupation (see Bennett 1976:231–2)? But not only does Harris reify broad categories of social types and work backwards down to individual cases, he also treats the categories of the Marxist analytical scheme as being *a priori* descriptive of institutions to which his own data must conform. This approach incorporates the common error of so-called vulgar Marxism in which an apparent hierarchy of institutions is confused with a determinate hierarchy of functions (see Godelier 1977:1–11). In minimizing the interplay between cultural and secondary features, Steward (and Mauss) made much the same mistake. But, while there are severe difficulties with Harris's non-dialectical materialism, his work is significant (perhaps paradoxically) as part of a more broadly based rehabilitation of Marxist thinking in anthropological theory after decades of neglect, hostility and caricature (see Frankenberg 1967).

THE CRITIQUE OF CULTURAL ECOLOGY

It is now possible to identify a number of weaknesses in the Stewardian approach, and in the approaches of those most closely influenced by him. These revolve around seven issues: the cultural core, the selection of significant correlations, linear determinism, function and adaptation, the relationship of ecology to human ecology, appreciation of ecological complexity and history.

Steward has attempted to avoid the problem of what variables to select by employing the notion of cultural core. However, he freely admitted that the variables composing the core were subject to considerable variation; and this is precisely the problem. The core may vary in terms of its institutional components, as well as in terms of the mechanisms of appropriation linked to such components. The so-called 'secondary features' may be in no causal relationship to the core, and Steward has been criticized by Harris for not permitting interplay between variables within and outside the core. Thus, those aspects of social organization seen as being in any way causally related to subsistence techniques are logically internal to the core. Similarly, the composition of the core for any given culture includes all those features 'closely connected with subsistence activities and economic arrangements' (Steward 1955:37), until such relationships observed by the investigator are exhausted. If so many features may be included in the core then the question arises as to when a core becomes an entire cultural pattern, and the concept dissolves into mere tautology. Lack of precision over what constitutes a core leads to difficulties in both empirical analysis and cross-cultural comparison.

Objections to this particular concept in Steward's work have been articulated principally by Marvin Harris for whom it is a 'core of confusion' (1968:661). This is somewhat ironic, since Harris himself employs analytical categories in a rigid and confusing way. Indeed, the very flexibility which he castigates in Steward shows at least some awareness that the categories should be functional rather than institutional ones. This is crucial. Nevertheless, both Steward and Harris see in second-order institutional abstractions – kinship, religion and so on – real-world phenomena. The problem is that the crucial terms of the analysis are not processes but entities, categories into which to sort data. Steward's types are second-order constructs, which may be appropriate and legitimate in archaeological studies where sociological data are absent, but which are misleading when used more generally (cf. J. W. Bennett 1976:227).

The theoretical positions of both Steward and Harris require that social relations of production be reduced to technical means of production, and for Harris, more than Steward, the most exotic of practices must be explained in terms of its mundane functions.[6] Such an approach necessarily denies that social systems can be transformed through determinate changes in social relations rather than material means alone. Effectively, it denies a role to history. This posed an acute problem for Steward who – as we have seen – affirmed the importance of the superorganic character of culture and was critical of both environmental and economic determinism on the grounds that they both contain their conclusions within the problem (Steward 1955:87). Thus, the criticism that he underestimates historical factors is not entirely warranted, although his attitude towards them is ambiguous. For Steward 'changes are *basically* traceable to new adaptations required by changing technology and productive arrangements' (my italics). Other factors are relegated to a vague residue of 'culture-historical factors'. History appears to be used to account for what his own method leaves unexplained, to explain those things which contradict what we might expect from the model.

While the large numbers of parallels in the evolutionary sequences discussed by Steward may be acknowledged (Steward 1955:178, 222), these are not in themselves proof of 'techno-environmental' determinism. There are other kinds of historical determinism (Friedman 1974:462). Indeed, history itself is only the product of numerous determining forces, with their proximate origins in both material and social relations, and of accumulated innovations which embody environmental responses. Moreover, rejection of a naive 'culture *sui generis*' idea does not require rejection of the notion that systems of social relations can create their own dynamic, a dynamic which may create its own contradictions and possibilities over time and may give rise to modified systems through the resolution of internal contradictions.

This brings us back to the notion discussed above that relations of production are best conceived in functional rather than institutional terms, since it allows for the recognition that elements which in one mode of production may be part of a superstructure may elsewhere be part of the base. Thus religion was to a large part drawn into the social infrastructure of the Inca state, providing key relations of *economic* production (Godelier 1977:63–9). Similarly, if ritual is perceived by participants as determining production – as, for example, in agricultural rites – then it may well have some real effect on productive cycles. But the inflexibility of the institutionally located determinism of Steward and Harris cannot cope with such subtlety, and the former's recognition of limited flexibility of core content only highlights the theoretical dilemma which results from such a position. Although they both begin by stressing that they are providing a strategy, they end up by confusing methodology with empirical reality.

Another problem relates to whether the significant correlations between cultural and environmental traits really exist. If Steward had been concerned to test the significance of such correlations by putting them to a cross-cultural test then things might have been different. However, he tended to choose just those cases in which environment–culture correlations which interested him were to be found. The routine is a familiar one in all academic work. We are not told therefore of those cases where an adaptation occurs to the same environmental and technical conditions through quite different social arrangements. Being primarily interested in origins, Steward first shows that features *co-vary* (are functionally interrelated), and that the same relationships *recur* in historically distinct areas. But this does not mean that the environmental features *cause* the cultural features. Sampling procedures are inadequate to eliminate the possibility of spurious correlations. Correlations do not necessarily imply cause and effect (see Chapter 1), and the relationship is not necessarily inevitable (Vayda and Rappaport 1968:483–7).

The errors are compounded by Steward's reliance on inadequate ethnographic literature rather than fieldwork specifically designed to test his hypotheses. The key variables are therefore those which appear *post hoc* (and at second hand) to be most significant. One attempt to highlight the inadequacies of Steward's typological approach in the context of fieldwork has been made by M. Freilich (1963). In a comparative analysis of Afro-Caribbean and Asian villages in Trinidad, he shows how their 'techno-environmental' bases are identical. Their landholding arrangements are similar, with freehold title and holdings dispersed throughout the village; for both the major cash crop is cocoa, while yams and sweet potatoes are grown for home consumption. In both, households are based on the nuclear family; work inputs on land, technology and crop yields are identical. Despite this Freilich reports no convergence in other aspects of social organization. Remaining basically sympathetic to the Stewardian approach, he attempts to circumnavigate the difficulty by distinguishing *specialized* cultures, functionally related to environmental conditions, and to which Steward's approach therefore applies, and *generalized* ones to which it does not; and between permissive and determinant 'ecologies'.[7] In Trinidad, he concludes, there is both generalized culture and permissive ecology. The problem with this is that there is no way of recognizing *a priori* the features of a generalized culture, and we are inevitably left with the conclusion that they are simply those cases which do not fit into the Stewardian types.

Then there are the related problems of linear determinism, function and adaptation. Steward continues to phrase the problems in gross terms – whether or not it is culture or environment which determines, and what such critical *a priori* 'techno-environmental' forces might be (Steward 1955:75). His concepts of cultural core and adaptation do not seem to allow for feedback operating between social factors and ecological adjustments: the human impact on nature, and human dealings with each other. His concept of adaptation is highly mechanistic, ignoring the intentional and manipulative character of human behaviour. Simple one-way cause-and-effect sequences are rare (see Chapters 2 and 5), and it is therefore important to take into account possible circular or reticulate relations between causes and effects (Vayda and Rappaport 1968:486).[8] Also, because certain cultural traits have effects which make them ecologically adaptive, this in itself is insufficient to make them inevitable (*ibid*.:486). In these terms adaptation becomes no more than a vague functionalism in which social systems are accorded no dynamic except that derived from 'techno-environmental' interaction (Netting 1974:4).

While emphasizing the necessity of an *ecological* formulation, Steward (like Forde) took the view that when we come to consider *Homo sapiens* as part of an ecological system the 'superorganic' character of human behaviour makes a biological approach to the human ecosystem inadequate. Moreover, he was clear that cultural adaptation had nothing to do with biological or genetic potential. Both Steward and Forde wished to segregate human ecology from the ecology of other organisms on the grounds that social and cultural patterns were evidently not genetically determined. Steward followed Hollingshead (1940:358) who contrasted culture (based on cooperation and communication) with ecology (based on competition). But Steward was fundamentally mistaken (as was Hollingshead) in this neat distinction. The difficulty is that what is achieved is the very thing that one is trying to avoid, namely the confusion of biological and social relationships. By introducing humans into an ecosystem the balance of that system is altered markedly, but it does not alter the *kind* of ecological relationships existing between different organisms. There is no qualitative leap involved.[9] Making and enforcing such a distinction seems also to have prevented Steward from appreciating the significance of detailed interconnections between cultural and environmental variables, and the ecological matrix composed of the interactions of a plurality of human populations both with each other and with other organisms. Steward's serious underestimation of the scope, complexity, variability and subtlety of those environmental factors relevant to an understanding of particular social forms, like his cavalier speculation concerning cross-cultural parallels, is in turn linked to the absence of fieldwork conducted within a specifically ecological framework. It is left to his students and other devotees to accomplish this transition. As we shall see, it entails a rejection of the notion of 'superorganic' and a movement from the general and gross to the specific and subtle.

4

Human ecology and the biological model

Some of those to whom I have attached the labels of environmentalism, possibilism and cultural ecology may have been inspired in their work by biological parallels. However, their Aristotelian assertion of the uniqueness of human culture, its dominance as an organizing concept, and its total analytical independence was certainly not conducive to an explicitly ecological approach to ethnographic analysis. Much of the early work was based on broad natural historical and evolutionary notions and was either indifferent to, or ignorant of, the rapidly developing disciplines of animal and plant ecology.

BIOLOGICAL AND HUMAN ECOLOGY

From the eighteenth century onwards 'normal' natural science had become increasingly non-Aristotelian in its organic view of the relationships between entities. This view was dramatically re-affirmed in Darwinism through the concepts of the interconnectedness of living matter and the 'struggle for existence'. The former became the basic meta-concept of a science of ecology (Glacken 1967:422), giving rise to a new definition of environment which included *all* factors external to the organism and provided for a highly complex set of conditions and adaptations. It was concerned with life as a system of dynamic interdependences, every organism being in a constant state of adjustment and readjustment to its external environment (topography, climate, other organisms and their activities). In short, it was concerned with what Haeckel saw as the universal life triad of environment, function and organism, and it was Haeckel who also appears to have been the first to use the term 'ecology' (*Ökologie*) (Haeckel 1911(1868):793–4). However, despite the circumstances of its origin, the subject as a distinct discipline is for the most part a product of the twentieth century, developed first by botanists and then by zoologists.[1]

Human ecology and the biological model

From the very inception of their science, animal ecologists have been writing about human ecology, either because they regarded themselves as professionally competent to do so, or because they felt under some moral obligation.[2] The legitimation for this inevitably springs from the dominant assumption of the continuity of life patterns of all organic forms (Adams 1935:328). If the ecological argument began with the simplest living systems, then it must necessarily culminate with the most complex, *Homo sapiens*. Given the thrust of this logic, it is perhaps paradoxical that ecological discourse concerning animals should have been so dependent upon terms and concepts of an unashamedly anthropomorphic kind, often drawn directly from the social sciences.[3]

It was this all-encompassing framework, a single scientific theory capable of assimilating human beings into nature, which attracted the interest of anthropological and social theorists. The vision of a *human* ecology as an extension of general ecology was first re-worked as sociology and as a tool for empirical analysis by the Chicago school of urbanists. In fact, it is to Park and Burgess (1924:559) that we owe the label 'human ecology'. The epistemological foundations of this particular model of community structure are spelled out by Alihan (1938) and Hawley (1950). For Hawley (1950:68), a second generation revisionist, it represents: 'a special application of the general viewpoint [of ecological theory] to a particular class of living things . . . In at least one of its aspects the human community is an organization of organisms adjusted or in process of adjustment to a given unit of territory.' The development of ecological studies is seen to rest on the conduct of intensive morphological investigation: 'no workable theoretical system can be built upon anything other than a coherent and inclusive classification of data' (1950:6). For Hawley, then, it is the logical extension of animal ecology; but in his hands, and in the context of social science, is reduced to rank empiricism, functionalist inductivism and conceptual analogy. There is little attention given to the causes and consequences of energy use, while a rarely used and naive concept of adaptation is expressed in terms of social 'competition'. Social ecology of the Chicago school is essentially spatial sociology employing organic analogies (Bennett 1976:71–2).

Among the chief difficulties of this approach, and that adopted by animal ecologists looking at *Homo sapiens*, is the use of superficial, vague and misleading biological analogies. Ecological concepts *can* be applied with profit to human populations. For example the idea of succession towards climax (introduced into the study of plant populations by Frederick Clements and others) is helpful in understanding the tendency of all human populations to change, other things being

67

equal, in the direction of that most suited for a particular habitat. The difficulty arises, however, when this becomes a notion of 'cultural climax' in which certain cultural patterns are explicitly seen as the culmination of some progressive accommodation with the environment, and by implication, therefore the best adapted to it (Dice 1955:150–1). The idea was worked out in respect to material culture by Wissler (see also Kroeber 1939). Now, while this involves an obvious truism, it is exceedingly difficult to apply it to particular ethnographic cases. Much more serious, is the fact that some writers have falsely equated such phenomena as mutation with innovation, diffusion with gene flow, and cultures with species. Analogies with natural selection and biological adaptation are particularly prevalent, and at times such writing dissolves into simple-minded and highly ideological biologisms (e.g. Dice 1955) and naive environmental determinism.

The general ecological approach to *Homo sapiens*, with and without its analogical fallacies, was early adopted by geographers. For some, their discipline became redefined as human ecology (Barrows 1923) and in this way directly contributed to the demise of determinism and to the emergence of a more sensitive treatment of environmental relations (Eyre 1964, Eyre and Jones 1966). Because of its broad overlap with biology in the areas of biogeography and geomorphology – indeed, because of the protean character of the word itself (Bates 1953:701) – geography rapidly incorporated the ideas and terminology of biological ecology. However, only in the last decade has the approach (aided by systems theory) been firmly endorsed, widely adopted as a methodological strategy and used in empirical investigations (Chorley 1973).

For similar reasons, prehistoric archaeology has also increasingly favoured an ecological approach, a view particularly encouraged by the natural-science orientation of many palaeolithic studies and the disposition of many archaeologists to participate within a 'scientific' mode of discourse (e.g. Meighan *et al.* 1958). As in geography, the main concern is with the *artifacts* of social life (rather than social life directly), the impact on the environment of social organization and the influence of the environment upon society. The point of view is made explicit by J. G. D. Clark (1954:22):

A more fruitful conception, and one increasingly shared by prehistorians and natural scientists, is to regard men and human societies as elements in specific ecosystems, the pattern of culture prevailing at any given moment in a particular society being viewed as the product of adjustment and interaction between specific social needs and aspirations and the possibilities of relevant climate, soil and animal and plant life.

Human ecology and the biological model

Eighteen years later David Clarke (1972:30) saw systems approaches as having led to a re-conceptualization of such key problems in prehistory as domestication, and permitted more specific prediction, simulation and focussed quantification.

By contrast, the social and cultural anthropology of the two decades beginning 1945 was dominated by theories which were either openly hostile to an ecological perspective or accommodated it only awkwardly. The major attempts to grapple with the culture–environment problematic – in the form of cultural ecology and environmental possibilism – assumed an axiomatic autonomy for social formations which prevented any easy assimilation of new ideas. However, the period was marked by a gradual receptivity to an ecological approach and a growing sensitivity to the character and complexity of environmental relations. These changes can be attributed to a number of developments, mostly related to the growth of ethnographic fieldwork.

The increasing amount of fieldwork being undertaken, particularly among populations with simple subsistence patterns with seemingly clear environmental correlates, was leading to an awareness of the more general significance of environmental relations. This awareness was, in part, fostered by possibilism. At the same time ethnographers were under pressure to enhance the respectability of their discipline by collecting more accurate and detailed (particularly numerical) data. For the first time attention was being paid to field measurement (Pospisil 1963:164–91), the provision of ethnographically useful and accurate maps, diaries of work effort (McCarthy and McArthur 1960, Freeman 1955), consequences of rainfall patterns on different subsistence topographies, the relevance of soil structure, the timing of planting, the implications of growing different cultigens and the distance of fields from villages (Bradfield 1971). Recognition of the importance of mapping and accurate description of the environment was accompanied by the development and systematic use of aerial and other forms of photography as an integral part of an analysis: to document the character of culturally modified landscapes, irrigation systems, cropping regimes, patterns of settlement, deforestation and so on (Scudder 1962, Conklin 1968, Sorenson 1972, Vogt 1974).[4]

The realization that information of this kind was essential encouraged a familiarity with the work of various non-anthropological specialists; in the fields of nutrition, agriculture, animal husbandry, geography and ecology. These disciplines provided ethnographers with accurate data on such subjects as the environmental requirements and productivity of particular species, maturation periods, seasonal availability and storage potential. All this is of direct (often crucial) relevance to an understanding of patterns of subsistence techniques, the organization of work groups, the allocation of effort and labour, the dispersion of settlements, patterns of resource utilization and appropriation, carrying capacity and diet. Occasionally, even more precise information may be useful: for example, on economically and culturally significant differences between crop varieties. At the same time access to such data, and contact with different regional and disciplinary specialists, instilled a more subtle appreciation of the effects of particular technical and social practices on domesticated species themselves and a greater respect for ecological complexity, and stimulated still more careful and detailed research in these areas. The work of Conklin (1961) on the environmental variation significant for an understanding of swidden cultivation is a good example of this.[5]

The extent to which it is possible to rely on existing regional records for weather, biogeography, soils, food values and rates of energy expenditure is, however, limited (Bates 1953:703). This is particularly so for the populations among which anthropologists have traditionally worked. Consequently, anthropologists had either to collect the data for themselves or to cooperate in the field with other specialists. During the sixties, for example, there began a continuing dialogue between ethnography and geography on their practical inter-relationships and on the necessity to share techniques and concepts (Ellen 1978:207–10). Geographers, too, were now interested in empirical investigations of small populations with small-scale patterns of agriculture (e.g. Lea 1964). Both disciplines were focussing on resource description, techniques for appropriating those resources, the social organization of food production, distribution and consumption, the extent to which groups achieve complete utilization of resources, what the selective factors which intervene to limit complete utilization are, and why some crops are grown and not others (L. Mason 1962:4). The work of Harold Brookfield and Paula Brown (1963) on Chimbu social relations and land use in the New Guinea highlands is an obvious product of such trends, and marks a significant watershed in the development of analysis and ethnographic fieldwork.

One of the results of a more sophisticated approach to the study of subsistence was an appreciation of the remarkable suitability of many environmental adaptations among small-scale populations. Steward (1938) had noticed that variations within basically similar culture patterns often represented local adjustments to differences in food availability and potential. But from the forties onwards fieldworkers provided empirical demonstrations of this: in terms, for example, of adjustments to soil fertility, available settlement locations and seasonality (Netting 1968:22). Among the most important pioneer studies of this kind was that of Richards (1939) on the *citimene* swidden practices of the Bemba. This technique involves the use of tree litter as a compost in a sub-humid scrub–woodland region of central Africa. Richards was able to show that, far from being wasteful as was widely thought by colonial administrators (including agriculturalists), it was the best possible solution in the circumstances. This was at least true with regard to millet, which produced yields far superior to those resulting from the application of introduced European methods (see Netting 1968:8–9). But although her book is greatly admired and frequently cited, it was not directly influential (Gluckman 1945).

Swidden cultivation more generally has often been regarded as intrinsically damaging to the environment, but that this need not necessarily be so has now been repeatedly demonstrated. Conklin's (1954a) pioneer study of Hanunoo swiddening in the Philippines is a notable example. In this study Conklin takes ten characteristics which have commonly been ascribed to swidden cultivation and then systematically rephrases them in the light of his own detailed examination of Hanunoo practice:

1. Swiddening is not a simple, uncomplicated, haphazard procedure involving an almost negligible labour input. It follows a locally determined, well-defined pattern requiring constant attention throughout the year. Although hard physical labour is involved, a large labour force is not required.

2. Swiddens are preferably not cleared from virgin forest and do not result in the loss of valuable timber but rather, wherever possible, are cleared from secondary growth.

3. Swidden fires seldom escape beyond the plots they are intended to burn, and often there are controlled firebreaks.

4. Techniques are not everywhere the same, details differing from area to area. This point has been elaborated for Southeast Asia by Spencer (1966).

5. Stoloniferous grasses such as *Imperata* are not always useless pests, but may serve (like other noxious weeds) as pasture and thatch. While *Imperata*, if dominant, may restrict swidden possibilities, its complete absence would occasion other hardships.

6. Swiddens are generally multicropped, rather than monocropped.

7. Efficiency can be evaluated only by taking into account the total yield per unit labour. It is impossible to gauge in terms of one crop yield per unit area.

8. Swiddens are not abandoned once the main crop is in and there is considerable intercropping. One harvest may allow others to mature in turn, while plantings and harvest usually overlap for more than a full year, and frequently continue for several.

9. Crop rotation is present.

10. Fertility is not lost, while destruction, erosion and permanent loss of forest cover do not necessarily result from clearing once-used swiddens after less than a universally specified minimum number of years of fallow. It is difficult to set a minimum fallow period as so many variables are involved.

A comparable detailed ecological refutation has been made of the assertion that cattle husbandry among the dominantly pastoral peoples of East Africa is inefficient and economically irrational, being based on the social value of cattle rather than their material uses. It has been shown (Netting 1971:13–15) that herding is generally dominant in those areas where water is scarce and unpredictable. Here agriculture is at its least productive, and dependable mobility enables herders to move towards more suitable locations. Pastoralism is a recurrent adaptation to dry savannahs, steppes and deserts, where there is insufficient food to nourish humans but sufficient for grazing animals. The comparison of several east African peoples has enabled the isolation of more specific factors determining the relative dependence on crops and herds (Goldschmidt 1965). Lower altitudes with an annual rainfall of between 25 and 51 cm are unsuitable for food staples and provide only grass, while in the upper part of the zone *Trypanosomiasis* is prevalent. By mapping rainfall probabilities and comparing these over a period of years with water requirements, the proportion of years for which there is adequate rain for crop maturation has been computed. For 90 per cent of the years there was an adequate precipitation to support a dense farming population, while 0.3 per cent of the population had chronic crop failure and famine and 0.1 per cent were largely pastoral and practised only intermittent cultivation. We are thus provided with a measurement of subsistence risk (Porter 1965). This does not mean that cattle are found in only marginal agricultural lands, but it is here that crops yield fewer calories than cattle. The highest development of the cattle complex is found in areas where cattle make the major contribution to sustenance.

Ecologically rational explanations have been provided for more specific and esoteric cultural practices. For example, Vayda, Leeds and Smith (1961) have suggested that the role of pigs in New Guinea is similar to that of cattle in east Africa: that of long-term storage. The theme has been developed by Rappaport (1968), who stresses that although pig-keeping is energetically inefficient it provides an adaptation to protein shortage. At a lower level it has been suggested by Conklin (1957:47) that the Hanunoo ritual in which a hollow bamboo is driven into the ground at a potential swidden site serves as a crude means of appraising the readiness of the soil for tillage. The practice is regarded as magical, but if the soil does not rise high enough inside the stick the site is discarded and one is chosen elsewhere.

The rational features of many subsistence practices had certainly been hitherto neglected, and ethnographic work of the kind described has done much to redress the balance. At the same time, the emphasis on the often-superior adaptation of traditional subsistence techniques (particularly) to specialized environments has been necessary to counter the uncritical worship of 'growth' and 'development'. On the other hand, it is necessary to avoid the primitivist fallacy which assumes that tribal societies are always in harmony with their environment and are consequently a source of remedies for the ills of contemporary industrial capitalism (Bennet 1976:12, 34). The idea that a culture necessarily comes to an accommodation with the environment has taken on a theoretical explicitness in much of the work described as cultural ecology or cultural materialism. Such approaches find their apogee in the work of Marvin Harris (e.g. 1965) and in what has been described as 'ecological functionalism'. The ideas associated with this label are treated at some length in Chapter 7. For the present it is sufficient to note that they tend to overemphasize the significance of the present conditions and are in great danger of finding any ecological circumstance adaptive (Sauer 1941). It has been argued that both Harris's 'new materialism' (a term coined by Sahlins, 1969:30) and ecological functionalism are in fact no more than a re-phrasing and development of older functionalist and empiricist ideas together with the ideological matrix in which they are embedded (Friedman 1974:455).

THE IDEA OF ECOSYSTEM

The sensitivity of a new generation of anthropologists to the intricacy of ecological relations, their increasing attention to environmental data and familiarity with the work of specialists from other disciplines encouraged a greater awareness of the conceptual language of biology. For some this was acquired via the analogical human ecology of the Chicago school, thus permitting writers such as Robert Redfield (1960:29–31) to maintain an essentially Kroeberian belief in the autonomy of the superorganic. A few writers, however, were beginning to absorb biological ideas independently and proved more flexible in their attitude. Bates (1953:701), for example, managed to eschew both a crude functionalism and the superorganic by viewing ecology less as a theory than as a perspective through which the organism could be regarded as functioning in an environmental context. Rather than adopting ecology as an unanalysed slogan, using its concepts in a vague and generalized analogical fashion, some were beginning to experiment with explicit concepts as a means of extending the explanatory repertoire of anthropology. As early as 1956 Frederik Barth was employing the notion of ecological niche to shed light on the relation of adjacent human groups occupying the same geographical area and in apparent competition.[6] The anthropological usefulness of the niche idea is examined in detail below, but the primary concept to which it is linked and which, historically, was instrumental more than any other in altering the character of ecological work in anthropology is that of 'ecosystem'.

The term 'ecosystem' was formally proposed by A. G. Tansley in 1935, as a general term for both the 'biome' – the total complex of interacting organisms – and its habitat (Tansley 1946:207):

All the parts of . . . an ecosystem – organic and inorganic, biome and habitat – may be regarded as interacting factors which, in a mature ecosystem, are in approximate equilibrium: it is through their interactions that the whole system is maintained.

For a later writer (Fosberg 1963:2):

An ecosystem is a functioning interacting system composed of one or more living organisms and their effective environment, both physical and biological . . . The description of an ecosystem may include its spatial relations; inventories of its physical features, its habitats and ecological niches, its organisms, and its basic resources of *matter* and *energy*; the nature of its income (or input) of matter and energy; its pattern of circulation of matter and energy; the nature of its losses of matter and energy and the behaviour or trend of its entropy level [my italics].

Even more recent definitions add a third essential component to matter and energy: information. An ecosystem – or ecological system – then becomes a relatively stable set of organic relationships in which energy, material and information are in continuous circulation, and in which all processes are seen in terms of their system-wide repercussions. *Specific* changes, which may theoretically begin anywhere in the system, trigger adjustment and re-adaptation among the other elements. The relationships between elements reflect the mutual adaptation of different local populations of organisms in their non-living environment. *Systemic* changes take place slowly through conjoint evolution that is biological, chemical and physical. The entire process is open-ended, constant, self-augmenting and versatile. It builds on itself, increasing the capacity of a site to support life. In doing so it stabilizes the site and the biota.[7]

Those who came to accord the ecosystem a central theoretical role in anthropology were, for the most part, both partial to the subject matter and explanatory power of cultural ecology, and dissatisfied with its specific theoretical remedy for the inadequacies of possibilism. In the vanguard of this approach were Clifford Geertz, A. P. Vayda and Roy Rappaport. In contrast to cultural ecology, some of these writers have preferred to describe their perspective as *general* ecology. It is worth listing some of the more important characteristics of the ecosystem approach.

1. *Monism*. The ecosystem approach is monistic; it *explicitly* seeks to analyse behavioural and environmental traits as part of a *single* system. Particular practices are seen as 'functioning' parts in the operation of systems which also include environmental phenomena (Vayda 1969:113). Culture becomes part of animal behaviour, to be interpreted in much the same way as the behaviour of other species. Consequently, it is unnecessary to use basically different principles in studying human behaviour in ecosystems and in studying the behaviour of other animals (Rappaport 1963:168–9). Thus, when examining the relations between populations of associated species in a food web, the relative positions which they occupy determine whether interactions are negative (predation, parasitism), neutral (commensalism) or positive (mutualism). In these terms the association between wild dingoes and aboriginal Australian hunters is one of symbiotic mutualism, since in return for tracking game the dingoes receive scraps of meat (Meggitt 1965a). Similarly, approaching food appropriation within the broader context of food chains, the milking of lactating stock by pastoralists (milch pastoralism) can be seen as introducing human parasitism at an earlier point in the food chain than when the animals are killed for meat (carnivorous pastoralism). Although milch pastoralism involves competition between a human population and the offspring of the stock for milk, its advantage lies in its greater carrying capacity than carnivorous pastoralism. This, together with the inability of humans to digest the plant food consumed by ruminants, makes it an efficient use of uncultivable grazing land (Ingold 1980:176). Indeed, much domestication of plants and animals can be seen as means of preventing species, populations and ecological systems from reaching maturity in order to maximize the biomass available for human consumption. The ethnographer must therefore understand a population not only in terms of its social organization, but as part of an ecosystem. This is not to confuse it with an ethological approach, where behavioural traits have precise analogues (indeed homologues) in non-human behaviour. Rather, it starts from the existence of behavioural traits and the assumption that it is impossible for them to exist in some form of splendid ecological isolation. It is axiomatic that environment and behavioural traits are bound by a complex web of interrelations. While *Homo sapiens* may be dominant in a particular system, it is argued, this

does not make him less subject to the forces which govern other species (e.g. Helm 1962:157). Accepting that culture might be an onto- logically distinct category does not necessarily imply functional auton- omy.

2. *Complexity*. In the context of anthropology the ecosystems approach is therefore linked to a reaction against the idea of culture as a reified closed system (Gray 1964:11), and to the assertion that culture is an unnecessary concept for understanding human ecology (Vayda and Rappaport 1968:493). A de-reification of culture and social structure has also found emphasis in the acknowledgement of the vast number of different factors upon which the functioning of an ecosystem may be contingent. The ecosystem approach stressed that 'environment' and 'behaviour' were merely convenient, and sometimes highly mislead- ing, labels for complex arrays of variables. It helped to do away with the view among geographers and biologists that social behaviour or culture represented a single 'master' variable, and the view held by anthropologists that environment was a single factor which could not be dissected.[8] Significance and cause in environmental relations were to be found in the web of finely interrelated factors rather than with general propositions at the level of gross categories, which could only ever yield gross answers (Geertz 1963:3). The concept of ecosystem assists in rejecting the treatment of culture and environment as quite different and separate spheres.

3. *Connectivity and mutual causality*. If behavioural and environmen- tal traits are part of a single system then they are connected with and affected by other components of the system, which are in turn affected by the presence of the behavioural traits. In the ecosystem view, all social activities impinge directly or indirectly on ecological processes and are themselves affected by those same processes. Fauna (including humans), vegetation, soil structure and microclimate are intricately related and mutually interdependent. The approach thus emphasizes the two-way character of causality and avoids the determinist–possi- bilist fallacy, although the relative influence in reciprocally causal relationships is never equal and may be very unequal (Kaplan and Manners 1972:79). The ecosystem approach therefore also brings together the work on environmental modification by geographers and possibilism on the one hand, and cultural ecology and determinism on the other.

4. *Process*. Analysis of ecosystems necessarily focusses on ecological and socio-ecological *processes*, and their system-wide repercussions. Not only does this add a new dimension to description, but it also allows for a more integrated approach. It avoids narrow correlations between environment and social organization, so easily refutable on

the grounds that the writer misinterpreted what constitute relevant environmental variables. So the emphasis is on the interaction of variables, all of which become of potential significance, irrespective of observed significance. An ethnographic accent on process has (among other things) enabled the specification of different kinds of succession, given particular cultivation practices, which is of importance in the analysis of a single pattern of settlement or in comparing different ecologically defined populations. The synchronic distribution of land types can be seen as representing different successional phases within a single system, a series of variable changes over time in their social and ecological significance.

5. *Populations as analytical units*. The local human population, usually a territorial group, can be specified as an *ecological population*. That is, it is an aggregate of organisms having a common set of distinctive means by which they maintain a common set of *trophic* (that is energy) relations within the ecosystem which they occupy. Ecological populations are identified in terms of the position or niche which they occupy in the ecosystem. The concept of ecological population is a useful one in human ecological studies because it is a more-or-less bounded unit, subject to some degree of quantitative description and analysis (Vayda and Rappaport 1968:494). Its characteristics can often be correlated with features of the physical, biological, social and cultural environment and change through the course of adaptation. Moreover, 'population' (rather than 'society') is a preferable concept to employ in studies of adaptation and evolution. There are enormous theoretical problems in attributing this capacity to social formations or ecological systems. Cultures and societies, unlike populations, do not occupy niches, are not fed upon by predators, limited by food supplies, or debilitated through disease; they are difficult to isolate and what is meant by their survival or adequate functioning or adaptation is highly problematic (Vayda and Rappaport 1968:494, Rappaport 1971a:243).

The above model assumes a basic similarity between *Homo sapiens* and other polytypic species. Distribution can be seen as a widespread network of demes, and overlapping ecosystems (Weiner 1964:401–2); a mosaic of simple, relatively isolated and self-sufficient groups. The conditions for observing their functioning are best met among groups of simple food-producers. The effective human ecological population is often a vast network of local groups spreading over several ecosystems, integrated through political, kinship and economic relations. Breeding populations are seldom small local groups. Ecological populations are in contact with others in the ecosystem or other ecosystems or niches; they usually exchange materials in the form of personnel, genes, trade goods and so on, and some of the processes which redistribute land are likely to involve two or more populations. The concept of ecosystem, because it is fundamentally one of trophic exchanges between populations occupying different ecological niches within a bounded area, accommodates, only awkwardly, non-trophic material exchanges between populations in separate localities. To overcome this problem, Rappaport (1968:226) has suggested a concept of regional population – resembling a geneticist's breeding population, which may be coterminous with a social formation. He suggests that the notion of clines may be useful in coping with the difficulty of boundary demarcation in such groups.

6. *Frameworks for description and analysis.* In fieldwork and empirical research the ecosystem provides a framework which accords recognition to the complex and varied interaction of environmental and cultural variables. It builds on the ecological approach in general and on specific techniques used by ecologists and geographers, some of which have been discussed above. Moreover, it brings ecological analysis to the ethnographic level. It is associated with methods and concepts which developed in biology in conjunction with empirical work. By contrast, the work of Steward involved *a priori* comparative categories and was concerned with particular variables and the question of their adaptability. The ecosystem concept emphasizes more firmly certain criticisms that had already been made and suggests a possible alternative approach.

More generally, the ecosystem serves as a conceptual framework and analytical unit, along with local (ecological) and regional populations (Rappaport 1969). It allows observation of the relationship of environmental to cultural factors in new ways, allows the formulation of new hypotheses and correlations. Ecosystems have become the new analytical and comparative spatial units rather than culture areas. With the ecosystem the problems created by the static character of the culture-area concept are reduced. Spatiality and temporality are built into the model.

DEFINING THE BOUNDARIES OF THE ECOSYSTEM

Because all living matter within the biosphere is connected spatially and temporally in complex ways, isolating a single ecosystem is, in effect, arbitrary. Wherever the boundaries are drawn, there will be connections across them. In general the boundaries of an ecosystem are determined by the research problem at hand, and it is impossible to define a system, identify its components or specify the character of its linkages without first making subjective judgements about which processes are critical for its functioning. Nevertheless some systems are more readily identifiable than others, being based on certain distinctly observable properties and discontinuities which mark them out from other systems. For example, we may speak of a pond ecosystem, or an estuarine ecosystem, or an atoll ecosystem. Similarly, we can select ecosystems in terms of geographical scale such that increasingly larger ecosystems can be identified like the layers of an onion. We may legitimately speak of a cell, a bodily organ, an organism, a puddle, a pond, montane-zone New Guinea, the Siberian Steppes or the biosphere as ecosystems in this sense. The entire terrestrial ecosystem is sometimes termed the 'ecosphere' (Cole 1958). Any unit which provides some basic empirical conditions for the existence of a boundary may analytically constitute an ecosystem. However, some ecologists have suggested that specific ecosystems may have distinctive *emergent* properties and undergo evolutionary change after the fashion of individual species (Margalef 1968).

When it comes to human populations the same criteria apply. Some ecosystems of which human populations are part are relatively well defined, for example, islands. These make ideal laboratories for the study of human ecology, for the system is generally more closed, in terms of both the human and the non-human components (Thompson 1949, Fosberg 1963, Bayliss-Smith 1977). But most ecosystems involving humans do not have such clearcut boundaries and the drawing of them becomes more arbitrary. Sometimes it is analytically convenient to portray human populations as being involved in several different relatively well-defined ecosystems. For example, Nietschmann (1973:63), in his study of the Nicaraguan Miskito, found the Caribbean coast to be a complex of ecosystems with various food-getting potentials. However, he found it convenient to divide it into just four large-scale systems: tropical rain forest, pine savannah, coastal complex of beach, lagoon and swamp, and coastal offshore waters, coral cays and reefs.

MICRO-ENVIRONMENTS

While, in theory, the ecosystem concept may be used at any level, it has traditionally, and perhaps most usefully, been used for environmental zones with a distinctive topography and vegetation: for example, savannah, desert, or tropical forest. Presumably, this follows older biogeographical notions of 'natural region'. But ecosystems are not simply composed of even mixtures of different organisms; they are patterned, and with an uneven distribution of features and processes. This is by no means clear from most ecological studies by ethnographers, which have not only tended to present normative descriptions

Table 4.1 *Major biotopes of the Miskito coast of eastern Nicaragua and niche-width calculations for Tasbapauni Miskito based on spatial resource variety (data from Nietschmann 1973:99, 169; calculations from Hardesty 1975:78)*

Biotope	Meat biomass (lb) butchered Oct. 1968 to Sept. 1969	(pi)	(pi)²
Tropical rain forest and gallery forest			
mature rain forest	340	0.003	0.000
secondary forest	2,640	0.026	0.001
old plantations	1,620	0.016	0.000
new plantations	1,790	0.018	0.000
gallery forest	596	0.006	0.000
banksides or *vega*: natural levees	764	0.008	0.000
rivers, open runs			
brena: dense bush, thicket	100	0.001	0.000
floodplains			
oxbow lakes			
Pine savannah			
creeks	295	0.003	0.000
creek edges			
wet low-lying savannah			
ridge and swamp	300	0.003	0.000
marsh	300	0.003	0.000
palm swamp	4,130	0.041	0.002
high savannah: *Pinus, Curatella, Brysonima*			
Beach–lagoon–swamp			
intertidal zone	700	0.007	0.000
beach	321	0.003	0.000
plantations: milpa or swidden			
old: little tended, partially abandoned			
new: currently worked			
beach forest, predominantly secondary			
swamp			
mangrove: various types			
palm: various types			
marsh: various types			
lagoon			
creek and river mouths	700	0.007	0.000
shoals, banks: shallow mud or sand flats bars: where lagoon empties into sea	400	0.004	0.000
sand bars	105	0.001	0.000
grass flats: along edges of lagoons, creeks and rivers	1,355	0.013	0.000
shallow borders	1,750	0.017	0.000
'banks'	2,750	0.027	0.001

Table 4.1 – *cont.*

Biotope	Meat biomass (lb) butchered Oct. 1968 to Sept. 1969	(pi)	$(pi)^2$
Offshore shallow waters, reefs, cays			
deep water			
cays: small coral islands			
shoals: shallow coral flats	28,550	0.280	0.078
reefs			
banks: turtle-grass-covered feeding	44,060	0.433	0.188
grounds			
mudset: shallow, mud-bottom waters	7,150	0.072	0.005
near shore			
close inshore waters			
surf zone	1,150	0.011	0.000

$\sum_{i}^{n} (pi)^2 = 0.275$

Niche width = 1/0.275 = 3.6

of obvious environmental features, but proceeded to match these typologically and abstractly with generalized characteristics of particular kinds of social and cultural organization (Winterhalder 1980:136). But variation may be crucial in an understanding of the functioning of human populations within ecosystems, to the extent that it affects such matters as the distribution of resources and yields and the selection of localities for cultivation. Moreover, human populations do not interact directly with their entire environment, or complete ecosystems, but with selected, well-defined species and components. These components – the smallest spaces characterized by a particular environment – may be termed 'biotopes', 'micro-environments' or habitats. They can be distinguished according to soil, vegetation, climate and their inhabitation by a definite and well-characterized animal community. They also provide definable segments of the environment which can be analysed in terms of subsistence yield, species and distance from settlements (Table 4.1; see also Nietschmann 1973:97). From an ethnographic point of view, biotopes are essentially resource clusters which may be recognized as such by human populations.

ECOLOGICAL NICHE AND SYMBIOSIS

The 'niche' concept has been used for a long time in biology but its modern definition we owe to Elton (1927:63–8). A niche is a distinct feeding strategy, position in a food web and share of available limited energy and nutrients separating ecological populations (Hardesty 1977:109).

Barth was the first anthropologist to employ the concept (1956:1079), as part of a more general experimental approach with specific concepts drawn from animal ecology. He found that the gross and mechanistic concept of culture area was unsatisfactory when dealing with south-west Asia, where societies form mosaics of different cultures displaying interrelations of varying degrees of intimacy. Barth describes three different ethnic groups as occupying different niches through a process of cultural adaptation. Because the groups were to varying extents materially and politically dependent on each other, sharing and overlapping different resource zones, Barth describes their relations as symbiotic.

In northern Pakistan, Pathans, Kohistanis and Gujars are engaged in plough agriculture in the high mountain valleys. They occupy those areas where two crops may be raised annually, though they also extend into the more marginal areas where only one annual crop is possible. Pathan political economy is multicaste, centralized and with special occupational sub-groups. Such a complex stratified structure requires a considerable surplus, which explains the necessity for double-cropping. Pathans maintain a dominance in the area through their military organization, a cohesive social system and their numerical preponderance. The Kohistanis are also in part agricultural people, but the equal importance of transhumant herding means that they are not as geographically restricted as the Pathans, and summer pastures are located in mountain areas. Correspondingly, their political organization is less cohesive and they live in compact, politically organized and independent villages. The Gujars constitute a floating population of herders of sheep, goats, cattle and water buffalo. They practise a little farming in marginal areas, but may move from transhumant herding to agriculture to true nomadism depending on their relations with other groups. They are the political clients of particular Pathans and Kohistani leaders for whom they supply milk, meat, manure, labour for the seasonal transplanting of wet rice and husbanding of animals. In exchange they receive grain, textiles, hardware, access to pasture and a reduced grazing tax.

Barth uses the concept of niche to refer to a subsistence system, the output of such systems, and a particular geographical range. Unfortunately, these things do not necessarily coincide. Barth provides no precise quantitative data, particularly on output. It has been suggested that the Pathans may actually produce less than other groups. In this case their dominance is essentially military, political and social rather than ecological and technical. The ranges of these groups are by no means agriculturally distinct. This is only so in certain places and at certain times of the year. The processes at work more closely resemble symbiotic mutualism. Hardesty (1977:158–9) has argued that Barth is dealing with micro-environments rather than niches and, like Bennett (1976:172–4), prefers to describe the relations as symbiotic. However, symbiosis generally refers to mutually acceptable complementarity between co-existing *species*. In the case of different human groups, the terms of what appears to be a mutually advantageous exchange relationship are often dictated by the balance of political power and control of the means and social relations of production and distribution. Even when dealing with the interspecies mutualism of human animal husbandry, the animals are entering into *social relations* of human dominance (Ingold 1980:88). For these reasons, the notion of intra-species symbiosis is perhaps best avoided altogether.

Coe and Flannery (1964) have followed Barth's approach in their work on Mesoamerican prehistory. Concentrating on the people of the Tehuacan Valley of Mexico and coastal Guatemala, they have demonstrated how two closely related populations inhabiting very different resource zones appropriate their respective environments through the utilization of a range of 'niches'. They interpret the archaeological material as showing how parallel adaptations were made to the available biotopes until the development of irrigation in Tehuacan permitted the development of full-time agriculture and permanent settlement.

A similar analysis for Mesopotamia is offered by Flannery (1965), in which he shows how different ethnic groups concentrating on different biotopes all contributed to a complex regional revolution in food production. The Mesopotamian neolithic is seen as the culmination of a long process of changing ecological relationships between local populations of humans, plants and animals, in which the shifting and seasonal appropriation based on species occupying different biotopes was transformed into a humanly modified system where certain grasses and ungulates were removed from their natural niches and placed in others where they were shielded from natural selection and underwent genetic changes.

This approach represents an extremely important advance, particularly when coupled with ideas drawn from systems theory (see Chapter 8). However, while the inspiration for it may have been biological, it has been the source of some confusion. What Coe and Flannery describe as niches are often biotopes; that is they are not so much unique feeding strategies of individual populations as separable resource clusters. More recent writers have attempted to develop an anthropological niche concept which more faithfully follows the original, emphasizing it as the total spatial pattern of resources appropriated by a given population. Hardesty (1975), for example, has suggested that, depending on the number of different biotopes which a local population uses, it might be described as either *generalized* (broad resource base) or *specialized* (narrow resource base). But Hardesty acknowledges that different biotopes are not appropriated with the same intensity. Table 4.1 indicates that marine and estuarine biotopes provide most of the meat consumed by the Miskito. Clearly, the niche is much more specialized than is suggested by simply counting the number of biotopes. Furthermore, what a biotope contributes may be as important in defining the niche occupied as *how much*. For example, a biotope contributing a large amount of starch may not be as critical for maintaining a nutritional level or culturally defined consumption pattern as one contributing high-quality protein. Similarly, seasonal availability of resources in a biotope may be more important in assessing the character of the niche occupied than the total annual amount available. Carrying-capacity calculations should take into account what is available during the poorest season. If food is not stored then food ordinarily ignored may become of critical importance. Thus a stable biotope may be more important to a feeding strategy than an unstable one.

Hardesty demonstrates how the niche of a human population might be calculated by measuring the number of different resources used and the extent to which each is relied upon. He employs the formula (adapted from Levins 1968:43):

$$\text{niche width} = \frac{1}{\sum\limits_{i}^{n}(pi)^2}$$

where *pi* is the proportion of total subsistence contributed by the resource *i*, and *n* the total number of resources used (Table 4.2). Niche width can also be calculated from the number of biotopes and the degree to which each is used (e.g. Table 4.1), or from different resource variables such as calorific and protein content. The latter may provide width measurements which are quite different; thus both the Tsembaga and the Miskito are much more specialized for protein than for calories. This is probably a general feature of human populations, although the opposite has been shown for the Panamanian Cuna. Levins (1968) and McArthur (1960) have stressed the importance of critical resources in defining niche-occupancy, although niche widths are not always comparable, and the problem involved in deciding what constitutes a critical resource has already been met in Chapter 2. A population's relative share of available resources can only be measured

Table 4.2 *Niche-width calculations from total mammal and bird resource variety for Mistassini Cree, Canada (data from Rogers 1972:104; calculations from Hardesty 1975:76)*

Resource	Biomass (lb)	*pi*	$(pi)^2$
Moose	4,000	0.448	0.202
Caribou	1,500	0.168	0.029
Bear	210	0.024	0.000
Beaver	2,120	0.237	0.058
Hare	114	0.013	0.000
Muskrat	240	0.027	0.001
Porcupine	60	0.007	0.000
Mink	33	0.004	0.000
Squirrel	8	0.000	0.000
Marten	5	0.000	0.000
Otter	110	0.012	0.000
Loon	44	0.005	0.000
Goose	67	0.008	0.000
Duck	231	0.026	0.001
Ptarmigan	150	0.017	0.000
Spruce grouse	38	0.004	0.000
Ruffled grouse	1	0.000	0.000
Owl	1	0.000	0.000
	$\sum_{i}^{n}(pi)^2$	–	0.291
	Niche width – 1/0.291	–	3.436

by comparison with that of other populations which are part of the same ecosystem. Its value is that is focusses attention on the relation of populations to their resources and is a measure of relative abundance. Hardesty suggests that human niche widths are generally broad compared with other species, and that this is related to populousness. Rare species might be expected to have a narrow niche width. He suggests that the comparison of human niche width with that of other competing animal populations in the same ecosystem would be useful; for example the partitioning of available protein in tropical rain forests where this is a critical resource. If a population expands its niche its resource share increases, as does its abundance. Humans can do this through the elimination of competing organisms and concentration of availability of specific resources upon which they are dependent. However, an approach which treats *Homo sapiens* as an equivalent species for such measurements is misleading on the grounds that human patterns of adaptation through productive specialization and exchange are unique. Also, niche is generally used by biologists to refer to the genetically adapted feeding strategy of a *species* rather than a local ecological population (Bennett 1976:167–75).

GENERALIZED AND SPECIALIZED ECOSYSTEMS

The notion of niche breadth described above is very similar to that of ecosystem diversity. In ecological terms, diversity is measured by the number of interacting organisms. Attempts to list the number of species used or recognized by different populations (Conklin 1954; Ellen 1973:446–64; Berlin, Breedlove and Raven 1974; Nietschmann 1973) have gone some way to measure diversity in ecosystems of which human populations are part. In all cases the attempts are necessarily incomplete. Diversity is measured theoretically by counting the total number of species present, and not those simply recognized or used. The task is even more formidable under archaeological conditions, due to the differential and partial preservation of organic materials. However, the data accessible can provide a reasonable idea of eco-system complexity, and permit some measurement of the degree of specialization or generalization, the connectedness of human populations with their environment and their susceptibility to hazard, as well as guide predictions about the changes which would follow an alteration in the variables.

Figure 4.1 shows the relationship between a number of the more abundant species associated with the cabbage, *Brassica oleracea*. Complex as the connections are, those for any human population would be infinitely more so. This is due to:

1. the large number of human parasites
2. the large number of species symbiotic with *Homo sapiens* (mostly as domesticates)
3. the large number of species not actually consumed as food but used for other purposes (traction, fabrication, sensory and motor purposes).

The number of interacting species gives some indication of ecosystem complexity, but, as we have seen from our discussion of niche, it is also necessary to take into account the relative quantities of each species and spatio-temporal dispersion. Ideally, it is upon this basis that we should distinguish between generalized and specialized ecosystems.

In generalized ecosystems there are many different species, but few individuals of each species. Complexity and a greater biomass have theoretically been taken to specify a more mature, stable and complex system, where a slight change is unlikely to destabilize the system owing to the large number of alternative energy and nutrient pathways and regulatory mechanisms. There is a low entropy rate. By contrast,

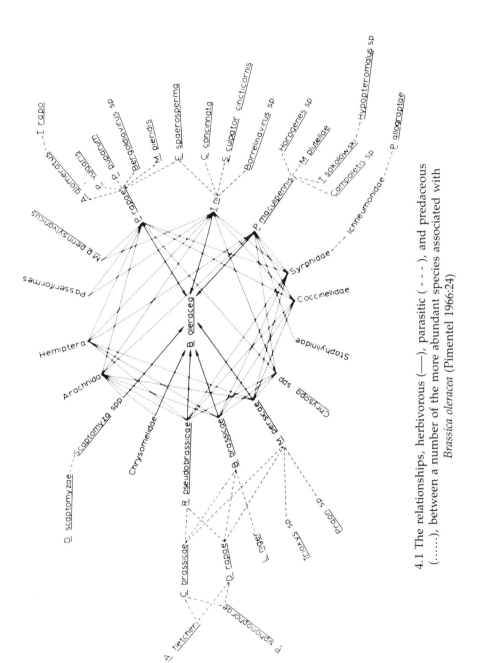

4.1 The relationships, herbivorous (——), parasitic (- - -), and predaceous
(......), between a number of the more abundant species associated with
Brassica oleracea (Pimentel 1966:24)

87

specialized ecosystems are those where there are few species, represented by many individuals, and a theoretically high entropy rate. In the first the diversity index is high, while in the second it is low.

The generalized–specialized distinction has been employed and developed for human ecosystems by a number of writers. Clifford Geertz (1963) and David Harris (1969) have made notable contributions to the discussion. It is suggested that species diversity has certain consequences for human subsistence and social organization. In a classic study, Geertz (1963) has contrasted the generalized ecosystem associated with much swidden cultivation in outer Indonesia with the specialized ecosystem of the wet-rice terrace of Java, Bali and Madura. He argues that swiddening maintains the natural ecosystem through crop diversity, rapid re-cycling of nutrients and the duplication of a protective plant canopy. Such polycultural cultivation is also claimed to aid stability. Such stability is, however, limited since all human-dominated systems are unstable in contrast to generalized natural systems such as the tropical rain forest. The hyperactive involvement of one species is necessary in order to prevent the system deteriorating. On the other hand, if human systems maintain their integrity over a long period they must be considered – objectively – as stable (rather than resilient). Human intervention tends to reduce the maturity of the ecosystem (Margalef 1968). Although there are cases of archaic subsistence strategies, highly focussed on a few species in specialized ecosystems (especially in the Arctic), the general trend for *Homo sapiens* is towards simplicity rather than complexity. This is in direct contrast to natural ecosystems. The already-limited autonomy of human populations is then further diminished through economic and political vicissitudes as well as environmental stress. 'Economic development', for example, accelerates the process of ecological simplification (Rappaport 1971:128–32).

The generalized–specialized distinction has also been applied with profit to the analysis of relatively autonomous food-collecting populations. In specialized ecosystems the problems are resource fluctuation and unpredictability (e.g. !Kung), while in generalized ecosystems the problem is complexity (e.g. Mbuti). According to Harpending and Davis (1977) the consequences of generalized ecosystems are small group size due to the minimal spatial variation in resources, dispersed settlement and minimal effort through sedentarism. Territorial behaviour is expected. Specialized ecosystems are associated with population aggregation into larger units with an in-phase occurrence of spatial variation in resources. Settlement is nucleated. Group mobility is required in order to use the full range of available resources, resulting in large annual territories with little local occupation of land. More generally, because specialized subsistence strategies concentrate on a narrower range of species, they must both use all those resources available and maintain flexibility if they are to survive in the long term. It has also been argued that specialized ecosystems permit cultural uniformity, while generalized ones encourage heterogeneity, and fragmentation of cultural forms where the environment allows for greater self-sufficiency (Yellen and Harpending 1972). Sahlins and Service (1960), clearly inspired by evolutionary biology, see less specialized subsistence strategies as having a greater potential for change than highly specialized ones.

OBJECTIONS AND LIMITATIONS TO BIOLOGICAL CONCEPTS

The employment of an ecosystems approach to *Homo sapiens* and the attempt to collect detailed relevant environmental data are not without their difficulties. The problems entailed in *describing* ecosystems, and the widespread lack of any recognition that such problems exist, are among the most basic. We still do not possess a complete picture of food relationships and interactions in any natural biotope. Pimentel (1966:23), for example, has attempted to trace the relationships between as few as fifty species, which represent only about one quarter of the total number of species in a relatively simple biotope. The diagram, reproduced here as Figure 4.1, is so full of lines that it becomes difficult to follow. It would be impossible to plot the relationships between the entire 210 known species of this simple community. Moreover, the relationships which are plotted do not indicate anything about the durational, quantitative or spatial dimensions, or the most important relationships between elements in the system. Indeed, every part of the system can never be accessible to direct observation, and the behaviour of large parts of a system is routinely a question of 'black box' assumptions (Ashby 1958) based on information about those parts of the system that are understood. It has been suggested (Woodwell 1970:26) that ecosystem complexity is so great as to preclude any simple single-factor analysis that is both accurate and satisfying.

In view of this it might seem that the extent to which a human ecosystem can be described in order that it might be useful for the purposes of ethnography is severely limited, and, given fragmentary data, virtually impossible to reconstruct from the existing literature. Consequently, it is seldom possible to confirm or reject empirical correlations without further extensive observation and investigation. This point has not been universally understood, and there is still a general tendency to over-interpret what little information is available. In any given project it is necessary to limit the field of analysis and the problems investigated. Description has to be directed and the system carefully defined. But, because boundaries are often arbitrary and drawn for convenience, they may become a source of artifacts which distort rather than facilitate analysis. Quantification of an incorrectly constructed or partially defined system may result in spurious precision and the placing of a misleading degree of confidence in any predictions. On the other hand, it has been repeatedly argued that the advantage of the ecosystem approach – whether in biology or in ethnography – is its stress on totality, interrelatedness and diversity (Watt 1966:3). The reconciliation of theory and practice would seem to hold out a daunting prospect.

Ecological analysis in ethnography is grounded in detailed fieldwork. But even with fieldwork the ethnographer, sometimes to a considerable degree, is straying outside his sphere of technical competence. Much analysis of environmental relations is worthless simply because it consists of observations which are either inaccurate or insufficient. At its most basic level this has meant a preference for native terminology and an infuriating absence of scientific nomenclature. No doubt, having some environmental data – however skimpy – is preferable to naive reports in which the environment, while featuring in explanations, is not discussed and not dissected. The solutions to such difficulties lie in recognizing the limits of disciplinary competence,[9] appropriate consultations, collaboration where the circumstances of fieldwork permit, and adequate preparation and training. Research in human ecology necessarily involves a high level of multidisciplinary activity and researchers must collect data which conventionally belong to other subjects. The alternative – team research – is hazardous and often does not work: the integration, coordination and synthesis of results are painfully difficult (Feachem 1977:4, 8). But the difficulties will not disappear by being ignored.

Ethnographers and archaeologists have also come unstuck in their borrowing of the key words and conceptual apparatus of modern biology. To begin with, confusion has arisen from the interchangeable use of such terms as 'ecological' and 'environmental', and the use of the word 'ecology' where 'natural environment' would have been more appropriate.[10] Ecology concerns the relations in which an organism is involved, not a separate material casing. *Ecological* determinism is therefore something very different from *environmental* determinism, and some might say a semantic impossibility. At the same time, jargon and concepts have been applied mechanically, such that mice and men become *a priori* ecological equals. Some of the worst excesses are found in the usages of the Chicago school (e.g. Mackenzie 1968), where 'habitat' is employed to refer to a class-dominated neighbourhood, and 'succession' to the replacement process in the same neighbourhood as families become more upwardly mobile. In the work of Bews (1935) fishermen and artisans become 'ecological types'. Neither are professional animal ecologists free from the fallacy of biologisms in their treatment of human systems. This simplistic transfer of concepts will just not do and often suggests the same kind of self-regulation and naturalness which have been rejected in the older organic models of sociological functionalism.

But terminological and conceptual difficulties are simply the more obvious reflection of an underlying theoretical discontent with subsuming human ecology under the rubric of general ecology (Cook 1973:41–3). The arguments are levelled at uncritical reasoning from animal to human ecology and recall the well-articulated objections of Kroeber, Boas, Steward, Forde, the Durkheimians and the Marxists. Such objections do not usually preclude ecological studies approached through biology via population genetics, epidemiology, nutritional ecology, biochemical and morphological variation, and the position occupied by human populations in a particular ecosystem. However, they do stress that the specific characteristics of human populations have often been suppressed through a desire to formulate a theory which embraces all living matter. These characteristics focus on five observations:

1. *Homo sapiens* is the only species which has evolved techniques for producing its own subsistence non-genetically, by directly manipulating and transforming the physical environment through organized social activity.

2. Interspecific exchanges have been emphasized and intra-specific exchanges played down (Cook 1973:41–4; cf. Godelier 1972:xxviii). This has tended to understress the crucial ecological role of human *labour* and the effect of those distributive relations which result from it, and define it.

3. The significance of the cognitive and affectual aspects of human behaviour has been disregarded. While, in other species biological transactions – predation, fighting, food intake and physical movement – tend to control population size and its pressure on the environment, in *Homo sapiens* population size and the character of appropriation are mediated and immediately governed by mental factors, which may have no necessary relationship with genetic programmes. A detailed consideration of this issue is reserved for Chapter 8.

4. Humans not only use and modify their environment through cultural activity (1) and organize it through categories (3), but accord

parts of it (including food) with value and symbolic meaning which may bear no necessary relationship to physical usefulness. Most specific values are arrived at through exchange (2).

5. The physical, social and intellectual products of production, exchange, cognition and value constitute the accumulated cultural tradition which in any one population determines the outcome of interaction with environmental variables.

The complexities of intra-specific exchange, the dominance of cognition and value together suggest that social structure have a dynamic of their own which is not described adequately or accurately in ecosystem terms. The unique character of human ecosystems has led some writers (e.g. Thompson 1949:266) to talk of 'ecocultural' systems, one of those unfortunate hybrids of little analytic potential. Human populations are parts of social systems and ecological systems. For the most part these must be treated as analytically separate, and with different properties. The implications of one for the other must be understood, not conflated. Where the ecosystem approach has been used most profitably is for simpler systems, where small populations are engaged in restricted environmental modification. This is because such populations most closely resemble the characteristics of those ecological populations of non-human species upon which classical ecological theory has been based. But the biological model cannot just be expanded to incorporate the complexity of modern social systems. The flow of capital, investment, technology, information and money cannot be reduced to energy units. Neither can dictatorship and democracy be usefully compared in terms of their distinctive energy networks, as has seriously been suggested (H. T. Odum 1971:202).

The ecosystem approach has found support and a moral legitimation for its excesses in the spread of the political 'ecological movement'.[11] Such excesses are well illustrated by the specific examples cited in the previous paragraph. In more general terms it has led to well-meaning but vague exaltations in favour of 'an adequate scientific humanism' (Anderson 1973:212, cf. Abbott 1970, E. N. Anderson 1972). This requires a concern with the survival of entire ecosystems, and a firm belief in the prophetic and salvationary role of an ecosystemic anthropology in tackling the otherwise inevitable environmental holocaust (Anderson 1973:181). In the words of Anderson (1973:214) it seeks: 'a humanistic ecology [which] would subvert the present orders of both capitalism and socialism. It is the revolution of revolutions – it would humanize aspects of the science–technology approach. [It is] a . . . touchstone for relevance.' It is not necessary to underestimate the dimensions of the current ecological crisis to realize that such dramatic prose owes a great deal to ideological fashion and political opportunism. Anderson speaks as one of the converted, and like the converted in so general a way as to obscure and avoid precise prescriptions. All we find are vague appeals for holism and integration; assertion, polemic, pretension, and a rhetoric which dissolves into a messy functionalism. His statements approach what Rappaport (1971b) has described as 'sanctity': dogma of a sufficient generality for the faithful to apply to most things, and at any event. But Rappaport himself (together with Bateson) has been criticized by Friedman (1979), who sees their well-ordered cybernetic totalities as suspicious ideological props (cf. Cotgrove 1976). Linked to such ecological utopianism is the theoretical primacy accorded to the concept of system. Anthropologists are criticized for focussing on the interrelationships between *Homo sapiens* in particular and the environment (autoecology), rather than on an examination of ecosystems as such (synecology) within which populations of *Homo sapiens* happen to dwell (Anderson 1973:209, 211–12). While this may emphasize the narrowness of existing ecological approaches, and, while the examination of systems in themselves is not only legitimate but vital, the replacement of autoecology by synecology would logically require the end of anthropology, underestimate precisely those species-specific properties which have enabled the modification of systems, and result in a theoretically naive and sterile 'ecosystemology'. Some writers seem so enamoured of the new ecology that they occasionally give the impression that we have reached an epistemological nirvana. It is implied that ecology provides a set of guiding principles beyond refutation, that if only the rules are applied correctly then an ecosystem approach will explain everything. The sad truth is that neither ecology nor 'anthropological ecology' provides us with any such panacea. Fortunately, the new faith already has its heretics.[12]

CONCLUSION

That the problems involved in ecological work are so formidable is no objection in itself to the techniques or theory, and should not detract from any potential light they may shed on human behaviour. If anthropology, or any other of the human sciences, has become pessimistic or nervous at the prospect that the behaviour of its object of study is varied, changeable, complex and population-specific, that it poses enormous problems of observation and description, then it should have given up the enterprise long ago.

The merits of the ecosystem appoach are of such importance that the difficulties should not be emphasized at their expense. Empirically, it has provided new techniques and data; it has enabled us to correct mistaken notions about often unfamiliar subsistence systems. Theoretically, it has stressed the necessity for holism while focussing on specific relationships between human populations and features of their environment. It has directed attention towards the existence of ramifications of particular relationships (even at the much-ridiculed 'box-and-arrow' level). It has shifted the emphasis away from the gross correlations of environmentalism, possibilism and cultural ecology towards more specific and integrated studies. It has stressed not only reciprocal causation but complex networks of mutual causality. It has focussed on system organization and properties: structure, equilibrium, change, the degree and forms of stability and the mechanisms which regulate the functioning of systems. It has emphasized the complexity of local environments and, technically, has focussed on the social significance of biological species. More generally, it has served to pave the way for the introduction and development of further systems concepts and ideas of energy flow and has revived an interest in Marxism and materialist dialectics.

5

The flow of energy and materials

INTRODUCTION

A great deal of our contemporary knowledge of the operation of ecosystems is based on the early work of Raymond L. Lindeman (1942). Drawing on the studies of Charles Elton in England and those of Clements and Shelford in the United States, Lindeman focussed on the fixation of energy by natural ecosystems and the quantitative relations that must theoretically exist between different users of energy as it is progressively disseminated among the various populations of organisms in an ecosystem. This concentration on the movement of energy and materials through a system was to consolidate ecology as a discipline and field of study; and it is the ecosystem approach which, over the past decade, has had most influence on the work of anthropologists interested in the articulation of biological and social systems. In this chapter I take up some of the general and theoretical concerns related to this approach, and in Chapters 6 and 7 specify the relevance of such ideas and techniques to an understanding of subsistence arrangements in particular.

Populations of organisms interact to form food webs, biotic communities and ecosystems. They are linked by flows of energy and nutrient materials which may be described and measured in quantitative terms. Although the complexity of ecosystems prevents a complete mapping of such flows, their examination in broad terms and the tracing of specific pathways enables us to learn much about the relationships between various components of the system and its overall structure.

Figure 5.1 illustrates the flow of both energy and materials in a generalized terrestrial ecosystem. There are two basic types of food chain: those involving grazing and those involving decay. In a grazing chain energy and nutrients accumulated by *primary producers* (mainly

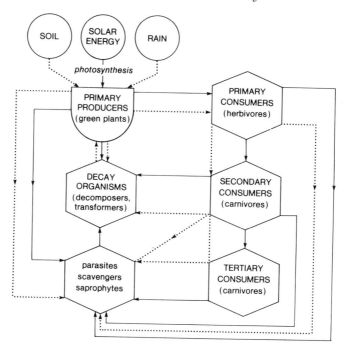

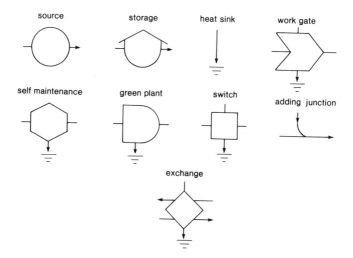

5.1 The flow of energy and nutrient materials in a generalized and simplified ecosystem. Continuous lines represent energy flows and broken lines flows of nutrients. The key is to conventions derived from Odum (1971) used in this and subsequent figures

plants) are used by *primary consumers* (herbivores) which convert some
of the energy to protein. Primary consumers are in turn used by
secondary consumers (carnivores). In this sense there are also *tertiary* –
and sometimes *quaternary* – consumers, while omnivores and certain
carnivores may occupy different levels of consumption depending on
the food they are eating at the time. As we move up the food chain,
feeding relations become more complex and consumers become increasingly dependent on a greater ratio of food to their own body
weight or biomass. This relationship expressed in terms of energy is
often illustrated in the form of pyramids (e.g. Parrack 1969:30). In the
decay chain, energy and nutrients from all kinds of organic matter of
producer and consumer origin are returned to primary producers with
the loss of energy and other nutrient matter to the immediate food
cycle. The transformation of energy (generally measured in kilocalories or kilojoules) from one form to another according to the laws of
thermodynamics and the circulation of materials are the two most
important principles underlying contemporary biological ecology,
applying to all organisms and ecosystems, including those containing
Homo sapiens. Figure 5.2 shows a schematic trophic structure of a
generalized ecosystem including humans, utilizing the concepts discussed in this section.

These general theoretical concepts have now been repeatedly and
fruitfully used to describe the workings of specific ecosystems by
biologists. An early and much-reproduced example is J. M. Teal's
classic study of a salt marsh in Georgia (1962). It was inevitable that the
concepts be extended to describe ecosystems of which *Homo sapiens* is a
part, and an early example of this is an analysis by Fosberg (1963) of
coral atoll ecosystems. Clearly, though, the specifically anthropological use of such concepts is concerned less with the broad description of
entire ecosystems than with a focus on those flows which directly
relate to human activities. This is a matter partly of technical competence and partly of theoretical interest.

THE CHARACTER OF HUMAN ENERGY RELATIONS

The energy structure of human populations is not duplicated exactly or
consistently by any other species. *Homo sapiens* is, for example, distinctive in the amount of energy derived at the tertiary level. This is partly
due to the use of technology and a capacity to organize the appropriation, transformation and transportation of external energy sources. It
is this ability to transform energy at exponential rates which determines the scale of the human ecological impact. While there are
enormous differences in the energy produced by food-collecting

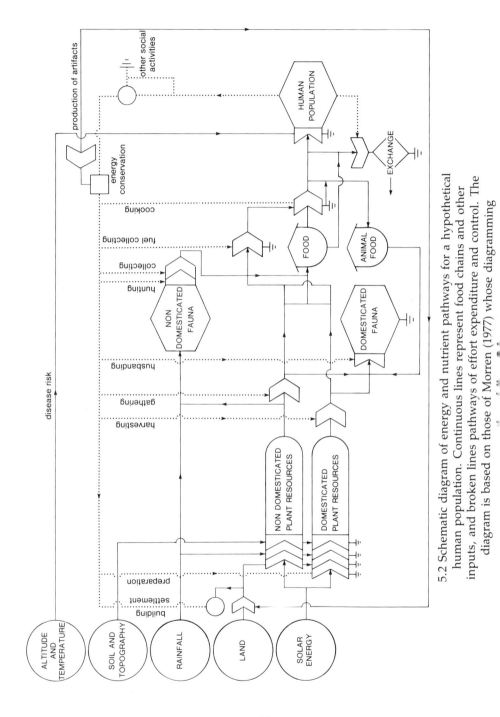

5.2 Schematic diagram of energy and nutrient pathways for a hypothetical human population. Continuous lines represent food chains and other inputs, and broken lines pathways of effort expenditure and control. The diagram is based on those of Morren (1977) whose diagramming populations and the thermonuclear industry, both exceed the amounts produced by any other species and the potential rate of increase is much greater. Moreover, the flow of energy and materials being transferred between both individuals and populations is *intra-specific* as well as *interspecific* (Anderson 1973:200). The combination of technology and exchange results in wide fluctuations and population:resource ratios (Foley 1977:168); this is in contrast to the fairly consistent population levels with respect to resources found in other species.

Some further aspects of human energy use compared with that of other animals can be seen if we distinguish six kinds of activity in the appropriation of food. Following Lawton (1973:62), these are the energy cost of: locating food supply, gathering or catching food, transport and storage, maintaining food supply, processing food and eating and swallowing. What is valuable about these activities is that they are neither anthropocentric nor culture-bound and they readily permit comparison between different species, including *Homo sapiens*.

The energy cost of food locating is probably of major importance among animals which have to hunt or forage for suitable food and hence move about actively; the energy cost of gathering or catching food, which covers chasing, catching, overcoming and killing prey and the energy used during grazing by herbivores, is important to all animals. The energy cost of transport and storage is probably small for most animals, but involves behaviour such as transport back to nest (bees, birds) or building winter food-stores. The energy cost of maintaining a food supply is generally small or non-existent in non-human animals, although the maintenance of aphid populations by ants, and territorial defence in some birds, might be included as exceptions in this category. The energy cost of processing food is also probably very small for most animals, but would include opening nuts (rodents), cracking snails (thrushes) or 'chewing cud' (ruminants). The energy cost of eating or swallowing food is probably very small for most animals, but may be important in species which swallow relatively large prey. Practically, it may be difficult to distinguish it from the processing of food.

Whereas in most non-human animal species such detailed differentiation is of little relevance, in *Homo sapiens* it is characteristic that within the species there is great variety according to subsistence strategy and economy. For this reason the categories listed are of some analytical interest in the comparison of different modes of subsistence. Accordingly, they are examined in further detail in Chapter 6.

Another respect in which *Homo sapiens* differs from all other animals is the variable ecological efficiency of energy use. This is generally measured as:

$$\frac{\text{energy assimilated from food/unit time}}{\text{energy expended (respiration while gathering food)}} = \frac{a}{r}$$

For any life to be sustained a/r must be greater than 1. But energy assimilated (a) is not the same as energy consumed (c) and most measurements collected under ethnographic conditions apply solely to consumption. However, under normal circumstances it is usually adequate to rely on the index c/r, that is, energy gained divided by energy expended. When calculated for individuals, the excess over and above 1 in the equation $a/r = 1+$ is available for other bodily functions, the growth of body tissues and reproduction. For all animals, including humans, c/r averages between 3 and 30. Some individual examples are shown in Table 5.1. On this scale, *Homo sapiens* is only moderately efficient and shows great variability. The fact of variability provides a further index of comparison between different subsistence strategies.

MATERIAL CYCLES AND NUTRIENT FLOW

In the same way as the flow of energy can be traced through an ecosystem, and the form of that flow and its measurement contribute to understanding human environmental relations, so nutrients and other materials can be seen in the context of their pattern of flow within the system.

Material cycles link organisms (including *Homo sapiens*) with the inorganic environment, generally via other organisms. Theoretically, material – unlike energy – can be re-used and moves through the system in cycles. However, some materials are part of cycles that are so long term that the resources might effectively be considered as nonrenewable. In many networks the path taken by materials is more or less circular and goes through biogeochemical cycles passing through several spheres. If carrying material essential for life, they are nutrient cycles (Odum 1963:53–64). Apart from calories, human populations require protein for growth and maintenance, and minerals and vitamins to ensure correct skeletal development and metabolism.

In addition to consumable materials, there are materials used for life-support purposes but not eaten, such as stone for construction. Some of these resources are a by-product of food-getting (e.g. skin, bone. . .), or may be specifically collected or grown. It is important to include them here, since in many ecological studies there is such an obsession with food-getting that other materials are often neglected. Such materials and their cycles may be critical for survival, limiting or

100

The flow of energy and materials

Table 5.1 *A summary of the ratios of energy gained to energy expended in animals including humans (adapted from Lawton 1973:72)*

	c/r
1. Dragonfly larva	1–4
2. Large-mouth black bass	4–10
3. 3 humming-birds in wild	4–30
4. Bumble bee	4–30
5. Dickcissel	20–25
6. Humming-bird in laboratory	6–75
7. Humans on coral island (no fossil fuel)	20–25
8. Modern cereal agriculture (human energy expenditure only)	5,000–7,500
9. Modern cereal agriculture (including fossil-fuel costs)	0.5–20

enhancing adaptation, or be necessary for maintaining food consumption (e.g. firewood). The depletion of such resources may have ecological consequences. Also, their appropriation and processing involves energy expenditure, which is all part of the system necessary to enable the population and social formation to reproduce itself. The exact organization of material cycles varies between ecosystems. Human adaptability depends ultimately on material cycles, and therefore long-term disruption (through pollution, mining. . .) could be disastrous. Also, essential materials are not distributed evenly, and this problem is overcome through transport, trade and exploitation. Thus, material flow in human populations in as much a social as a physical process (Hardesty 1977:72–4).

The possible limiting effect of such materials has not been subject to the kind of detailed ecological analysis which its importance deserves. However, something which has been of considerable interest to ethnographers, geographers and others is soil fertility. This has been discussed in Chapter 2 in particular connection with swiddening. The early generalization that soil fertility is limiting in swiddening populations has had to be revised in the light of more recent detailed work, which has approached the problem in terms of nutrient cycles in the ecosystem and provided empirical evidence to the contrary (e.g. Geertz 1963; see also pp. 39–41).

Even more recent work has explored the possible limiting effects of protein. It has, for example, been noted that in many small populations the energy cost of obtaining protein is high. It has been assumed, therefore, that the quality of protein must be important, as is the time when it is consumed. For example, Nietschmann (1973:218) reports that traditional Miskito foodstuffs encourage the availability of essential amino acids and increase the percentage of ingested protein which can be absorbed by the body. He also suggests that the intermittent high consumption of meat allows for rapid recovery from periods of low calorie intake, and may help to resist infectious disease. Rappaport (1968) had earlier suggested that for the Tsembaga the intake of high-quality protein on culturally specified occasions provided energy just at those crucial times when the body was under stress or ill. Nietschmann's argument is so similar to Rappaport's, including the suggestion that the dietary pattern is somehow a result of adaptive accommodation, that it is surely its inspiration. But, even if these patterns do have the physiological effects described, there is no need to explain them as adaptations.

ETHNOGRAPHY AND HUMAN ENERGETICS

Anthropologists have been drawn to the mapping and measuring of energy and nutrient flows partly through their central place in modern ecosystem theory, which, as we have seen, has had great influence. But the concerns of economic anthropology over the last few decades with measuring production and consumption, and with nutrition, and a longer history in American anthropology of concern with the capacity of different human societies to harness increasing amounts of energy (White 1949, 1959; Cottrell 1970), have helped to establish the techniques as legitimate and useful. But modern ecosystem research, and its anthropological offspring, could not get off the ground until the practical calorimetric problems of measuring energy flow, productivity, the biochemistry of foods and food values, especially of tropical foods, had been effectively removed.

Following Foley (1977:166), we can distinguish seven variables that are of interest in the examination of human energetics:

1 all energy in the system; in practical terms, the amount of primary production (P)
2 P in terms of its various parts as they affect human populations – e.g. edible/non-edible, animal/plant – species composition. . . (P_1, P_2, P_3 . . .)
3 energy which can be extracted without damaging source populations; defined in relation to the structure and population dynamics of the parts (e)
4 energy necessary to support an individual or population, usually human (s). This value is a function of metabolic rate
5 energy which it is physiologically or technologically possible to expend in unit-time; defines the potential of the system (o)
6 energy extracted from environment in unit-time (p)

Table 5.2 *Relationships between energy flow variables of relevance to ecological work in anthropology (after Foley 1977:167–8)*

1 Primary production divided by the amount of energy extracted in unit-time, that is, the percentage of available energy utilized. In practice, this must be considerably greater than 1, as the amount extracted is always negligible in relation to total primary production. The necessity of this solution to the equation has been noted above with respect to specific animal populations (Phillipson 1973).

2 Energy which can be extracted without damaging the system, divided by energy actually extracted. This is a measure of stability, indicating the likelihood that the system will persist in the long term.

3 Energy extracted from the environment in unit-time divided by energy necessary to support an individual or population. This is a crucial test of ecological success. In a situation where extracted energy is vastly greater than needs, then a surplus will occur.

4 Energy extracted from the environment in unit-time divided by energy which it is physiologically or technically possible to expend in unit-time. If this index falls below 1 then the system loses the capacity to expand without technological or physiological change, or discovery of new resources.

5 Energy extracted from the environment in unit-time divided by energy expended in extracting the energy.

6 Index of the potential for maximum stable appropriation and productivity; measured by noting the productivity of energy that may be extracted without damage to the source populations to amount of primary production.

7 Primary production will always exceed energy necessary for supporting a population, but it is useful to know by how much. This is also the case for the relationship between primary production and possible energy expenditure.

8 Energy expended in extracting energy divided by primary production. This index should represent energy-exchange efficiency.

9 Energy extractable without damage to source populations divided by energy necessary to support a population. This is an alternate to index 5, in terms of availability rather than actual extraction.

10 Energy necessary to support a population divided by energy which it is technically or physiologically possible to expend in unit-time. When a system is at capacity, this index will approach 1.

11 Energy expended in extracting energy divided by energy necessary to support a population. This is the coefficient of extractive efficiency.

12 Energy which it is physiologically or technologically possible to expend in unit-time divided by energy expended in extracting it: a measure of the technological pressure on the system.

7 energy expended in extracting this energy (r).

Given these variables, there are then a number of relationships between them that are of interest in ecological work in ethnography. These are listed in Table 5.2, but few of them have been systematically calculated for human systems. Primary production and total biomass have only been estimated crudely in ethnographic studies (Parrack 1969). In archaeological work (Shawcross 1972, Foley 1977) trophic models have been drawn from animal ecology in palaeolithic studies, and from anthropological and geographical studies of specific communities in post-Palaeolithic work. They remain largely of theoretical interest, rather than an empirical preoccupation. Attention has generally concentrated on gauging the energetic efficiency of various populations, comparing the efficiency of different techniques and tracing the flow of energy through human populations. There are now several studies of this kind (Kemp 1971, Morren 1977, Thomas 1973), but the earliest and perhaps most influential has been the work of Roy Rappaport (1968) on the Tsembaga, a Maring clan group of the New Guinea highlands.

THE FLOW OF ENERGY IN A MARING POPULATION

Given that energy flow in all human ecosystems is complex, swidden cultivation as practised in the humid tropics provides a relatively simple case. As part of his work on the Tsembaga, Rappaport kept detailed records of the activities involved in transforming an area of 11,000 square feet of secondary forest into garden. He conducted time-and-motion studies, and estimated crop yields, from daily weighing of harvests from some 25 gardens over a period of almost a year, using various standard sources for calculating the food value of produce. Using the findings of Hipsley and Kirk (1965) on individual metabolic rates for the performance of everyday tasks by Chimbu New Guinea highlanders, he estimated that the energy input of each sex is approximately equal, some 28,314 kilocalories per acre (69,966 kcal per hectare). Rappaport calculated energy inputs for clearing underbrush; clearing trees; fencing gardens; weeding and burning; placing soil retainers and other similar tasks; planting and weeding until the end of harvest; other maintenance; and harvesting sweet potatoes, taro, cassava and yams; and cartage. These twelve major inputs in gardening amount to some 561,313 kilocalories per acre (1,387,054 kcal per hectare) and are illustrated in Figure 5.3. Combining all the inputs and comparing the sum with yields Rappaport found that the ratio of yield to input was about 16.5:1 in taro-yam gardens and about 15.9:4 in sweet-potato gardens.

Tsembaga devote a substantial proportion of their principal crops to feeding their pigs. Pig populations are culled at periodic year-long festivals, reducing the population to one-sixth of its former size in terms of liveweight. Rappaport estimated that about 45,000 kilocalories of human energy per pig were spent in a year on growing pig food and managing the animals. He calculated that the energy yield to input, because of the ten years required to increase the population for

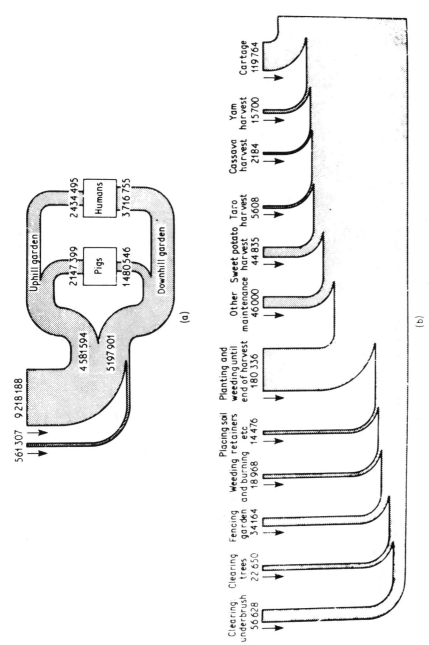

(a)

(b)

5.3 Some features of energy flow among the Tsembaga, measured in kcals per acre, of a pair of gardens, and showing (a) inputs required to prepare and harvest gardens and (b) biomass of crop yield (from Rappaport 1971:120–1)

105

the next festival, was in the region of 2:1 and 1:1. So, swiddening and pig-keeping provide the Tsembaga with both an adequate daily ration of energy and an emergency source of protein. The garden produce provides the men with some 2,600 kilocalories per day and the women with some 2,200 kilocalories.

In this brief summary, it is clear that Rappaport is concerned with a number of matters:

1 achieving some overall comprehension of energy flow in a system through simplification, measurement and diagramming using the ecosystem model discussed in Chapter 4.
2 measuring energy intake and comparing the quantities from various sources.
3 measuring energy input for different sections of the population and for different activities.
4 gauging overall efficiency and the efficiency of various activities.

We can now examine each of these issues in more detail.

DESCRIBING ENERGY AND NUTRIENT FLOW

The complexity of ecosystems requires that they must be simplified for the purposes of description and analysis. In doing this minor flows can be eliminated, although precisely what is eliminated depends on the key variables of interest. It has become standard practice to represent ecosystems as diagrams. The conventions used tend to vary from self-explanatory pictures to highly stylized diagrams based on the 'box and arrow' principle and employing standardized symbols (Figure 5.1). An example of how these techniques might be used to model a hypothetical human population is shown in Figure 5.2. Figure 5.4 compares gross energy flow and control diagrammed in this way in four ethnographically very different populations. From such models it is possible to move to algebraic formulations upon which the operations of calculus can be performed. These may permit an examination of the dynamic interaction of energy flow and information by means of computer simulation and mathematical analysis. In practice, though, the mathematics has seldom proceeded beyond the relatively simple level of handling variables and defining problems (e.g. Dow 1976).

Diagramming can be a useful procedure, but there are a number of points which should be remembered. Firstly, diagrams are there to simplify, to communicate broad features and mechanisms involving parts of a system, and to indicate rapidly relationships which might otherwise prove awkward to describe. Obfuscation due to complexity and reduction to unstandardized algebraic and graphic conventions should be avoided, although this has not always been the case.

The flow of energy and materials

Secondly, diagramming ecosystem flows inevitably tends to emphasize the static character of systems, while not always adequately con-
veying the degree to which they are changing. Thirdly, diagramming
itself is very much part of an analysis, in as much as it may portray
unforeseen relationships and patterns, and eliminate detail.

For the anthropologist it is neither feasible nor usually necessary to
map and measure energy flows for all components of an ecosystem,
although it may be useful to trace part of the pattern as it directly affects
human activities. What these are will largely be determined by the
requirements of a specific research problem. However, it may be an
important part of an investigation to estimate energy consumption and
expenditure. The physiological relationship between these can be
shown in terms of a number of elementary equations (Lawton 1973:59–
60). In the formulae

$$c = g + r + f + u$$
$$a = c - f$$

g is energy used for the growth of body tissue and in reproduction; a is
the food assimilated (absorbed); r is that part of absorbed energy used
in respiration; c is that consumed (eaten); f is that lost as faeces; and u is
that lost in urine. Total energy loss is therefore

$$(u + f) c - (a - g + r).$$

This particular computation is of little use in ethnographic work, and is
anyway virtually impossible to measure under fieldwork conditions.
But as has already been noted it is both useful and possible to estimate c
and r.

ENERGY YIELD, CONSUMPTION AND DIETARY STUDIES

The estimation of food yields, consumption patterns and diets in
small-scale populations has been going on for about four decades.
Some of this work has been pioneered by ethnographers, for example
as illustrated by the work of Richards (1939) among the Bemba and
those specifically concerned with food habits (e.g. Bennett 1946, Mead
1945). Other work has been approached from a more specifically
nutritional angle (e.g. Hipsley and Clements 1947). Both kinds of study
have tended to suffer from their particular disciplinary orientation.
Anthropologists have lacked technical knowledge about nutrition
while nutritionists have often tended to be sociologically naive. Biologists and nutritionists, in attempting to extend their techniques and

(a)

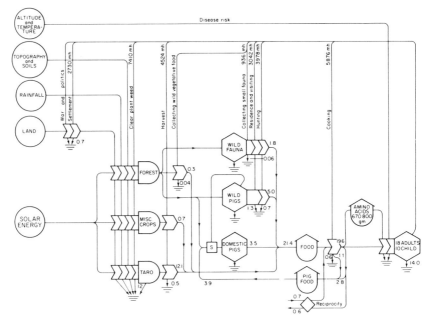

(c)

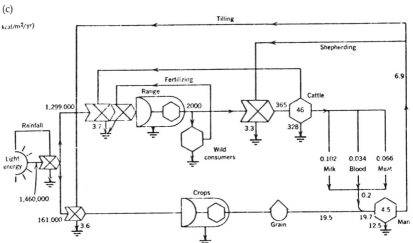

5.4 Comparson of energy flow and control in four populations: (a)
Miyanmin, New Guinea highlands (Morren 1977:288), (b) Dodo, Uganda
(Odum 1971:109), (c) Nuñoa Quechua, Peruvian Andes (Thomas 1974,
redrawn by Little and Morren 1977:66), and (d) Lamotrek atoll, Micronesia
(Odum 1971: fig. 4–1, based on data in Alkire 1965)

108

(b)

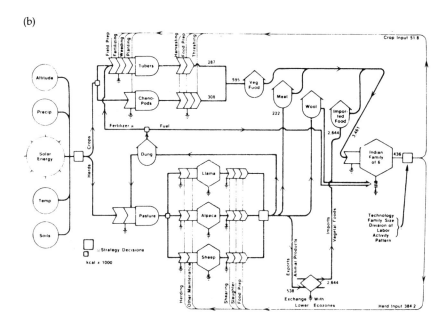

(d)

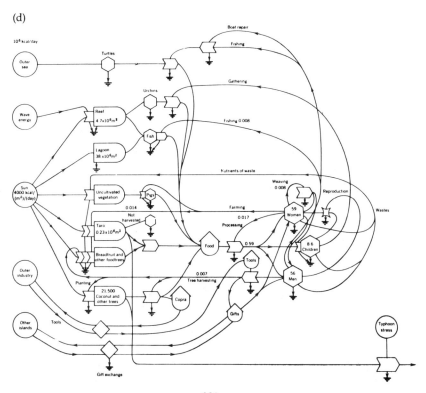

109

paradigms to man, have been inclined to make unwarranted assumptions concerning the uniformity of behaviour patterns in given contexts and the reliability of published ethnographic descriptions and production statistics. In general, they tend to underestimate the extent of the intrusion of the social into the biological domain (Gerlach 1965). Sometimes skills have been combined, as in the work of Margaret McArthur (1960); but all work in this field has relied upon, and has only been as good as, the groundwork undertaken by food biochemists, physiologists and laboratory nutritionists. For example, much of the work has been based on standard sets of energy and food-value equivalents. But, however inadequate the groundwork, such information is better than none at all. It is important to differentiate the quality of different foods, since mass or weight may be a poor guide to their nutritional value. For example, concentrated and easily accessible energy is found in fat, and in some populations this is a major energy source. Fat is the most concentrated form of energy, yielding 9 kcals per gram compared with 4 kcals for carbohydrate. Similarly, small quantities of certain plant matter may be important sources of particular vitamins, and the absence of such plant matter may present a limiting condition.

Nutritional work in small-scale populations took on a new impetus with the influence of ecological energetics and the new ecology. Not only was it crucial to obtain large and accurate samples of dietary records, but comparison of consumption from different sources and comparison of actual human consumption with yield became of central interest. The focus remained on humans, but quantitative information on surrounding flows became of significance. Thus it became important to discover what proportion of the energy yield of a garden plot was consumed by pigs and what proportion by humans, and what proportion of food waste decomposed and what was consumed by scavengers such as domesticated dogs. These questions were important because the object of analysis was not simply the human population, but the system, whose functioning was regarded as having certain implications for humans whose behaviour, in turn, had implications for the functioning of the system. Also, it became important to compare the contribution of different food chains and resources, to assess their relative importance in subsistence.

ENERGY EXPENDITURE

As with dietary studies, the physiological study of subsistence effort goes back several decades (e.g. R. H. Fox 1953). Ethnographers have been keeping diaries of work effort (though not always systematically) for even longer (e.g. Richards 1939). As with the analysis of diet, ecological approaches have led to renewed interest and a wider appreciation of their relevance. There has also been a similar tendency for physiological field studies to suffer from inadequate ethnographic and ecological back-up (Norgan, Ferro-Luzzi and Durnin 1974, Hornabrook 1977). For example, sometimes gross labour-time data are translated into calories (Lawton 1973). From the point of view of an anthropologist, not only does this procedure often involve uncritical use of sources, but frequently the very advantage of calorific data is that as a measure of effort they differ from the index of time in taking into account variation in the intensity of work. Equally, ethnographic studies tend to underestimate the technical difficulties of measuring effort. Ideally, such measurements should be made with proper equipment (Thomas 1973), but much of the work has been based on the use of tables of constants for various activities for a relatively limited number of populations. The reason for this is lack of time, lack of necessary skills and the fact that physiological investigations are cumbersome and easily antagonize local populations. As energy expenditure for a given task is variable, estimates may be as accurate for long periods as detailed measurements for only a brief period. Such estimates are made from careful time-and-motion studies for particular activities involving a record of the number of movements of the same type and noting the size, sex and age and number of individuals engaged in the task. All these may affect the amount of energy expended per movement. This is illustrated in Table 5.3, from the work of Roy Rappaport on the Tsembaga Maring. It then requires access to data on the number of calories expended over time for each type of movement and for each body size, sex and age. I have already mentioned that these are seldom available for small-scale populations. Rappaport used data from other New Guinea groups. I have used New Guinea data in analysing work effort on Seram (Ellen 1978). This is questionable, but sometimes unavoidable. It may be possible to justify the use of such equivalents, as I have done, where population biology, subsistence and ecology suggest a general similarity. Clearly, though, this is an area in which there is room for enormous technical improvement.

Once measured, energy expenditure provides a convenient common denominator for the comparison of effort expended on different tasks, the calculation of efficiency ratios and the undertaking of comparative studies between different populations and techniques. In this respect it may be an advance on time-and-motion studies, since, in recording energy input for different activities, periods of inactivity do not count as effort. Similarly, different parts of an activity – say

Table 5.3 Results of a time-and-motion study on the clearing of underbrush by selected Tsembaga Maring individuals (Rappaport 1968:258)

Worker's name	Sex	Est. age	Weight in lb.	Time	No. strokes	Time	No. strokes	Time	No. strokes	Comments
Akis	M	20	88	10:37–10:43	296	11:14–11:20	250	12:14–12:20	248	Only one 3-minute break during period. Next longest break: 15 seconds
Aũmp	F	50	85	10:55–11:01	244	11:30–11:36	209			No breaks longer than 20 seconds during working period
Avoi	M	55	94	11:02–11:08	177	11:50–11:56	190			Slower than other workers because of short breaks, and slower strokes
Meñ	M	28	120	6 min.	233					Longer strokes than any of the others
Wale	F	35	76	9:53–9:59	246	10:58–11:04	260			No breaks longer than 20 seconds during working period
Nimini	M	18	96	6 min.	246					
Mer	M	40–5	94	6 min.	316					Stated that he was in a hurry

hunting – require different amounts of effort, which measurement by time fails to indicate. The chase is not energetically equivalent, for example, to the journey home, though it may last the same length of time. Such measurements may involve comparison of different subsistence activities, or of subsistence with non-subsistence activities, such as ritual.

PROBLEMS AND TECHNICAL DIFFICULTIES IN THE COLLECTION OF ECOLOGICAL DATA

It must now be clear that, whatever other deficiencies the analysis of ecosystem flows may bring with it, it can make extraordinary demands on the time, care, patience and skill of the investigator and his back-up facilities. There are problems with regard to methods and at the level of interpretation of results.

It is understandably difficult for fieldworkers whose primary focus is on human behaviour to obtain the kind of data and results which biological research into non-human ecosystems and nutritional–medical surveys can often provide. This is in part a problem of professional competence and in part a problem of limited time and resources. Collaborative research between behavioural and biomedical disciplines has occasionally proved possible (e.g. Gross and Underwood 1971), but it has been much more common for fieldworkers to undertake their own work in consultation with specialist assistance and in conjunction with available scientific reports and technical field manuals (Netting 1971:24). However, even with the intelligent use of such data and aids, much work suffers because the relevant, detailed support studies in plant ecology, zoogeography, dietary composition, energy expenditure and geomorphology are unavailable for the area concerned. In such circumstances workers have tended to rely on a strategy which combines the compilation of their own records with recourse to reports on well-documented areas with close similarities in ecology, subsistence economics and population biology.

The extent to which an ethnographer can rely on existing basic regional records is limited, while collecting this kind of material under ethnographic field conditions is time-consuming, painstaking and depressingly repetitive. Human subjects cannot be expected to behave in ways convenient for the ethnographer's field schedule, or for his techniques of measurement, while the ethnographers themselves can seldom maintain the necessary daily routine of measurement over a sufficiently long period of time. Moreover, we have already noted that the standards for energy expenditure and food values, even when available for the localities in question and presented according to categories useful to the social scientist, are only as good as the techniques used by physiologists and nutritionists to determine them in the first place.

The early work on energy expenditure and food intake in New Guinea, and probably in many other parts of the Third World, now looks pitifully inadequate by modern standards. It was often based on inadequate samples and might have been a little more useful had it not been so often ethnographically naive in assumptions made about the social and cultural context of obtaining food and expending energy. Temporal changes, in particular, have frequently been underrated. It is always necessary to take into account the fact that the features of the biotic and physical habitat which affects humans are continually fluctuating. The fluctuations are often cyclical, as between night and day, and between the seasons. There are also non-cyclical critical periods, marked by disasters such as tornadoes and severe droughts.

Biological ecologists have now recognized some of the problems associated with calorimetry used in the measurement and interpretation of energy equivalents. Cummins and Wuycheck (1971) have actually listed the kinds of variability linked to the character of the material being analysed, e.g. season of collection, life-history stage, sex, reproductive conditions, nutritional history and diet of animals prior to collection. Very often, where an attempt has been made to hold some of the variables constant, standardized methods of measurement have just not existed. Under field conditions the problems multiply, and the logistical problems of preparing and organizing a large-scale systems measurement study alone are overwhelming (Watt 1966:7). Woodwell (1970:31–2) has described the formidable task of measuring the total respiration of an oak–pine forest on Long Island. This involved a detailed description of the structure of the forest, including the total amount of organic matter, the weight and area of leaves, the weight of roots and the net amount of production. The principal techniques employed to measure energy flow were (a) the rate of accumulation of carbon dioxide during inversions of temperature and (b) a precise measurement of the rates of respiration of various segments of the forest (including the branches and stems of trees) and the soil. Such work is tedious, laborious and time-consuming and requires virtually unlimited financial support. The determination of the biomass of tropical forests, where trees often exceed 30 metres in height, presents problems of an even greater magnitude. Certain short cuts have been advocated to speed up the means of biomass estimation, for example allometric regression analysis (Manner 1977:217), but even these cannot eliminate a great deal of difficult groundwork. There remain problems in measuring flows in all complex ecosystems (Woodwell and Smith 1969).

The flow of energy and materials

When it comes to ecosystems involving *Homo sapiens*, the problems of description are far greater and the degree of possible accuracy much less. Human beings are not ideal laboratory animals and respond poorly to calorimetry. An analysis equivalent to those described for pristine ecosystems, even one containing a small human population, would be a mammoth operation. Measurement of energy consumption and expenditure is a particularly acute problem in ethnographic ecology.

As with the analyses of pristine ecosystems, however careful and sophisticated the fieldwork, our understanding of the energetics can only be very partial. Most existing information is extremely patchy and there is a constant tendency to overinterpret sparse nutritional data.

The problems of reseach of this order should not be underestimated, even for trained experts devoting all their time to gathering such data. The practical difficulties involved in measuring energy flow for lower animals (McNeill and Lawton 1970) are magnified in human communities under field conditions. Anthropologists and geographers are obviously prone to underestimate the technical problems involved. Roy Rappaport has admitted as much in a recent spirited theoretical defence of his *Pigs for the ancestors* (1977:155). Rappaport's analysis has been criticized on the grounds of the inadequacy of the techniques used to collect the kind of data necessary to test his hypotheses, and he has admitted himself that some of his data leave much to be desired (McArthur 1977:95). It is instructive to specify some of these objections.

1. McArthur (1977:98–122) has pointed out that for five months the amount of food given to pigs was not weighed and that there are weights for vegetable foods only, although these appear to constitute 99 per cent of the usual diet.

2. Rappaport weighed the food of a group of 16 individuals (6 males, 4 females and 6 children) over an eight-month period. McArthur regards the duration of this sample as good, but not the sample itself. The individuals are too closely related genealogically, and the population has a higher proportion of children than in the sample. The problem with samples of this kind is that we do not know how big an error they embody.

3. There is a difficulty with regard to conversion ratios. Foods in small-scale rural societies vary considerably from place to place in composition and therefore food tables are unlikely to be a good guide. Moreover, Rappaport's data are useless for his purposes, since we have no way of estimating the validity of protein in the diet of different age and sex groups. Even if his data were reliable, comparison with amounts recommended would not tell us how well nourished Tsembaga individuals are.

115

4. Rappaport argues that the availability and distribution of pork in contexts of stress may be important as Tsembaga achieve nitrogen balance at a low level. McArthur notes that it is clear that formulated protein requirements are not applicable to traditional New Guinea lifestyles, while any hypothesis about ritual consumption enhancing the value of pork should not ignore the well-documented evidence of the ill-effects of gorging at festivals.

5 Finally, McArthur criticizes Rappaport for suggesting that salt intake immediately prior to fighting enhances the value of the pork that has previously been consumed. She notes that many New Guinea people have successfully adapted to a low sodium intake, and use potassium salt. It is unwise to assume that their physiological response would be the same as those with a high intake. Changes in blood volume, rate of sweating, development of thirst and production of energy from pork fat, even if we grant that they occur, would be unlikely to last for more than a day or two.

But even if we acknowledge the failings of Rappaport and others (among whom I must include myself), there are still very good reasons for anthropologists to collect their own data and for paying some attention to existing data. As with many other fields, data collected in these areas by non-specialists may not be as accurate or useful as they might otherwise have been – but they are often the only data that exist. Furthermore, the variables considered and the categories selected are often not those normally used by biologists themselves, but they may be of particular importance in the investigation of the sociology of subsistence economies: output considered by geographic area, inputs for particular social groups, categories of activity and so on.

Clearly there is a need to be enormously careful in choosing samples, selecting methods and collecting data. But the collection of data always depends on what is going to be done with them. One of the few field investigations of energetics in a human population in its environment to have combined precise measurements of dietary intake and energy expenditure with a realistic model of energy flow and control is Thomas's study of Peruvian Altiplano Indians (1973). As in many biological studies, it is more important to focus on a realistic and general model than to be precise, and to have a detailed record of the pattern of daily life than to undertake laborious expensive measurement (Norgan *et al.* 1974:343). If this is true for physiological work, it must surely also be true in ethnographic work. Here precise and detailed physiological measurement is generally of secondary interest and some studies have explicitly denied that they should be understood as studies of dietary intake and energy expenditure (Morren 1977:284, Ellen 1978). Rather, what is important is to focus on the gross

outline structure of energy pathways, control mechanisms, broad relationships and critical ratios of effort and intake according to selected
social and economic variables. This does not mean that accuracy and
careful description are of no consequence. Indeed, it is essential to
strive continually for the improvement of field techniques. One solution might be the careful design and conduct of some research projects
with limited goals, rather than more 'total' ecological ethnographies
supported by suspect data or methods. The danger here, though, lies
in research formulations which conceal wider structural factors, the
attribution of unwarranted autonomy to partial systems and the return
to a fanciful empiricism.

ENERGY, MATERIALS AND ADAPTATION

Many attempts to measure energy and nutrient-capture and use in
human populations have been associated with attempts to measure
efficiency of energy use. This in part reflects the preoccupation of
cultural ecology with technology, effort and subsistence defined in
narrow terms (Little and Morren 1977:20). Apart from the technical
difficulties in measuring energy and material flow under ethnographic
conditions, there are major theoretical problems centring around the
extent to which social life can be reduced to calories and energy-
efficiency computations, the extent to which energy balance reflects
cultural adaptation, and to which either energy or protein can be
regarded as limiting. The matter has already been given some consideration in Chapter 2.

In its more extreme form (White 1959:39, Dow 1976:954), the proposition that culture is simply a mechanism for processing energy and
materials is manifestly ludicrous. Technology and social organization
certainly modify the rate and amount of energy transfer, but also
generate change and activity which have no necessary relationship
with maintenance of biological existence. In the case of *Homo sapiens*
individual or collective action may be instigated for reasons originating
within the social system where energy transformation is not the end
but the means. Human behaviour is therefore purposeful, and not
simply the effect of genetic instructions to transfer energy and materials. Not all energy transformation is purposive, however, and
much is simply the incidental by-product of human activities. Nevertheless, in *historical* terms the great increases in the amount of energy
transferred by *Homo sapiens* have been purposive and largely a means
to other ends. This point is developed further in Chapter 11.

The difficulties in handling biological and behavioural variables in
the same analysis arise from there being no comparable measures of

such phenomena. Attempts to make such comparisons are therefore bound to become either explicit or implicit analogies, interesting but often misleading. Power, in its social and cultural sense, is in no way reducible to 'the rate of flow of useful energy' (H. T. Odum 1971:26), neither are monetary or other economic transactions the equivalent of physical flows (H. T. Odum 1971:174–205, Dow 1976). Re-phrasing the fundamental questions of economics, law and religion in terms of calories is both absurd and dangerous. The downgrading of economic production to the expenditure of calories, for analytical reasons, or simply to dress up ethnography as hard science, is what Brookfield (1972:46) has called the 'calorific obsession', echoed elsewhere as 'nutritional reductionism' (Cook 1973:45–6, Vayda and McCay 1975:4–6). 'Man', remarks Scott Cook (1973:44), 'must produce more than calories if calories are to be produced.' For calories to be of any use in economic analysis they must be converted or carefully related to use and exchange values. Even the technical concept of 'effort', as distinct from the ideological concept of 'work', involves more than the disposal of undifferentiated energy; it relies upon such things as organizational intricacy, patterns of intensity, number of tasks, rate, duration and the objects being produced. Physical exertion makes more demands on the body than the burning of calories.

This critique reflects a similar one among biologists themselves. Slobodkin (1972), implicitly arguing against the reductionism of Lindeman (1942), points out that it is erroneous to see the evolution of plant and animal species just in terms of their adaptation as efficient users, collectors and converters of energy. The pressures of natural selection are as much concerned with the efficient use of nutrients, the ensuring of mating, safe overwintering, swift growth and dispersal. In fact (Slobodkin 1972:293–4):

> there exists no uniquely generalizable maximum energy efficiency which can be used as a rule of thumb in biological resource exploitation . . . the empirical data do not indicate the existence of such a maximum . . ., [and] the combination of the mathematical form of calculation of ecological efficiency, and certain basic considerations of evolutionary process, make it theoretically impossible for any such constant maximum ecological efficiency to exist . . . we must clearly distinguish between adaptive effectiveness, ecological efficiency and population efficiency . . . the concept of efficiency as such relates to energy, while the concept of effectiveness relates to adaptation.

Slobodkin (1972:305) concludes that the empirical evidence shows that ecological efficiency is not maximized while population efficiency is. He points out that biological systems are the end results of a long evolutionary process, which has:

for the last several billion years operated through a system of intensive variables, and has not been guided by any external agency which interfered with the process and which maintained a global view. It is only with the development of human control of the environment and particularly with the development of conservation theories that global goals have become significant in ecological systems.

Despite this it remains clear that energy may – under certain conditions – be a major limiting factor. In the analysis of a Quechua district of the high *puna* of the southern Peruvian Andes, R. B. Thomas (1973) describes various practices contributing to the efficient use of limited energy:

1 appropriation from a spatially dispersed and multiple-resource base of energetically efficient crops and domestic animals
2 trading surplus resources in the district for high-energy-yield foods from lower regions
3 the assignment of a large proportion of herding to children for whom it is energetically less expensive
4 restriction of daily activities to sedentary tasks wherever possible. We may also add:
5 the use of sheep, llama and cattle dung for fertilizer and fuel.

(Winterhalder, Larsen and Thomas 1974)

And where energy is not limiting, an increase in its availability may still permit more time to be spent on activities more directly relevant to adaptive success (Smith 1979:63).

Because certain patterns of food consumption or work effort are beneficial does not mean that they are adaptive, in neither a purposive nor a non-purposive way. In societies where energy is not a limiting factor there may still be periodic shortages of calories – such as famines – and these may sometimes represent major hazards. But, even in populations where such hazards do not occur sufficiently frequently for there to be culturally developed strategies for dealing with them, energy measurement can tell us a great deal about basic subsistence behaviour, about the conditions in which technical relations of production develop and change, about the character of surplus, perception of work, and the comparative importance of different foods and activities. Nevertheless, abstract empiricism and statements of the patently obvious which this kind of quantification may be in danger of encouraging must be avoided, and it should be recognized that empirical data can only be properly understood in an adequate theoretical framework. Nor must we reflect a crude technicist position, where production is no more than the provision of calories. It is not necessary to endorse the view that efficient use of energy is paramount to recognize the practical value of such data in the analysis of systems of social relations.

119

Environment, subsistence and system

The measurement of energy in ethnographic studies is useful for several reasons.

To begin with, energy has the advantage of being a fundamental and neutral measure of quantity (Bayliss-Smith 1977:318, cf. Shawcross 1972:616). The energetic approach enables a high degree of inter-subjectivity and quantification (Morren 1977:277) and although calories are not the only thing to be looked at in terms of yields or nutrition they do represent a convenient standard of measurement (Nietschmann 1973:189). For example, it is possible to compare the calorific yields of different cultigens, or assess the relative significance of plant and animal species. Measurement of energy is more accurate and meaningful in comparative terms and in discussing evolutionary trends than labour time since, in recording energy input for different activities, periods of inactivity can be programmed by assuming certain constants.

Secondly, energy expended may be considered as part of a *system* of energy exchanges. It can be compared with energy consumption to give some indication of the energetic and ecological efficiency of different activities, and for localities, groups or entire populations. But, while such measurements may be useful, it should not necessarily be assumed that such efficiencies are socially, economically or ecologically critical or functional. At a descriptive level, such data illustrate the danger of characterizing particular subsistence economies as being dominated by one particular mode of subsistence or technique when, in fact, if energy gain and loss were to be measured, the situation might look rather different. More generally, such measurements permit useful comparison between the food-getting and social activities of *Homo sapiens* and those of other species. They are therefore significant in evolutionary studies, offering a broader perspective and baseline for the analyses of human productive processes and social systems, by emphasizing that the expenditure of calories (human or non-human) is a necessary (though insufficient) condition for production, and that these productive activities form part of a wider system of energetic (or trophic) relationships involving exchanges with other species and other human populations. It is therefore a necessary part of any general ecological and ecosystematic analysis of groups of *Homo sapiens*. Local systems, in turn, are part of wider regional and global systems. So, while it is valid to undertake an analysis at a specified level, the fact that production and consumption activities are linked into wider ecological systems should not be forgotten.

Thirdly, the effort devoted to a particular food-getting activity and

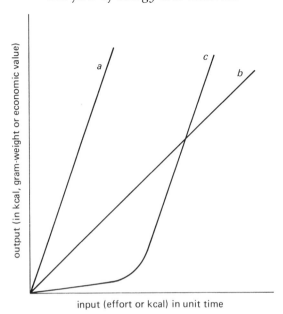

output (in kcal, gram-weight or economic value)

input (effort or kcal) in unit time

5.5 Input–output curves for three types of food-getting activity in relation to the formation of work groups. For explanation see text

the relative yield determines to a certain degree the formation of *technical* relations of production and work groups. By this I have in mind the size of work groups, their duration and the character of their internal technical divisions. If a particular technique is energy intensive with little return for effort, there is not much to be gained by increasing the size of work groups. Unless technological or social factors require otherwise, such activities are generally conducted at an individual level. Equally, if a task is relatively energy free with a high return for effort, specialized and group effort may be unnecessary. On the other hand, work that is energy demanding with a high return for effort (however this is measured) tends to be linked to collective activities. The use of groups is in a general way related to the appropriation of resources which do not become economic unless they are employed. This point is made graphically in Figure 5.5. An example of curve *a* would be the various activities involved in gathering accessible and reliable non-domesticated plant resources among the Nuaulu, where output tends to rise steeply with little energy input. I suspect that !Kung gathering of *Ricinodendron* nuts would also approximate to this kind of curve. Activities where output rises steadily with energy input (*b*) would include Nuaulu sago extraction which, while expensive on calories, is also highly productive. Activities related to domesticated resources characteristically involve an initial heavy input of effort before rewards become apparent. We would therefore expect that plant cultivation techniques would generally conform to curve *c*. It is, however, interesting to compare swiddening and advanced intensive cultivation in this respect. Swiddening is at the lower end of the range of energy inputs for different techniques of plant cultivation (Table 6.3). Although, compared with a large number of strategies for gathering non-domesticated resources it is initially relatively energy intensive, this is not so when compared with the initial inputs associated with some of the more intensive agricultural techniques involving meticulous land preparation and forms of non-human traction. Swidden plots also tend to be productive rather sooner than many monocrop permanent plots, and stay continuously productive much longer. This is not to say that swiddening is therefore *economically* more productive in terms of output per worker or hectare. But, it does go part of the way towards explaining why swiddening is generally associated with small work groups, rarely exceeding two or three individuals. By contrast, wet-rice cultivation, quite apart from the effort necessary to lay out and maintain plots, requires minimal inputs of effort of a much higher level before output begins to rise to an energetic and economically efficient level.

Arrangements for production and consumption are generally the most energy-intensive aspects of both human and non-human behaviour. All other behaviour is ultimately dependent upon their success. All biological organisms are systems of energy production, utilization and exchange. It is this which is the material basis of human existence, and which underlies an adequate materialist explanation of human social relations and the history of those relations.

6

Ecosystems and subsistence patterns I

The task of describing and analysing different patterns of human subsistence is a complex matter, and one which has been very much underrated. The bulk of contemporary anthropology has concerned itself with the discovery and elucidation of elaborate hidden networks and subtle symmetries, whereas subsistence activities have been regarded as simple, undifferentiated and tediously repetitive wherever they are found. This is a fatal error. Much of what we say about the operation of specific social systems must hinge on an accurate appreciation of how social relations articulate with patterns and techniques of subsistence. One of the most important contributions which ecological approaches have made is to provide the tools and information for the analysis of subsistence. In this chapter and the next I explore the kinds of anthropologically relevant data which can be collected on the ecology of subsistence, and which facilitate productive analysis of specific populations and comparative enquiries. I have selected illustrative material from a large number of studies. Some of the material is undoubtedly unsatisfactory, and some forms part of wider analyses which are highly problematic. This, however, should not detract from their didactic value.

VARIATION IN HUMAN ECOLOGICAL SYSTEMS

Ecosystems of which human populations are a part vary enormously in their distinctive characteristics. They do so not only because populations find themselves in different environments, but because they solve the problems of biological reproduction and the reproduction of social structures in different ways. This is done through population control on the one hand, and management of food and non-human material resources on the other. The various mechanisms have been conveniently listed by Little and Morren (1977:19, 23–26). Population

123

control may operate through any one or a combination of the following: (a) social and territorial behaviour: e.g. social ranking, migration, courtship and marriage patterns; (b) reproductive behaviour: e.g. post-partum sexual prohibitions and coital frequency; (c) gestational term: factors affecting probability of a successful pregnancy; (d) growth and socialization: factors affecting degree of sexual maturity: e.g. child care; (e) longevity and mortality: Malthusian checks, such as senilicide and suicide. Adequate food and other non-human material resources can be ensured through:

  (i) movement: e.g. settlement patterns, warfare, nomadism
 (ii) environmental modification: e.g. intensification, irrigation, breeding
(iii) areal specialization
(iv) technology: e.g. traction, harnessing non-human energy.

It is these latter kinds of strategy which have tended to dominate in classifications of human ecosystems. The effects of such control and management mechanisms in particular ecosystems gives rise to distinctive ecotypes, characterized by a dominant subsistence technique or combination of such techniques (D. R. Harris 1972:245). But ecotypes are very variable and difficult to define, and cannot easily form the basis of a rigid typology.

A better start can be made towards understanding variation in resource management by employing a simple three-phase model based on the degree to which a specified population has manipulated the ecosystem (Table 6.1). The term 'manipulation' involves such processes as the shifting of resources, control of breeding (genetic engineering, pesticides, livestock rearing), building, land use and alteration of topography. The model distinguishes three phases on a continuum: *pristine ecosystems*, in which there is appropriation but only minimal manipulation; *partially altered ecosystems*, in which appropriation is sustained through temporary and periodic manipulation; and *artificial ecosystems*, which can be maintained only by constant human interference.

It should be made quite clear, however, that this is simply a scheme to assist in unravelling the complex diversity of human ecosystems; it is not a typology and serves only as an awkward basis for classification. The boundaries between what I have deliberately called phases are imposed for convenience on a model in which there are no real discontinuities, just a gradation of imperceptible changes. The terms 'artificial' and 'pristine' must be used with care, and are employed here as labels for two contrasting extremes of a continuum of increasing domination of ecosystems by populations of *Homo sapiens*.

In broad ecological terms the continuum of the model progresses

Table 6.1 *A three-phase model of the relationship between ecosystems and human subsistence techniques*

SUBORDINATE	PRISTINE ECOSYSTEMS	appropriation with minimal manipulation	all resources undomesticated	food-collectors hunting fishing
	PARTIALLY ALTERED ECOSYSTEMS	periodic manipulation	partial domestication of resources	some fixed field horticulture and swiddening elementary animal husbandry
DOMINANT	ARTIFICIAL ECOSYSTEMS	only maintained through human participation	almost total domestication of food resources	all advanced cultivation, pastoralism industrialism

from high biomass and species diversity with a theoretically low entropy rate (that is, degree of energy disorder) to an increasingly low biomass and species diversity with a theoretically high entropy rate. This is the result of human populations controlling and encouraging certain species at the expense of others, and represents a shift from *generalized* to *specialized* ecosystems, examples of which have been presented in Chapter 4. Thus, as we move towards the artificial end of the continuum, so the amount of energy flowing into human populations from other parts of the ecosystem increases. (We will be returning to this issue shortly.) Greater energy flow is partly, though by no means entirely, linked to population density, which tends to increase the more altered the ecosystem becomes. The point has been made more generally by Murdock (1969) on the basis of ethnographic atlas data. Table 6.2 presents data on population density for some of the populations used for illustrative purposes elsewhere in this book.

In a given human ecosystem, the same phase model can be applied to different components, such as biotopes or species. Thus human ecological systems may contain species which are subject to no direct interference at all, some which are appropriated but not manipulated, and some both. The reason for this is the degree of synchrony between the different criteria by which we may compare different subsistence systems is very low. We can only talk in the most general and approximate terms of the correlation between degree of physical modification, species diversity, net energy inflow and population density. In any one case there is considerable variation in the configuration compounded from different criteria. For example, some swidden systems maintain or even increase the species-diversity index, while at the same time increasing population density and energy flow into the

125

Table 6.2 *Base data on selected populations profiled for energy characteristics. Some additional populations are included for comparative purposes*

Location	Subsistence pattern	Population (number of food producers)	Population density per km²	Source (study period)
1. !Kung San, Botswana	gathering, hunting, collecting	336(20)	0.2	Lee 1969 (1963–5)
2. Hadza, Tanzania	gathering, hunting, collecting	800	0.5	Woodburn 1972 (1958–60)
3. Baffin Island Eskimo, Canada	hunting, fishing	15		Kemp 1971 (1967–8)
4. Arnhemland aboriginal Australians	hunting, collecting, gathering			McCarthy and McArthur 1960
5. Nuer, southern Sudan	cattle herding, millet cultivation	144,000		Evans-Pritchard 1940 (1930–1)
6. Dodo Karimojong, Uganda	cattle herding, sorghum cultivation	20,000	5.5	Deshler 1965, calculations: Pimentel and Pimentel 1979
7. Tsembaga Maring, New Guinea	extensive root cultivation, pig husbandry	204(122)	26	Rappaport 1968 (1963)
8. Miyanmin, New Guinea highlands	extensive root cultivation, pig husbandry, hunting	28(18)		Morren 1977, Little and Morren, 1977
9. Bomagai Angoiong Maring, New Guinea highlands	extensive root cultivation, pig husbandry, hunting	154(71)		Clarke 1971, 1977 (1964–5)
10. Hanunoo, southern Philippines	extensive rice cultivation	128		Conklin 1957 (1952–4), calculations: Weiner 1972
11. Yaruro, Venezuela	extensive root cultivation, hunting	24		Leeds 1961
12. Ruhua Nuaulu, Seram, Indonesia	extensive root cultivation, gathering, hunting	180(79)	70	Ellen 1978 (1969–71)

No. Location	Type			References
13. Iban, Borneo, eastern Malaysia	extensive rice cultivation	9–18	615(366)	Freeman 1970 (1949–51), calculations: M. Harris 1971
14. Tasbapauni Miskito, Nicaragua	extensive root and rice cultivation, fishing, hunting		997(488)	Nietschmann 1973 (1968–9)
15. Tepozoztlan, Mexico	extensive maize cultivation		4,000(2,280)	Lewis 1963, calculations: Pimentel and Pimentel 1979, M. Harris 1971
16. Lamotrek atoll, Micronesia	intensive root cultivation, fishing		201(115)	Alkire 1965 (1962–3), calculations: Odum 1971
17. Ontong Java, Solomon Islands	root and coconut cultivation, fishing		850	Bayliss-Smith 1977 (1970–1)
18. Nacamaki, Koro, Fiji	root and coconut cultivation, fishing		309	Bayliss-Smith 1977 (1973–4)
19. Nasaqalau, Lakeba, Fiji	root and coconut cultivation, fishing		265	Bayliss-Smith 1977 (1974)
20. Raiapu Enga, New Guinea highlands	intensive root cultivation, pig husbandry	96	45(34)	Waddell 1972 (1966–7), calculations: Morren 1977, Bayliss-Smith 1977
21. Nuñoa Quechua, Peru	intensive root cultivation, herding		7,750	Thomas 1973 (1967)
22. Genieri, Gambia	cereal and peanut hoe cultivation	34	494(334)	Haswell 1953 (1947–9), calculations: Harris 1971
23. Kofyar, central Nigeria	intensive dryfield cultivation	112	72,946	Netting 1968 (1960–2)
24. Pul Eliya, Sri Lanka	irrigated and dryfield cultivation	227	146(67)	Leach 1961 (1954)
25. Luts'un Yunnan, China	irrigated rice cultivation	436	611(418)	Fei and Chang 1945
26. United States of America	intensive grain agriculture		5×10^6	Clarke 1977, Harris 1971

human population. Here species diversity is maintained through increased manipulation. On the other hand, in some marginal or otherwise low-diversity ecosystems (such as grasslands), the number of
species can be increased. Also, the degree of physical manipulation is
not always correlated with high population density. Large areas of
forest and grassland can be destroyed by small populations with low
energy needs, while relatively high population densities can be maintained by some subsistence strategies – for example swiddening and
collecting – which alter the ecosystem only temporarily, or less than
many lower-density populations.

MODES OF SUBSISTENCE AND SUBSISTENCE TECHNIQUES

Every human population employs techniques in order to appropriate
resources from the environment. Each technique is a combination of
material artifacts (tools and machines) and the knowledge required to
make and use them. Usually a single population will employ a range of
such techniques which together constitute a mode of subsistence or –
emphasizing its adaptive and coping aspects – a subsistence strategy.
The concept operates at the level of technical relations of production
(*contra* Ingold 1980:86). It indicates little about the *social* relations of
production, which can only be understood once information has been
provided on the number of persons involved in given productive and
non-productive activities, the social division of labour and occupa-
tions, and the exchange relations between groups and individuals
involved. As part of a wider economy the mode of subsistence
becomes functionally incorporated into the means of production.

Part of the explanation for the variety of human ecological systems
lies in the large number of different subsistence strategies which a
population may adopt. But, although the number of strategies and
specific techniques is very large (the number of strategies almost
infinitely so), the number of basic types of subsistence technique is
relatively limited. At any rate, it has been usual to distinguish only a
small number. Viewed this way the variation is attributable not so
much to the number of distinct techniques recognized as to the ways in
which they are combined together.

If we adapt a widely recognized scheme, it is useful to distinguish six
basic types of technique: 1. gathering of vegetable species; 2. collecting
of animal species and their products (small game, insects, honey, . . .);
3. fishing; 4. hunting and trapping; 5. animal husbandry (including
fish farming); and 6. plant cultivation. The first four involve the
procurement of *non-domesticated resources*, the last two the procurement of *domesticated resources*. If we now return to Table 6.1 specific

techniques can be plotted against a graph of increasing artificiality. Roughly speaking, gathering, collecting, hunting and fishing are techniques predominantly associated with pristine ecosystems, largely because sustained yield depends on allowing decimated populations to recuperate. Intensive appropriation of non-domesticated species and the extensive appropriation of domesticated species (e.g. swiddening) tend to be associated with partially altered ecosystems, while the intensive appropriation of domesticated species is necessarily linked to artificial ecosystems. However, because of the different combinations of techniques in any one subsistence strategy, it is difficult to plot population density on this continuum in the same way (Table 6.2).

There is a degree of arbitrariness in assigning particular techniques to the categories listed in the previous paragraph. For example, are we to understand the appropriation of shellfish as collecting or fishing, the appropriation of small reptiles as collecting or hunting? Clearly, the categories used depend on the criteria adopted and the significance attached to them. Here they are based on a mixture of narrowly technical features (that is, kinds of tools), the kind of species involved (plants, animals; terrestrial, acquatic . . .), and the degree of manipulation, through breeding and control of life-support mechanisms. A classification could be established for any one of these sets of criteria; or categories of an equivalent order of generality, but based on quite different criteria, could have been selected (e.g. energy or protein capture). But although no single overall classification is possible (or perhaps desirable), the one adopted does have the considerable advantage of being familiar, relatively unambiguous, and consisting of categories which may be defined so as to contrast significant technical and ecological variables. They also have a degree of cross-cultural objectivity, while frequently being recognized indigenously as distinct types. For these reasons it is a useful framework for the presentation of some basic ethnographic and ecological generalizations.

Techniques are only one of a number of key variables which must be considered when analysing and comparing different subsistence patterns. In addition to the gross physical manipulation of an ecosystem by a particular population, these are: input of effort, ecological output, time, spatial variation and fraction of human population. The pairing of these variables provides us with different insights as to the operation and structure of a particular subsistence pattern, and its relation to social organization. The relationship of input of effort to ecological output provides a measure of efficiency, and the pairing of spatial variation with output tells us something about the relative productivity of different areas or components of the ecosystem. I have found it convenient to discuss these variables under the following headings:[1]

1 total ecological production
2 total ecological effort
3 relative and absolute ecological efficiency
4 patterned ecological production and technique
5 patterned ecological effort according to activity
6 patterned ecological efficiency
7 yield, effort and efficiency over time
8 output, effort and efficiency distributed spatially
9 output, effort and efficiency according to population fraction
Headings 1–6 are discussed in the present chapter and headings 7–9 in
Chapter 7. Clearly, this approach involves a degree of overlap.

TOTAL ECOLOGICAL PRODUCTION

Ecological production may be defined as the creation of organic
materials resulting in species and population reproduction. It is not to
be confused with *economic* production, which is the creation of value
in order to reproduce social and economic formations (Ingold 1979:
274–7).

The total amount of *energy* produced by a human population has
been of interest to anthropologists since Leslie White first speculated
on the relationship beween energy levels and cultural organization.
For White (1949:367), the functioning of culture as a whole rested on,
and was determined by, the amount of energy produced and the ways
in which it was put to work. During the last thirty years much more
data have been accumulated than were ever available to White, and
our analyses and calculations have become more sophisticated. Tables
6.2, 6.3 and 6.4 attempt to summarize, in comparative form, some of
the data now available from various ethnographic studies. The exercise
is a hazardous one, and the figures presented are for the most part
crude estimates based on original data of variable quality. They should
be interpreted with extreme caution. Having said this, I provide in
column 2 of Table 6.3 some examples of total energy production,
expressed as kilocalories of energy value of food produced per person
per day. Several points should be noted in connection with these
figures in order to place them in their correct perspective.

Human ecological production should ideally be examined in the
context of a specific ecosystem. Much ethnographic work has tended
to adopt an *autoecological* rather than a *synecological* perspective, concentrating on the energy inputs and outputs of *Homo sapiens* alone
rather than on the patterned relations between different species. Such
a narrow preoccupation is in danger of obscuring the total impact of
energy balances on a human population.

Table 6.3 *Energy production, consumption and expenditure in selected populations*

Population	p Kcal food produced per person-day (per adult-day)	c Kcal food consumed per person-day (corrected for age imbalance)	r Kcal expended per person-day extracting food energy (per adult-day)
1. !Kung San	(3,194.4)	2,140	335.4
3. Baffin Island Eskimo	979.6		
7. Tsembaga Maring	2,680.5	1,958.4	167.5
8. Miyanmin	2,321.4		248
	(3,611)		(386)
9. Bomagai Angoiong		2,650[a]	139.5[b]
12. Ruhua Nuaulu		3,085	
14. Tasbapauni Miskito		2,000–2,800	
16. Lamotrek		2,935	149
17. Ontong Java	3,363	2,558	94.2
18. Nacamaki	8,250	3,728	116
19. Nasaqalau	4,680	3,542	61.7
20. Raiapu Enga	6,703	2,253	426
			(564)[c]
21. Nuñoa Quechua	22,081	1,198.2	
22. Genieri	3,825.7		342
25. Luts'un	25,200		470
26. United States of America	144,444.4		714

a excludes energy expended in purchasing
b assuming $p \simeq c$
c males only

The total energy yield of an ecosystem is the amount of energy produced by all organisms within the system. This is not the same as the total energy available to a human population. In order to obtain this it is necessary to distinguish (following Foley 1977:171–2):
(a) between organisms which are edible for humans and those which are not
(b) organisms edible for any domestic stock (or various animals in general)
(c) organisms serving any other than a directly nutritional function (e.g. for housebuilding, artifacts, medicines)
(d) between a hierarchy of calorific values for various organisms, and their nutritional qualities
(e) a hierarchy of abundance.
Even then, energy which is *culturally available* will ordinarily be far in

excess of the amount actually appropriated by a given population employing a particular subsistence strategy.

The *total* amount of energy produced by a population consists of the energy content of the food yield and the calorific equivalent of other things produced or appropriated, such as crops produced for export and consumed as fuel. Most ethnographic studies have been concerned with *food* energy. Some work provides estimates for energy produced in animal feed (e.g. Lee 1969:73, Rappaport 1968, 1971:349, Kemp 1971:336) and consumed as fuel. The work of Kemp (1971) on a population of Baffin Island Eskimo, R. B. Thomas (1973) on Peruvian Indians of the High Andes and Morren (1977) on New Guinea highland populations is exceptional in this latter respect.

The most convenient and satisfactory measure of energy transferred to a human population is that actually *consumed* as food. This is shown in column 3 of Table 6.3. Although not all food consumed is *assimilated*, the difference between consumption and assimilation, and between assimilation and the proportion of energy entering the food chain actually converted into human biomass, is unimportant for practical ethnographic purposes. In isolated low-energy populations the amount of energy produced and consumed by humans (and also by domesticated animals) is a reasonable proxy for the total amount of energy produced. But as populations use energy, so an increasingly greater proportion is involved in the use of fuel and the creation of non-food products.

The relationship between production and consumption becomes more problematic as populations become involved in trade: energy exported may not be equivalent to that imported. The value different populations attach to products does not necessarily reflect their calorie content. High-energy sago, for example, may be exchanged for low-energy (but high-protein) fish, or for valuables and other items which have no direct significance at all in terms of key calorific equations. This may result in a net energy loss. On the other hand, low-energy food products, such as tobacco, may be exchanged for high-energy food products and result in a net energy gain. Depending on amounts produced for exchange in relation to their value and the effort put into production, import–export relations may have a considerable effect on the calorific efficiency of a human population (Table 6.4).

Appropriation from the environment involves, or is contingent upon, the making or importing of artifacts which permit energy conservation, either as tools in the processes of appropriation themselves, or as artifacts to prevent human energy loss (e.g. houses, clothes). As noted in the previous paragraph, under certain conditions of unequal exchange, this can result in a net energy loss.

Table 6.4 *Calculations of energy efficiency for selected populations*

Population	$\dfrac{c}{r}$	$\dfrac{p}{r}$	per capita energy harnessed $\dfrac{360p}{10^6}$	$360p$ $10^6 \times \dfrac{p}{r}$	$\dfrac{p + \text{kcal imported}}{r}$	$\dfrac{\text{kcal exported}}{\text{kcal imported}}$	$\dfrac{p}{r + \text{kcal imported}}$
1. !Kung San[a]	6.38	9.5	1.5		9.5	0	9.5
3. Baffin Island Eskimo			0.3				
7. Tsembaga Maring	11.69	16(10.2[b])	0.96	15.36	12.6[c]		13.4[c]
8. Miyanmin		9.36	0.84	7.9	7.1[c]		8.3[c], 7.8[d], 3.8[e]
9. Bomagai Angoiong	19		0.95[f]	18.05[f]			
11. Yaruro		8–9	1.1[f]				
12. Ruhua Nuaulu		10					
13. Iban							
14. Tasbapauni Miskito							
15. Tepozoztlan		12.5–29.0	0.72–1.0[f]				
16. Lamotrek	19.7		1.05[f]	20.7[f]			
17. Ontong Java	27.15	35.7	1.2	42.8	11.2[c]	15.9[c]	12.2[g]
18. Nacamaki	32.1	73.5[g]	2.97	218	8.5[c,g]	37.25[c,g]	24.6[c,g]
19. Nasaqalau	57.4						
20. Raiapu Enga	5.3	15.7	2.4	37.68	15.8[c]	0.6[c]	13.2[c], 5.3[d], 3.4[e]
21. Nuñoa Quechua							6.75[d]
22. Genieri		11.2	1.38	15.5			
25. Luts'un		53.7	9.1	488.7			
26. United States of America		202.3	52	10,519.6			

a value of *p* calculated for adult day
b includes production of pig fodder (Little and Morren 1977:79)
c includes all life-supporting effort
d assumes $p \simeq c$
e mean for years 1972–3 and 1973–4
f Little and Morren 1977
g Bayliss-Smith 1977:353

133

Environment, subsistence and system

Ecological production is generally presented in weight or calorific terms. Concentration on either of these, or both to the exclusion of others, may be insufficient and misleading. Both conceal protein and other necessary nutrients and materials produced by a population. Energy is seldom the only limiting factor, and its production should not be confused with ecological production in its entirety.

The concept of *total* ecological production conceals its patterned character according to time, space, fractions of a human population and different subsistence techniques. Estimates of ecological production have sometimes confused that of a total subsistence pattern with that of a particular (though dominant) technique. This is not possible where consumption is used rather than production, but is often the case where the yield of a main crop is used as a measure of the ecological production of a cultivating population. Although in some cases the yield of a major crop may be a reasonable proxy for total production, it often hides other important factors.

TOTAL ECOLOGICAL EFFORT

Total energy expenditure of a population also varies between patterns of subsistence, tending to increase with the extent of human manipulation. Thus the total energy required to maintain one square kilometre of wet rice is much greater than that required to maintain the same area under swidden cultivation. There is a more marked increase in effort as subsistence techniques intensify if all energy inputs (including animal and mechanical traction) are considered. This is also the case if energy expenditure is calculated per food producer (M. Harris 1971: 252–3), but this reflects social division of labour much more than technical necessity.

The energy expenditure of a human population is usually understood in terms of the number of calories expended by individuals in the performance of food-getting activities (Table 6.3, column 4). Work time has been widely used to estimate effort, and is often translated into calories. The work of Lee (1969) on the !Kung Bushmen is a well-known example of this. However, the collection of data on effort generally, and this practice in particular, is subject to the difficulties already discussed in Chapter 5.

Many of the remarks which I have made in relation to the concept of total ecological and energy production also apply to the concept of total ecological and energy input, although they must be modified in certain respects. (1) Human energy expenditure should be set in the context of a particular ecosystem and seen in relation to that of other significant interacting species. (2) Energy may be expended on many activities

134

which might not ordinarily be considered as subsistence, but which have an impact on subsistence activity. In fact, total ecological effort, as opposed to total *subsistence* effort, must strictly speaking include *all* energy expended by a population. (3) Energy may be expended in the appropriation or production of items not consumed by the population itself. (4) A population expends not only energy but also protein, and other nutrients and materials. (5) energy output, as much as input, is patterned over time and space, and according to technique and different fractions of the population. (6) Total subsistence and ecological effort is not represented by human work alone. Biological energy may be employed in the form of animal traction, and in other ways (e.g. hunting dogs); and mechanical energy used in the form of fuel. These are finite forms of energy which have to be replaced. Other forms, such as the appropriation of wind or water energy, represent no energy loss. The reliance on non-human forms of energy increases with technological sophistication.

ECOLOGICAL EFFICIENCY

Energetic efficiency calculations for a number of human populations are set in Table 6.4. A standard measure of efficiency is energy production divided by total *human* energy expenditure (p/r). M. Harris (1971) divides energy production by the energy expenditure of food-producers (column 3). This is a more sensitive measure of the technical efficiency of food production itself, the size of the work force and the hours of work (Little and Morren 1977:20), but it can be misleading. First, much human effort involved in life-support activity may occur outside the food-production sector; in transportation, food preservation, preparation and so on (Morren 1977:277). Little and Morren (1977:75) have suggested that this is also a narrow and inadequate measure of efficiency, since *all* expenditure of energy by a population indirectly affects the equation. Rather than speak of 'subsistence' these writers prefer to substitute 'life support system'. Secondly, p and c do not distinguish imported and exported energy, that is, take account of trade in food products. For many populations $p = c + kcal\ exported$, while $c = p - kcal\ exported + kcal\ imported$. Bayliss-Smith (1977:350–2) has attempted to indicate the possible sources of error by distinguishing, in addition to p/r, $p + kcal\ imported/r$ (indigenous efficiency), $kcal\ exported/kcal\ imported$ (exogenous efficiency) and $p/(r + kcal\ imported)$ (total efficiency). How this may affect efficiency computations is indicated in Table 6.4.

All the measures of efficiency considered so far are, in terms of the performance of ecological systems, *relative* and autoecological. That is, they are all concerned with human inputs and outputs alone. To obtain some measure of *absolute* energy efficiency it is also necessary to incorporate non-human inputs in food-getting. Some writers have claimed that absolute ecological efficiency should be measured by dividing the total yield by the solar energy striking the earth's surface within the area from which a population appropriates *plus* any energy imported into that area. Alternatively, since consumption is the only effective measure of energy transfer, it has been suggested that feeding effectiveness must be calculated by dividing assimilated food by the input elements (Hardesty 1977:38–59).

Low-intensity applications of the use of mechanical energy to reduce human effort (wheels, pullies, the harnessing of physical energy in water flow or wind or the use of animal labour) are found widely in small-scale societies. They are also often the only non-human sources of energy use available in many centralized complex societies, where traction animals obtain at least part of their energy supply from a food source unused by humans. High-intensity applications of non-human energy are those available from fossil fuel (coal, oil or gas), or atomic fission and fusion. A comparison of the energy inputs involved in using technologies of different levels of intensity is provided in Table 6.5. When the level of technological input is increased, absolute ecological efficiency declines. From Table 6.6 it can be seen that the index of energy gained to human energy expended in modern cereal farming lies between 3,000 and 6,000, that is about 300 to 1,200 times greater than for technologically less-intensive subsistence patterns. However, if all energy inputs are included (particularly those derived from fossil fuels) the index is dramatically reduced to between 3 and 14.

We are accustomed to associating economic development and cultural evolution with an increase in productive efficiency, but this is only the case if measured solely in terms of human energy expenditure. Similarly, it has generally been assumed that progressive attempts to specialize and improve food production have led to ecosystems with a higher primary productivity than natural ones; yet we now know that some pristine ecosystems are more productive of energy per hectare than artificial ones (Phillipson 1966:47). Both relative and absolute indices have their place in anthropological analysis, but both present enormous obstacles in calculation, and must be understood in relation to other characteristics of a population. In no sense, for example, can they be seen as a simple measure of adaptation. But efficiency always depends on the criteria which are judged to be important.

Table 6.5 *Comparison of energy inputs for tilling 1 hectare of soil by human power, oxen, 6-hp tractor and 50-hp tractor (from Pimentel and Pimentel 1979:46)*

Tilling unit	Required hours	Machinery input (kcal)	Petroleum input (kcal)	Human power input (kcal)	Oxen power input (kcal)	Total input (kcal)
Human power	400	6,000	0	194,000		200,000
Oxen (pair)	65	6,000	0	31,525	260,000[a]	297,525
6-hp tractor	25	191,631[b]	237,562[c]	12,125		441,318
50-hp tractor	4	245,288[d]	306,303[e]	2,400		553,991

a each ox is assumed to consume 20,000 kcal of feed per day
b an estimated 191,631 kcal machinery was used in the tillage operation
c an estimated 23.5 litres of fuel was used
d an estimated 245,288 kcal machinery was used
e an estimated 30.3 litres of fuel was used

PATTERNED OUTPUT AND TECHNIQUES

Output, however measured or defined, varies within a population according to the techniques or basic food chains employed. Table 6.7 presents some data on the output of calories according to different techniques for a number of small populations, while Figure 6.1 graphically illustrates variation according to technique for three selected cases. Such information has revealed the significance of techniques hitherto regarded as secondary, while testing assumptions as to the dominant position of particular techniques in total subsistence strategies.

There is now considerable evidence to suggest that hunting, gathering and collecting have been consistently under-valued in studies of populations of cultivators, in terms of their provision of energy, protein and other nutrients; and also in terms of effort, spatial significance and trade (Boserup 1965:54; Barrau n.d.:28, 30; Nietschmann 1973; Morren 1977:310). This is partly because of methods and emphasis in fieldwork. Dwyer (1974:278) has been able to show from his data on the Komonku-Siane of the New Guinea highlands that Salisbury (1962) underestimated the importance of hunting and non-domesticated animal food. Dornstreich (1977:256) reports for the neighbouring Gadio Enga that although hunting, gathering and collecting contribute less than 10 per cent of the total weight of food consumed, they supply more than 20 per cent of protein, and a greater proportion of higher-quality protein. Dornstreich (Table 6.8) has also been one of the few

Table 6.6 Comparison of gross energy characteristics[a] for cultivation techniques at different levels of technological intensity

kcal ha^{-1}	Nigerian maize production (Pimentel and Pimentel 1979:65)	Iban rice production (Pimentel and Pimentel 1979:73)	Guatemalan maize production (Pimentel and Pimentel 1979:64)	United States maize production (Pimentel and Pimentel 1979:69)	United Kingdom cereal production (Lawton 1973:69–73)	Tsembaga Maring swidden cultivation (Pimentel and Pimentel 1979:38)	Mexican maize production (Pimentel and Pimentel 1979:40)
1. human effort	319,300	625,615	728,725	5,580	1,100	686,300	494,950[b]
2. tools	16,570	16,570	16,570	558,000		16,860	16,860
3. fossil fuel and electricity (including drying)	0	0	0	2,084,709	440,000–649,000	0	0
4. added nutrients and chemicals	183,300	0	0	2,543,830		0	0
5. irrigation	0	0	0	780,000	0	0	0
6. seeds	36,608	392,040	36,608	525,000		36,000	36,000
7. transportation	0		0	34,952		0	0
8. total input	555,778	1,034,225	781,903	6,532,071	441,100–650,000	739,160	548,410
9. yield	3,564,200	7,318,080	3,784,300	19,148,700	1,151–1,611 kcal m^2	11,384,462	6,901,200
10. $\dfrac{\text{output}}{\text{human effort}}$	11.16	11.69	5.19	3,431.7	4,233–5,926[c]	16.6	13.9
11. $\dfrac{\text{all imputs}}{\text{yield}}$	6.41	7.08	4.84	2.9	7–14	15.4	12.5

a ha = hours per hectare

b includes calories expended while at rest and conducting other activities

c Lawton does not include the calorific costs for tools, seeds, irrigation and transport. This partly accounts for the difference between the index for the United States and the United Kingdom

138

Table 6.7 *Output (p) according to technique in selected populations*

Population	Hunting kcal per person-day (percentage)	Collecting kcal per person-day (percentage)	Gathering kcal per person-day (percentage)	Fishing kcal per person-day (percentage)	Cultivation kcal per person-day (percentage)	Animal husbandry kcal per person-day (percentage)
1. !Kung San[a]	690 (32.2)	←[b]	1,450 (67.8)	0	0	0
3. Baffin Island Eskimo	979.6 (100)	← or[c]	0	0	0	0
7. Tsembaga Maring	0	0	0	0	2,519.7 (94)	160.8 (6)
8. Miyanmin	178.6 (7.7)	← or 0	29.8 (1.3)	0	1,270 (54.7)	843 (36.3)
12. Ruhua Nuaulu[a]	145.97(4.73)	0	1,097.45(35.6)	28.33(0.9)	1,813.23(58.8)	0
17. Ontong Java	0	0	0	372.2 (28.4)	933.33(71.2)	5.5 (0.4)
18. Nacamaki	0	0	0	144.4 (9)	1,455.5 (90.3)	11.1 (0.7)
19. Nasaqalau	0	0	0	250 (23.1)	819.4 (75.6)	13.8 (1.3)
20. Raiapu Enga	0	0	0	0	6,704 (99.5)	37 (0.5)
21. Nuñoa Quechua	0	0	0	0	206.6 (72.8)	77.08(27.2)

a figures refer to consumption (*c*) only
b ← = incorporated in adjacent column
c 0 = insignificant

139

Table 6.8 *Percentage of nutrients supplied by different Gadio Enga subsistence techniques, 3 June to 20 September 1968, involving 53 recognizable kinds of food (modified from Dornstreich 1977:257)*

Food-getting activities									Percentage of nutrient supplied				
	edible grams	calories	protein	fat	calcium	iron	vit. A	vit. B₁ thiamine	vit. B₂ ribo-flavine	niacin	vit. C ascorbic acid	phos-phorus	potassium
Gardening	63.9	42.4	52.6	8.3	72.5	65.1	45.5	70.4	60.1	71.9	74.5	79.6	49.4
Sago making	23.7	47.4	2.8	1.0	9.9	12.9	0.4	1.8	3.5	1.7	3.3	1.5	30.8
Silviculture	1.1	1.0	2.2	7.5	0.4	0.3	–	1.4	0.5	1.8	0.6	0.2	–
Plant gathering	7.1	2.3	14.2	8.2	12.9	17.7	54.1	11.1	14.2	10.4	21.6	11.0	19.7
(Total) Plant-food getting	95.8	93.1	71.8	25.0	95.7	96.0	100.0	84.7	78.3	85.8	100.0	92.3	99.9
Animal husbandry	0.5	1.5	3.4	19.4	0.1	0.6	–	3.2	1.2	2.6	–	–	–
Trapping	0.3	0.3	3.1	3.0	0.1	0.3	–	0.5	5.5	2.5	–	0.7	–
Fishing	0.6	0.4	5.9	1.4	3.4	0.6	–	0.4	2.8	1.9	–	2.4	–
Animal collecting	1.5	1.6	6.3	14.3	0.4	0.7	–	4.8	6.5	0.4	–	3.6	–
Hunting	1.3	3.1	9.5	36.9	0.3	1.7	–	6.3	5.6	6.8	–	1.0	–
(Total) Animal-food getting	4.2	6.9	28.2	75.0	4.3	3.9	–	15.2	21.6	14.2	–	7.7	–
Total	100.0	100.0	100.0	100.0	100.0	100.0	100.0	100.0	100.0	100.0	100.0	100.0	100.0

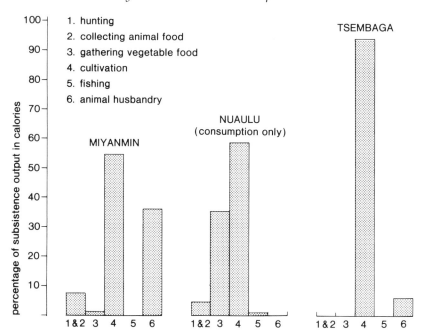

6.1 Percentage subsistence output profiles according to technique for three
populations, based on data provided in Table 6.7

scholars to indicate the significance of different techniques in providing a wide range of other nutrients. Similarly, by most conventional
ethnographic standards, the Nuaulu might be described as swidden
horticulturalists. In fact, the total energy derived from domesticated
resources per head per day is in the region of 1,813 kcal compared with
1,272 kcal derived from all non-domesticated resources. Thus more
than 40 per cent of their daily calorific intake is from non-domesticated
resources, and 64 per cent of all protein; while at least 56 per cent of all
energy expended in subsistence activities relates to the procuring of
non-domesticated species (Ellen 1978:291). On the other hand, within
the category of food obtained from non-domesticated sources,
available data now suggest that the nutritional importance of hunting
in particular tropical populations has been exaggerated (Dornstreich
1977:256 *contra* Carneiro 1970). This is particularly clear from the data
of Woodburn (1968) on the Hadza and Lee (1969) on the !Kung.

In the cases cited above, non-domesticated foods constitute a normal
part of appropriation for *use*; but for populations in the Malayan rain
forest they have long represented an important means of appropriation for *exchange* (Dunn 1975). Elsewhere such resources may be particularly important in offsetting seasonally induced hunger, as among

Table 6.9. *Food output according to fractions consumed, allocated for animal feed, imported and exported*

Population	Kcal produced per person-day for local human consumption (percentage of consumption)	Kcal produced per person-day for animal consumption (percentage of production)	Kcal per person-day exported[a] (percentage of consumption)	Kcal per person-day imported[a] (percentage of production)
1. !Kung San	2,140 (≃100)	0	0	0
3. Baffin Island Eskimo	979.6(41.2)	0	0	1,398 (58.6)
7. Tsembaga Maring	2,680.5(≃100)	226 (27)		
8. Miyanmin	1,875 (96.4)	386.9(16.7)	59.5(2.6)	69.4(3.6)
12. Ruhua Nuaulu	3,085[b] (≃100)	0	*0*	*0*
17. Ontong Java	1,736.1(67.9)			822.2(32.1)
18. Nacamaki	2,122.2(56.9)			1,605.5(43.1)
19. Nasaqalau	2,111.1(59.6)			1,430.5(40.4)
20. Raiapu Enga	2,216.9(98.4)	4,370.4(65.2)[c]	61.7(0.92)[c]	36.1(1.6)
21. Nuñoa Quechua	817,000[d] (23.5)		538,000[d] (39.7)	2,664,000[d] (76.5)

a Includes cash transactions

b Represents actual consumption

c Subtracting all consumption and export from production leaves 54 kcal which can most probably be explained as waste

d Figures relate to actual sample used

the Gwembe Tonga of the Zambian woodland savannah (Scudder 1971).

The data I have been able to provide on output according to technique are clearly incomplete and present difficulties in comparison. Different workers have presented their data in different ways: as figures per head or for a total population, for a single day or for an entire year. The subsistence characteristics of particular populations, and the particular concerns of different ethnographers, have meant that data for techniques regarded *a priori* as of little significance are not collected at all. Also, some workers have based their estimates on overall calorie production, others have taken human consumption as a convenient and more readily calculated proxy. But not all food produced is consumed. There is always a proportion of waste, which is very difficult to calculate. Additionally, some of the food produced is often exchanged, while some may constitute animal feed. Sometimes this may be of crucial sociological significance. Table 6.9 includes figures for energy exchanged with other populations and that used as animal food. For the Miyanmin, Raiapu Enga, !Kung and Nuaulu the energy gained or lost through exchange is small or non-existent. This is what we would expect in small-scale populations producing most of what they require. The high figure for imported energy in the Eskimo case is unusual for a food-collecting population, but is entirely explained by its participation in and dependence on a modern cash economy. This also explains the high import figures for the three Pacific island populations of Ontong Java, Nacamaki and Nasaqalau. In contrast, the very high percentage of imported energy of Nuñoa reflects that population's specialized position in the complex exchange relations between different environmental zones in a precolonial Andean economy.

Table 6.9 also indicates relatively large fluctuations in calories for animal food. For the Nuaulu, who rarely keep domesticated animals, except a few fowls and dogs which are fed on waste matter, the figure is negligible. Among the Tsembaga Maring, where the consumer role of pigs plays an important part in Rappaport's explanation of the functioning of the entire ecosystem, animal food constitutes 27 per cent of the total appropriated. But this is very low compared with the staggering figure of 65.2 per cent for the Raiapu Enga.

PATTERNED ECOLOGICAL EFFORT ACCORDING TO ACTIVITY

Most anthropologists have been preoccupied with energy expenditure in the sense of total energy yields (e.g. White 1959, Parrack 1969, Lee 1969). Much less attention has been paid to how this is patterned according to types of subsistence activity or 'work gates' (Morren 1977:279). Physiologists (Durnin and Passmore 1967) have undertaken considerable work on rates of energy expenditure for various subsistence activities in different populations, and there are a handful of early time-and-motion studies and exhortations on the importance of examining temporally distributed effort (Digby 1949, McCarthy and McArthur 1960). Only in the last decade have social anthropologists seriously tackled the issue as it relates to their own concerns. Again, the pioneer work is that of Rappaport on the Tsembaga Maring (Figure 5.3 and Table 5.3). Table 6.10 gives some idea of the variation in effort according to different food-getting activities (and for food-getting activities compared with other activities) in actual populations for which there are numerical data.

The collection and comparison of such information presents the same kind of difficulties as that on patterned output. It is not routinely available; ethnographers have been selective in the activities for which they have collected data; categories of effort are not always comparable and distinctive activities not always separated. Perhaps the most notorious weakness has been the failure to provide data on the energy and the time cost of food-processing (to a large extent the work of

Table 6.10 *Effort expressed in kcal or unit time per person-day according to different food-getting activities for selected populations*

Population	Percentage of effort involved in all food appropriation						Percentage of total effort recorded		
	hunting	collecting	gathering	fishing	cultivation	animal husbandry	food preparation, including cooking and collection of firewood	other productive activities, including wagework, maintenance, manufacture, cash transactions	other non-directly productive activities, ritual, recreation, war, politics
1. !Kung San	→	↑	100	0	0	0		*0*	
3. Baffin Island Eskimo	324(100)	←*0*	←*0*	←	0	0	76.2	←	10.3
4. Arnhemlanders	31.2		40	28.9	0	0	2.8	22.7	
7. Tsembaga Maring			←	0	73	27			
8. Miyanmin	33.6	7.9			58.5		25	←	24.7
12. Ruhua Nuaulu[a]	27.7	←	32.6	1.4	38.3	*0*			
17. Ontong Java	0	↑	0.37	22[b]	70.34		32.6	←	
20. Raiapu Enga					96.7	3.3	7.1	*1*	
21. Nuñoa Quechua					11.9	88.1			33.8

italics indicate percentage effort expressed in hours rather than kcal

a males only

b includes collection of shellfish, turtling and *Trochus* cleaning females), together with the neglect or under-estimation of other activities technically and socially necessary for subsistence but not 'food-getting' in the strict sense. But the figures do show that variation in terms of effort expended between different subsistence activities, and between subsistence and other activities, is important for understanding political economy. For example, data on the Nuaulu reveal that non-domesticated resources (procured by the gathering of fruits and vegetables, the extraction of wild sago, animal collecting, hunting and trapping) involve a greater proportion of effort than domesticated ones (from the cultivation of gardens and groves). The percentage of work-days devoted to activities involving the appropriation of domesticated resources is 44 compared with 56 for non-domesticated resources. In energy terms this is 39 per cent compared with 61 per cent. Data of this kind add a further dimension to the point made in the preceding section concerning the under-estimation of the role of non-domesticated resources.

Another way of looking at the expenditure of subsistence effort is not in terms of contribution to different food-getting techniques but in terms of effort expended on different processes which cut across these techniques. These processes, standard analytical categories in the work of animal ecologists (Lawton 1973), are: location of food supply, gathering or catching food, transport and storage, maintenance of food supply, food processing and eating and swallowing. The last of these – eating and swallowing – is hardly measurable except under laboratory conditions and can be ignored for most practical purposes. Some idea of how the energy cost of these processes varies is provided in Table 6.11. Table 6.12 gives a more general impression of how energy cost varies for different techniques. There are a number of points worth noting. (1) Certain of the contrasting features of the energy-use profile for different techniques are linked to the degree of domesticity of the resource. Domesticated resources do not usually have to be located, but *by definition* have to be maintained. (2) The shape of the energy-use profile also varies according to technical factors, social organization, cultural values and the species involved. Thus, gathering green fern fronds for vegetable food is very low in calorie expenditure, while gathering palm sago may be very high indeed. (3) Though we may argue that the categories of subsistence technique are too broad, it is also the case that the subsistence strategy of most populations is a combination of a number of these. Clearly, it is necessary to see them in operation for specific populations. (4) The categories are difficult to apply under ethnographic field conditions. The first three – location, gathering and transport – merge in many hunting, gathering and collecting activties; while some may be concealed (e.g. transport costs

Table 6.11 *Variation in effort according to grouped food-getting processes, expressed in kcal and percentage of total*

Population	Location of food	Hunting, collecting, gathering and harvesting	Transport and storage	Maintenance of food supply	Food processing
7. Tsembaga Maring		2,304(16.5)	2,022(14.4)	9,672(69.1)	
8. Miyanmin	→	4,524(65.2)		2,410(34.8)	
12. Ruhua Nuaulu	→	(10–20)	(10)	(70–80)	
20. Raiapu Enga	→	14,270(48.7)	←	15,045(51.3)	

Table 6.12 *Subsistence techniques compared in terms of the energy cost of their different processes*

	Hunting	Collecting	Gathering	Fishing	Cultivation	Animal husbandry
Location of food supply	high	variable, higher than gathering	variable	generally low	very low to non-existent	very low
Appropriation	high	generally low	highly variable	low to medium	medium to high	low to medium
Transport and storage	very variable	low	very variable	low	highly variable, very high for systems involving industrialized agriculture and long-distance trade	low to medium
Maintenance of food supply	negligible	negligible	negligible	negligible	medium to very high in advanced cultivation	medium
Processing	variable	low	variable	low	variable, but high in industrialized systems	medium

in hunting). For the purpose of data collection it may be necessary to modify the scheme. Thus, since for the Nuaulu the extraction of *Metroxylon* sago is such an economically, socially and ecologically important part of the gathering both of wild vegetable resources and of silviculture, it makes analytical sense to separate it from other gather-

146

ing and cultivating activities. Table 6.13 illustrates the percentage use of energy for these various categories in the village of Ruhua. (5) Travel and transport tend to be major variables in agricultural effort (cf. Nietschmann 1973:143), and yet they have been appallingly neglected in studies of tribal and peasant economies, and their economic consequences seldom subjected to detailed analysis. The cost of travel and transport varies according to the dispersion of resources, the techniques employed, the degree of nucleation of rural populations and so on. Input of agricultural effort is sometimes expressed in terms of person-unit area, but such expressions often ignore travel time (e.g. Conklin 1957:150, Lewis 1963:155).

Calculation of energy expenditure may sometimes be of interest at a more detailed level than food-getting technique and energy process, namely at the level of the use of individual tools or technical processes. By specific technical processes I have in mind, for example, the component activities involved in maintaining subsistence through swidden cultivation: clearing underbrush, fencing, weeding, burning, seeding. Table 6.14 compares the relative effort involved in these various activities for the Tsembaga Maring and rural Mexicans. Such techniques vary in complexity, according to the implements employed, energy source and input, character of somatic actions and degree of necessary cooperation (that is, in terms of the technical relations of production). Watson and Watson (1969:81) distinguish three levels of tool complexity: (1) simple tools (e.g. cutting-stones, digging-sticks . . .) (2) compound tools (axes, ploughs . . .) and (3) tools which enable the more efficient use of other tools; by harnessing non-human energy (e.g. bows, pulley systems, combine harvesters). Tools with moving parts can be defined as machines.

Archaeological and ethnographic analyses of material culture may usefully employ data on the energy expenditure involved in using various kinds of tools, to classify them and to gauge their efficiency. Any tool can be characterized by the amount of effort involved in making, using and maintaining it, and that saved compared with not making or using it at all. In this sense a tool represents condensed effort. Whenever a tool is used, the real energy cost of the activity should theoretically take into account the cost of manufacturing the tool. Therefore the real energy cost of an activity is

$$Nu + m$$

where u is the cost of use, m the cost of manufacture, and N the number of times a tool is used without repair. In most cases the number of times a tool can be used makes the relative energy cost of its manufacture insignificant, but this is not always so. Nuaulu sago adzes may be

147

Table 6.13 *Effort according to energetic process in Nuaulu subsistence activities, expressed as a percentage of total effort for an activity*

	Hunting	Collecting	Extracting non-domesticated sago	Gathering other plant species	Fishing	Swiddening	Extracting domesticated sago	Cash-cropping
Location of food supply	95	↓	0	0	95	0	0	0
Appropriation of food supply	↑	↓	50	95	↑	10–20	80	80
Transport and storage	5	↓	50	5	5	10	10	5–10
Maintenance	0	0	0	0	0	70–80	10	10
Mean work-group size	1–25	1–2	3–7	2–5	1–5	1–5	1–2	1–5

Table 6.14 *Effort per hour–hectare for different technical activities involved in maintaining Tsembaga Maring and Mexican swiddens. Calculations based on Pimentel and Pimentel (1979: 38, 40), from original data in Lewis (1963) and Rappaport (1968, 1971)*

	Tsembaga Maring kcal ha^{-1} (percentage)	Mexicans kcal ha^{-1} (percentage)
Clearing underbrush with machete and knife	70,000(15.3)	128,000(41.9)
Clearing trees	27,200(5.9)	↑
Fencing	42,000(9.2)	38,400(12.6)
Burning	23,400(5.1)	19,200(6.3)
Weeding	↓	72,000(23.6)
Planting, seeding	222,600(48.6)	38,400(12.6)
Reseeding		9,600(3.1)
Placing soil retainers	17,600(3.8)	
Other maintenance	54,800(12)	

used on one or two occasions only, and thus the ratio of cost of manufacture to cost of use is relatively high. Much of this information can be collected relatively easily and accurately under controlled experimental conditions and careful observation. There are a number of ethnographic studies of this kind (e.g. Townsend 1969, Godelier and Garanger 1973, Hames 1979) in addition to those of physiologists (e.g. Hipsley and Kirk 1965).

Occasionally studies of the kind described above have assumed theoretical significance in scholarly debates, as in the studies of the effects of technological change in New Guinea (cf. Salisbury 1962 and Townsend 1969), or in experimental reconstructions of the efficiency and impact of European Neolithic tools (Coles 1973). As we move from simple to compound tools and then to machines, human input decreases overall and the input of non-human energy increases. This, as we have noted, is linked to an increase in the effectiveness of harnessing energy. However, the energy cost of tool-making also rises, until more efficient tools are introduced for making other tools. As tools become more complex, so the amount of ecological effort put into their manufacture increases. Related to this are key changes in the materials used. Manufacture which involves complicated preparation of materials (as in metallurgy) will raise the overall energy input. This must be set against human effort, which increases overall until the impact of industrial techniques begins to raise the proportion of non-human to human energy involved. The ratio of cost of manufacture to

149

Environment, subsistence and system

cost of use is much more difficult to compute. In simple tool manufacture this index may be very variable. The Nuaulu take between 7 and 10 minutes to make a bamboo adze for working sago, which may have an active working life of 32 hours. An arrow-head which takes 14 minutes may have a much shorter one, and anyway is in constant need of repair. McCarthy and McArthur (1960:190–1) calculate that aboriginal Australians in Arnhemland took 1 hour to haft an axe and 4 hours to make a fishing line (cf. Coles 1973). In modern industrially made farm equipment, the cost of use rapidly outstrips the cost of manufacture since the fossil-fuel cost of using a combine-harvester may be 51,870 kcal per hectare per annum (Lawton 1973:70). However, attempts to estimate gross energy costs at particular technological levels (e.g. Hutterer 1976) have not been very successful (Ellen 1976).

THE PATTERNED CHARACTER OF ENERGETIC EFFICIENCY

Calculations of the total efficiency of entire populations and subsistence strategies tend to conceal remarkable sociologically significant variation in efficiency according to different subsistence activities, localities, periods of time and fractions of a population.

Efficiency has been shown to vary according to crop regime. For example, Rappaport (1968:52) reports an energetic efficiency of 15.9 for Tsembaga Maring sugar and sweet-potato gardens, but 16.5 for taro and yam gardens. Little and Morren (1977:79), basing their calculations on Rappaport's data, estimate the energetic efficiency of Tsembaga cultivation at 18, pig-herding at 1.5 and the net energetic efficiency of subsistence at 10.2. For the Miyanmin (1977:77–8), they calculate the energetic efficiency of cultivation at 7.5, hunting and collecting at 8.9, and pig-herding at 6.4. The Raiapu Enga (1977:81–2) have energetic efficiencies of 16.2 for cultivation and 0.13 for pig-herding. The same authors (1977:67) calculate that among the Peruvian Quechua of Nuñoa the energetic efficiency of cultivation is 11.5, the gross energetic efficiency of herding (including exports) is 2 and the net energetic efficiency of herding (including imports) is 7.5. Data collected by Bayliss-Smith (1977:342) and presented in Table 6.15 suggest that, on Ontong Java, mixed gardens and coconut collection are by far the most efficient subsistence activities engaged in. Nietschmann (1973:228–9) has shown that, among the Miskito, cultivation has a calorie productivity many times that of other forms of food procurement. Not only does it have the high calorie ratio of 30.4:1 (calories returned: calories expended), it also has a fairly *dependable* calorie return. Dependability of a resource may, over time, be more important than average yield, and

Table 6.15 *Relative effort and energetic efficiency for various subsistence activities: Ontong Java, 1970–1 (modified from Bayliss-Smith 1977:342)*

Activity	Relative effort[a]	Energetic efficiency[b]
Colocasia cultivation	13.7	6.0
Cyrtosperma cultivation	6.96	19.3
Turmeric cultivation	2.46	
Village crop cultivation	0.48	44.7
Coconut collection	2.35	43.6
Copra, plantation work	26.9	10.4
Copra, village work	25	
Collecting birds, eggs, wild fruits	0.37	9.3
Fishing	15.9	8.6
Shellfish collection	1.01	1.2
Trochus diving	1.23	8.2
Trochus cleaning	1.3	
Collecting turtles and their eggs	2.59	0.5

a Expressed as percentage of total effort expended on listed activities
b Energy gained divided by energy expended, where energy input is calculated from hours of work multiplied by energy-expenditure rates supplied by Hipsley and Kirk 1965

may encourage appropriation. Miskito calorie returns for hunting (7.1:1) are higher than turtle fishing (5.5:1), or gathering shellfish of the species *Donax* (2.1:1), due to a hunting focus on the high-calorie-yield white-lipped peccary (*Tayassu pecari*). Food-getting through participation in the market economy gives the second highest calorie ratio (11.5:1). This substantially augments subsistence effort and reduces risk by decreasing the amount of food a family must procure directly. However, procurement of cash may disrupt the timing of subsistence activities and thus lower their efficiency. The degree to which exchanges contribute to Miskito diet is sensitively adjusted to market demand for declining species, over which the Miskito have little control.

In more general terms, the variable efficiency of Nuaulu subsistence techniques is shown in the high-energy cost of maintaining gardens compared with their relatively small contribution to overall energy needs. Rappaport (1968:63) has suggested that very few techniques employed by human groups primarily for the purpose of obtaining food energy will have efficiency ratios much below 10. If they do, then they may be important in other respects, such as sources of protein, or, as in shellfish collection and turtling on Ontong Java, for their economic value. But Rappaport's measurement of efficiency seems very generous, and appears to relate to a narrow definition of energy input for specific activities. Using figures for energy expended for the entire period during which Nuaulu informants were focussing on particular activities, I recorded efficiencies of 0.26 for hunting, 1.0 for fishing, 1.7 for gathering and 2.4 for cultivation.

Of course, efficiency is not to be measured in energy ratios alone. The energy expended on husbanding New Guinea pigs is little different from that which a population receives back in food. Nuaulu hunting, and that of many other peoples, provides a negative calorie return. The importance of the activity lies not in calories but in the provision of high-quality protein and nutrients (e.g. Rappaport 1968 cf. Dornstreich 1977:226), quite apart from any culturally determined use and exchange values encoded in furs, plumes, bulk and bone. In this respect it is of some interest to assess the energy cost of obtaining protein. To illustrate this I wish to return to Dwyer's study of the Komonku Siane. Dwyer (1974:285) undertook an in-depth study of hunting in conjunction with his own zoological investigations. From this he was able to determine the various species hunted and undertake a sex and bag-weight analysis of mammals. His data show relationships between the proportion of available nights spent hunting and the mean number of hours spent hunting per night; that hunters who hunt on average for longer periods each night are also likely to hunt more frequently (and this is independent of success); hunting effort and return for individual hunting; and that one mammal is obtained for every 26.1 man-hours of effort, or 25.1 man-hours for each kilogram (bag weight) of game. Effort, it seems, is not the sole or primary criterion of success. Skill is important; often only a few men are expert hunters, and spend much time in this activity.

Dwyer's calculations of efficiency are based on an assumption that the basal metabolic requirement for a male is about 1,500 kcal per day. An equivalent of 100 kcal per hour during nocturnal hunting probably underestimates mean energy requirements of this activity. A return of one kilogram bag weight of game for 25.1 man-hours of hunting effort is equivalent to 39.8 grams (bag weight) per hour of effort. Using Lee's (1969) figure of 3,000 kcal per 100 gram cooked, and an edible:waste ratio of 2:1 for game of this kind, we get an estimated return of 79.6 kcal for an expenditure of 100 kcal, making no allowance for shrinkage in cooking. In energetic terms nocturnal hunting of mammals is a costly activity. In contrast, he notes that estimates of return for effort in flying-fox hunting suggest energetic gain for this activity. Similar calculations on my Nuaulu data also show an overall energy loss on hunting, which has to be subsidized by other activities (cf. Kemp 1971). But energetic efficiency is not necessarily an accurate measure of return for effort.

vwv

Ecosystems and subsistence
patterns II

In Chapter 6 I assumed a model of synchrony, and for many purposes this is acceptable and profitable. But variation in yield, effort and efficiency through time and its use and allocation between different activities may be of the greatest importance in understanding the operation of particular subsistence patterns, and in comparing populations.

YIELD, EFFORT AND EFFICIENCY OVER TIME

All populations experience differential availability of food, and therefore variation in consumption patterns, depending on phases of the agricultural calendar, the seasonal movement of animal species, growth cycles of animals, maturation periods of plants, and climatic and other temporally patterned ecological hazards. Figure 7.1 provides a simple example of this: the frequency of use of different foods in an African peasant population. Figure 7.2 gives a general indication of energy availability, consumption and expenditure over a period of one year for a Gambian population. From this it is clear that input of effort may also be closely tied to prevailing seasonal conditions. Nuaulu time spent in the gardens is correlated inversely with the amount of rainfall, and the difficulties of communication which this gives rise to (Ellen 1978:131–2). Clearly, efficiency will vary concomitantly, although balance is generally maintained over an entire cultivation cycle.

Patterns for the appropriation of non-domesticated resources may be similar. In their classic essay, Mauss and Beuchat (1979:55) were able to show how the seasonal availability of different animal species is directly linked to Eskimo patterns of nomadic movement and settlement (cf. Damas 1969, Rogers 1972, Thomson 1939). In his work among the Miskito, Nietschmann (1973:166–7) carefully computed

Ecosystems and subsistence patterns II

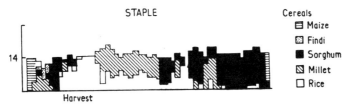

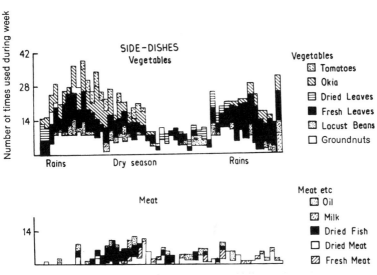

7.1 Frequency of use of different foods in an African peasant economy
(from Weiner 1964:429)

variation in the numbers of most important species hunted each month
to illustrate seasonal variation in resource appropriation and meat
yields. He was able to show that yields in marine fishing, like Nuaulu
garden effort, were inversely proportional to rainfall. Here, however,
the relationship is more complicated. Periods of heavy or light rainfall
are accompanied by differences in the velocity of offshore currents,
changes in wind direction, and rearrangements of fish and game
populations, most markedly the migration of green turtles. Rain,
therefore, is simply a convenient proxy for other environmental
variables (cf. Birdsell 1953). Dwyer (1974:265) has also related his
Komonku Siane data to seasonality and prevailing weather conditions,
and is able to show that effort is greater in the dry season than in the
wet, and in clear conditions rather than rainy. But, while return for
effort is greater in the dry season, the most productive hunting is that

155

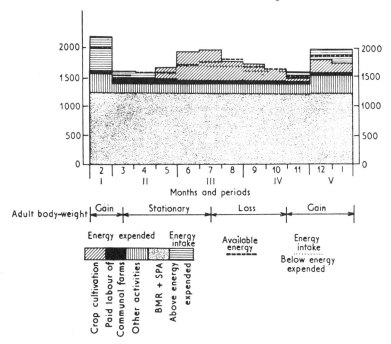

7.2 Energy consumption, availability and expenditure variation over a one-year period in a Gambian village (from Weiner 1964:431, adapted from Fox 1953)

conducted during wet spells in the dry season. This appears to reflect the behavioural traits of the animals being hunted. In hunting, as in cultivation, efficiency may be negative for any one occasion or run of occasions, but may prove positive over a longer period of time. However – as we have seen – hunting is not necessarily a primary and reliable source of calories (or even protein) and may consistently provide negative energy returns. Toleration of this will depend on the existence and significance of hunting in providing other valued materials, and its ideological role. In this respect, it would be interesting to compare hunting in populations where it is nutritionally vital (e.g Eskimos) with those where it is not.

Seasonality is generally linked to the changing foci of resource appropriation. During the dry season much of Miskito food-getting is focussed on marine resources while in the wet season it shifts to terrestrial resources (Figure 7.3). The actual loci of hunting, fishing, agricultural and gathering activities radically shift during seasonal extremes. In the dry season food resources are generally more diverse, and this is related to depletion of agricultural foodstuffs. In the rainy

156

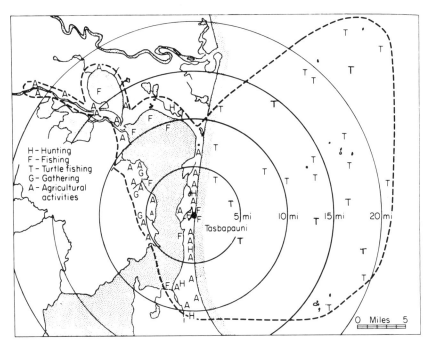

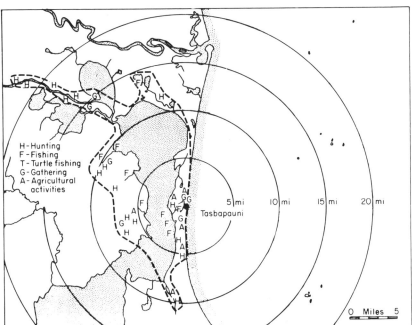

7.3 Location of appropriated food resources and associated activities
during (a) April and (b) July in the Miskito village of Tasbapauni,
Nicaragua (from Nietschmann 1973:120)

157

season resources are more limited in quality and kind, but the distances travelled to obtain them are reduced due to weather, hunting conditions and animal migration. Fishing activities increase to offset the loss of meat supplied through hunting. Nietschmann (1973:119, 121–2, 160, 236) argues that the range and density of biotopes, the changes in their fauna and flora, and varying fruiting and crop maturity periods (many with overlapping phases) give rise to seasonal changes in the appropriation patterns of villagers, which permit a qualitatively and quantitatively balanced diet under subsistence conditions. By focussing on different means of food procurement at different times of the year, an average calorie consumption could be maintained between 2,000 and 2,800 per day for an adult, despite major changes in the Miskito environment. On the other hand, Buchbinder (1977:127) reports that in a Maring population she studied the diet was richer in protein during the wetter months, owing to an increased consumption of greens and marita, despite an increase in starchy taro at the expense of the more proteinaceous sweet potato.

Profiles of effort expenditure over the course of a year enable us to locate dominant activities characterizing a particular mode of appropriation as a whole, and thus help to specify the minimal essential technical relations of production. Figure 7.4 compares graphs for the temporal distribution of effort in (a) multicrop swiddening, (b) monocrop (rice) swiddening and (c) irrigated rice cultivation. Although the curves are only rough approximations of the total population effort involved at particular periods, and exaggerated for purposes of presentation, each clearly indicates a distinctive pattern with necessary social consequences. Both (a) and (b) begin the sequence in a similar way: effort-intensive cutting followed by a lull before burning and then planting. From there on the curves differ markedly. In multicrop swiddening weeding is generally minimal, while harvesting of certain species may begin as little as 25 days after planting. Harvesting then rises steadily towards the end of the year when it merges with replanting. In contrast, weeding is important in rice swiddening and harvesting is concentrated during a short period. The curve for irrigated rice cultivation is different altogether, involving a continuously higher level of effort from initial dyking through to harvesting.

Seasonal fluctuations in the flow of energy, nutrients and materials make it important for the ethnographer to think carefully about problems of sampling over time, collecting information which reflects all significant seasonal changes. Any long-term information is difficult to obtain and this is particularly so where crops are harvested over many months, and where plots may continue to yield 1–2 years after initial

Ecosystems and subsistence patterns II

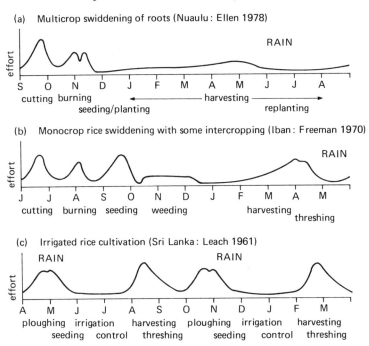

(a) Multicrop swiddening of roots (Nuaulu: Ellen 1978)

effort

S O N D J F M A M J J A

cutting burning ◄——————— harvesting ———————►
seeding/planting   replanting

(b) Monocrop rice swiddening with some intercropping (Iban: Freeman 1970)

RAIN

effort

J J A S O N D J F M A M

cutting burning seeding weeding   harvesting
                                              threshing

(c) Irrigated rice cultivation (Sri Lanka: Leach 1961)

RAIN   RAIN

effort

A M J J A S O N D J F M

ploughing irrigation harvesting ploughing irrigation harvesting
     seeding control threshing seeding control threshing

7.4 Comparison of seasonal distribution of effort for three different
subsistence patterns

planting, as in certain swidden patterns (Nietschmann 1973:140–1,
Ellen 1978).

There are few studies relating to cyclical temporal fluctuations other
than seasonality, and ethnographic studies of time allocation tend to
be impressionistic rather than exact (Johnson 1975). Nietschmann
(1973:176) has noted variation in Miskito meat consumption according
to the day of the week. Watanabe (1977) and others have paid some
attention to the daily rhythm of different food-getting activities.
Ohtsuka (1977), for example, provides data on the average number of
hours per day for particular activities, daily activity rhythms and the
average time spent per head per day in Oriomo Papuan food-getting
activities. McCarthy and MacArthur (1960) provide similar data for the
two groups of Arnhemlanders they studied, inadvertently giving
Sahlins (1972) ammunition for his attempt to demonstrate the
'affluence' of hunting, gathering and collecting populations.[1] A little of
this kind of information is also available from the work of physiologists
and nutritionists. There are many studies of varying quality on yield
and effort per household which enable us to get some idea of the

(a)

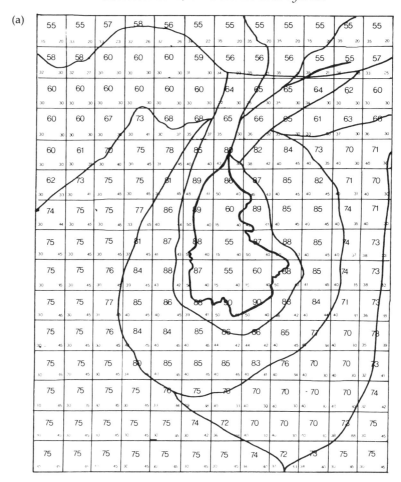

7.5 Measuring the spatial productivity of an ecosystem. (a) Model area with grid, showing productivity for each quadrat. The large central figure is the total productivity value. The left-hand corner value represents plant productivity, the right hand animal productivity. Practical applications would normally be in units of g/m² dry weight per unit of time, or kg/km² live weight per unit of time. Figures used here simply illustrate the method. (b) Productivity contours (total productivity) of a model ecosystem. The values are absolute and do not take account of energy costs. Contour interval = 5 (after Foley 1977:173)

(b)

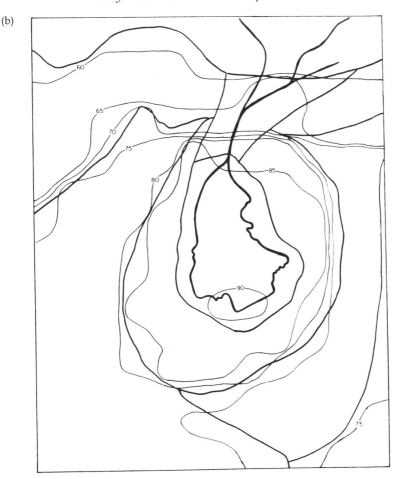

character of their relation to the developmental cycle of domestic groups.

SPATIAL DISTRIBUTION

Resource usage is distance dependent. The areal distribution of resources acts as a determinant of subsistence strategies, and such strategies influence both settlement and mobility patterns.[2]

Ecological production varies spatially. If a map showing ecological zoning is gridded into between 1 and 10 km² quadrats, then energy production can be measured per quadrat (Figure 7.5). Primary production can be measured through an analysis of vegetation and secondary production through animal biomass. Figure 7.5(a) illustrates such a gridded area (following Foley 1977:171–2, 175), in this case a hypothetical lake basin. Production is shown for each quadrat, the central figure being the total productivity value, that in the left-hand corner plant productivity, and that in the right-hand corner animal productivity. The figures are ordinal numerals on a percentage scale to show relative productivity of different habitats from which it is then possible to construct productivity contours.

Foley's work has been specifically concerned with the reconstruction of palaeoenvironments, but the methods are just as applicable to contemporary ones. Total ecological production does not, of course, represent the amount of food or materials *potentially* available to a human population, but figures can be adjusted to take this into account. However, the geographical distribution of available resources is clearly going to affect the potential for human extraction.

It has long been hypothesized, following von Thünen, that yields rise the nearer one gets to the focus of settlement. It has been shown for rural European communities, for example, that as average distance increases so the per-hectare yield declines (Chisholm 1962:49–53). Very little comparable material is available for populations of small-scale societies. Lee (1969) has shown that the energy cost to the !Kung San of gathering *Ricinodendron* nuts rises sharply at distances of between 15 and 20 km from a campsite, giving a characteristic 'S'-shaped curve. Under Nuaulu swidden cultivation there is a general decrease in yield (measured through approximate size of plot) the more distant the location from the hamlet. However, this does not hold for locations less than one kilometre from the hamlet (owing to land fragmentation and soil depletion), while the overall correlation is not as striking as in the European data (Ellen 1978:139; cf. Nietschmann 1973:144–5).

While the von Thunen pattern may hold reasonably well for yields from cultivated plots, the situation begins to deviate markedly for yields of non-domesticated resources. Nuaulu hunting and collecting takes places mostly in the area circumscribed by the outer limit of cultivation, and this may be fairly common for swiddening populations (cf. Ohtsuka 1977:252). But with non-domesticated resources geographical distribution cannot be guaranteed to be uniform: certain resources are only available from particular locations. Faunal populations, in particular, are not distributed evenly throughout an area. They occur in restricted areas, under specific ecological conditions and at certain times of the year. For this reason what we tend to find is that appropriation becomes focussed more sharply with increasing distance from the settlement. This is the case with Miskito hunting and fishing, where appropriation is concentrated on assured meat-yielding biotopes or species and where yields tend to increase with increasing distance from the settlement because of less general human pressure on resources (Nietschmann 1973:170–1, 231, 234–5).

Foley (1977:179, 184) has suggested a method by which distortion in the von Thunen model caused by differential resource availability and effort might be graphically represented. Yield and human effort are calculated for animal capture, plant cultivation or the appropriation of particular species in each quadrat of an area exploited by a population. The yield:effort ratio can then be calculated for each quadrat. Linking quadrats with the same extractive value for the same species or activity gives *isocals* (Figure 7.5(b)). Within each isocal the home range (area where extraction of resources shows a positive energy balance) will vary depending on, among other things, levels of demand, balance of animal and food-plant species, seasonal availability, and technological efficiency. However, animal and plant resources will generally have very different configurations and fall-off rates.

The spatial distribution of effort and intensity of appropriation have been computed in a few ethnographic studies. Ohtsuka (1977:253) has shown how the latter varies spatially among the Oriomo of New Guinea by plotting the number of times km² quadrats were appro-priated from during the course of various activities over a 26-day period (Figure 7.6). Nuaulu data on work-scheduling for a 524-working day period (Table 7.1) show that the appropriation of non-domesticated resources occurred in 13 localities of varying size and importance defined in indigenous terms. However, the cumulative area of all localities (214 km²) does not match the entire area which the Nuaulu maintain that they use. There is a lack of congruity between Nuaulu ideals and practice, although the boundaries of the area appropriated clearly vary over time. The differential intensity of appropriation for various parts of this area as a whole indicates that the larger part is really of very limited direct ecological or material rel-evance in Ruhua Nualulu subsistence. More time was spent in two localities – 1 and 8 – than in all other localities put together (some 62 per cent of the total number of man-days). Together, these areas occupy about 62 square kilometres. Compared with the total area appropriated by the Nuaulu (say in the course of one year) this is small, and it might be concluded that its productivity is therefore high. In a sense this is correct, but if productivity is measured by a day–area index a some-what different picture emerges. While real productivity by locality proves a difficult index to compute accurately, the numerical data do emphasize the simple (but nonetheless often overlooked) fact that patterns of appropriation often vary considerably spatially, according

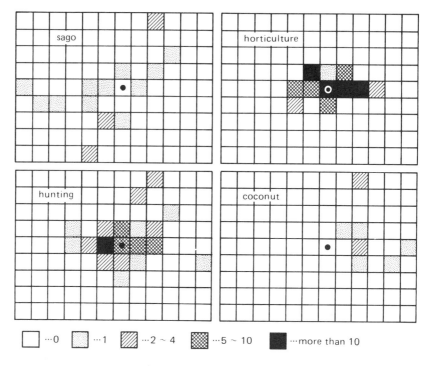

7.6 Space used for four food-getting activities by an Oriomo village (represented by central dot), New Guinea. The key indicates intensity measured as the number of occasions a particular square in the grid was used during a 26-day test period (Ohtsuka 1977:253)

to vegetational cover, faunal composition, topography and relative accessibility (Ellen 1978:61–3, 78–9).

The spatially patterned distribution of production and effort relates directly to the ecological structure of the exploitative area. Table 7.2 shows Dornstreich's analysis of Gadio Enga subsistence in such terms. For comparison, I have presented Nuaulu data in Table 7.3 in the same way. In both tables the number and character of resource areas indicate the degree of environmental diversity and their relative dietary contribution. Some habitats or biotopes are more important than others. The tables also illustrate the difficulty of achieving exact comparability. In order to represent Nuaulu resource areas and distinctive subsistence techniques accurately and informatively, I have felt bound to alter Dornstreich's categories.

Table 7.1 Differential appropriation of non-domesticated resources by locality, Ruhua Nuaulu (modified from Ellen 1978:63)[a]

Locality	Hunting	Various gathering activities	Extraction of non-domesticated sago	Fishing	Total no. man-days	Percentage total	Approximate area (km²)	Work-day–area index
1. Upa river area	81	56			137	28	14	10
2. Sama	15	33			48	8	8	6
3. Mon river area	26	7			33	6	8	4
4. Awao river area	9	2			11	2	0.5	22
5. Ruhua village vicinity	17	20		18	55	11	1.5	36
6. Lihuru river area	1				1		0.75	1
7. Lahati	26	4	1		31	5	25	1.25
8. Somau	1		165		166	34	48	3.5
9. Lata river area	30				30	5	48	0.6
10. Joko river area	2	2			4		0.25	16
11. Samna-ukuna	1				1		0.5	2
12. Turiaro	5	1			6	1	0.25	24
13. Ruatan river area	1				1		60	0.01
TOTALS	215	125	166	18	524	100	214.75	
Percentage totals	41.5	23.5	31.5	3.5	100			

a For a discussion of the sample used, see Ellen (1978: Appendix D)

165

Table 7.2 *The relationship of resource areas to food-getting activities among the Gadio Enga of the New Guinea highlands (after Dornstreich 1977:249, 250)*

Resource area (or biotope)	Altitudinal range (m above sea level)	Food-getting activities[a]									Total number of activities
		a	b	c	d	e	f	g	h	i	
1. Hamlet site – current	450–750			+		+	+		+		4
2. Hamlet site – abandoned	450–750			+	+				+		3
3. Living site – current	350–900			+		+			+		3
4. Living site – abandoned	350–900			+	+				+		3
5. Garden – in production (i.e. fenced)	450–750	+		+			+		+		4
6. Garden – staple foods exhausted	450–750	+		+					+		3
7. Garden – abandoned	450–750	+		+	+				+		4
8. Fruit tree stands	450–750			+							1
9. Sago swamp	300–600		+			+	+	+	+		5
10. Sago stand	300–900		+						+		2
11. Stream or river (lower altitude)	350–600							+	+		2
12. Stream (upper altitude)	650–1,050						+	+	+		3
13. Streambank	450–750				+				+		2
14. Rainforest	450–1,050				+				+	+	3
15. Mountains	900–1,200								+	+	2
Total number of resource areas		3	2	8	5	3	4	3	14	2	

[a] a, gardening; b, sago making; c, silviculture; d, gathering (plant foods); e, animal husbandry; f, trapping; g, fishing; h, collecting (animal foods); i, hunting

Table 7.3 *The relationship of resource areas to food-getting activities among the Nuaulu of south central Seram*

Resource area (or biotope)	Altitudinal range (m above sea level)	Food-getting activities[a]										Total number of activities
		a	b	c	d	e	f	g	h	i	j	
1. Hamlet site – current	0–200				+		+		+			3
2. First-year garden	0–400	+						+				2
3. Old garden – staple foods exhausted	0–200	+			+			+				3
4. Abandoned garden	0–200	+		+	+	+		+	+	+		7
5. Sago swamp and domesticated sago groves	0		+	+					+	+		4
6. Other groves	0–50				+				+	+		3
7. Mixed secondary forest	50–400				+	+		+	+	+		5
8. Mature rain forest	200–1,000					+			+	+		3
9. Montane rain forest	1,000–4,000									+		1
10. Rivers	0–200								+		+	2
11. Streambank	0–400			+		+			+			3
12. Littoral	0								+		+	2
13. Sea	0										+	1
Total number of resource areas		3	1	3	5	4	1	4	9	6	3	

a a, swiddening; b, starch extraction from non-domesticated *Metroxylon* (sago) palms; c, starch extraction from domesticated *Metroxylon* palms; d, silviculture; e, gathering non-domesticated plant foods; f, animal husbandry; g, trapping; h, collecting non-domesticated animal foods; i, hunting; j, fishing

Ecological production and yield can be calculated in terms of specific biotopes, localities within an exploitative environment, or in terms of the distance from the settlement nucleus. Nietschmann (1973:168–70), for example, has calculated Miskito meat yields according to the biotope from which they are derived (Table 4.1). Within the shallow offshore water environment, the most productive areas are the shoals, banks and mudsets, yielding 79 per cent of the total annual weight of butchered meat catch. On land, the palm swamps, old and new plantations, and secondary forests have the highest meat yield. In the lagoon–river-resource sphere, the shallow-water shrimp banks, grass flats and shallow water borders provide most of the meat. In all, approximately 87 per cent of their meat is obtained from water, and 13 per cent from land. Biotopes within the land and water zones are appropriated in terms of cultural meat preferences, recognition of various species' habits and habitats, available technology, and degree of subsistence risk.

There is also the question of the total amount of land required when employing different subsistence strategies. Calorie and protein yield per square kilometre is clearly going to depend on the composition of the diet, available resources and the distribution of those resources, and the efficiency with which they can be appropriated. For example, hunters, relying principally on secondary sources of energy, require a substantially larger area than cultivators, relying on primary energy sources. This is because game animals in turn require a greater biomass than their own to satisfy their energy requirements. This means a large exploitative area, although the ratio of individual to potential food sources may remain fairly constant. This fact is consonant with their low density, though it is rarely the only factor determining it. Pimentel and Pimentel (1979) suggest that under ideal conditions food-collecting populations require about 40 hectares per person, although Clark and Haswell (1971:29–30) quote figures ranging from 250 hectares in favourable zones to 14,000 in more marginal subarctic lands.

FRACTION OF POPULATION

Less attention has been paid to the yield, effort and efficiency of different members of a single population than to any other single set of variables (cf. Ruyle 1973a:606). This crucial flaw points to the sociological naivety of much ecological work, and to the subtle intrusion of ideology. The notions of total production, effort and efficiency conceal the relative input and output of different sectors of a population: people do not all produce or consume the same, or work as hard.

Variation according to age and sex is acknowledged in numerous physiological and ethnographic studies (e.g. Lee 1969:71–2; Nietschmann 1973:217, 220; Thomas 1973:66–8). But usually the discussion relates to the process of arriving at generalized figures per head, rather than to an interest in the differences themselves (e.g. Rappaport 1968, Ellen 1978). It is clear that to a certain extent age- and sex-linked figures are related to physiological, anatomical and psychological capacity. Children neither require the same bulk of food as adults nor are capable of the same effort. To a lesser extent this is true for old people, and for women as opposed to men. But actual intake and patterned effort is to a large degree socially determined within the limits of physical possibility. Over-consumption may result from cultural conventions as to physical form, child-rearing lore, and rules relating to domestic food distribution. Dornstreich (1977:259) reports that Gadio Enga women and children receive a disproportionate share of available protein, whereas Nuaulu women and children receive less protein than adult males. Under conditions of labour and food shortage, the role of children may become relatively more important (B. White 1975).

Relative effort may be affected by local conventions as to the appropriateness of the technical division of labour, combined with the significance in yield and input in terms of the various activities involved. Such factors may result in disproportionate efficiencies between the sexes. The fundamentally social character of the sexual division of labour is now too well attested (Edholm, Young and Harris 1977) to require further elaboration here, but it is worth noting that food-getting activities will tend to have different temporal and spatial patterns of effort depending on gender. Thus, if Figure 7.4(b) is understood to refer to the Iban agricultural calendar then the first two peaks in the graph reflect for the most part male effort, while the central trough and the final peak reflect for the most part female effort. For other societies the same or similar graphs annotated for gender will look very different.

Inequality in effort, yield and consumption may exist between fractions of a population defined in other ways; between kinship groups, groups of specialists and classes. This kind of inequality is principally dependent on *exchange* between constituent groups, and the possibility of differential relative efficiencies brings us to the creation of *surplus*.

In order to support sectors of the population which do not engage in productive activities it is necessary for the ratio of energy gained to *human* energy expended to be greatly increased. Many small populations have been unable to break out of these energetic restrictions because a large part of the population is directly and permanently

involved in food production. However under-productive such populations may or may not be (Sahlins 1972), this sets a technical outer limit
on the development of an unproductive sector. These limits are only
removed by using some other source of energy in addition to that used
directly by human beings in producing food.

Data are available for some populations which have reached these
technical limits, in the form of studies of under-nutrition and protein
deficiency. What is interesting about many of these cases is that the
areas of high population density, where such populations are most
typically located, are parts of complex social formations with significant unproductive and under-productive sectors. Malnutrition is frequently a consequence of differential access to strategic resources, and
may itself lower work capacity, result in permanent physical damage,
and so impose further strain on the productive sector of a population
(Greene 1977:280; 1977a). Thus it seems that in many societies surplus
energy is created at the cost of the health of producers. Gross and
Underwood (1971:1), for example, analyse the process by which sisal
leaves are transformed into exportable fibre by Brazilian agricultural
labourers. They examine two representative household budgets in
detail to determine the impact of sisal labour, and conclude that energy
requirements are so great in relation to wages that the systematic
energy deprivation of non-productive dependants is unavoidable.
Rapidly growing children are particularly affected, a process which is
revealed statistically in a sample population by relative retardation in
the growth rate of these workers.

PROBLEMS IN DESCRIBING SUBSISTENCE

It must be clear from a reading of Chapters 6 and 7 that the description
and analysis of subsistence are not quite the straightforward matter
that some have confidently considered them to be. Much confusion
has been caused in the ethnographic and comparative literature by
assuming ostensibly predominant subsistence techniques to represent
total subsistence strategies, and by a general use of excessively simple
criteria for the description of life-support techniques.[3] For example,
we happily describe Eskimo, Hadza and Tasaday as 'hunter-
gatherers', the Nuaulu, Gadio Enga, Iban and Hanunoo as 'swidden
cultivators', when the difference between them *in purely subsistence
terms* are of as much social and ecological significance as those
between populations to which we attach different labels.

In some cases labels are quite misleading, and such broad terms may
conceal critical variation. Often an illusion of uniformity is sustained
(as in the New Guinea highlands) by a common repertoire of useful

species (Little and Morren 1977:73). Thus, although for certain purposes the Miyanmin and Maring might be usefully placed together
(Brookfield and Hart 1971), a more careful and broader examination of
their food-getting activities shows them to be very different. Among
the Maring, swiddening and pig-raising are more intensive (as was
competition for territory in the pre-colonial period) than among the
Miyanmin (Morren 1977 cf. Dornstreich 1977:248). It is characteristic of
systems involving swiddening that it is only part of a broader and more
complex strategy linking together a range of techniques. If it were
otherwise, cultivation would have to be intensified to compensate for
the loss of subsidies, the existence of which maintains its viability.
Similarly, populations which subsist through hunting, fishing, collecting and gathering range from those where trophic relations and
efficiencies are similar to those of large ungulates or other mammals
(Table 5.1), to those where human influence over environmental
balances exceeds that of some populations of cultivators. The term
'pastoralist' has been used in a particularly slovenly fashion, to include
many peoples (e.g. Maasai and Mongol) not wholly dependent on
livestock for survival. The Dinka, also, are not entirely 'pastoralists'
since they rely on sorghum, bulrush-millet and fish. On the other
hand, the nineteenth-century plains Amerindians described as
'hunter-gatherers' relied on herds of horses and were therefore strictly
speaking pastoralist-hunters. Ingold (1980:200) has pointed out that
milch and carnivorous pastoralism are very different in terms of the
ecological and social relations between humans and animals, and has
suggested that lumping the two together is grossly misleading.

Such terms as 'hunter-gatherer', 'swiddening' or 'pastoralist' are
often meant to suggest that according to certain, usually unspecified,
criteria (but often including physical visibility, indigenous importance,
calculations of food mass or weight), the techniques to which they
refer appear to be the most important or *dominant* ones. This is the
sense in which the subsistence designations in Table 2.1 are used, and
since the characterization of populations by their dominant technique
is such a widespread and convenient practice it can hardly be avoided
entirely. But this assumption obscures the relevance of other techniques employed, which although secondary may have a critical and
necessary role in an overall subsistence strategy. They may, indeed, be
limiting. Also, time apportionment or energy contribution may be less
important for health and survival than the effectiveness with which a
strategy copes with the problem (Vayda and McCay 1977:414).
Moreover, to establish the dominance of any one technique there must
be some recognized criterion by which to measure it. Statements by
informants on the importance of a particular technique are of little use

here, since they may be corrupted by cultural ideals, although cultural ideals themselves may be important in determining the pattern of subsistence activity. More useful are measures of gross yields, by mass or weight, according to particular nutritional quanta; and measures of temporal and calorific effort, and the use of space. But concentration on any one may result in distortion if taken as the sole criterion in analysis. Likewise, to describe a subsistence strategy in terms of the degree of dependence on particular resources is likely to obscure overall long-term adaptive characteristics.

It is somewhat surprising that, despite their obvious importance, methodologies and techniques for analysing subsistence are so poorly developed. There are no standard or widely accepted formats for description, other than the most elementary and naive. What typologies exist tend to obscure the character of actual ecological adaptation and lead to the posing of spurious problems (Dornstreich 1977:248). More preferable is an attempt to outline a subsistence strategy in terms of the profile resulting from a combination of features. The results of recent empirical research discussed in this chapter and Chapter 6 go some way towards achieving this end, though no simple formula is possible. For some populations dominant techniques will always be clearly identifiable from any competent ethnographic examination (e.g. Hadza, !Kung). In others it will always be necessary to look at several criteria (which may be contradictory) before arriving at a reliable statement of the relative importance of techniques. In some populations it may be quite impossible to describe as 'dominant' any one technique, or complex of techniques, without distortion. The Nuaulu, for example, obtain most of their calories from wild sago, spend most of their time and energy procuring non-domesticated resources, but still make their greatest impact on the environment through, and expend most calories on, swidden cultivation. Similarly, in a few populations raising animal stock is the only significant technique in terms of human effort, nutrition and ecological relations. Among those populations unusual in this respect we may include arctic reindeer herders, some Bedouin and central Asian nomadic peoples. But in most populations it is an important source of protein in a broader strategy which includes cultivation, as in the East African cattle area (Gulliver 1955), or among the Fulani of northern Nigeria (Stenning 1957).

A more balanced assessment of subsistence strategies avoids the receding obsessionalism that has characterized much ecological work in anthropology: an obsession solely with calories, with protein, with other nutrients, or with dominant or apparently dominant techniques. Differences *between* populations may be enormous. For example, the six basic subsistence strategies listed in Chapter 6 can be combined in 720 different ways, even before we begin to consider strategies combining fewer than six. Each combination has different implications for an overall pattern of subsistence and necessarily articulates in a different way with social relations.

The same balanced assessment of subsistence strategies also emphasizes diversity within populations. An examination of a total configuration brings out adaptive patterns which would otherwise be concealed. For example, among those who have a wide variety of possible resources to choose from, it may make sense to specialize in terms of a subsidiary food focus. This is particularly so where food has to be searched for (as in hunting), and where advantage lies in pursuing prey which can be captured efficiently. Alternatively, a particular pattern of resource appropriation may maintain the environment in a favourable state for a given population. By focussing on green-turtle hunting, the Miskito of Nicaragua relieve pressure on terrestrial animal populations which, under other conditions, would receive more hunting attention (Nietschmann 1973:166). Nuaulu hunting of a wide range of smaller game (e.g. python, monitor, cuscus, bat) has the same effect with respect to wild deer and pig populations. In the arid climate of Karimoja where poor crop yields are expected every five years, and complete failure every ten, large cattle herds are an insurance against famine. The Karimojong also grow a drought-resistant sorghum. Although this does not store for more than a year, its usefulness is extended through social relations – ceremonial redistribution, begging and trading – rather than technical innovation (Dyson-Hudson and Dyson-Hudson 1970). Subsistence diversity encourages good nutrition and health, minimizes the impact of failure in a particular sector and thus enhances adaptability (Dornstreich 1977:263). The concept of subsistence diversity is a useful way of comparing different subsistence patterns, and a possible means of measuring it has already been discussed under the heading of ecological niche.

Another reason why categorical statements cannot be made about different subsistence strategies, dominant or non-dominant techniques, is that the species subject to appropriation by a given technique may vary from place to place, and the same species may be appropriated by different techniques. As we have already seen in Chapter 4, different species entail different ecological consequences, make different demands on a population and possess different food and resource properties. For example, rice may be grown under intensive hydraulic conditions and extensive swidden conditions, yet, in both cases, possesses similar nutritional qualities. Equally, grains and root crops grown under the same swidden conditions may make quite different demands on a population and open up an entirely different set of possibilities. What cultigens are grown may make the difference between, for example, high population densities and sparse habitation.

The ecological consequences of appropriating particular species are bound to vary, but we know little of the impact of subsistence activities on animal populations, and on the types of species appropriated over time. The survival of several species of terrestrial and marine animal is threatened by over-appropriation, for the most part as a result of global market demand. Faunal depletion not only requires that populations alter their subsistence strategy, but can lead to cumulative ecological disruption (Nietschmann 1973:163, 177). Nietschmann (1973:202) has noted, in connection with his analysis of Miskito subsistence, that increasing dependency on a declining resource can only lead to a downward socio-ecological spiral.

It should be noted that by 'subsistence' I mean all the uses to which a species may be put. Some recent ecological work in anthropology has paid so much attention to the food-getting aspect of subsistence that it has played down the total life-support role. This narrow focus on the energy relations of subsistence activities themselves is misleading (Morren 1977:227). M. Harris (1971) and Sahlins (1972:57) have perpetuated this fallacy by using a very narrow range of activities in calculating labour inputs (cf. Johnson 1975:305–6). Subsistence also involves appropriation for non-edible resources, and edible and non-edible resources for exchange. Such activities often have very significant ecological consequences (such as when forest is cut for building materials), which themselves may be important in an analysis of the ecology of sustenance. Depletion of forest affects the availability of certain food species, while the collection of firewood (itself necessary in the preparation of food) involves the expenditure of calories and releases calories as fuel.

Any one subsistence pattern is a complex and unique combination of variables, and its accurate description and analysis is a legitimate end in itself. But it does not exist in a vacuum, as something apart from the social relations of the population which is responsible for it. We cannot simply compare subsistence system with subsistence system, narrowly defined. Social relations as much as any environmental or technical characteristic determine the form taken by subsistence. Generalizations, therefore, about the determinate character of specific techniques must be made with care. Accurate specification of the importance of different techniques, their spatial and temporal concomitants, and the configuration to which they give rise is vital for a

174

proper understanding of both the technical organization of labour and the larger social formation. For example, it is clear that the technical demands of irrigated cultivation will have a distinctive impact on work organization at the local level and allow for the possibility of a high return for effort. But the precise impact very much depends on the position of irrigated cultivation in an overall subsistence strategy. Similarly, the character of Nuaulu relations of land use (especially flexibility) only begins to make sense when placed in the context of reasonably accurate observations on the significance of different techniques of appropriation, in terms of output, effort and visible impact on the landscape (Ellen 1977). It is no good attributing a dominant structural role to a particular kind of technical relation of production if, on closer examination, it is found to contribute only peripherally. In general, the more intensive the food-getting pattern, the more complex particular technical activities tend to become, involving more specialization and an increase in the demands on effort. This development is inconsistent with overall subsistence diversity. Consequently, a narrowing of food focus implies greater productivity, but not ecological efficiency or adaptive flexibility (Dornstreich 1977:263, Morren 1977:281). An increase in the human effort devoted to one activity reduces that available for other purposes.

In conclusion, I wish to return to a matter discussed in Chapter 6, but which still occasions considerable confusion. This is the theoretical distinction between modes of subsistence and modes of production, which may or may not be based on particular subsistence techniques or combinations of such techniques. The general labels I have employed for the description of subsistence specify technical and ecological relations, and the modes of subsistence which arise from their combination are similarly specified. Both techniques and patterns necessarily imply the existence of social relations (indeed, they may be determined by them), but they can never predictably specify their character. The categories used to describe and analyse subsistence do not always make this important distinction, often through the naive technicist assumption that what is being described is simply a technical and ecological matter. Alternatively, the social underpinnings of particular subsistence forms may be recognized but assumed to be the necessary condition for their existence (e.g. Ingold 1980). This latter approach blurs the theoretical issues by confusing analytical designations with complex substantive cases. For example, to define hunting theoretically, in ecological and technical terms, as human predation on large animal species involving a high energy expenditure may be imprecise, but it most definitely does not imply social sharing, common access to animals or land. On the other hand, 'pastoralism', in as much as this broad category can ever accurately reflect actual practice, is an aspect of a mode of economic production using the technique of animal husbandry (involving degrees of taming, herding and breeding). But over and above this, and following Ingold, it describes a situation where animal populations are allowed to increase naturally under human protection, are periodically used parasitically or predated upon, and where social relations involve divided access to animals but common access to land. Similarly, ranching is a form of economic production where animals (often bred) accumulate through un-protected natural increase only to be periodically killed, and where social access to both animals and land is divided. It is characteristic of a market economy. However, in technical and ecological terms alone (that is, as a generalizable theoretical subsistence form) it is a combina-tion of both hunting and husbandry. By defining subsistence in terms of general categories used to describe actual empirical cases Ingold has made it seem as if particular human technical and ecological conditions necessarily entail particular social relations. Unfortunately, the ethnographic evidence is unable to sustain such an assertion.

8

Systems and their regulation

SYSTEMS THEORY AND THE ANALYSIS OF ECOSYSTEMS

An aspect of ecological theory which has generated great interest and which is now commonplace in the analysis of small-scale human populations stems from the theory of general systems developed by Ludwig von Bertalanffy (1968). The applicability of this approach rests on the assumption that ecosystems are types of general system and therefore possess their properties; that they are open systems with processes tending towards a harmonious and coordinated 'steady state'. As such they are held to follow the laws of open-system thermodynamics. Many of the features of ecosystems which suggest this tendency – the idea of climax in vegetation, maturity in soils and grade in geomorphology – have been recognized for much longer; but in the light of systems theory it has become possible to reinterpret such concepts in a dynamic rather than a static manner.

The ideas of systems theory have been employed by geographers (Stoddart 1969:305), archaeologists (D. L. Clarke 1968, Flannery 1968) and anthropologists, as well as biologists, within an ecological context, and with varying degrees of faithfulness, precision and success.[1] Although implicit in some earlier work (Forde 1970:19), among the most influential pioneer work in anthropology has been that of Roy Rappaport, and I will be referring to this in some detail in subsequent sections of this chapter.

Formal and empirical definitions of a system are curiously difficult to formulate, although intuitively the idea is not a difficult one to grasp. What it is not is a collection 'of entities which share some ontological characteristic' (Rappaport 1971b:59), such as a belief 'system'. This usage, which still persists in anthropology, is perverse and misleading and reflects sloppy thinking. The definition provided by Hall and Fagan – 'a set of objects together with relationships between those objects and their attributes' (quoted in Langton 1973:128) – has also been criticized for being too vague. Rappaport (1968:4) defines it as 'any set of specified variables in which a change in the value of one of the variables will result in a change in the value of at least one other'. This seems hardly sufficient but is generally similar to Watt's 'an interlocking complex of processes characterized by many reciprocal cause–effect pathways' (1966:2). For Millar (1965:200) a system is 'a set of units with relationships among them. The word "set" implies that the units have common properties. The state of each unit is con-strained by, conditioned by, or dependent on the state of other units.' And therefore (Langton 1973:128): 'The relationships are thus causal, functional or normative; the set is in some way "organised" through the interrelationships between the units. It is in this sense – in the possession of organisation – that the units exist as a "whole" which is "greater than the sum of its parts".' The variables of such a system are any of its measurable properties, such as size, number, spatial arrange-ment or rate of change (Millar 1965:203). As we have already noted, for ecosystems in particular, any one system contains a very large number of variables, and any one analysis can select only a small number of these for investigation.

COMPLEXITY, CLOSURE AND PROCESS

Central to systems theory is the recognition of 'the complexity of interaction, of the numerousness of parameters which must be in-cluded in an analysis of any set of variables, and of the multidirectional and often indirect, yet ordered, links which exist between par-ameters and variables' (Langton 1973:131). In fact, the main reason for using systems analysis in ecology is the complexity of the processes involved, originating from the number of variables, *types* of variable (e.g. genetic, ecological, exogenous, endogamous), levels of organiza-tion (e.g. population, social formation), and the non-uniform and non-homogenous distribution of entities spatially and through time (Watt 1966:6).

In order to reduce the work load in research and subject a system to analysis, it is necessary to simplify it (Harvey 1969:448). Once the important variables are simplified it is necessary to structure them into a model which accurately describes the behaviour of a complex system and can be used in simulation studies to show how the system can be manipulated in order to reflect the situation for different human populations.

The necessary process of simplification has four aspects. First, over-all complexity must be reduced by shedding variables and causal pathways that provisionally or *a priori* are of no relevance to the analysis at hand. In some analyses these variables will already have been measured, and their significance tested statistically, using multiple-variance and regression techniques (Watt 1966:9). However, such an approach is seldom employed, and often impracticable, in ethnographic studies. Secondly, the relationship between the variables considered must be represented in a way convenient for analysis. This can be done either graphically or mathematically, and some of these techniques have already been examined in connection with the discussion of energy flow in Chapters 5, 6 and 7. Another formal technique which has been employed in systems modelling, and which is amenable to topological and other means of mathematical treatment, is the conversion of 'box and arrow' diagrams into 'signal flow graphs' or 'phase space' description (Langton 1973:162).

The third aspect of simplification is system closure. Thus, according to Hagen (1961:145):

> For use in analysis, a system must be 'closed'. A system which is interacting with its environment is an 'open' system: all systems of 'real life' are therefore open systems. For analysis, however, it is necessary in the intellectual construct to assume that contact with the environment is cut off so that the operation of the system is affected only by given conditions previously established by the environment and not changing at the time of analysis, plus the relationships among the elements of the system.

The notions of complexity, interaction and order have emerged independently in ecosystem studies, but this explicit emphasis on organization and the need for analytical closure provides greater focus.

As has become evident from ecosystem studies, the definition of any particular ecosystem is arbitrary; that is, it is largely an association of diverse elements into which the researcher has infused a unifying structure. The universe can be seen as being composed of systems of different kinds (e.g. social systems, information systems, ecosystems) and systems contained within successively larger systems, that is, systems of different levels of complexity. The search for degree of *systemness* rather than arbitrary definitions remains an important issue in the interpretation of human behaviour patterns in general (Buckley 1967:42). It is practically and intuitively relatively easy to isolate 'systems' which make sense of data and which may be used for the investigation of a wide range of different research problems. However, it is empirically complicated to specify them in terms of numbers of connections or intensity of flow. The boundaries of systems may often be modified from an original *a priori* delineation, so as to conform with emerging data, or to make data conform with a model. Moreover, as

Friedman (1976) points out, the difficulty of guaranteeing closure under empirical conditions is that local societies are rarely closed reproductive units. Where closure is demonstrably weak, local societies are no longer sufficient units of explanation.

Once analytic closure has been satisfactorily achieved, analysis can proceed through the construction of models linking variables as part of causal processes. Process is therefore the central concept of any analysis which attempts to find out in what conditions the system changes and when it remains static: 'Processes . . . occur in systems only when a stress or threat has created a strain which pushes [a parameter] beyond its range of stability' (Millar 1965:224). The kinds of processes which occur in systems and their identification in ecosystems containing human populations are discussed in the following sections.

NEGATIVE FEEDBACK AND HOMEOSTASIS

It was noted in Chapter 1 that linear causal sequences rarely occur in human environmental relations. The logical explanation of this must now be clear; that the connectedness of any empirical system makes this extremely unlikely. Rather than causality being simply uni-directional ($a–b$), it is often circular (e.g. $a–b–c–a$). The idea is formally similar to the logical basis of functionalism. Condition a produces condition b, which in turn produces others which may themselves become conditions for the recurrence of the first condition (Nagel 1956, Gellner 1970). In its ecological context reciprocal causality was certainly acknowledged by earlier writers, such as Forde (1970:19) and Steward (Kaplan and Manners 1972:79). But despite such acknowledgement its effective use in analysis was precluded by inadequate theoretical development and empirical studies.

Loops of circular causality are known technically in systems theory as *feedback*, a term which we owe more specifically to cybernetics. In a feedback system causal loops are therefore closed. Any change in a is looped back to a, and a stimulus represented by a change in a is subsequently altered by the feedback. In an environment which is constantly changing, and where there is therefore continuous change in the constraints acting on the system, feedback operates between the subsystems to cause mutually adaptive changes within them. Let us take a particular example of this.

If the demand for meat increases in a Nuaulu population then this will tend to stimulate greater output. But an increase in output requires more effort, effort which must be withdrawn from other important productive activities, such as sago extraction. Since sago possesses a high cultural value – equal to if not surpassing that attached to meat –

very little effort can be withdrawn from its appropriation while maintaining production at a culturally acceptable level. So, demand for sago in turn feeds back to limit any further growth in activities connected with the supply of meat. This has the added effect of controlling the size of populations of hunted animals, allowing them to maintain themselves at viable breeding levels. The entire process is accentuated at times of important festivals, when demand for both products rises. The essence of the argument can be represented graphically as an inverse supply curve, where, to maintain output of both sago and meat at an optimal level, labour and time inputs for each product must not exceed x. But this does not help us in following through all the causal chains. The model is, of course, highly simplified, and it could be argued that effort might be drawn in to increase the level of meat production from elsewhere. This is true, but it is worth noting that the male labour involved in sago-gathering and hunting combined comes to about 57 per cent of person-days involved in all food-getting activities. While labour might be withdrawn from other sectors (such as gardening, where a drop in production can be tolerated and where anyway labour can be subsidized by the employment of females), with such a high proportion of the labour time invested in hunting and sago extraction periodic reallocation of effort in one is bound to have some effect on the other.

The link between fluctuating levels of Nuaulu meat and sago appropriation provides an example of *negative feedback*. Systems which behave in this way are said to be homeostatic, and the property is *homeostasis*. The loop a–b–c–a is a homeostatic system of a very simple kind. We can therefore say that homeostasis serves to regulate a system, by maintaining the state of variables included in it within a range or ranges which permit the continued existence of the system (cf. Rappaport 1971b:59). Ecosystems in a steady state possess such a property of self-regulation, and this is similar in principle to a wide range of mechanisms such as homeostasis in living organisms, feedback principles in cybernetics and servo-mechanisms in engineering.

THE CULTURAL REGULATION OF ECOLOGICAL RELATIONS

In the last decade there has been great interest in the possibility that human social or cultural behaviour might regulate material relations within an ecosystem through homeostasis. In particular, there has been some emphasis on how maintaining certain crucial variables, such as the amount of land under cultivation, population size, calorie intake and energy expenditure, ensures the survival or 'adequate functioning' of the system. Among that work which has been most influential in encouraging this type of approach is that of the zoologist V. C. Wynne-Edwards (1962), while the tradition of anthropological functionalism provided an essential theoretical disposition. Wynne-Edwards noted that animal populations on the whole maintain an optimum population size. In order to explain this he suggested that social behaviour acted as a form of homeostatic control, and there have now been a number of attempts to demonstrate that cultural practices previously regarded as irrational do indeed have significant ecological functions. This enterprise is wholly consistent with the tendency noted in Chapter 4 for ethnographers to become morally involved with their objects of study. A fine example of this approach is Marvin Harris's (1965) attempt to show that the contemporary pattern of husbanding the religiously venerated cows of Hindu India functions to provide cheap traction, dairy products, dung for fuel and construction, and a famine food reserve. A similar kind of hypothesis had been suggested some years previously by Andrew Vayda, Anthony Leeds and David Smith (1961), namely that pig slaughters in certain New Guinea festivals regulate ecological balance between humans, crops and the environment. This idea was subsequently taken up by Roy Rappaport (1968) and elaborated in his analysis of Tsembaga Maring environmental relations.

At the centre of this argument is a very specific circular causal sequence. Periods of hostility between local groups – clan hamlets – are terminated by the planting of the sacred *Cordyline* plants to mark new territorial boundaries. There then ensues a period of fifteen years or more during which there is peace and the size of local pig populations increases. The pigs are fed on yam tubers and consume roughly half the number of calories required by the human population. One third of the land area is used for growing tubers for pigs. Eventually the pig population becomes so large as to be unmanageable for the women and threatens to become a garden pest and degrade the environment through foraging. This triggers the slaughter of all except a few of the pigs and the holding of a festival. The festival ends with the uprooting of the *Cordyline* and the restoration of hostilities. Fighting ends only when new boundaries can be drawn which presumably reflect the numerical strength of the groups involved and therefore their land requirements for both humans and pigs.

Rappaport characterizes this as a homeostatic process in which the Tsembaga employ a digital device – to plant or uproot *Cordyline* – to regulate the analog relationships of the system in which they live (1968:70). The benefit of pigs is seen not only in terms of the protein and calories they provide, but also in terms of their role as part of the means by which relations between autonomous local groups are regulated. The frequency of warfare is regulated by the ritual cycle, but the timing of the cycle itself is a function of the speed in the growth of the pig population. So the main part of Rappaport's argument is that, through ritual, the relations between people, pigs and gardens are regulated, and that this operates directly to protect people from the possible parasitism and competition of their pigs. Indirectly, it protects the environment by helping to maintain extensive areas of virgin forest and assuring adequate cultivation : fallow ratios on secondary forest. But additionally, and specifically, Rappaport (1968:3–4, 1971a:128) suggests that the cycle: 1. enhances the value in pork through the slaughter and distribution of pigs; 2. enhances the value of non-domesticated animals to the population as a whole by regulating their consumption; 3. conserves the marsupial fauna; 4. redistributes the population over land and also land among territorial groups; 5. regulates the frequency of warfare and mitigates the severity of intergroup fighting; 6. facilitates the exchange of goods and personnel between local groups; and 7. encourages re-establishment of forest through the role of pigs in the detritus food chains where they consume garbage and human faeces, root up unharvested tubers in abandoned gardens and eat herbs but not tree seedlings.

The approach has been among the most sophisticated attempts to cope with the complexities of human–environment relations in small-scale populations. It avoids naive reductionism to culture and environment, resolves certain epistemological problems concerning determinants and limiting factors, accommodates the findings of a number of diverse fields within a single framework, and offers a stimulating theoretical perspective. But it is precisely because it is a sophisticated and integrated approach, and because it claims so much (ranging over the borders of carefully cultivated bourgeois disciplines), that the many theoretical objections and problems it raises must be considered very seriously. Some of the specific technical difficulties have already been mentioned in Chapters 4 and 5. In the following sections I discuss the more important general criticisms.

CANONS OF PROOF, ETHNOGRAPHIC OMISSION AND SOCIOLOGICAL EXPLANATION

In many cases the necessary data required to support analyses couched in systems terms have been shown to be wanting. Rappaport has been criticized on the grounds that the scale of his Tsembaga study is too small for us to understand many ecological processes, such as material cycles and other limiting factors; that his use of quantitative data is not sufficiently sophisticated and his use of systems theory incomplete;

and that he does not extend the study of energy flow to include exchanges among human groups (J. N. Anderson 1973:199–200). These are criticisms of a type we might expect from among those generally sympathetic to the approach.

But Rappaport has also been criticized on his presentation and interpretation of very specific Maring ethnography. Much of this suggests that he has understressed the significance of social factors in his explanations. For example, in non-festival years the Kauwasi Maring kill more pigs for the purposes of affinal prestations than to deal with misfortune or warfare (Lowman-Vayda 1971), while Tsembaga pigs were well below carrying capacity when slaughtered in the year of Rappaport's observations (McArthur 1977:95). One type of big man – the Ancestor Spirit Man – had power to affect clan policy in war and pig sacrifice, contrary to the claim that sanctity is the functional alternative to political power (Lowman-Vayda 1971). It has been noted that women succeed in complaining in some New Guinea highland societies when the pig population is much smaller (Waddell 1972). It has been suggested (McArthur 1977:124) that the wastefulness of the ritual cycle must be explained in terms of prestige accumulation as well as protein, and that had Rappaport paid more attention to the disadvantageous aspects of ritual he might have been led to examine the wider political aspects of intergroup relations. Among the numerous Chimbu, with their vast interlocking exchange cycles, such regulatory devices are inconceivable. Ceremonies are not primarily to dispose of pigs, but have complex objectives in the maintenance and reinforcement of the whole system of social relations (Brookfield 1972).

Buchbinder (1977:110, 137–8) has suggested that the Tsembaga are neither nutritionally nor in terms of resources as well off as Rappaport has suggested. The various Maring people of the Simbai valley respond to the stress of introduced infectious diseases according to differences in their nutritional status with regard to energy and protein. Nutritional stress adversely affects the ability of populations on the highlands' fringe to cope with the period following culture contact. Introduced stresses have proved most lethal in those populations which have traditionally been subject to highest stress. A relation of positive feedback exists between a population's biological and behavioural response to stress. For Buchbinder the various Simbai Maring local populations occupy various stages in a dynamic regional population cycle: an initial pioneering stage, population build-up, resource depletion and population decline due to a greater susceptibility to infectious disease. She suggests that the outcome of intergroup conflict might be predicted on the basis of the health and nutritional status of antagonists. The ritual time interval following conflict allows for regeneration of resources and therefore of population.

Despite the wealth of data presented by Rappaport there are still criticisms which can be made at a practical level. Some of these have already been mentioned in Chapter 5. Work of the kind necessary for studies of this type in remote areas far from laboratories is extraordinarily difficult, especially for one individual to undertake with some degree of success. The assumptions permissible in biological ecology are not always so in human ecology. The demonstration of complex feedback requires a fuller and more complexly specified quantification. Rappaport's observations were for only 11 months, but he provides no information on the time required for the system to emerge, nor how long it might last after the period of observation. His nutritional data are taken from a small, unrepresentative sample (McArthur 1977:125). It seems very possible that such systems were quite unstable and likely to be altered through either environmental or human factors on a scale exceeding the previous limits (e.g. Sahlins 1964).

The time factor is crucial since activities in balance are not necessarily under the simultaneous control of the same forces or institutions. They can change at different rates and magnitudes, although it is at least feasible that this should be less so in relatively isolated small-scale populations. It is also unclear how the perception of the Tsembaga is linked to the impersonal properties of the cycle. Rappaport assumes that purposive human behaviour is assimilable to natural processes, and that human behaviour for the most part emerges from a kind of bio-environmental complex. Perhaps he would maintain that humans consciously respond to perceived environmental factors, although physiology triggers that response. The built-in controls may only be a half-conscious affair. As Rappaport has implied, it is the consequence of mutual reinforcing of many cultural and economic patterns. But such control can often be entirely rational and planned; it is possible for societies to develop controls over environmental use with self-conscious methods based on a particular ideology (Bennett 1976:183).

THE PROBLEM OF CLOSURE

Analytical closure poses a particularly acute problem for systems analysis, although it is by no means unique to it. The boundaries of groups and ecological populations are not always clear and local human groups are seldom economically independent. Steward (1955) noted this, particularly as a feature of modern populations, and it led him to consider the notion of 'levels of integration'. Strictly speaking, the term 'ecological population' refers to all those participating in an exchange network. Rappaport's analysis is based on an assumption that the Tsembaga represent a closed spatial and temporal system, at least as far as the variables which he discusses are concerned. He had to assume that the Tsembaga and Maring are relatively isolated and constitute a population in dynamic balance with its environment. The empirical data clearly suggest that his assumptions are not valid.

We cannot automatically assume the ecosystem to be a closed system, but how to deal with the effects of exogenous factors remains unresolved. With thermodynamic closure, where there are no outside connections, no processes can occur and progress is towards a state of maximum entropy, or disorganization. Theoretically, then, analytical closure is the only kind we can imagine. In practice, as we move from mechanical to organic systems we move to increasing openness, and human social systems are the most open of all. The more connections there are in a system, the more sources of inputs, external stimuli and therefore of organization (Langton 1973:140). Although human systems may sometimes be seen to maintain a degree of systemic integrity, they are almost invariably engaged, to a greater or lesser extent, in transactions with an ambiguously demarcated wider environment. They receive information which may modify their operation and alter their output. Since material exchanges rarely, if ever, discontinue abruptly at any border, it is usually necessary – as we have seen – to demarcate ecosystem boundaries more-or-less arbitrarily, with reference to the research problem at hand. For example, the territory of a local group can usually be considered an ecosystem. It is sometimes useful to see a population as encompassing two ecosystems, or to break the ecosystem down into its composite biotopes.

EQUILIBRIUM MODELS

One of the most vociferous criticisms of the systems approach is of its alleged concern with static equilibrium, with balance and symmetry between culture and resources.

The equilibrium notion is found in several guises. At its crudest it is expressed in such phrases as 'ultimate ecological adjustment' and 'man must be a balanced part of nature if he is to survive on earth' (Watson and Watson 1969:14, 131). Such trite statements explain nothing, nor does unspecified talk of 'ecological stress'. In its more insidious form such language, like the earlier functionalism, has been employed in support of conservative and eugenic ideologies. The democratic process is seen as a regulatory mechanism, while ecological populations are regarded as being 'essentially democratic'. Birth control is not advised, on the grounds that it reduces the more intelligent and 'prudent' members of society. One source of such dangerous nonsense is Dice, for whom 'only by cooperation and by mutual tolerance and respect among its economic and social classes can a community achieve the highest success' (1955:106). Fortunately most recent work is not as naive as this, and is less blatantly ideological.

As a description of empirical phenomena, the concept of ecological balance is at best highly relative and at worst misleading. The notion of a perfectly balanced ecosystem is incompatible with the empirical evidence for species extinction, population depletion and under-nutrition. While approximate balance may be the result of short-term adaptive processes, no biological mechanism is perfect. The isolated populations traditionally studied by anthropologists might seem to fit such a model rather well, but even in relatively closed small-scale populations there is evidence that this balance is frequently upset – through innovations, migration, conflict and resource depletion. The more complex ecosystems become the less equilibrium assumptions hold true.

It has been suggested by some that because it is a closed-system energy concept, the notion of system equilibrium should be restricted to thermodynamics and mechanics (Wilden 1972:139). Among biologists, Holling (1973:2) finds that equilibrium models provide

little insight into the transient behaviour of systems that are not near the equilibrium. Natural, undisturbed systems are likely to be continually in a transient state; they will be equally so under the influence of man. As man's numbers and economic demands increase, his use of resources shifts equilibrium states and moves populations away from equilibria. The present concerns for pollution and endangered species are specific signals that the well-being of species is not adequately described by concentrating on equilibrium and conditions near them.

Nature is not, then, in a state of balance but is subject to periodic upsets, due to climatic and other geographical processes. And if all systems fluctuate to varying degrees then the extent to which they can be relied upon as regulatory systems also varies.

Holling has suggested that a useful insight might be obtained by viewing the behaviour of ecological systems in terms of the probability of extinction of their elements, and by shifting emphasis from equilibrium states to the conditions for their persistence. In earlier work equating stability with systems behaviour, it had been argued that stability is approximately proportional to the number of links between species in a trophic web, that stability and diversity go together (Holling 1973:17–18). This is a view that has been accepted by anthropologists and has implications for the work of such writers as

Geertz (1963), Rappaport (1968) and D. R. Harris (1969, 1973). In ecology this has caused confusion since, in mathematical analysis, stability has tended to assume definitions which relate to conditions near equilibrium points, a simple convenience dictated by the analytical difficulties of treating the behaviour of non-linear systems at some distance from equilibrium (Holling 1973:17). Moreover, a recent analysis by May (1973) has indicated that even on a linear model the probability of stability generally decreases with an increase in the degree of connectedness among the parts of a system. It seems that randomly assembled complex systems are generally less stable (never more stable) than less complex ones, and fluctuate much more (Holling 1973:19). Though systems always tend towards stability in accordance with the second law of thermodynamics, no ecosystem is actually stable. Systems fluctuate over time and this can be theoretically measured.

To avoid these difficulties Holling (1973:17) has suggested that we redefine ecological systems in terms of the distinct properties of resilience and stability. Resilience is that which

determines the persistence of relationships within a system and is the measure of the ability of these systems to absorb changes of state variables, and parameters, and still persist . . . resilience is the property of the system and persistence or probability of extinction is the result.

Stability then becomes

the ability of a system to return to an equilibrium state after a temporary disturbance. The more rapidly it returns, and with the least fluctuation, the more stable it is . . . stability is the property of the system and the degree of fluctuation around specific states the result.

These definitions allow a system to be very resilient and still fluctuate greatly, that is, have a lower stability. Simple systems, such as those dominated by plant cultivation, may be stable for very long periods as long as major changes do not occur. If they do change then the system lacks resilience and may rapidly collapse. It appears that it is this which Geertz, Rappaport and Harris are concerned with. Equilibrium processes keep the system from fluctuating too much while resilience acts to prevent the system's self-destruction, to ensure that it persists. Fluctuating systems may therefore be more advantageous under certain conditions. Vayda and McCay (1975) suggest that we should shift from equilibrium studies to resilience studies.

The capacity of an ecological system to remain stable depends on its diversity and interconnections. Diversity, which to a certain extent must be linked with generalized systems (Chapter 4), might be expected to permit more rapid and smoother switches in strategies, given resource depletion of particular resources or other technical, social or economic hazards in subsistence appropriation, production and exchange. Netting (1968) describes how the Kofyar of central Nigeria, with access to vacant plains land, were able to switch from terracing, basin listing and managing on homestead farms to swiddening, depending upon the state of hostilities with neighbouring peoples. Similarly, I argue below (pp. 196–9) that the structure of trading networks and subsistence patterns in the Moluccas over several hundreds of years has permitted a switching between rice and local sago, trade in spices and subsistence production, depending on political forces controlling the character of the spice trade. Such systems have managed to maintain their general structure and therefore might be said to possess the characteristic of resilience.

Despite the persuasive elegance of such hypotheses, the link between diversity and stability has not been consistently supported by empirical findings, and the relationship is unlikely to be a simple one (Goodman 1975:238–9). There has been no experimental or mathematical demonstration that complex predator–prey systems involving many organisms are more stable than simple systems. For example, ecological studies in tropical forests are quite inadequate to show that extreme fluctuations do not occur; in fact there is some evidence to suggest that they may be quite violent. Furthermore, the mathematical theory is weak, and some other measure of diversity is necessary before the arguments become convincing.

One kind of diversity – habitat heterogeneity – does suggest a link with stability. This is measured by the number of resource clusters available to an organism. Any non-uniformity which separates the future condition of one segment of the population from another should decrease the probability of simultaneously bad periods (May 1974). Similarly, a vast array of interconnections in a system opens up alternative pathways for energy, material and information flow in the event of blockage of normal routes, buffering unexpected changes in the environment. Increasing interconnectedness does seem to stabilize a system, but, when couplings become so complex that routes are opened between all or most parts of a system, change in one part is more easily relayed elsewhere, removing the advantages of buffering. The phenomenon of too many connections resulting in rapid transfer of local environmental problems has been called by Flannery (1972:40) 'hypercoherence'. It is found typically in complex political systems. However, since over-connectedness may also have beneficial effects (Hardesty 1977:43–5), it cannot be treated as a general condition and must be related to a specific problem.

Environment, subsistence and system

Closed systems in dynamic equilibrium logically depend upon negative feedback for their maintenance. Both equilibrium assumptions and the notion of negative feedback have formed the backdrop for recent work on the cultural regulation of environmental relations, where it is argued that equilibrium is maintained through homeostasis.

Critics of equilibrium models have seen such analyses as an unwelcome historical development of sociological functionalism, and have labelled them with such implictly pejorative epithets as 'neo-functional ecology' (Friedman 1974:455), the 'new functionalism' (Murphy 1970:164), and 'ecological functionalism'. At least in terms of British anthropology, environmental relations were at last brought fully and acceptably within the realm of social theory. Earlier sociological functionalism had either been openly dismissive of their relevance, or regarded them as theoretically insignificant. Certainly, sociological ethnography had treated the environment as peripheral, giving rise only to constraints; now it was at the forefront of the ecological argument. After all, social anthropologists had also claimed to be interested in 'systems', although, with the possible exception of Parsons, they had been inclined to use the word loosely or as a synonym for ontologically similar kinds of social relations. Whereas functionalists had previously been concerned to demonstrate the rational character of the institutions of those societies under examination, they were now concerned to show the rationality of institutions with respect to their environment. Friedman (1974:455) has noted that, in their most modest form, such analyses dissolve into pure description, telling us that the function of x is what it does; while more sophisticated attempts at explanation make claims for the adaptation of societies which are acutely problematic. The trend finds its apogee in notions of 'control hierarchy' as applied to social systems; that is, where special-purpose institutions adopt a more general regulatory purpose with respect to the wider system of which they are part. In the Tsembaga case the ritual cycle is the control hierarchy, reinforced by unfalsifiable sanctifying propositions (Rappaport 1971b:71).

In the various ecological re-analyses of *potlatch* ceremonial exchanges in the societies of the Amerindian northwest (e.g. Piddocke 1965), we are never told if the institution operates to transfer food from rich to poor groups. If the potlatch functioned to equalize distribution it would be necessary for food automatically to be transferred from areas of high to low productivity. For Friedman (1974:459), a critical weakness of functionalism is that it identifies the rationality of elements while ignoring the rationality of systems. If, by negative feedback, we are to understand those variables which maintain others within crucial limits through further variables whose function is dependent upon reaching such limits, then Rappaport's Tsembaga data (for example) do not support this interpretation. Rappaport suggests that the principal limit is the point when stress on women builds up. He indicates that his evidence suggests that it is this which triggers the cycle. His explanation assumes, however, that it is the ritual cycle which regulates labour and not the reverse. If labour is regarded as the dependent variable instead of being constant then it is social relations which determine the limit of labour input. Sahlins (1971) has shown that women's labour is much nearer the minimum. Rather, it is often exchange relations which control the size of pig herds. The environmental limit is not involved at all and the cycle is triggered below carrying capacity. While it is valid to describe the ritual cycle as keeping the pig population below a certain level, it does not follow that it is necessarily a homeostatic mechanism. For this to be so a relationship between the limit and the triggering of the cycle has to be demonstrated. Causal statements must follow rational ones.

There are more general problems with the notion of feedback. Feedback loops involving animal behaviour are less complicated to describe than those involving human behaviour. The number of purely behavioural elements in the loop is generally limited in the first place, as are the intrinsic behavioural factors affecting the performance of the loop. In *Homo sapiens* the complexity of social relations and the dominance of culture makes it difficult to isolate simple uncontaminated loops, which are not interrelated and subordinate to others. Homeostasis is too simple a concept to account for the complexity of learning, adaptation and dynamic process in human and social systems. The number of feedback loops in human systems is almost infinite and no particular feedback loop is inevitable. This hardly provides for the high degree of closure which negative feedback requires if it is to be effective.

But there is something to be salvaged from the notion of negative feedback if it is used simply as a description of a structural state of affairs and is shorn of the implication of purposive cybernetic regulation. As an ethnographic case in point, Burnham (1979) has contended that for the Gbaya of east central Cameroon, ease of residential mobility is a major element in 'triggering' a causal cycle which results in the maintenance of a complex conservative nexus of social relations. It is this process that, for Burnham, relieves pressure on individual autonomy which might otherwise lead to structural transformation. He sees residential mobility serving as a regulator but, rather than being the end product of a process of adaptation, it is no more than the effect of a particular arrangement of variables within given limits.

The openness of human systems is in part related to the complexity of objective linkages between components, but, more important, it is related to the character of information flow. An ecology of human social relations cannot just consider the mechanistic properties of objective systems, it must also take into account

> patterns of purposive behavior involving a matching of resources with objectives, a transforming of natural phenomena in order to meet these objectives, and a capacity to think about this process objectively without actually going through the physical steps. This form of behavior also contains the capability of becoming aware of the disturbances created by humans in the milieu, and how these might be avoided if there is evidence of danger.
>
> (Bennett 1976:35)

From this it follows that much human behaviour regulating environmental relations is conscious, taking the form of spontaneous decision making and innovation, triggered by autonomous direct action, compulsion, persuasion or manipulation. Most techniques of population control and ritual measures of resource conservation can be adequately explained in this way, although they may well be enmeshed in a web of values and beliefs. For the most part, it is necessary to invoke homeostatic mechanisms only secondarily. Although the latter may sometimes emerge in isolated populations when the historical sequence of events has reached a stable phase, there is no foolproof mechanism linking conscious planning and Malthusian checks (Bennett 1976:259).

Rappaport does not appear to have considered this distinctive characteristic of information flow in human systems, or realized that overt communications and rational decision making are perhaps an important part of feedback processes. He seems to want to find his regulator at some covert level below the interplay of human discourse and actual behaviour, rather than in Tsembaga social organization, suggesting that feedback states are maintained without conscious awareness of underlying consequences and causes by the actors. Rappaport might reply that he has not neglected purpose or intention, and knows full well that actors are aware of the specific effects of their actions, if not of the long-term balance, but that the processes (whether perceived or unperceived) have systemic properties. Without more details, it is impossible to resolve the problem (Bennett 1976:184). But it is difficult to see how Tsembaga rituals function serendipitously as controls, and to discover whether or not they were developed for this purpose. Nor is it clear whether the members of the society are aware of the functions of their ritual. If such subliminal regulations exist they have not been sufficiently effective to maintain control over populations and resources for long historical periods, to prevent systems from abuse and overuse (Bennett 1976:52, 62). It is odd that something as mundane as the size of a pig population should be regulated through indirect, automatic, higher-order symbolic and ritual communication (Rappaport 1971b). Certainly it would be more effective to have such things under rational conscious control (Bennett 1976:205–6).

CAUSE AND EFFECT

The underlying theoretical weakness of much of the work claiming to find non-meditated cultural regulation of environmental relations is the logical fallacy of demonstrating that certain practices have effects and then assuming that this is their purpose, either in the conscious minds of sentient human beings or in terms of some evolutionary dynamic. It is, of course, the fallacy of functionalism. Showing how things work is explaining neither why they came about nor why they persist. It does not provide a causal explanation (Friedman 1974). Shoulder-blade divination among the Naskapi may indeed serve to randomize the selection of hunting localities and as a consequence prevent depletion of caribou herds (Moore 1965), but to suggest that it is done for this reason is a more complex matter. Likewise, the Miyanmin may well have a protein problem, but to describe their activities as a coordinated response to it is, following the apt analogy of Vayda and McCay (1977:44), like saying that celibacy in Catholic priests is a response to a problem of venereal disease. The occurrence of Tsembaga pig feasts may have the effect of limiting environmental deterioration, but this does not explain why the feasts occur. While warfare may have ecological consequences which, in environmental terms, are regulatory, this does not necessarily explain specific outbreaks of war as a phenomenon; any more than the fact that warfare depends upon and channels the aggressiveness of individuals (which may or may not be imperative) denotes it as an expression of a territorial instinct. Analysis may show how a trait functions under particular conditions, but this is not to present an explanation of historical origins, to be able to predict future behaviour, nor necessarily to see a trait in its entire functional perspective, in relation either to environment or to social relations.

GROUP ADAPTATION

Anthropologists adopting a systems-regulation approach have drawn heavily on the notion of group adaptation developed by Wynne-Edwards (1962). However, the idea that ecological systems are somehow natural entities, units of adaptation, with survival strategies like individual organisms and operating in a self-regulatory and self-determining way is now rejected by many ecologists and zoologists. I have already pointed out that it is empirically difficult to discover discrete ecosystems, let alone ecosystems with self-organizing properties (cf. Vayda and McCay 1975:14). The question of closure is crucial. If systems are not closed then their existence is more a matter of analytic convenience than any reflection of their existence as objective biological entities.

If we assume that group adaptation and selection are valid for animal populations, to what extent can they be applied to *Homo sapiens*? The problem is that human population-control methods are essentially social and not genetic. While certain conventions may maintain population balance under certain circumstances, changed circumstances will not automatically create a new optimum. The only ultimate check is starvation. New technology may allow for a higher population density, but not necessarily. Many societies have a low population density in otherwise rich environments (Douglas 1966). Here there may be other proximate limiting factors, such as disease (Woodburn 1972) or social conventions which act as birth-control methods. However, few populations actually maintain optimum populations and are either comfortably within their limits or at them. This is simply because of constant changes, population movement and so on. So if there are homeostatic mechanisms they work rather ineffectively.

Another problem specifically related to the concept of adaptation through homeostasis is that it is defined in negative terms, in terms of the compatibility with environmental conditions. To insist that the potlatch is adaptive, points out Sahlins (1969:30), is a weak form of functionalism which accounts merely for its feasibility rather than its existence.

As we have seen in Chapter 4, it is not difficult, with a little ingenuity, to describe the most seemingly pointless, wasteful or exotic cultural practice as rational or adaptive in some way. Much the same may be said for the more specific notion of adaptive homeostasis. This is in part due to a concentration on synchronic analysis. But simply because a system functions it does not make it adaptive. In many systems studies of adaptation, the links between the variables are just

too good and the feedback controls too smooth to be quite real in a
world where failure and waste are essential parts of continuing evolution (W. C. Clarke 1977:366).

CHANGE AND POSITIVE FEEDBACK

Human populations and their various social arrangements and cultural regularities are in a constant state of flux, coping with new
environmental problems by 'disturbing' rather than maintaining systems. It is therefore not necessary to determine *whether* a population is
changing, but to determine *how* and at what rate. The critique of
equilibrium models and homeostasis is very much tied to the observation and accusation that this simple point is not always grasped by
those who investigate socio-ecological systems. Indeed, the theory
itself sometimes seems inadequate to cope with the possibility of
change, specifying the change as an interruption of stability rather
than the other way round. Homeostasis (based on an assumption of
non-temporal relations) in effect reduces all change to mechanical
oscillation and endless repetition (Waddington 1970:1–32, Wilden
1972:140). Moreover, in ignoring historical change, the question of
origins is also neglected. In one sense this might be held to be
irrelevant since the function of an element in a present system may
bear little relation to its part in the circumstances of its genesis. However, if we are to posit that certain institutions and practices have adapted
to serve a particular function then we must at least supply a plausible
explanation as to how this came about. Rappaport (1971a:261) has
admitted that how the regulatory elements of Maring cosmology develop remains a profound mystery.

Now, there is nothing in the basic tenets of systems theory, or in the
study of systems and their operation, which is inimical to a consideration of change. This is quite clear from theoretical discussions of the
notion of 'positive feedback', by which is meant the cumulative effect
of feedback processes in amplifying the deviations of a system in a
particular direction away from a pre-existing goal (Maruyama 1963).
Positive feedback is to be distinguished from maturation changes, such
as the process of socialization, ageing and the developmental cycle of
domestic groups, which may operate to maintain a steady state. It has
been suggested that it is a basic property of social systems that
processes of uncontrolled feedback begun by an exogenous stimulus
will eventually, if undisturbed for long enough, become negative, as
the system progresses from morphogenesis to homeostasis (Langton
1973:150).

Positive feedback and so-called dysfunctions in socio-ecological systems have received less theoretical and empirical attention than negative feedback and homeostasis (Anderson 1973:199). A concern with inter-species relations and system-maintaining devices has encouraged the neglect of the empirical investigation of fundamental but potentially system-destroying contradictions between material and social pressures, as between forces and relations of production specified in terms of 'the limit of . . . functional compatibility between structures' (Friedman 1974:446–8), which set the limits on the development and stability of the system as a whole. One of the reasons for the neglect of such processes is that, while effective negative feedback requires a high degree of closure, positive feedback logically requires more open systems. Systems approaches in anthropology have generally assumed a high degree of closure for the systems being studied, and therefore it is logically difficult to see how changes might take place. Moreover, functional (and certainly functionalist) analyses have a built-in tendency to play down dysfunction. In all systems analysed explanation is marred by the existence of maladaptive aspects which are conveniently ignored. For example, whatever Harris may claim to be the case at the village level, viewed nationally, Indian sacred cows are undeniably dysfunctional (Heston 1971).

Some studies employing the notion of positive feedback do exist, and others have been stimulated by the critique. Vayda, who has been among those criticized, has noted in his defence that he has always warned against automatic assumptions that systems always interact to the advantage of human populations, and, tautologically, that because they do so they are necessarily the best possible system (Vayda 1969:117; Vayda and McCay 1975). He argues that, on the contrary, ecosystem studies can lead to the analysis of imbalance and dynamism. Among those analyses explicitly concerned with positive feedback, ecological instability and disruption are Rappaport (1971c, 1977a), Lee (1969), Flannery (1972) and Vayda (1970, 1974). More recently, David Harris (1977) has shown how an initial change in one variable amplified through the socio-economic system of a small mobile band of hunters of migratory herd ungulates results in a larger population which establishes a new equilibrium based on a broader-spectrum pattern of resource use while remaining residentially mobile. This self-amplifying process of subsistence and demographic change is illustrated in Figure 1.3.

Other studies have been ethnographically and historically more focussed. For example, a model of this kind is helpful in explaining the relationship of the appropriation of starch from the *Metroxylon* palm to growth and fluctuation in the production and trade in nutmeg, mace and cloves from the sixteenth century onwards in the Moluccas (Ellen

1979). The model assumes an elementary self-subsisting economy (EMSU) which is progressively drawn into increasingly wider exchange systems and, as a result, larger and more complex modes of production, exchanges and total reproduction. When matched to the data it shows how local patterns cannot be understood except in relation to progressive ecological change and external links, as relatively independent populations were absorbed into more extensive systems, through local polities, petty states, Javanese and European hegemony, and finally total colonial control.

The first phase of the model is dominated, for the most part, by simple relations of production. Small amounts of spices are collected and exchanged for a variety of material items: valuables in particular, and usually not food. The process steadily accelerates as external demand for spices and internal requirements for the valuables of traditional local exchanges increase. This results in a second formative exchange phase, recognized by an upswing in the level of production and the full domestication of spice trees. Trade becomes of increasing political significance to both producers and traders. The control of the growing volume of commodities by individuals and small kinship groups forms a growth-point for class differentiation. The process is amplified through external support for indigenous rulers through whose hands the trade passes. A mature phase is marked by a further increase in the scale of cultivation and, most important, growth in the local trade of foodstuffs, particularly sago, along traditional communication routes into areas hitherto self-sufficient. On the way, further subsistence populations are drawn into the trade system. There is a corresponding growth in the population of spice-producing areas. Growth continues in spice production, local trade in food staples and population. The pattern is consolidated and the communities are drawn within a global exchange sphere of which they are a quasi-dependent element. This phase of consolidation is characterized by two self-amplifying loops of dependence, more generally a feature of those emerging relations of unequal exchange which result in under-development. These are illustrated in Figure 8.1. In the first loop (a) the increasing area devoted to production for exchange leads to more intensive use of available land for subsistence crops but eventually a net decrease in land available and output of production for use. This, in turn, leads to more reliance on production for exchange and consequently to a further expansion of production activities in this sector. The second loop (b) is functionally similar but concerns human effort. As more time and labour are devoted to cultivation for exchange, so there is a drop in subsistence production. Under other conditions this might be directly related to increasing inputs of labour in the exchange

(a) LAND

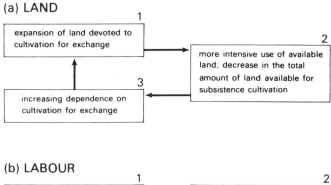

(b) LABOUR

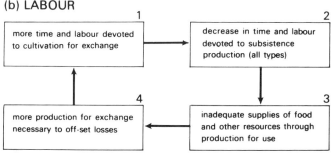

8.1 Self-amplifying loops in the process of integrating local economies into wider systems of exchange (Ellen 1979:45)

sector. However, the increased effort required in this case is minimal. What seems most significant in accelerating the cycle is the relatively high return for labour compared with subsistence production.

The processes described above may be partly modified by shifts in technical arrangements, and in the social division of labour, but ultimately decisions are made which result in the allocation of progressively less effort to subsistence crops. Less subsistence activity results in a drop in the level of production for use, which in turn leads to more production for exchange to make up losses of food in the subsistence sector.

Now while these loops may be operating in their classic form in particular localities and at the level of gross generalization, the traditional Moluccan pattern of subsistence based on sago, and the peculiar trade nexus which developed, significantly altered their shape and the rate at which they were circuited. Subsistence on sago delayed and altered the character of the dependent relationship by preventing the immediate depletion of arable land, rapid deforestation and competition over land between subsistence and trade crops. The relative drainage of resources in particular areas was offset by local trade in sago along traditional pathways. It was only the intervention of European mercantilism and capitalism to break this trading network which increased the speed of change in the direction of dependency and which resulted in chronic ecological instability. These processes are summarily diagrammed in Figure 8.2, loop 3–4–5 representing the potential ability of the system to delay the onset of dependency.

A late exchange phase is characterized by a rapid decline in the trade in spices in the context of an artificial control of spice production and trade. Local trading is resumed, alleviating to some degree the problems of unequal resource distribution. The system becomes a relatively stable, but deteriorating, combination of dependency and self-sufficiency until the mid-nineteenth century. From this period onwards, there is a gradual resumption and geographical extension of the processes dominant in the formative and mature exchange phases.

Sago subsistence both allowed for the rapid growth of clove production and prevented the immediate negative economic consequences that are usually associated with rapid expansion of agricultural production for the exchange of crops that have no local subsistence value. The communities were able to tolerate the erratic and wide fluctuations in spice production and sales. However, it was precisely sago dependence, plus external pressure, that paradoxically maintained and increased the rate of expansion of clove production in some specific localities, such that an initially adaptive pattern finally proved inadequate. On the small islands heavily involved in spice production, the system adjusted to the depletion of traditional subsistence resources by importing food, particularly sago, from other islands less directly involved in the spice trade. However, this made the communities still more dependent on clove production, although they were partly cushioned through payment in locally produced commodities rather than imported items and food.

SYSTEMS LANGUAGE, CONCEPTS AND REPRESENTATIONS

Among the criticisms of systems approaches is that they are doing no more than dressing up existing theoretical ideas in new jargon. Jargon can be confusing at the best of times, but systems theorists themselves do not use terms uniformly or define them in the same way. There is confusion between analytical and thermodynamic closure. Similarly, 'system', for some, refers to the variables and 'environment' to parameters; for others 'system' is the variables plus the parameters, and 'environment' those factors external to the system influencing the values given to parameters (Langton 1973:130, 160). Some of the jargon transferred from general systems theory and natural science to sociological discourse is arguably sufficiently confusing, without making it

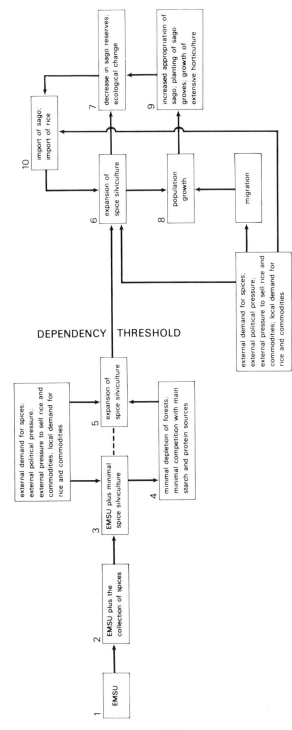

8.2 A general model of aspects of ecological and economic change in the Moluccas (Ellen 1979:46)

200

doubly so by transferring terminological muddles as well. Likewise, flow diagrams can be illuminating, but they are only as useful as the information put into them. Some complex diagrams and catch-all boxes seem hardly worth the effort and ingenuity required in their creation. They give the illusion of accuracy and comprehensiveness and an impression that the cells somehow constitute real bounded entities. The problem is compounded by cells whose content is unexamined or unknown – the so-called 'black box'. A common set of representations has suggested that systems approaches are truly interdisciplinary. But the elements of a system selected and emphasized still reflect the disciplinary bias of the investigator. Thus, those whose primary interest is not 'social organization' tend to lump this in a single box (e.g. Bayliss-Smith 1977a:328) and underplay the systemic connections between different social factors and their interrelationship with various environmental variables.

There is also sometimes a blurring of concepts drawn from different bodies of theory. General systems theory, ecological theory, systems analysis (that is, empirical attempts to discover interdependences or energy flows), organic functionalist and mechanical equilibrium approaches are to varying degrees conflated and confused with each other. These are not the same and the implications of applying them to human systems vary.

SYSTEMS AS FRAMEWORKS AND EXPLANATION

Not only is the analysis of systems remote because of its language, but it has also been suggested that its relevance to specific empirical investigations is limited. Approaches from general systems theory inevitably lead to conclusions versed in terms of formal theoretical statements about the properties of different types of system, emphasizing the theory of systems rather than systems themselves (Langton 1973:127). The testability and predictive usefulness of some of the models used to date is severely limited. In anthropology, systems frameworks have been developed largely with reference to microsystems which have been assumed to be highly integrated. Such an approach, even if adequate for small, closed, rapidly disappearing systems, cannot readily be extended to more complex systems, with their many subsystems and exceptions (Bennett 1976:184, 234). Considerable modification is required. Even biologists have come to the conclusion that mathematical systems models cannot account for certain organic processes, partly because of the specificity and opportunism of evolution (Slobodkin 1961:81).

To indicate the limitations of models is not necessarily to criticize their usefulness, but merely to point out the considerable difficulties involved in putting uncontrolled feedback models into operation. Thus, although many interesting properties of feedback systems can be ascertained if it is assumed that one variable is independent, auto-correlation among the error terms of the equation can give rise to difficulties in application, and is only really feasible if regression slopes are linear (Langton 1973:166–8). While it is a relatively simple exercise to draw double-headed arrows for reciprocal causation and insert arrows feeding back to the original independent variable, it is another matter to test these theories in a definitive way. Considerable method-ological sophistication is needed to formulate and test more complex theories (Langton 1973:164). The problems are of two kinds: (1) devis-ing techniques to translate data into terms relevant to the theories, and (2) collecting the necessary data in the first place. In the analysis of systems, as in other areas of social and economic theory, our techniques are growing faster than our capacity to collect relevant data.

For some writers it has been sufficient that a systems approach supply a framework or perspective, and serve as a general set of organizing principles, or as an *aide-mémoire* in data collection, a means to avoid the 'existential dilemmas' between emphasizing synthesis or analysis, theory or observation, generalization or specificity. That it should provide explanations has not always been demanded or expected. Others, while recognizing that it may indeed have explanatory power, hold that it is not primarily aimed at the formulation of generally applicable theory but may simply define boundaries and generate an awareness of the linkages between the components of historically specified societies (e.g. Geertz 1963).

Despite all the problems, systems approaches have undeniably led to a greater awareness of the limits imposed by variables on other variables, and of the possibility of contradictions between elements or subsystems (Friedman 1974:460). At the same time, systems theory can provide an integrated framework for the analysis of change and for directing the search for explanations (Langton 1973:170), but without making assumptions as to the character, direction or implications of specific causes. In this sense the system is much more than just a framework to be filled out with data, a means of sustaining an abstract empiricism. In most science, as practised, it is the specific correlations which are the testable elements of theories and which are subject to refutation. But the system is a model which is not subject to refutation after the fashion of simple correlation. That the model reflects an objective reality depends on its general utility in explanation and prediction. If it is not useful, then it can be said to falsify reality

(Watson and Watson 1969:140–1). In this sense the Popperian condition is met. Generalizations can be extracted on the basis of the model, checked and used as a test for the validity of the model, requiring its adjustment or rejection.

9

Information and the manipulation of the environment

> Man's contact with nature has never been direct; it has always been mediated through knowledge structures via his senses and his intellect. We have no other means of knowing the world around us.
>
> Moscovici 1976:145

INTRODUCTION

Most of the older formulations of the ecological problematic ignore the theoretical significance of human *interpretation* of the environment, treat it as irrelevant or assign it to some unexamined (perhaps unexaminable) 'black box' which mysteriously mediates between humans and their environment. It was generally assumed that social organization and culture responded mechanistically to environmental stimuli. The impact of the capacity and limitations of *Homo sapiens* in interpreting the environment, handling information in complex ways and using information to direct behaviour went unappreciated; as did the fact that societies, groups and individuals see their environment in noticeably different ways, with varying implications for ecological interactions. This was so even for possibilism, despite its stress on the explanatory priority of social behaviour and collective representations.

Systems approaches provide a convenient theoretical means of understanding the function and effects of environmental perception. Information, energy and materials are distinct interacting and integral components of a system, although, in the last instance, information is dependent on some physical base. In social systems, flows of matter and energy link and articulate physical elements, and information does likewise for their images (Langton 1973:132). The sensed environment is no more than the sum total of images of material things, largely organized through categories, and is the source of all information. In the analysis of exchanges within a population it may be analogous to the 'memory' of a computer in an automated system, primarily concerned with the regulation, control and triggering of energy in the interests of a goal.

The simplest information is transmitted chemically, as in the action of a genetically coded enzyme in transforming one protein into another. Much information regulation in living systems, including human behaviour, is of this type, and is often linked to negative feedback circuits. Thus, if intense light hits the retina information is transmitted to the brain which responds by contracting the pupil. This reduces the amount of light, and things return to normal. But what is distinctive about humans is the capacity of the brain to manage *semiotic* information, comprising learned abstract signs. Because of this, the relationship between energy and information is a highly complex one. For example, the minute amount of energy needed to send certain simple messages may be quite disproportionate to their behavioural consequences. Huge amounts of energy can be released through information flows, without the spatial and temporal proximity found in simpler systems (Wilden 1972:142).

Learning itself well illustrates another characteristic process of information systems, namely feedback. The ear picks up sound signs which are recorded by the brain. This stored information enables a growing child to communicate through speech, which itself increases the ability to acquire still more speech signs. Learning a language is therefore a self-amplifying process, although it may also involve cybernetic loops which correct inaccurate information, both internally and through external communicators, such as teachers.

Signs (and symbols) are the most important kind of information storage and communication used by *Homo sapiens*. They are superior to chemical means, in terms of the potential complexity of messages, and in overcoming space and time limitations (as in telecommunications and written records). Also, humans learn rapidly and may quickly enlarge and correct environmental knowledge. Similar techniques are found in animal populations, but they generally lack the ability to link signs in original premeditated ways. Human beings possess this ability through language, which profoundly affects all means of communication (Sebeok 1970:614–27). It consequently affects ecological relations. But we are not merely 'filters of information' about environmental conditions. Images of nature are always simpler than nature itself and therefore often an incorrect reflection of environmental reality. As information is perceived, recalled and transmitted from person to person, it changes perceptibly. In this sense cultural information flows are not as reliable or precise as chemical pathways, and as many theoretical constructions might suggest. Nevertheless, people's perception of their environment is a significant part of the complex mechanism producing the actual physical behaviour by which ecological relations are directly manipulated. In this chapter I review some of the attempts to understand how this takes place.

INTERPRETATIVE AND COGNITIVE MODELS

The distinction between what is objectively so and what is an indigenous construction has always been explicit to varying degrees in anthropology, and is by no means restricted to ecological studies (e.g. Kula 1968). It is given formal recognition in a number of contrasting terms. The world as described and understood from the point of view of the ethnographer has been variously called the interpretative, operational, observer's or analyst's model. The world as described and understood by the informant has been called the home-made, cognitive, cognized or folk model (see Ellen 1978b for references). The differences were first clearly distinguished with respect to environmental relations by Rappaport (1963:159, 1968:237), for whom the local environmental model is composed of all phenomena arranged into categories by a population. This is sometimes referred to as the perceived environment (Brookfield 1969). In general, and following Rappaport, I shall employ the terms 'interpretative' and 'cognitive'. In practice, they may overlap in their recognized elements, but they contrast radically in the way the elements are connected. This is what we might expect, since the discontinuities of the environment are so numerous and diverse that they permit many different cognitive constructions. To comprehend and make decisions with respect to the environment (or certain parts of it), it is necessary to superimpose a selective model of discontinuities, with artificial (and sometimes distorting) cultural boundaries to categories. In this way the natural environment is reworked in cultural terms (Douglas 1972).

It is because we see nature in terms of cultural images, and because it is to these that we respond, that a proper understanding of indigenous knowledge and cognitive structures is theoretically crucial to the analysis of ecological relations. And it is also because of this that, more than two decades ago, Harold Conklin began to urge us to adopt an *ethnoecological* approach and to study *ethnoecology* (Conklin 1954a, 1957:20). Conklin was adopting the prefix 'ethno-' to indicate that the area of knowledge specified was that of the observed rather than of the observer. In this sense, we understand ethnobiology as 'the study of human conceptualization and classification of plants and animals, and knowledge and belief concerning biological processes' (Bulmer

1975:9). Generically, the different kinds of indigenous knowledge (e.g. ethnobotany, ethnoecology) have been subsumed by some under the term ethnoscience (Sturtevant 1964). It is perhaps unfortunate that this term has come to specify a quite separate methodology and approach to the analysis of cultural data.

In another, earlier (and probably more widely understood) sense, compound words such as ethnobotany, ethnohistory or ethno-geography refer to the general study of the botany, history or geography of a particular 'ethnic group' (Sturtevant 1964:99). Ethnobiology, for example, is thus concerned with 'The determination of the biological species, cultigens and cultivars which are of significance in human ecology, and the study of the ways these relate to men on the objective biological dimension' (Bulmer 1975:9). This meaning is reflected in the usage by some botanists, such as Barrau (e.g. 1965) and other scholars associated with the Laboratoire d'ethnobotanique, and geographers and archaeologists primarily concerned with problems of domestication (e.g. D. R. Harris 1973). Here it overlaps with the traditional interests of economic botany. Ethnoecology therefore refers to that body of knowledge concerning the interaction between a population and its environment, primarily meaning uses, practices and techniques.

Any comprehensive study of the environmental relations of a given human group must clearly involve both types or 'levels' of enquiry, and fortunately they have often been interfertile. However, and despite the fact that this is a more recent usage, I prefer to restrict terms such as ethnozoology to indicate the study of cognitive worlds. The main reason for this is that in the second sense the prefix is superfluous. It conveys as much information to talk about the history of a group as to talk about its ethnohistory. Similarly, many of the traditional concerns of ethnobotany are reflected in the concerns of economic botany. To avoid confusion, I use ethnoecology and its cognates in the first sense only.

THE ANALYSIS OF CLASSIFICATIONS AND ITS CRITIQUE

Much of the work conducted on cognitive models of the environment has been concerned with eliciting local categories for different parts of the environment, and how these are arranged in classifications. The importance of investigating these has been recognized for a long time (de Schlippe 1956: xvi, 37–47; Conklin 1967:207), but the main growth in interest has occurred during the last fifteen years. The literature on folk classifications is now large and expanding rapidly, as evidenced by Conklin's recent monumental bibliography (1972), the periodical bibliographies issued by CNRS, and various editions and readers (Tyler 1969, Ellen and Reason 1979). Among the most influential ethnographic studies have been those of Brent Berlin (1974) and Ralph Bulmer (1968, 1972–3, 1975) and their various co-workers. Much of this research has been conducted using specific eliciting techniques to discover and describe cognitive structures, some of which are claimed to be semantic universals.

This approach is largely the result of a convergence of interests in cognition, classification, linguistics and human relations with various elements of the environment. Many of its practitioners have been anthropologists trained in linguistics who were attracted by the apparent descriptive and predictive power of contemporary language analysis. Other work, primarily in the European Durkheimian tradition, has been more sociological. Its concern is with the congruence of classificatory structures and other collective representations and social practices and with the way in which society assimilates nature into itself. Some of the writings of Mary Douglas (1972) are a good example of this (and for a more detailed discussion of these contrasting approaches, see Ellen 1979a).

Parallel developments have meanwhile been taking place in geography. Here an interest in environmental perception can be traced back to the idea of *genres de vie*, to Ratzel and Vidal de la Blache (Sorre 1948), but the past decade or so has seen a particularly marked rise in the investigation of such issues. Some of this work has involved fieldwork in subsistence and peasant economies, and has been explicitly concerned with the kinds of data discussed later in this chapter (Brookfield 1968, Nietschmann 1973). Because of their interest in many of the same substantive problems, anthropologists and geographers have been able to profit from a considerable exchange of ideas and information. Elsewhere, studies have taken their inspiration more from qualitative notions of 'landscape' or have concentrated on psychologically influenced investigations of cognitive mapping and spatial behaviour, looking at spatial learning, urban perception, topographical orientation and distance concepts (Goodey 1971).

Much of the work undertaken on classifications, particularly that of a formalist character, has been subject to severe criticism. Nevertheless, if we are to evaluate the relevance of cognitive data for analyses of objective ecological relations, the various objections must be properly examined.

Some critics – and perhaps the most vociferous of these is Marvin Harris (1968:591–2, 1974; but see also Keesing 1973) – have claimed that some formal approaches have received a quite disproportionate quantum of attention given the profound triviality of their initial problems.

Information and the manipulation of the environment

It is suggested that there has been such an obsession with 'correct' methodology that content tends towards the banal, with articles being published in professional journals on such peripheral subjects as firewood categories (Berreman 1966:351). Moreover, the method itself is now beginning to look a little inadequate, viewed from recent developments in linguistics and classificatory studies (Keesing 1972, Ellen 1979a).

The kinds of formal techniques employed, and the acceptance of certain widespread ethnographic fallacies, have often given the impression that the classifications elicited are invariable. There is a hidden assumption of a high degree of homogeneity and stability in categorization. Cultural constructs are typically based on information from few informants, who are then held to be representative of *the* culture. One thing is certain: decisions about environmental relations are not made by some omniscient, omnipresent speaker–hearer, but by mere mortal individuals. Fortunately, we now realize that classifications are extremely flexible, vary considerably within a culture, contain different and contradictory organizational structures and appear generally pretty messy. But this is not to suggest that they are somehow without structure (Ellen 1979).

It has also been pointed out that stress on informants' verbal statements leads to idealistic, as opposed to realistic, descriptions of environmental phenomena, ones of little importance to actual behaviour (M. Harris 1968). There are two important points to unravel here, both about the relationship between theory and practice. First, words (or conscious recognition) do not necessarily reflect mental operations or practical mastery. They are therefore not always a reliable guide to the understanding of decision making (Burling 1964). Also, terms are notoriously difficult to translate, and the use of formal lexicographical definitions, which contrast beautifully, may nevertheless be misleading or even downright inaccurate. Overuse of local terms can lead to confusion and stultification. Secondly, there is a subtle distinction to be made between models *of* the environment and models *for* behaviour directed towards the environment. This is the difference, for example, between an ideal phylogenetically based plant taxonomy and the key of a flora. Models of the environment may be to varying degrees ideal, but they may still influence environmental behaviour. Where the analytical problem lies is in distinguishing between the two types of model and in not mistaking the ideal reconstruction by an ethnographer of 'a folk model' for the ideal conceptions which individual decision-makers possess, even less for practical guides to action.

If we assume that formal techniques reveal something of the rules and categories of choice relevant to an understanding of ecological relations, this does not exhaust an analysis of ethnoecology. It only tells us about classification (Vayda and Rappaport 1968:469). If, for instance, I were to describe how the Nuaulu discuss, explain and react to soil erosion, exposure and the effect of horticulture, this would be just as much a statement about Nuaulu ethnoecology as if I were to list in detail their categories for soils and minerals, the criteria for their recognition, and their arrangement in classifications. Ethnoecology cannot be based on local classificatory models alone, for they are intricately interrelated with a more discursive indigenous knowledge of environmental phenomena and the technical theory and practice associated with them.

Moreover, folk classifications, and other ethnoecological knowledge and practice, do not exist in isolation. Presented as such, they can easily become esoteric and meaningless. It is important to specify the social context of particular classifications, techniques, statements of knowledge and practice. General statements always lack a certain degree of credibility. The subject of variation has already been touched on, and we would do well to remember that informants (not always wilfully) provide data that are to varying degrees incomplete and inaccurate. Indigenous models (or even parts of them) can never be described completely, or with absolute veracity. This is partly due to the limitations of ethnographic method, but is also because they are in their very character inconstant. How much more impossible, then, is the recreation of total 'cognized worlds' of the structuralist or ethno-science variety, even if the mechanism by which they affected the operation of ecosystems could be demonstrated. Enormous amounts of information, drawn from the entire cosmology accessible to an individual, may affect his environmental interactions. Of this we can fully understand only a fraction.

Perhaps one final point should be mentioned in this section. In their review of anthropological ecology, Vayda and Rappaport (1968) note that concentration on perceived environments and cognitive models can result in failure to describe ecological processes and environmental relations of critical importance but which are not the subject of cognition. Such latent functions of behaviour may, it is suggested, facilitate population dispersion or resource utilization, as Rappaport claims is the case for certain Tsembaga rituals. The issues raised by such analyses have already been tackled in Chapter 8. It seems obvious that certain behaviours have ecological consequences that are not a result of conscious decison making. What we are concerned with here is something different: the way in which the cognitive organization of recognized environmental phenomena affects (consciously or unconsciously) ecological interactions.

Information and the manipulation of the environment

I shall return to some of these criticisms in the conclusion to this chapter. What I shall first try to show is how specific kinds of ethnoecological data might be of use in more conventional ecological analyses. In particular, I shall pay attention to ways in which it has been suggested that we might analyse how cultural rules, conventions and determinants transform information about the environment into practices which affect ecological relations.

THE RANGE AND RELEVANCE OF ETHNOECOLOGICAL DATA

Some idea of the range of ethnoecological information is provided by Table 9.1. The types of data listed are illustrative rather than exhaustive, while column headings and numbered sections are largely arbitrary and not mutually exclusive. For example, in many folk schemes topographic surfaces and vegetation types are combined into a single set. This is so with the Ifugao terms given in Table 9.2. There are also overlaps. Thus, certain plant diseases, such as insect infestations (A.6), would also be included in a listing of animal biology (A.4); while the suitability of different kinds of soils for different crops (C.3) is also an aspect of crop ecology (A.4) and cultivation techniques (A.5). The role of birds and mammals in the propagation and dispersal of plants might be listed under A.4 twice, for both plants and animals, and also under A.5. Further, in the light of some of the objections discussed in the previous section all these data must be understood as being subject to interindividual variation within a group, and as varying over time and according to changing contexts for the same individual. A final general point to note in connection with Table 9.1 is that all information is handled by an indigenous population in terms of local linguistic classifiers and units of measurement (numerals, units of weight, volume, length, value . . .). Consideration of such matters is an essential part of any ethnoecological study.

A cursory glance at the Conklin bibliography (1972) indicates the large amount of ethnoecological material now available, although many studies listed are very fragmentary. The most thoroughly worked area is ethnobiology, which includes the important work of Berlin on the Tzeltal plants of the highland Chiapas of Mexico, and Bulmer's work on Kalam vertebrate lore in highland New Guinea. However, the bulk of recent contributions have been made as minor adjuncts to more general projects undertaken by geographers and ethnographers of horticultural systems (e.g. Lea 1964). Some have been made by professional zoologists and botanists in connection with their own researches (Diamond 1966, Dwyer 1976). Analyses of soil

Table 9.1 An outline of the main kinds of ethnoecological data

A Plants (including fungi) and animals	B Rocks and minerals	C Soils
Both domesticated and non-domesticated species		
1. Names and total numbers of terminal categories known and recognized, names and numbers of categories in successively more inclusive groups; and compared with scientific designations for the same locality	1. Names and total numbers of terminal categories known and recognized, names and numbers of categories in successively more inclusive groups; and compared with scientific designations for the same locality	1. Names and total numbers of terminal categories known and recognized, names and numbers of categories in successively more inclusive groups; and compared with scientific designations for the same locality
2. Structure of classifications and types of cognitive device employed	2. Structure of classifications and types of cognitive devices employed	2. Structure of classifications and types of cognitive device employed
3. Uses:	3. Uses:	3. Uses: e.g. suitability for different kinds of crops
(a) food	(a) salt	4. Knowledge of properties and distribution of different soils and of their formation
(b) other economic uses e.g. artifacts	(b) other economic uses	5. Knowledge and techniques of soil management e.g. use of fertilizers
(c) medicinal	(c) social and mystical	6. Other beliefs related to soils
(d) social and mystical	4. Knowledge of properties and distribution of different rocks and minerals, rock formations and geological landscapes	
4. Knowledge of biology and ecology of different species e.g. life-histories, means of reproduction	5. Other beliefs related to rocks, minerals and geological formations	
5. Knowledge and techniques of animal and plant domestication, propagation and appropriation		
6. Knowledge of plant and animal diseases and their remedies		
7. Other beliefs related to animals and plants		

212

D Topographic surfaces (including aquatic)	E Land use and vegetation types (including aquatic)	F Meteorological features
1. Names and total numbers of terminal categories known and recognized, names and numbers of categories in successively more inclusive groups; and compared with scientific designations for the same locality	1. Names and total numbers of terminal categories known and recognized, names and numbers of categories in successively more inclusive groups; and compared with scientific designations for the same locality	1. Names and total numbers of terminal categories known and recognized, names and numbers of categories in successively more inclusive groups; and compared with scientific designations for the same locality e.g. cloud, rain and wind types
2. Structure of classifications and types of cognitive device employed	2. Structure of classifications and types of cognitive device employed	2. Structure of classifications and types of cognitive device employed
3. Uses: e.g. suitability for different kinds of crops and settlement locations	3. Uses: e.g. suitability for cutting for gardens and as locations for different kinds of resource	3. Uses: e.g. suitability of different weather regimes for various crops
4. Knowledge of properties and distribution of different surfaces and geomorphological features	4. Knowledge of structure, properties and distribution of different vegetation types, and their formation	4. Knowledge of meteorological process and effects, spatial distribution of forms and temporal occurrence
5. Knowledge and techniques of topographic management and manipulation e.g. erosion control, irrigation	5. Knowledge and techniques of wild vegetation management and manipulation e.g. cutting forest	5. Knowledge and techniques of weather management e.g. forecasting and flood control
6. Other beliefs related to land and water forms	6. Other beliefs related to vegetation types	6. Other beliefs concerning weather forms

knowledge are fewer. Some general studies (Rappaport 1968) have included relevant details, while a number of more specific treatments exist, for example, the analysis by Ollier, Drover and Godelier (1971) of actual samples in relation to soil categories and knowledge of the Baruya of the New Guinea highlands. Much the same applies to the examination of topographic surfaces, vegetation types and land use (Conklin 1957, 1968, Ellen 1978), and rocks and minerals (Ellen 1978).

What is known and how we classify are important because they have consequences for the way in which we use the environment. In assessing factors delimiting energy, protein or other sources for a particular population, perception and desirability are as important as spatial availability, seasonality, dependability and productivity. Cultural considerations may encourage utilization of some resources while discouraging others. For example, local classifications may determine what is considered food, and the scale, intensity and frequency of appropriation of particular species (Nietschmann 1973:104–5).

Information on the names and total numbers of known and recognized categories, and the names and numbers of categories in successively more inclusive groups, reveals something about the cultural significance of species, types, zones and phenomena, and something of their significance in ecological relations. In cultures where there are large numbers of categories recognized this is often, though not always, linked to cultural significance. For example, a large inventory and body of associated knowledge of wild plants may indicate the importance of gathering in otherwise cultivating societies. That Mongol pastoralists distinguish many kinds of steppe (Krader 1955) and Eskimo many kinds of snow (Basso 1972) is in this sense predictable. Conversely, we might expect limited inventories, inconsistently applied terms and poor knowledge to reflect absence of relative material importance. In some cases the combination of such data enables us to trace recent subsistence histories. Thus, the Nuaulu have a list of terms for frogs which approximately corresponds to what is objectively known of the fauna in their exploitative area. The terms, however, are applied inconsistently and (compared with other related groups) they have a poor knowledge of amphibian natural history. This is associated with the fact that such minor sources of protein have become unimportant in recent years with the increasing availability of more reliable and larger game animals (Ellen, Stimson and Menzies 1976), although they remain important for groups at higher altitudes.

Regional differences in classification, preferred varieties of domesticates and seed selection may be closely associated with minor changes in soil composition and terrain. The number of varieties reflects seed quality, comparative yield and other ethnobotanically important characteristics. For two Abelam villages alone, in the Sepik river basin of New Guinea, Lea (1964:90) recorded 108 different varieties of yam. This testifies not only to the importance attached to yam cultivation, but also to the sophisticated appropriation of the potentialities of the crop under minutely varying conditions and for different purposes.

Although the link between lexical diversity and cultural importance holds widely, especially for domesticated biota, it does not do so invariably. To a large extent the numbers of categories distinguished will reflect the objective diversity in local ecology, irrespective of differential material significance (Ellen 1978b). Conversely, extremely broad and apparently unsystematic and unspecific categories may be used which in no way reflect actual knowledge and significance (Morris 1976). If soils are classified into two categories which serve as the basis for all planting decisions, then it might be thought that such decisions are less discriminating and useful, and ultimately less adaptive, than a 10-category scheme where differences are recognized according to such criteria as pH and nitrogen content. However, such differences may be so slight as to provide little advantage over a simple binary discrimination, given the cultigens involved.

A further problem in relation to data such as these is the pitiful inadequacy of the concept of cultural significance. In part this relates to the issue of variation: what is significant depends on who you are and in what context you are operating. For this reason it has been suggested that it should be applied to roles rather than to entire societies. Cultural significance is such a general term that it fails to indicate in what way environmental components may be significant. Some plants are significant because they provide important construction materials, others are only significant in the sense that they are to be avoided (e.g. noxious fungi). In most cases high differentiation reflects material significance, that is plants and animals used for food or manufacturing purposes. But categories may be socially significant in other ways, as in the case of totems. Also, many named plants and animals are materially important to a population only in a secondary sense, in that they are components of food chains of which primarily significant species are part. If significant animals and plants exist in significant relations with other significant species then these are sufficient grounds to classify such forms (Lévi-Strauss 1962:8). If such a broad definition of significance is adopted, then the total number of significant categories brings us very near to the total number of categories given recognition simply in terms of the reflection of local objective ecological diversity.

Simple numerical indices, moreover, do not indicate the varying significance of different distinctions within a classification. Some distinctions may have few ecological consequences, others many. Hunn

(1977), for example, reports that the Sahaptin people of Washington State have many categories for edible roots, particularly desert parsleys of the genus *Lomatium*. One distinction separates two varieties of *L. canbyi*, termed 'luksh' and 'shkulkul'. The first refers to the bulk of the species, the second to plants growing in an isolated region to the north, originally occupied by Sahaptin speakers. These latter plants are so much valued that people will travel over 250 kilometres into neighbouring tribal territories to obtain them. Such behaviour has had significant ecological consequences, in that it tends to increase the range of social contacts and material exchanges.

Accepted uses of significance, then, fail to differentiate between quality and quantity. Many categories may be recognized because they are all significant in the sense that they have at least one minor use; whereas less differentiated classifications may be of far more materially significant categories, in the sense that they are used more regularly, in greater volume and for culturally more important purposes. Such measures do not distinguish between categories of varying importance within the same classification. But weighted measures which do give some idea of differential significance can be obtained. Hays (1974), in his work on the plant classification of the New Guinea Ndumba, has derived an index from the number of different uses for each species. This, of course, depends on a highly problematic definition of a single *use*. In measuring significance for particular kinds of usages more precision is possible, as in the employment of weights for different food species consumed (Ellen 1978), the volume of different timbers used in construction, the number of times a resource is used in the course of a year, or even exchange value as measured in cash return. General measures of degree of significance may be calculated by bringing together a number of separate indices.

Indigenous terms may also be valuable because they facilitate succint and accurate description and analysis of cultural and technical processes and areas of knowledge as they are locally understood. Vernacular terms can rarely be translated as brief glosses (Conklin 1957:30).

Because of the problems of inferring significance from formal analyses of words and categories, the context in which distinctions and classifications are employed must be carefully specified. Decision making, too, is not entirely dependent on formal distinctions, and this is where the evidence relates back to Harris and Burling. Listing categories and their differential significance is not the sole object of an ethnoecological enquiry. Actual discursive knowledge of natural processes and relationships is also an important part.

The degree to which different populations are informed varies, but ethnographers have habitually stressed the often extensive and detailed working knowledge of local ecology. For example, Nietschmann (1973:123, 126) has emphasized the importance of Miskito knowledge of animal behaviour. It is this which assures advantageous turtling conditions, increases the probability of high returns, and permits appropriation in other resource spheres during turtling periods. Richards (1978) has shown that detailed entomological research into *Zonocerus* infestation in Ghana has simply replicated what was already known by the local population. In some cases communities had detailed knowledge of the severity and geographical extent of specific outbreaks, the range of crops attacked and their local significance not available to the research team. Many eastern Nigerian farmers hypothesize a connection between rainstorms and the spread of cassava bacterial blight, and in so doing have correctly identified rainsplash as a major vector. A number of authors have drawn attention to indigenous awareness of decline in soil fertility through an examination of plant cover, and the effects of slope, ash, anthills, and rotting timber on soil variation (Netting 1974:26). In the Virgin Islands (Morrill 1967:411) knowledge of types of reef formation and other marine habitats involves recognition of food-chains, the long periods required for reef growth, the complexity of shape, diversity of niches and small significant differences in depth and clarity of water, currents and sunlight.

That explanations or interpretations of phenomena are technically in error need not be important. Thus, Virgin Islanders note that while lobsters are usually found in sheltered spots, the female moves into turbulent areas for the purpose of egg-laying. This is said to be because young lobsters need more 'air' in the water, whereas objectively the purpose is to scatter the young and therefore reduce predation. Similarly, for the Naskapi (Moore 1965), patterns on caribou scapulae are understood (falsely) to encode information about the environment. This information is used by hunters to locate game, although in fact shoulder-blade divination has simply had the effect of randomizing choice. On the other hand, false information may have negative consequences for environmental interactions. For example, Arctic Alaskan Eskimos avoid what might otherwise be good summer fishing, superior locations for caribou hunting and excellent campsites because of beliefs in malevolent spirits (Burch 1971). The criterion of adequacy for a cognitive model lies not in its accuracy but in its functional and adaptive effectiveness (Rappaport 1971a:247).

It is also important to remember that information about environmental states is culturally transmitted, both transgenerationally and laterally. Transmission entails the possibility of introducing error, but, more importantly, it makes possible a pooling of knowledge and comparison of information. Various social occasions serve as clearing houses for environmental information.

There are numerous recent studies which shed light on local ecological knowledge and attempt to relate this to subsistence practice (Basso 1972, Bulmer 1965, 1968, Forman 1967, van Leynseele 1979). Such analyses have often shown that subsistence and other cultural practices, which (adopting highly generalized or inappropriate assumptions, or making inadequate observations) seem either disruptive or inexplicable, do in fact have a rationale when examined closely, and with care, from an ethnoecological angle. The classic example of this is Conklin's study of Hanunoo swidden cultivation (1954), although earlier studies anticipated it (Richards 1939). In this analysis, which has been discussed in Chapter 4, Conklin stresses that swiddening has a rationality in terms of local needs and perception, and that the horticulturalist sometimes knows more about the interrelations of local environmental and cultural phenomena than we may realize. Some statements about local ecological knowledge and its rational nature have often been inspired, and some may have been distorted, by ethnographer loyalty to informants, commitment to Rousseau's 'noble savage' or modern ecological utopianism. For this reason, while folk classifications may often be more sensitive to ecological differences in key areas, may be a very necessary corrective to older and uninformed opinion and may have important contributions to make to our understanding of the operation of human ecosystems, they occasionally require scepticism and critical judgement.

Ethnoecological information enables us to learn more of objective ecological relations: data on animal behaviour and distribution, plant geography, the structure of ecotones, food chains; the discovery and description of distinctive features of new species and varieties, and new properties of phenomena. It has been a major source of evidence for reconstructing environmental changes, human migration and history, and the spread and introduction of new species, especially domesticates (Barrau 1960). On these grounds alone it would require no further justification.

INDIGENOUS CLASSIFICATIONS OF LAND AND VEGETATIONAL SURFACES

There is little point here in discussing in detail the problems and methods of analysing folk classifications, or of systematically examining each of the substantive domains of knowledge through the comparative ethnography. This has been done elsewhere. Moreover, I am anxious not to reduce ethnoecology to formal studies of classifying behaviour, but to examine the cognitive environment as something that is relevant to ecological analysis in general. However, some exemplification is useful, and in this section we look at classifications of land and vegetation, since these are frequently of central concern in understanding the environmentally significant decision-making of cultivating populations. The examples chosen here are those of the Ifugao of the northwestern Luzon cordillera (Conklin 1968) and the Nuaulu of south central Seram in eastern Indonesia (Ellen 1978).

Ifugao and Nuaulu producers distinguish a large number of land forms, involving variation in type and combination of rock, soil, water and vegetation. Classifications range from broad general categories of terrain to highly specific particulars. In both cases, many of the terms are used to refer to special qualities, aspects or components of the domesticated environment, rather than to contrasting types of land surface in general. For wet-rice cultivators, such as the Ifugao, this is particularly so, with the most important group of land forms, possessing the most intensive and complex set of distinctions, being those concerned with lands already subject to some degree of cultivation. For swidden cultivators, such as the Nuaulu, who rely to a considerable extent on non-domesticated resources, the classification tends to be a mixture of primary and secondary land forms and vegetational associations; that is, both natural and culturally determined terrains.

Table 9.2 shows an intermediate set of eight 'contrasting' categories covering all major Ifugao land-surface types which are of horticultural or botanical importance. The main Nuaulu categories for topographic surfaces and vegetation can be represented in two intermediate and cross-cutting sets, presented in Table 9.3. Figure 9.1 shows the boundaries of cultivated areas on a contour map superimposed according to local topographic categories. Most land cultivated falls into the category *sanane*, which may contain cultivated slopes of around 35 degrees. The Nuaulu prefer to cultivate *watane*, but because this is already claimed by other non-Nuaulu, turned over to coconut or sago groves by themselves, or is unsuitable in other respects, they are forced onto *sanane*. There are advantages of sloping land, in terms of drainage and clearance, and these may well have been more emphasized formerly. In most inclusive terms, the Nuaulu classify vegetation into two contrasting categories: forest (*wesie*), in which no land rights are held, and cultivated land, or land which has recently been cultivated and in which rights are held (*wasi*). *Wasi* itself refers to all cultivated land and parcels in which rights are held. Actual cultivated plots are termed *nisi*, the three basic types of which are outlined in Table 9.3. Definition of

Table 9.2 *Ifugao categories for major agriculturally and vegetationally significant land types (extracted with modifications from Conklin
1968:105–8)*

Category	General description	Dominant species
1. *mapulun*	short, low, open grassland	*gūlun – Imperata* sp. *tanlag – Themeda* sp.
2. *qinalahan*	public forest, distant forest	mid-mountain climax forest pine forest
3. *mabilau*	cane grassland, high grassland second growth, *runo* association	*bilāu – Miscanthus* spp. (canegrass)
4. *pinūgu*	private forest or grove	timber and fruit trees erect palms, rattan
5. *hābal*	slope swidden fields	sweet potatoes, taro, yams, manioc, corn, millet etc. little rice
6. *lattan*	residential hamlet terrace	
7. *qilid*	drained terrace	sweet potatoes, legumes etc.
8. *payo*	pond field, rice terrace	rice, taro and some other crops

these is based in part of the state and content of the plots, and in part
on the time period since they were first cleared.

Table 9.3 brings the two Nuaulu classifications together and provides figures for the areas of the different combinations of types under
cultivation during 1970–1. The pattern shows a close correlation between ideal Nuaulu statements about garden-land preferences and
what they actually do. A similar kind of exercise has been undertaken
by Johnson (1974) in which he has attempted to show a statistical
correlation between the planting behaviour of sharecroppers in northeast Brazil, their classification of 'land types' and ideas concerning the
most appropriate land for different crops. Three terminologically distinguished land types for swiddens (new, second year and old) are
recognized, three topographic zones (sandy hillside, river margin,
river bottom) and four field types based on soil fertility and moisture.
Dry fertile lands include new and second-year gardens, wet fertile
areas include the river margin and low moist lands. The contrasting
dry infertile lands are the old swidden and sandy hillside locations,
while the wet infertile areas are confined to the river bottoms and
saline lands. Johnson computed the number and percentage of fields
according to this classification, recording relative fertility and moisture
preferences of various commonly planted species, including squash,
manioc, beans, potatoes, rice and maize grown on different kinds of
land. He then counted the number of plants in the fields of six cultivators and computed percentages of plants in each of the four field types.

Table 9.3 *Basic Nuaulu categories for topography (shown horizontally) and land use (shown vertically), showing areas (in hectares) classified in terms of them (based on data provided in Ellen 1978)*

	watane flat areas, coastal margins, valley floors, alluvium	*sanane* valley sides	*pupue* ridgeland, crests, higher reaches of valley walls	*tinete, pupue tinete* mountains, peaks	Total area of cultivated land	Percentage land area
nisi honue recently cleared garden plot up until end of first year	3.15	7.24	0.11		10.49	10
nisi monai garden after first year including sago, clove and coconut groves – each representing a separate sub-category and which may (as in the case of coconut) be up to 60 years old	20.36	46.82	0.68		67.85	67
nisi ahue secondary growth of various kinds, discarded gardens *niane wesie* dwelling areas, mature forest, advanced secondary forest	7.16	16.46	0.24		23.85	23
Total area of cultivated land	30.71	69.64	1.84		102.19	
Percentage land area	30	69	1			100

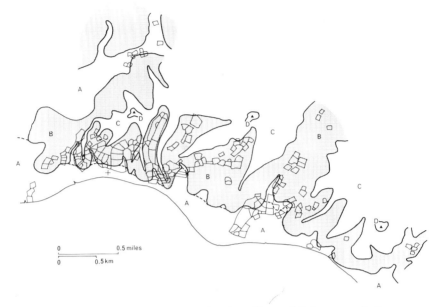

9.1 Distribution of garden plots for the village of Ruhua, south Seram,
   superimposed on land classified in terms of Nuaulu categories of
                              topography
A. *watane* flat areas, coastal margins, valley floors, alluvium
B. *sanane* valley sides
C. *pupue* ridgeland, crests, higher reaches of valley walls
D. *tinete, pupue tinete* mountains, peaks
   The broken line represents the approximate boundary between coastal
   watane and the *watane* of valley floors. The are no Nuaulu terms to
   distinguish between these two manifestations of *watane* (Ellen 1978:
                              map 10)

He found high agreement between the field classifications, actual
planting practices and informants' statements about the requirements
of different species. In this case at least, people do what they say they
do, and local categories are closely related to actual practice on the
environment.

While the contrast between categories in the land-form classifications of many societies is certainly there, its emphasis does tend to
detract from an appreciation of the dynamic successional relationships
between categories. The key successional links between Ifugao and
Nuaulu categories respectively are:

222

It is the fluidity of category boundaries, often their 'fuzziness', and the recognition of continua, successions, tendencies and cycles which a static model of a 'classification' cannot portray. As they are also developmental stages, land-use categories can also be used to record changes in the status of land through time, and therefore shed light on actual decision-making processes. In the ecology of swidden cultivation such an approach can be valuable as a measure of land-use intensity and productivity, and as a guide to other significant changes in subsistence history and environmental relations.

INFORMATION AND DECISION MAKING, THE IMPACT OF INFORMATION AND SCHEDULING

In trying to relate our perception of the environment, decisions made with respect to it and the implementation of those decisions through activities which materially affect ecology, we are concerned with two kinds of theoretical process. The first is how the decisions are arrived at, and the second how information actually affects environmental relations. I say 'theoretical' because in practice the two are closely bound together. However, for analytical reasons they are often considered apart. I believe that there are dangers inherent in doing this.

One suggestion for integrating environmental information into the analysis of ecological systems has been to use conventional systems-modelling techniques. The procedure is to isolate the analytic system, the sources of material and energy; follow the flows; note the points where human action affects flows; and consider the effect of information systems. The model is then constructed, ensuring that the flows are followed completely until they leave the system. Finally, elements and flows that are too small to affect the dynamics of the system, and those that do not affect the variables of interest, can be eliminated. An elementary example would be how the knowledge of, say, resources of a given plant species affects decisions regarding whether or not to gather, where to gather and what to gather. Information inputs of this kind can then be fitted into larger diagrammatic or mathematical models, given specific subsistence techniques. In this way the model is held to generate more realistic predictions about the behaviour of the system (Dow 1976:964).

There are problems with such modelling techniques. They remain *models* of a very limited kind, not descriptions of parts of ecosystems of analytic significance. Their usefulness as models depends on strict rules of closure, and the handling of a relatively small number of variables. In view of recent criticisms of the misuse of analytical closure in the analysis of local systems, and the evident complexity of interacting variables, we might be justifiably suspicious of them. Such models are generally too simple and 'macro' to shed light on many of the processes of interest to anthropologists, though they may help with carefully specified parts of systems, which have been fully described in other ways. The analysis of admittedly basic theoretical systems may also provide general 'clues', such as may interest the prehistoric archaeologist. There are other difficulties, though, and I shall return to these shortly.

Studies of how decisions affecting ecological relations are arrived at are still relatively scarce. One influential example is Frake's suggestion that an ethnoecological approach should be a description of cultural behaviour in terms of what it is necessary to know to be able to respond in a culturally appropriate way in a given social and ecological context (1962). This is an underlying axiom of ethnoscience. Unlike much work characterized by this epithet, Frake has been concerned with understanding actual decison-making processes rather than simply describing classifications. He accepts that one of the most important prerequisites of an adequate field analysis is that it should be closely geared to an understanding of the rationale of indigenous decison making and resource evaluation. This may entail a consideration of folk classifications for a wide variety of domains, but beyond this it must seek regularities in the formulation of practice based on these classifications. These he calls 'rules'. For example, the formulation of three rules permits us to understand the pattern of settlement of the Subanan, a people of the southern Philippines. These are: (1) minimum number of wild vegetation boundaries to a swidden, consistent with other site requirements; (2) minimum distance between house and swidden; and (3) maximum house-to-house distance. Rules 1 and 2 appear to be explicitly geared to the protection of swiddens from animal pests, with a minimum of time and energy in such tasks as fence-building and the construction of garden houses and daily travel to fields. Rule 3 stems directly from the importance attached to neighbours' not overhearing conversations and family quarrels. Frake sees the consequences as (a) a clustering of swiddens together with a maximizing of common boundaries and the grouping of new swiddens next to old ones, (b) nuclear family households, with new houses being built actually within the swidden perimeter and (c) a maximizing of the distance between households. He suggests that the advantages and disadvantages will be found to be weighted differently in other communities of swidden cultivators in southeast Asia, with different consequences for the pattern of settlement.

For any given decision-making sequence the area of choice is circumscribed. Those factors which delineate the area in which rules operate are constants or givens. These may be social, cultural or environmental. For example, for the Nuaulu these include non-Nuaulu land ownership limiting choice of garden sites, the knowledge and categories of land use, and a rainfall regime which prevents the planting of some crops and allows the planting of others. Givens are not, of course, timeless, but their rate of change is much slower. They alter through the social revolutions which permit access to previously prohibited lands, through education and accumulated cultural experience of new knowledge and through the slow non-reversible change of microclimates. The degree to which rules are implemented, and the existence of recommendations which act as if they are sanctions, make some rules seem pretty much like givens, but then the evolution of one to the other is a part of the general evolution of human ecosystems.

As I emphasized in the introduction to this chapter, human beings are not simply filters of information about resource conditions. Unfortunately analyses in the ethnoscience tradition have tended to reduce decision making to an ideal and mechanical process. The approach seems to be claiming too much, with its stress on the reconstruction of cognitive worlds, total explanation and the rigorous use of formal methods. Frake's work, for example, tends towards naive maximization and use of linguistic analogies. Ethnographic description can never resemble linguistic description. People just do not conduct their lives in such pre-programmed ways.

Similarly, the impact of information on the structure of ecological relations is not as straightforward as many empirical and theoretical systems analyses suggest. They cannot show how perception and decision making develop as processes ultimately acting on, and then continually interacting with, the environment. They only indicate the effect of technical practice on a system. The 'black box' remains unopened. We still need to know how the mental machinery creates representations and memories, which, through social interaction and technical praxis, are then translated into individual or collective patterns of response.

It is difficult to separate the making of decisions from their ecological impact. Information is not a resource which is always prior to action; new information gathering may accompany it. Information itself is not homogenous; some of it is incorrect and its transmission imperfect; it may come from different sources, and be available at different times. It cannot be separated from the structure of a group. Some people make decisions, others may simply implement them. Some decisions are beyond the control of a single producer, such as where people do not control their own means of production. Some people's knowledge is better than others, but for social reasons has no effect; some knowledge is used privately, although sometimes it is shared.

The problem is that what is actually done to the environment is generally not simply the outcome of rational decision making. Because of this I prefer the term 'scheduling' (Flannery 1968, Cook 1973) to refer to all those considerations which result in a particular course of action. The term refers to decision making as we might narrowly understand it, the weighing of the merits of different courses of action, while avoiding the suggestion of simple maximization and transactionism. It covers active calculation and actions which stem from habit; it is the process through which rules and givens interact to give rise to actual behaviour.

GENERATIVE ANALYSIS OF ECOLOGICAL END-STATES

We cannot model entire systems so that the character of information inputs is sociologically realistic, or construct scheduling sequences as statements of ideal behaviour and the implementation of formal rules. However, it is possible to bring environmental perception, scheduling and ecological relations into sharper focus.

One way of doing this is by isolating a specific nexus of information, behaviour and environmental variables which can be shown to be interrelated in a way which has significant ecological consequences; another is to concentrate on the end-states of behavioural processes. I shall briefly discuss the first using Rappaport's analysis of Maring pig festivals in New Guinea, and the second with reference to my own work on Nuaulu settlement.

Rappaport has explained, in his much acclaimed and now much criticized book *Pigs for the ancestors* (1968), that Maring ritual cycles serve, among other things, to regulate warfare between adjacent groups and prevent environmental degradation. In so doing he has made an explicit attempt to resolve the problem of the relationship between

226

the perceived and objective environments using systems concepts of information. I do not wish to return to the problems associated with his general analysis here, and shall simply assume that the cultural practices Rappaport describes have the effects he says they have without claiming that this system is either maintained or developed in order to do these things.

Whatever the ecological effects of Maring ritual cycles, the Maring themselves see them as necessary in order to maintain and transmute their relations with spirits (Rappaport 1971a:253). The performance of Maring subsistence activities closely interconnects with numerous cognitive models, which in turn are connected to more abstract conceptions of cosmological relations. For Rappaport these are regulators, and the relation of the cognitive model to the operational model is similar to that of a memory of an automated control device in the physical system it regulates. It is in terms of understanding encoded in the cognitive model that the ritual cycle is undertaken, but the ritual cycle itself has the effect of regulating material relations within the local ecological system. The operation of the entire cycle is cybernetic. There are signals from the ecosystem: for example, women begin to complain that the pig population is getting too large to look after. This indicates that there are sufficient beasts for the performance of sacrifices to spirits. But these in turn have a corrective effect on the ecosystem through the reduction of the pig population: the immediate environment is not degraded. This is not a simple single chain of events but a complex one in which the same messages are reinforced through repetition. There is a continuous interaction between the cognitive model, the ritual cycle, the regional system and the ritual cycle, the regional system and the ecosystem (Figure 9.2). There is no doubt that if the interrelations are as Rappaport describes them then this is a supremely adaptive codification of reality. But how they could have developed as an integrated homeostatic mechanism of such complexity is difficult to comprehend.

Rather than attempting to reconstruct whole systems, it is also possible to examine in relative detail all those proximate processes which result in one fragment of a system as it is described. Such a generative approach selects patterned sets of ecological relationships or phenomena of interest, configurations of social relations, or their commensurable artifacts, such as settlement patterns and meat consumption. Observed patterns at any one point in time may be seen as end-states of the cumulative interaction of social and ecological processes and scheduling sequences, where the end-states are represented by spatial structures – such as patterns of settlement (Ellen 1978) – or other analytically defined social structures (social

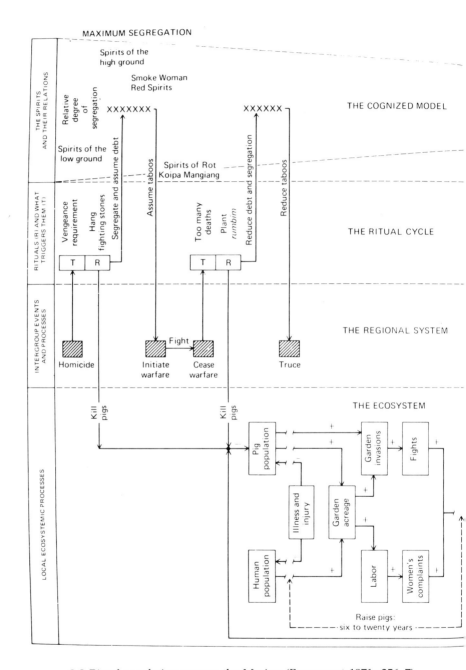

MAXIMUM SEGREGATION

THE SPIRITS AND THEIR RELATIONS

Spirits of the high ground

Smoke Woman
Red Spirits

Relative degree of segregation

XXXXXXX   XXXXXX   THE COGNIZED MODEL

Spirits of the low ground

Segregate and assume debt

Spirits of Rot
Koipa Mangiang

Reduce debt and segregation

Assume taboos   Reduce taboos

RITUALS (R) AND WHAT TRIGGERS THEM (T)

Vengeance requirement

Hang fighting stones

Too many deaths

Plant *rumbim*

| T | R | | T | R | THE RITUAL CYCLE

INTERGROUP EVENTS AND PROCESSES

Homicide

Fight

Initiate warfare   Cease warfare

Truce

THE REGIONAL SYSTEM

LOCAL ECOSYSTEMIC PROCESSES

Kill pigs   Kill pigs   THE ECOSYSTEM

Pig population

Garden invasions   +   Fights

Illness and injury

Garden acreage

Human population

Labor   Women's complaints

Raise pigs: six to twenty years

9.2 Ritual regulation among the Maring (Rappaport 1971a:256–7)

228

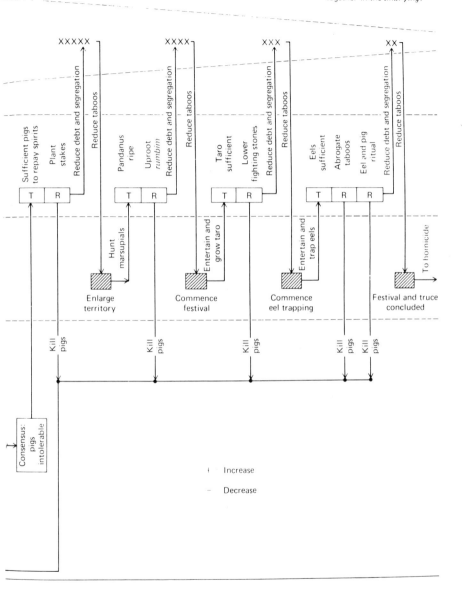

MAXIMUM INTEGRATION
(Koipa Mangiang and
Smoke Woman brought
together in the *timbi ying*)

Sufficient pigs to repay spirits

Plant stakes

Reduce debt and segregation

Reduce taboos

| T | R |

XXXXX

Pandanus ripe

Uproot *rumbim*

Reduce debt and segregation

Reduce taboos

| T | R |

XXXX

Hunt marsupials

Enlarge territory

Taro sufficient

Lower fighting stones

Reduce debt and segregation

Reduce taboos

| T | R |

XXX

Entertain and grow taro

Commence festival

Eels sufficient

Abrogate taboos

Eel and pig ritual

Reduce debt and segregation

Reduce taboos

| T | R | R |

XX

Entertain and trap eels

Commence eel trapping

To homicide

Festival and truce concluded

Kill pigs

Kill pigs

Kill pigs

Kill pigs

Kill pigs

Consensus: pigs intolerable

╁ Increase

─ Decrease

229

formations, modes of production, means of subsistence, economies). Thus, if a settlement pattern is seen as an artifact of a human-dominated ecosystem (Langton 1973:131), the observed pattern can be explained in terms of the processes which generate it and how these are influenced by both culturally ordered information and non-cultural matter and energy. This approach allows us actually to 'test' the contribution of selected cognitive models and knowledge in generating an outcome by comparing the actual outcome with that predicted solely from interpretative data, as embodied (for example) in classical locational analysis.

Frake's paper on Subanan settlement is a useful example of the kind of practical procedures involved in a generative analysis, but – as I have already explained – his analysis and theoretical assumptions are in other respects inadequate. My own monographical treatment of Nuaulu settlement (1978) is an explicit attempt to use a modified generative approach. A large part of this analysis is concerned with the selection of garden sites as an outcome of numerous but identifiable processes, the interplay of ideas about the ideal location of gardens, landscape classifications, and how such ideals have to accommodate factors such as topography, soil quality and vegetative cover. Some of these will be what I have called rules, others givens. It is, however, impossible to select one class of factors – ideational, relational, or economic – as being collectively more important than another so that a hierarchy of preferences might be established. Rather, it is a question of tendencies, with individual micro-factors interacting with others in a particular situation. The classes of factors – topography, soil, ritual, and so on – are simply convenient second-order constructs.

For any one fragment of the pattern not every factor is relevant, or is not relevant to the same degree. This can be shown by tracing scheduling pathways for particular groups of gardens, generalized pathways typical of particular conditions, or schematic pathways for entire settlements. Scheduling pathways, the importance of particular factors and the impact of their effects vary according to time and place, dependent on such factors as season, year and the type of vegetation from which gardens are cut. Micro-ecological and social conditions are constantly in flux.

An observed pattern of gardens will be the outcome of decisions made at different times, when perhaps different conditions were operative, and the effects of decisions made at any one time will have consequences for different phases of future action. I have already stressed that in looking at synchronic patterns we are also looking at developmental phases. Depending on the phase, there will be different implications for the future development of a garden and the land around it, affecting vegetational cover, the character and intensity of appropriation in the vicinity, and the dispersal of such specific artifacts of settlement as paths, fences, dwellings and garden huts. Decisions affecting a given cluster of gardens may have been taken as many as sixty years previously, the life expectancy of a coconut palm. But these decisions do not all have the same consequences for ecological and social relations; some are more important than others. A decision about where to locate a garden hut, which then becomes a focus for a new garden complex, will lead to many derivative scheduling pathways for individual gardens of less consequence. But this decision may have been largely the result of the presence of an old coconut grove in the vicinity. This example is diagrammed in Figure 9.3(a). The same figure also illustrates the qualitative difference between different scheduling pathways. Junctions indicate the cutting of new gardens from forest; but changes in the status of particular cut plots represent scheduling of a different order. These are changes which occur by the following through of social and ecological successions and cycles. They involve minimal cultural modification, but no dramatic ecological breaks, unlike clearing. The number and structure of such transitions can usually be specified quite accurately and in detail, in both botanical and ethnobotanical terms. These are shown schematically for the Nuaulu in Figure 9.3(b). The periodicity of junctions and the duration of lines between them in such diagrams indicate the intervention of other factors, such as the developmental cycle of domestic groups, demographic trends and environmental disasters. Site selection is not an easily differentiated phase in the horticultural cycle. There is a constant reassessment of the potential of new sites and the rejection or loss of old ones.

Clearly, it is impossible to reconstruct every scheduling pathway which may be involved in generating a given pattern of settlement. But, in the light of the kinds of issues raised in the two preceding paragraphs, more realistic generalizations can be made. For example, it is possible to arrange the factors involved in site selection in terms of interpretative schemes, such as whether their net effect is integrative or disintegrative (Ellen 1978:159). Such routines permit the construction of more specific generative pathways. Figure 9.3(c) illustrates this for some of the processes resulting in the clustering of land around villages. The actual pattern for a particular settlement can be shown by introducing deliberate asymmetry into the structure of junctions (as in the other diagrams) or by varying the thickness of line. It is equally possible to construct scheduling chains of this type which result in contrary processes: the dispersal of land, or garden-hut orientated patterns. Recognition of opposing, parallel or integrative processes

(a)

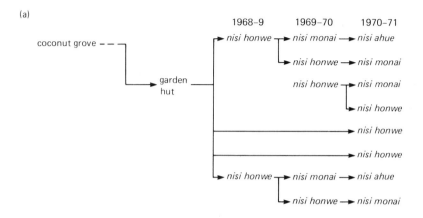

(b)

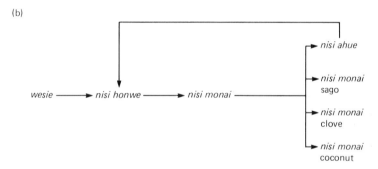

(c)

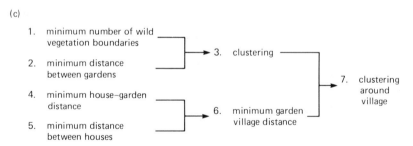

9.3 Diagramming various aspects of the generative analysis of Nuaulu settlement patterns, eastern Indonesia. (a) Generative history and developmental phases for gardens in a garden-hut complex (Ellen 1978: map 12); (b) principal succession possibilities for Nuaulu gardens; and (c) generative processes resulting in the clustering of cultivated land around the village (Ellen 1978: fig. 10)

allows for the estimation of deviation from ideal patterns, and the extent to which they are reflected in actual ones.

Generative analysis is not a theory but a framework and set of techniques which enable us to comprehend the operational relationship between diverse factors contributing to particular end-states. It reveals historical processes, not those that are 'synchronic' and 'universal'. Depending on the rate and kind of change, historical precedent permits an element of predictability, but primarily it is an approach which aids the sometimes underestimated problem of description, analysis and the formulation of specific hypotheses. The processes reconstructed are not, however, evidence of operations taking place in the minds of individual 'decision-makers'. Rather, they reflect a complex dialectical interrelationship between scheduling activities and environmental constraints accumulated over time.

REASSESSMENT

Many of the criticisms levelled against formal methods in ethno-ecology are valid, and much work has not noticeably advanced our knowledge of the human ecological condition. The obsession with methodology has often gone hand-in-hand with the analysis of trivial ethnographic issues. Variation, flexibility and the social context of classification have, until recently, been ignored; while a concern for categories, and particular kinds of contrast and arrangement, has been widespread. The differences between practical and ideal and ideological classification, as well as other complexities, have been submerged in naive mechanical exercises in elicitation. But, paradoxically, it is continuing research into classification which has revealed such shortcomings and made attempts to rectify them. The analysis of classifications has, with some justification, and under the influence of individuals such as Conklin, Berlin and Lévi-Strauss, become an important theoretical area in itself. Perhaps, then, we should not simply judge it in terms of its contribution to the understanding of man–environment relations, although it would severely retard that understanding if work (especially recent work) on classification were to be rejected altogether. Ultimately, it is as necessary to relate classificatory questions to the objective structure of social formations and eco-systems as it is to have objective information on biota for ethnoecological studies.[1]

Confining observations to actual physical behaviour can, of course, facilitate a substantial degree of explanation and prediction of ecological states and processes – as the preceding chapters have indicated. But, if no attention is paid to cognition and scheduling, human ecology

233

is limited to general interpretations of phenomena on a scale far removed from individual actions,[2] where the social realm can tidily be
relegated to black boxes, and mechanistic explanations reign supreme.
Such approaches actively prevent us from understanding what is
distinctively human about human ecology, and from transforming
Forde's dark 'middle term' into identifiable variables amenable to
empirical investigation (Vayda and Rappaport 1968:490).

The justification of ethnoecological analysis is as straightforward as
the empirical processes involved are complex. We perceive the environment through sensory perception which is necessarily selective,
organize information through simplification, and identify problems in
terms of cultural categories *through* social organization. Every somatic
human action which results in an environmental change (however
small) is preceded by, and undertaken in relation to, a process of
interpretation and specification which is culturally coded and socially
situated. This process of 'self-description' (Diener, Nonini and Robkin
1980) itself affects our behaviour towards the environment. Our sense
data are ordered through classifications, some of which are accessible
to study through ability of conscious recall and terminological expression. The criteria of significance in classifying often reflect matters that
are crucial when making 'decisions' about subsistence policy and environmental resources. Indeed, in one sense, resources themselves are
simply those parts of the environment accorded significance by cultural perception (Brookfield and Hart 1971:41). Classifications, then,
embody information about the environment; but alone they are insufficient. More discursive knowledge, notions about the cognitive environment, technical and social practices, are also necessary. Technical
practices reflect accumulated environmental knowledge, and therefore tools and technology are a function of information. And among
the social practices is the according of certain resources – those we
might objectively describe as significant – with value. Value is information given a very particular social construction and in some systems
can be represented semiotically. Money is an example.

Once the ethnoecological data are accepted as relevant, there remains
the more complicated task of showing *how* they affect the objective
environment. I have discussed scheduling – or, more narrowly, decision
making – and, although it is indisputable that decisions can be made only
in relation to the perceived environment, delineating actual scheduling
pathways and showing how these interact with environmental variables
are extremely difficult. Ethnographic information of a more precise kind
than has generally been collected hitherto is required, as are analytical
techniques which shed light on the kinds of processes involved, the
integration of factors and their relation to actual ecological end-states.

234

It is possible that generative analysis may be of some assistance here.

It is impossible to reconstruct entire cognitive environments, and fortunately symbolic universes are not much use in understanding mundane scheduling and man–environment relations. The more inclusive a classification and the more general environmental knowledge,[3] the more open it is to ideological invasion and complete sociological reconstruction (Ellen 1979a), and the less likely it is to correspond to interpretative scientific schemes. But some classifications, models, areas of knowledge, and scheduling pathways are more relevant to key environmental relations than others. It is perhaps upon these that we should concentrate. What fractions of data on cognitive environments we do possess can be used intelligently, to design and to scale research problems in order to make best use of them. The analysis of classifications, the collection of ethnoecological data and techniques such as generative analysis are, in the end, of use only to the extent that they render interpretations more meaningful. What is important ethnographically is not so much the abstract conception of the perceived as the operational relationship between it and the interpretative environment, as mediated by a particular social context. In this way it is possible to focus attention on the articulation between ecosystems and the intentional behaviour of sapient information-bearing individuals.

vwvwvwvwvwvwvwvwvwvwvwvwvwvwvwvwvwvwvwvwvwvwvwvwvwvwvwvwvwvwvwvwvwvwvwvwvwvwvwv

Adaptation: a summary and reconsideration

For the knowledge of historical phenomena in their concreteness, the most general laws, because they are most devoid of content, are also the least valuable.

Max Weber 1949:80

INTRODUCTION

It would have been impossible to avoid introducing the concept of adaptation in the preceding parts of this book, given its central explanatory role. Nonetheless, I have reserved a more specific treatment until some of the major anthropological approaches to the ecological problematic have been presented. In this way it is possible to clarify certain discussions in the literature which might otherwise appear unnecessarily complicated, polemical and abstract. As might be expected from the structure of that discourse already examined, the limits of the debate are set by, on the one hand, those who adhere to a strict Darwinian model and express amazement at its neglect in contemporary anthropological theory and, on the other, those who insist that definitions of adaptation must be framed with specific reference to the human condition. It is hardly surprising that empirical case material suggests that the appropriate theory lies somewhere in between; not in the form of some woolly minded compromise, but as a subtle conceptual articulation.

It is possible to identify four distinct types of adaptation among biological organisms:[1]

1 *phylogenetic*, in which a genotype (the genetic constitution of an individual) adapts trans-generationally through natural selection;
2 *physiological modification* of the phenotype (the outward physical constitution of an individual) during the course of a life span, but within the range made possible by the genotype;

3 *learning,* adaptive behaviour acquired during the life span; and
4 *cultural modification* through a combination of learning and use of
  culturally transmitted information.

The last three can be distinguished from the first in that they are
adaptive modifications manifested when two populations with the
same basic genotype develop different physiological and behavioural
characteristics in response to particular ecological conditions. The last
two are behavioural modifications requiring the participation of the
central nervous system. The first three are common throughout the
animal kingdom. Non-cultural learning is an important part of all
animal behavioural development. Cultural modification is not unknown among non-primates (Thorpe 1963), is recognized and well
documented for certain species of non-human primate (Kummer 1971,
Boehm 1978), such as chimpanzees and Japanese macaques, but only
becomes supreme in *Homo sapiens,* where cultural adaptation and
transmission of information must be said to constitute the dominant
species characteristic. Humans are born with a capacity to learn any of
a virtually unlimited set of social and cultural conventions, and this
must ultimately be seen in terms of the enhancement of biological
survival and the ability to transmit genetic material.

Examples of phylogenetic adaptation in humans are the sickling of
the red blood cells in certain tropical populations which promotes a
high degree of resistence against malaria (Wiesenfeld 1967), and
sweat-gland distribution and skin pigmentation in hot climates
(Weiner 1964:445). Physiological modifications include adaptation to
high-altitude living among Andean and Himalayan populations, and
more temporary individual responses to cold, such as shivering, an
increase in the metabolic rate, and the constriction of peripheral blood
vessels to prevent heat loss. In the same category as physiological
modification we should also consider developmental plasticity (Weiner 1964:447–52, 479–80; 1964a). However, the forms of adaptation that
are of central concern here are learning and cultural modification.

The four types of adaptation differ in the speed with which they can
be effective. Phylogenetic adaptation is limited by the rate of reproduction and fecundity of a population. Physiological modification is more
rapid, but it is dependent on somatic changes and accommodation
linked to physical growth and the reorganization of body tissue. Learning is simply dependent on sensory-motor coordination in the central
nervous system; it may be rapid (as in escaping from a predator), but it
is often through processes of trial-and-error which vary in learning
time depending on the kind of problems to be solved. Learning may
often provide more rapid and temporary solutions to hazards often
accommodated to through physiological means. For example, heat

loss may be prevented not only by reducing excretion, but by moving away from the source of cold. Cultural adaptation may be very rapid indeed, since drawing on the experience of others (either synchronically through diffusion or diachronically through locally accumulated tradition) enables the trial-and-error stage to be omitted. Thus, the learned adaptive responses of individuals can be transmitted to others independently of genes. In cultural terms, heat loss can be avoided by wearing clothes, the manufacture and appropriateness of which have been discovered by preceeding generations. The superiority of such cultural mechanisms in terms of rapid accommodation, and adaptation to temporary conditions (together with learning) enables them to act as a bulwark against the necessity for physical change (Slobodkin 1968:187–205).

In practice, overall human adaptation to particular environments may involve combining these different basic types of modifications. For example, the Quechua employ a wide variety of means to cope with such hazards of high-altitude living as energy scarcity, cold and low-oxygen tension. In addition to the more obvious cultural practices, these include the custom of coca-chewing, and such physiological responses to hypoxia as changes in the respiratory and cardiovascular system (Vayda and McCay 1975:13).

MECHANISMS OF CULTURAL ADAPTATION

Cultural adaptation may take place through: differential survival of populations, perceived hazards and conscious responses, and chance.

Adaptation through the differential survival of populations is based on the observation that there is *variation* in cultural traits from which individuals and cultures *select*. Since the selection of certain traits rather than others may prove more adaptive under certain conditions, this may affect the chances of survival of a given population. Alland (1970, also Alland and McCay 1973:170) has argued that cultural traits have coefficients of selection, since there is variation, differential natality and mortality, and culture traits operate within a biological system. Unadaptive variation therefore tends to be eliminated. An example of this form of adaptation is found in a comparison by Wagley (1951) of the effects of outside influence on the Tenetehara and Tapirapé peoples of Brazil. Among the Tenetehara, population levels appear to have remained steady over a period of some 300 years of close contact with colonial and post-colonial settlers, while the Tapirapé population has been constantly reduced over a period of only 40 years of intermittent contact. The subsistence pattern of the two groups is broadly similar, but their population policies and social organization contrast. Tapirapé notions of family size have remained unchanged despite a higher mortality rate caused by introduced disease. This, in turn, disrupted the system of production, distribution and ceremonial organization. Tenetehara social organization was sufficiently flexible to survive the initial impact of contact until the population was able to adjust to the new circumstances.

Processes of this kind, however, can only explain a fraction of known cultural adaptations, and are largely restricted to those practices directly affecting mortality and natality, such as food preparation (Burnham 1973) and factors influencing disease susceptibility. Moreover, we must be careful not to confuse them with natural selection of genes. Those cases where entire populations decline or become extinct due to disadvantageous cultural practices must be extremely rare, and one would expect maladaptations to be recognized and countered, even if the avoiding behaviour is not always successful.[2] It is only when such coping measures fail that this form of selection of cultural practices operates. Cultural adaptation can never be entirely equivalent or analogous to natural selection. Variation and selection are not remotely similar to biological processes. Cultural variation is due to invention, discovery, borrowing, plans and unconscious accidents (Service 1971:10). Culture cannot replicate and transmit traits between individuals and generations precisely, and traits are subject to infinite blending and reinterpretation.

The differential survival of a population theoretically specifies adaptation as a passive effect of the presence of certain conditions. It is also possible for the individuals and population actively to modify their behaviour to maintain certain conditions, cope with hazards, adjust to new conditions, or improve upon existing ones. Clearly, this can happen only if there is an awareness that a problem exists, if it is diagnosed properly and responded to effectively. Because of the inadequacy of human sensory perception, cerebral coordination, cultural information and ability to respond, adaptations frequently fall short of a goal or have no adaptive effects at all. This form of adaptation can respond to the world only as it is perceived and in ways which are culturally possible. Not only are human perception and response physiologically constrained, they are also culturally conditioned. The level of deprivation required to initiate new adaptive strategies is related to tolerance induced by socialization, while our perception of reality is often an illusion and our means of response predicted by mystification. For example, we pray to avoid the consequences of some unknown disease. But most cultural adaptation is of this form, and sometimes even illusory or incorrect information may lead to individual or group action that is adaptive, though it is generally a response based on adequate technical information.

Some adaptations are the chance, unconscious effects of social and cultural practices. If the Tsembaga ritual cycle does have some effect on environmental conservation, it is very probably of this kind. Equally, the mere presence of an adaptation does not mean that it is necessary. At the genetic level it might simply be that the genes which augmented its development survived at a greater rate than those which did not (Williams 1966:29). Culturally it may be a fortuitous by-product of some other innovation. Its effect may well be to extend adaptiveness, but this is not to say that it was therefore necessary.

Actual adaptive processes may be a combination of any of the previous three. For example, variation in a cultural practice may arise by chance or by pressure on resources or groups. The new variants are then recognized and the adaptation is encouraged, and modified to a more suitable form. The same process may take place through the observation that the presence or absence of certain practices results in the extinction of local populations. These are characteristically interrelated processes. Similarly, problems may not be directly apparent, only reflected in conditions of organization or belief. Such information can be quite arbitrary. All that is necessary is that there should be a change in their condition which acts as a signal, resulting in the undertaking of an activity which is adaptive. This is what is happening when Tsembaga women complain about the size of the pig herd.

No other mechanisms are necessary to explain human adaptive processes through culture, and it is difficult to see how other suggested mechanisms might actually work. The notion of 'gross structural pressure' can be explained by other means. For example, it is true that if a particular species is appropriated to the point of extinction, a population will be compelled to increase its appropriation of other species. But this is not a simple mechanistic consequence; the situation gives rise to complex processes of decision making in the context of a series of constraints of varying degrees of significance. Adaptation is therefore an active strategy and falls into the second category above. We have already considered the difficulties of a model of adaptation which regards it as being fortuitous.

DEFINITION AND MEASUREMENT

The confusion surrounding the concept of cultural adaptation stems from its very definition. For this and for other reasons some writers have preferred to avoid it altogether, speaking instead of 'adjustment', 'fit', or 'accommodation' or omitting terminological specification altogether. But such coyness reflects an unwillingness to come to grips with the problem, and just adds to the confusion.

Let me make my own position quite clear. To say that a genetic, physiological, individually learned or cultural trait is adaptive is simply to describe what its effects are under a given set of conditions. It says nothing of how it came into existence. Put this way, it is more specific than describing fitness, aptness or suitability, and broadly follows the Darwinian notion of a process of modification which results in either maintaining the conditions for existence of an individual or extending them. Much behaviour and change is not adaptive, in the sense that its effects cannot be categorically specified in these terms. More generally, though, any change or trait has some net contribution to the state of adaptiveness of an individual or population. Statistically, under a given set of conditions, it must contribute negatively or positively to the state of adaptiveness. So-called 'neutral' change simply has the effect of reinforcing the adaptive *status quo*.

I have said that an adaptation may often be seen as a means of maintaining conditions of existence in the face of change. This view of adaptation is derived from systems theory, where behaviour is adaptive if it maintains essential variables within physiological limits. Rappaport (1968:241, 1971c:24) has developed a cybernetic definition of adaptation in which organisms maintain homeostasis in the face of short-term environmental fluctuations and long-term permanent changes. He follows Romer in suggesting that the initial survival value of a favourable innovation is conservative, in that it renders possible the maintenance of a traditional way of life. Adaptation is therefore regulation, usually through negative feedback. But, while this particular formulation is appropriate within the context of physiology, it is highly problematic when discussing social and ecological systems. The problems have already been discussed at length in Chapter 9, but the point to emphasize here is that much adaptive behaviour, even if explicitly designed to maintain certain conditions of existence, may very well have the effect of disturbing others. Also, adaptation frequently operates to extend the conditions for existence of particular individuals and groups only.

Beyond this it is unnecessary and futile to find single-factor definitions of adaptation. Unfortunately, some writers have talked in terms of 'general adaptation', usually referring to the increasing effectiveness of a species over time, where effectiveness is measured in terms of some single factor such as energy use. Notions of general adaptation are really evolutionary theories indicating the broad course of change. It is possible that such features may serve as useful indices of some theoretical notion of adaptation if they could be empirically demonstrated, but this has been the case neither for biology (Williams 1966) nor (convincingly) for anthropology. Treating features in the course of evolution as adaptive responses really begs the question, and it would seem that no general theory can really predict what will be a 'prime mover' in any one case (Service 1971:25; Alland and McCay 1973: 156–7[3]). The processes of adaptation are almost as diverse as the traits through which it takes place, and certainly anthropological uses should not be judged appropriate or inappropriate solely in terms of the extent to which they conform to those used by biologists. Biologists disagree among themselves, and there is an absence of consensus as to whether a general concept of adaptation can apply to social systems and cultural traits (Collins 1965, M. Harris 1960). But to avoid too specific a definition is no excuse for employing it imprecisely. It is always necessary to specify the processes by which a trait or action is adaptive, the population involved, and any empirical consequences.

The problem of definition is closely linked to measurement, since we require some means of recognizing when adaptation has taken place and to what degree it has been successful. There are a number of possibilities:

(1) survival
(2) relative abundance (adjusted for area, stage in life-cycle, ecological type and so on)
(3) rate of increase in size of population
(4) reduction in population, or numerical stability
(5) ability to tolerate wide fluctuations in population level
(6) ecological versatility (number of environments in which a population can survive)
(7) geographical range
(8) degree of assurance of long-term population survival.

That a population or individual survives is no measure of its adaptiveness, although it has been argued (Holling 1973:18) that evolution is simply a game in which the one reward is to remain in it. However, this does not help us in comparing the evidently variable fitness of different populations and species, and is a position which has been resisted (Mazess 1975:10).

Among the most popular measurements in anthropology has been relative abundance or variations upon it. A number of writers have measured effectiveness in terms of the increasing efficiency of energy use – the efficiency with which food is converted into human biomass (White 1949, Sahlins and Service 1960), the ratio of food yield to work done (M. Harris 1971:203), or the total food yield (Hardesty 1977:26). In these terms, in comparing two groups with the same means of subsistence, the larger is the more effective. Alland and McCay (1973:150) favour an emphasis on differential reproductive success since they argue it frees the concept from the clichés of survival and struggle.

There are numerous difficulties with this approach. To begin with, those who adopt variations on this theme do not always operate within the same conceptual framework. Much work assumes that 'societies' or 'cultures', rather than populations, are the adaptive unit. I have already demonstrated how this cannot be so. Secondly, it is difficult to know where to stop bringing in the correction factors (Williams 1966:103). Size of population is clearly no indication of adaptive success in many human populations, where the retention of a small population may be more adaptive than a large one.

The other measures are similarly unhelpful in measuring human adaptivity (Alland 1970:150). Environmental versatility itself may well be an adaptive characteristic though not simply the number of environments in which a given social organization is found, or its geographical range. Ultimately, versatility may be crucial but, in human populations, short-term survival may often be guaranteed only by rejecting flexibility in favour of a more productive specialization. The adaptation of a population as a whole is more of a compromise resulting from various selection pressures to which it is subject and from varying degrees of resistance to adaptation in different directions (Mayr 1949:517). Adaptation does not always related to normatively defined environments, but in many instances to the *pattern* of the environment or to extreme conditions only (Winterhalder 1980:136). The contradictions – such as between measuring the rate of change in size and measuring the degree of population stability – reflect different theoretical meanings of adaptation (Alland and McCay 1973:152). No single measure is adequate for measuring cultural adaptation, since they have no *a priori* comparative applicability. It is possible that the evolutionary biologist may find them useful at the level of species comparison, but they cannot be applied to human populations characterized by particular cultural strategies. They may all be marks of success under certain conditions. Moreover, problems of measurement have tended to determine definitions of adaptation and thus lead to tautology. Consequently, adaptation must be seen as any cultural response, or an open-ended process of modification, which copes with the conditions for existence by selectively reproducing and extending them (Hamburg, Coelho and Adams 1974, Slobodkin 1968, Mazess 1975, Hardesty 1977:22). As such, the measures employed depend entirely on the adaptations involved, and, more importantly, on the hazard for which such changes are adaptive.

Environment, subsistence and system

LEVELS OF ADAPTATION

In biological systems also, but particularly in social ones, what is adaptive varies according to the level of organization under discussion. Unfortunately, the level intended is not always made clear, and often the implication is that entire populations are adapted to environments defined in normative terms. Such an approach comes dangerously close to marrying abstract typological descriptions to environmental causes which are, in any case, incorrect (Winterhalder 1980:138). In discussing processes of adaptation it is always necessary to ensure that the mechanisms, population units and range of environmental features involved are clearly specified and identifiable.

It has already been made clear that populations, rather than cultures and societies, are the units of adaptation (Chapter 4). Cultures cannot adapt since they are no more than the sum of attributes of a population and second-order constructs used to describe similarities in the knowledge and practice of individuals. Only when an adapting population is identical with a putative culture unit might the culture be said to be adapting, and then only figuratively. Similarly it is a nonsense to characterize social institutions, such as religion or art, as adaptive, since these are second-order abstractions made by the analyst. It is possible that a particular ritual is adaptive in a particular context and for a particular population, but that is all. Similarly, general social strategies cannot be said to be generally adaptive. Even to claim that certain subsistence strategies are adaptive to certain environmental conditions requires considerable qualification, since how a population adapts depends on the techniques and resources available at a particular time. Similarly, as we have seen, no single strategy maximizing efficiency or a particular reward (e.g. protein, carbohydrate) is necessarily adaptive, or the most adaptive.

But if it is populations which adapt rather than social formations, cultures and their component institutions, this is not to say that populations adapt as wholes. The issue of group versus individual selection has been discussed widely in the biological literature (Williams 1966, 1971), but its full implications for studies of cultural adaptation have yet to be fully realized.[4] The issue is crucial for putting the basic character of cultural adaptation into perspective. Group selection, as argued by such zoologists as Wynne-Edwards (1962), is the theory which claims that populations of not necessarily related individuals of the same species adapt super-organically; that is, the population acts as a unit for the purposes of natural selection. It may possess population-limiting devices, keep the population below carrying capacity, and through altruistic behaviour promote the repro-

244

ductive success of others (Alland and McCay 1973:152–3). It has been argued (Alexander 1974) that local human social groups are highly appropriate for the operation of group selection as they tend to be hostile, rapidly develop enormous differences in reproductive and competitive ability through culture, and are uniquely able to act and plan as units. The concept of group selection has been extended to ecosystems, and even the entire ecosphere, by some writers claiming that systems evolve as super-organisms, are subject to natural selection and respond in much the same way as individual beings. At the very least we may object to this argument on the grounds that most ecosystems are essentially analytic units whose boundaries are to a large extent arbitrary. Organocentric approaches of this type have clearly sustained the more extreme forms of anthropological ecosystemology discussed in Chapter 4.

Group selection has its vociferous critics. It is claimed by Williams (1966:252) that there is no need to look beyond the level of the individual, that the only adaptations which are clearly expressed and therefore susceptible to scientific scrutiny are individual. Selection is seen as acting upon individual living things, or perhaps groups of very closely related organisms bearing the same genes. The goal of visible adaptive mechanisms is the perpetuation of the genes responsible. If group selection takes place at all, it is regarded as a relatively insignificant process.

It is now becoming clear in anthropology, as well as in biology, that group selection and adaptation are theoretically difficult to account for and empirically difficult to describe. The critique is a useful and instructive one for a number of reasons. Firstly, there is a great deal of vague generalizing which assumes that it is groups that are the adaptive units, often without indicating the processes by which group adaptation might take place. This problem at the level of social formations, cultures and institutions has already been mentioned. Secondly, group selection has recently become analogically fashionable, as in the notion of population homeostasis entertained by Rappaport, considered and rejected in Chapter 8. That population size may be checked by density-dependent factors does not in any way prove that populations have adapted consciously or through selection to this state; that something is beneficial does not mean that it is the *purpose* of the adaptation. On the other hand, it is impossible to rule out completely the idea that altruistic behaviour in small groups of related individuals, where much of the genetic material is shared, serves to maintain the genes of close relatives (Dawkins 1978). But there is no non-conscious mechanism which can anticipate or prevent such hazards as resource collapse or disease.

245

The only solution to the immense difficulties presented by the anthropological concept of group selection is to understand cultural adaptation as taking place, *in the first instance*, at the individual level. It is only individuals who adapt to changing environmental circumstances, though they may do so through social relations, cooperation, exploitation or conflict (Ruyle 1973:211). It is *through* social structures that individuals or collectivities adapt; it is impossible for such structures to have this capacity themselves (Friedman 1974:455). So perhaps we can speak of the adaptation of groups only in the derivative sense, that it is the product of either *cumulative* adaptation of individuals, or the *manipulative* adaptation of powerful individuals or collectivities within a group.

First of all, adaptation occurs through the *cumulative* practice of individuals. For example, individuals may adapt to a cold environment by manufacturing and wearing suitable clothing. They may also adapt through cooperation with other individuals to build appropriate dwellings. Subsistence adaptations, such as the use of new crops or the development of new strains, are the result of individual practice, although this may be predicated by collective knowledge and be practised by many individuals in a population who exchange information concerning it. If an adaptation spreads from one individual to all members of a population it becomes a characteristic of that population. In this sense it is legitimate to describe the population as adapting. Similarly, if individuals in a population cooperate with the intention of maintaining their collective conditions of existence or extending them, this too may be described as population adaptation.

Manipulative adaptation through the exploitation of other individuals may operate between individual dyads or larger groups. Such collectivities may include those based on sex, age, locality and kinship; or those defined in terms of their position in the technical and social relations of production. They may, therefore, include social classes. For example, Ruyle (1973a:607) has recently argued that ranking and potlatching are not means by which the Kwakiutl population as a whole adapts to its environment, as suggested by Piddocke (1965), but means by which a ruling class can exploit the surplus value produced by others. In other words, classic Marxist class analysis can be seen in terms of competition between interest groups, or even in terms of predator and prey. One population in a system is manipulating the subsistence base so as to maximize the flow of materials and value towards itself. However, any social relation of exploitation embodies a contradiction: that if exploitation is carried to extremes the exploited may cease to be exploitable. If, as is often the case, the exploited group is one of the conditions of existence of the exploiting group, then the fitness – indeed, survival – of that group is threatened. This contradiction applies in an obvious way to sex, age and class relations. In small-scale tribal societies, manipulative adaptation is less than in complex, technically and socially differentiated and politically centralized ones: the locus of production is the household or family group, where effort is collective and the social product distributed relatively equally (though there may be some age- sex- or status-linked differences). The interests of the individual coincide much more with those of the collectivity in band societies and those organized around an essentially domestic mode of production (M. Harris 1971:370–2).

TEMPORAL CONTEXT

Natural selection does not always promote the long-term survival of populations, since, in cases of increasing specialization, adaptation might be concomitant with increasing vulnerability to extinction (Williams 1966:106). Much the same situation applies to cultural modifications, and in specifying adaptations it is crucial to take into the account the time period over which they are effective. It is convenient to talk in terms of long-, medium- and short-term adaptations, although we should be wary of assigning to them particular durations or considering them as anything more than a rough-and-ready descriptive device. Here I take short-term adaptations to be those whose life span is within an annual cycle, medium as having a life span within a single life cycle, and long-term as those promoting population survival over any longer period of time, although in evolutionary terms these may often seem relatively short. Of course, adaptations described in any of these three ways may be transformed into each other under certain circumstances.

Cultural adaptations with a short life span may include responses to particular hazards at specific times, as in the formation of *ad hoc* groups following cyclones or hurricane damage. Such behaviours may disappear after the problem has been controlled. Alternatively, responses may be available for recurrent hazards. In this case knowledge of the adaptation is long term while operational use is short to medium term. Alternatively, social organization may embody features which are adaptively responsive depending on environmental condition. Such responses include the adjustment of band size among food-collectors following periodic changes in resource distribution. Recurrent adaptations that are operationally short term but which are permanently encoded are often seasonal.

Recent developments in systems theory have emphasized how adaptation may be accomplished through graded sets of responses to hazards of increasing magnitude with a distinct temporal structure, depending on the duration and severity of conditions which threaten individuals or populations (Berrien 1968:67–8, Vayda and McCay 1975). Vayda (1974) has shown how warfare can be seen as a set of graded processes where escalation is a phased response to pressure, particularly that of populations. Similarly, in an analysis of how Fringe Enga people of the New Guinea highlands cope with recurrent, and sometimes severe, plant-killing frosts, Waddell (1975) points to a structured temporal ordering of responses related to the timing, recurrence and severity of frosts. This series of graded and interrelated responses ranges from sweet-potato mounding (short to medium term) to migrations of varying degrees of permanence (medium to long term).

Cultural adaptations vary according to how long it takes to implement them and the degree to which they are sustained. Rapid actions can be taken which have immediate beneficial consequences, as in population movement to avoid flooding or volcanic eruption. Others may only have the required effects if they are sustained over a period of time. But adaptations to some environmental conditions may be delayed for several months or into the medium term. Others still are essentially long-term adaptations, such as developing disease-resistant domesticates, population control to avoid rapid decline in resources, or the development of certain forms of pastoralism to cope with the problems of arid zones. Most discussions of cultural adaptation have been concerned with such relatively long-term trans-generational forms. But if it is the case that certain social arrangements and technical practices have a long term rather than a short or medium term adaptive advantage, we are forced back to the problem of how such adaptations originate and how they are maintained. The degree of consciousness of ecological consequences will vary, but consciousness must always have been an important factor in both origin and maintenance. The complexity of an adaptation depends also on an awareness, not necessarily of intricacies or interconnections, but of approximate end–means relationships. Long-term adaptation may periodically be re-affirmed through its occasional protrusion into consciousness, particularly at those critical periods when it is clearly operational. This is well exemplified in the case of kinship.

Because particular adaptations are time-phase specific, it often happens that those which operate in the short term may be disadvantageous in the long term. For example, a farmer may increase short-term yield by applying fertilizer which in the long term will cause damage. The repeated application of short-term measures to solve a chronic environmental problem may make matters worse rather than improve them (multiplier effect). At the same time, established strategies may be employed not because they are effective but because other social and cultural conditions maintain them (buffering), only to be discarded when the problem has become considerably worse (Bennett 1976:285–6). On the other hand, long-term adaptations may make little short-term sense. Viewed in favourable years, certain kinds of herding may be uneconomic, although in years of critical famine animals may use available vegetation more efficiently than humans, turning otherwise unavailable calories and nutrients into consumable food. Animals may therefore carry human populations through drought periods in a way which cultivation cannot match. At the level of relations of production, it has been suggested (Bloch 1973) that the adaptiveness of kinship under particular conditions only becomes effective in the medium to long term, and that the very significance of extensive kinship networks may stem from their morally sustained residual permanence and flexibility. Extended networks are maintained for those occasional periods when it is useful to employ certain specific ties. In class societies time specificity may be crucial in maintaining the position of individuals or groups within the system. It may be in the long-term adaptive interests of a person to be ideologically consistent and risk subsistence failure, rather than risk losing his class identity for the sake of short-term subsistence gain. Similarly, returning to the intrinsic contradiction of manipulative adaptation, a superordinate group may prefer to decrease exploitation in the short term rather than risk the destruction of the system through permitting its internal contradictions to be played out. On the other hand, the long-term incremental exploitation of a subordinate class may increase the willingness of the latter to accept short-term risk in order to overthrow the system. Alternatively, a superordinate class may improve the conditions of the subordinate class in the interests of medium-term productive efficiency, only to create precisely those conditions which make their own destruction possible. Adaptation within subsystems always has implications for the stability of higher systems over time. Marx – of course – understood all of this weil.

CONTEXT AND CONTRADICTIONS

Much confusion in discussions of cultural adaptation has arisen from *a priori* judgements as to what is adaptive, and *post hoc* generalizations as to what has been so. It must be emphasized that whether a particular kind of behaviour is adaptive revolves very largely around the question of context. Viewing a population as a whole, specific adaptations may appear to contradict each other. Apparent conflict between adaptations to different time phases has been discussed in the previous section, while the existence of conflicts between different groups and levels of adaptation have also been intimated. Most social formations are complex structures, in which the interests of individuals, individuals and groups, and different groups do not always coincide. What may be adaptive for one group, in as much as it maintains or extends its conditions of existence, is not necessarily so for another. It is not invariably true that the maximization of friendships minimizes antagonism and so confers evolutionary advantage, as argued by Alland and McCay (1973:302). Such a naive view of the character of social altruism and adaptive dynamics does not take into account the possibility that antagonism or competition might be specific strategies through which individuals and groups adapt to particular situations, while a person who does maximize his friendships may do no more than conspire in his own exploitation.

Given what has been said of contradictions between adaptations at different levels of organization, between different individuals and groups and with respect to different time periods, it comes as no surprise to discover that the same technique or social practice may have adaptive advantage for some purposes though not for others. For example, the Nuaulu garden-hut system is adaptive in as much as it permits greater garden productivity. On the other hand it is disadvantageous in that it has to be periodically abandoned, is at a great distance from the village, and so on. In this case, as in others, people have to make decisions as to whether it is worth maintaining. As social and cultural practices may have both adaptive and maladaptive consequences depending on context, so environmental hazards may be differentially significant for individuals in a population. Plant-killing frosts may be beneficial for farmers who profit from the increased prices paid for surviving crops and lower labour expenditure but cause hardship for migrant farm-workers through reduced wages and unemployment (Vayda and McCay 1975:19). Objectively, whether a practice or social arrangement is adaptive – for an individual or a population – depends on the cumulative effect of positive features out-weighing negative ones.

If it is accepted that at least some environmental adaptations in small-scale populations are mutually contradictory at least some of the time, then it follows that the more complex the infrastructure and the more socially differentiated the population becomes the more adaptations (of particular collectivities, or with respect to different phenomena) will tend to conflict. Under such conditions information about resources becomes more distorted and responses less immediate. This is particularly so where institutional subsystems reduce overall flexibility through their domination of the workings of more inclusive systems (Rappaport 1971a, 1977a).

Adaptation: a summary and reconsideration

CONCLUSION

A human population observed at a particular point in time is therefore in part a web of (often conflicting) adaptive strategies (Blurton-Jones 1975:89) employed by individuals and collectivities of different degrees of inclusiveness to cope with present and possible future conditions. These adaptations arise in specific contexts which make them appropriate, but are not necessarily the most adaptive possibility in the circumstances. Cultural adaptations are seldom the best of all possible solutions and never entirely rational. Because adaptive processes involve scheduling, and therefore ensure a crucial role for human choice, there is considerable room for error and manipulation. Also, because a population plans through culture for future contingencies, it can never be fully adapted to the present. If it were it would simply risk extinction in the future, since environmental and social conditions change in both predictable and unpredictable ways. The situation at any one time is a dynamic compromise between individuals and groups, and their interests as perceived for different phases of future time.

11

The reproduction and evolution of social and ecological systems

History itself is a *real* part of *natural history*, and of nature's becoming man

Karl Marx 1975:355

MATERIAL FLOW AND THE FLOW OF VALUE

All species require and assimilate energy and materials. Non-human primates, for example, appropriate calories, nutrients and other material substances from the environment around them. Because parts of the natural world are used as food and for other purposes, they may be said to have *use values* (although to employ this concept does not necessarily imply a uniform means of measuring it). Use values are not *produced*, they occur naturally, are appropriated and then consumed on an individual basis. Although tools and cooperation may be present, their role is secondary. Dominance hierarchies also exist, but these are based on the strongest individual appropriating the most choice resource, not on the exploitation of labour. *Homo sapiens* also requires and assimilates energy and materials which can be seen in terms of use values. Although some of these (air, water, certain foods) may be directly consumed on an individual basis, most are obtained through social relations of production whose scope for proliferation and modification is enormous (Ruyle 1973a:606). In short, social production both dominates and determines the character of human appropriation.

Humans not only appropriate use values through social production, but additionally attribute meaning to their environment. Specifically, use values are created not only through the expenditure of effort, but also through the cultural transformation of nature. Thus the attribution of meaning cannot easily be separated from the existence of production as a process which materially changes the environment, its

252

fundamentally social character and the ability of humans to conceive, in abstract terms, of such processes as transformations. Values arise out of cultural arrangements internal to social organization and cannot emerge independently from objects. Whatever is produced necessarily has value. Human environmental representations (Chapter 9) are therefore at the centre of an anthropological study of ecological relations, at that point where the rationality of systems meets the rationality of individual sentient beings. Food is accorded meaning: it is consumed, altered, displayed, distributed and destroyed. These are all social rather than nutritional activities; they are not solely for the creation of calories and materials. Human appropriation of other species and substances involves a semiotic transformation. Objects *become* 'natural resources', consciously so regarded, and are then used to produce and transform energy and other materials. Expenditure of effort becomes a conscious process, one that is objectified and given culturally valued form as labour or 'work' (Faris 1975:235). For the most part it is the exercise of labour which is involved in appropriating different parts of the environment and which therefore accords it value, although this is not to say that 'labour value' therefore provides us with a convenient cross-cultural standard of comparison.

Homo sapiens is the only species with the certain ability to conceptualize substances, and it is the act of conceptualization which changes substances into something more than is evident from an examination of their material characteristics. The translation of objective entities into culturally conceived forms involves a process of valuation, designation and representation. These result in varying degrees of reification of material phenomena. Processes of classification, for example, create abstract generic categories such as 'birds' or 'stones', which have no material existence. All that exists are individual birds and stones. In formal terms we might say that a is transformed into a^v, where a refers to a specific material substance defined in terms of its ecological characteristics and the superscript v to the value accorded it by a particular individual or population at a given time. In human terms, a can never exist simply in its ecological sense, but only as a^v. The value of v can change depending on time, context and individual, while a remains constant. Such values or representations, as well as the things they represent, are, in a very real economic sense, produced (Bourdieu 1977). Indeed, they are treated as if they were active agents in control of a situation. Money, of course, is the supreme example. Such fetishism is not simply Marxist mystification.

There are, therefore, two fundamental processes underlying the ecology of human social systems: (1) the appropriation of materials from the environment, their alteration and circulation through social

253

relations; and (2) the according of such materials with value which in turn affects the dynamics of the objective process of appropriation, alteration and circulation. The character of circulation of materials and value in any one population specifies its structure, its mode of production and reproduction and its position in any wider social formation. For Marx (1970:217) differences between systems of production and reproduction could be more specifically represented in terms of the way in which surplus is extracted from the labour of the producer. An ethnographic illustration of the form that this might take can be seen from a re-analysis of the Kwakiutl social formation by Ruyle (1973a:607). Figure 11.1 shows how traditional Kwakiutl stratification was generated and maintained through a particular flow pattern of material surplus and value.[1]

ECOLOGICAL SYSTEMS AND SOCIAL FORMATIONS

An ecological system is defined in terms of mutually interacting and adapting populations of organisms. Human populations are a necessary and integral part of most, if not all, present ecological systems; while the condition of many ecosystems is a direct result of human activity. Moreover, the ecological characteristics of human populations are comparable to those of other species, and in this sense culture is part of the distinctive means by which a human population maintains itself in the ecosystem. As with the population characteristics of other species, they may contribute to the reproduction of the ecological system, by either maintaining or altering its structure. The ecological reproduction of a human population is clearly a prerequisite of biological survival.

A social formation is an empirical configuration of processes and relations between human individuals and populations through which value is exchanged, and which is sufficiently bounded to possess an identifiable dynamic which ensures its independent survival and (under the right conditions) dictates the course of its transformation. It reproduces itself not simply by maintaining resources at a level that would permit the population involved to reproduce itself, but by processes which maintain the circulation of value in a way which preserves the basic relations of dominance and dependence. An example of this is the developmental cycle of domestic groups (Goody 1958). The cycle is part of a mechanism of overall social reproduction. It involves norms and patterns of social natality, kinship, socialization, dispersion and interaction, which are fundamentally conservative and combine to reproduce a series of stages of the same kind generation after generation. Although reproduction of a social formation is ulti-

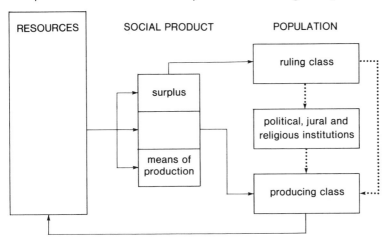

11.1 Flow of materials and value in a stratified population. The continuous
line indicates the flow of productive materials and value through the
expenditure of effort; the broken line indicates the flow of exploitative
effort (control of production, exchange, distribution) (modified from Ruyle
1973:607)

mately dependent on adequate ecological reproduction and may be
specifically linked in a determinant relationship with particular ecological variables, it may at the same time control socially adequate rates
of reproduction (Kunstadter 1972:320). This is because overall and
differential population figures may in themselves be important in the
viability of particular social formations.

Although ecological relations underpin any one social formation,
social reproduction is for the most part dependent on the circulation of
value. The dynamic for this may be located conceptually in a mode of
production or complex of interrelated modes of production. A social
formation need not contain within itself all the determinants necessary
to ensure its own reproduction, but necessarily alters the precise
determinate character of all interacting extrinsic factors. Internal relations and processes mediate the impact of causal factors external to the
system. Systems which *are* capable of reproducing themselves can be
theoretically specified as total systems of reproduction (Friedman
1976). These may be social formations comprising one or a number of
delineable modes of production (which may depend on how they are
defined), or may consist of interlinked social formations. Reproduction
is determined by the forces of production: environmental materials
and the cultural value attributed to them, the means of production and
a specific organization of labour. Local conditions do, of course,

constrain and limit, determine the limits of local productivity, surplus extraction, intensification and so on, in the short term (Friedman 1974); but local conditions are themselves the result of the total reproductive process which may affect the distribution of those conditions. There are two distributions of local constraints. It is possible to conceive of systems where the material constraints are only technology and environmental conditions. These Friedman calls primary distributive systems, and they correspond to systems which are largely self-reproductive and exchange only finished products. Systems of secondary distribution are those which involve technical interdependence. This is the most characteristic situation encountered historically, and in such cases the technological base and the environmental conditions are those of the larger reproductive totality, not of the local population. Here local material constraints depend on the properties of the larger social system (Friedman 1976:8, 10). The structures of reproduction in particular social forms are, then, those processes which dominate production and circulation. They constitute the socially determined form by which populations reproduce themselves as economic entities. Such relations of production are not simply relations in the organization of work, as with Steward and Harris, but relations which organize the entire labour flow of a population, its immediate work processes and the appropriation of environmental resources within the limits set by a particular body of techniques. Following Friedman and Rowlands (1977:203), we can visualize a population as existing in four concentrically nesting spheres. The outer and largest of these is the ecosystem, the next the system of productive forces, the next the system of social relations of production, and the innermost the system of superstructural relations. Each can be considered as structurally autonomous in the sense that its properties cannot be reduced to another level of organization (cf. Waddington 1970:180–3), although linked in the material process of reproduction by two types of relation. Each sphere constrains the limits of functional compatability between spheres, and therefore of their internal variation. Working outwards, relations of production organize and dominate the entire process of social reproduction. Now, this presents us with a much more satisfactory theoretical formulation than the simple determinism of Ratzel, Steward or Harris, while at the same time taking us beyond those systems approaches which manage to neglect the interposition of social relations and to avoid the attribution of relative significance in causal pathways. It is a dialectical determinism which ultimately plays-off social relations of production against culturally mediated environmental forces, and it is the outcome of this conceptually deduced interaction which (not only in the last instance, but frequently more immediately) determines the conditions of social life.

To observe the social, material, cultural and spatial arrangements of a particular population at a given point in time is not to identify the components of the system. Visible surface relations and features are artifacts of a system which also includes hidden functional components. Representations and artifacts often conceal the hidden dynamic of a system. The language of abstract second-order categories encourages the location of causes and effects in entities, which are often merely products of analysis. Particular phenomenal forms may be surface relations only, suggesting the impossibility of an ecology of particular institutions – an ecology of 'religion', 'warfare' or whatever. And it is because *adaptation* is a concept at the level of functional analysis that an approach based on the adaptation of institutions, subsistence types or entire social formations is inaccurate and grossly misleading. The dynamics of a system lie in functional components not in any material or institutional forms which they might take (Godelier 1977). It is for this reason that those who insist on examining the interface of social and ecological systems must understand the characteristic dynamics of both.

Now, any ethnographic study examines the ecological and social system at a particular stage in its development. At any one time the *observable* pattern of social relations, practices and settlement is generated through the interaction of a large number of variables. For example, a settlement pattern is generated through the interaction of social and ecological processes which are limited to a number of interrelated cycles: annual and longer-term cultivation cycles, the reproductive and growth cycles of animal populations; the developmental cycle of domestic groups, village cycles, kin-group fission and fusion; microclimatic cycles, exchange, ritual and other structurally determined production cycles, as well as non-reversible ecological successions. Depending on the conjunction of different phases in these cycles and trends, there will be different generative possibilities. In the case of populations of cultivators, these have implications for the succession on particular plots of land, and for the development of land surrounding such plots; which affect vegetational cover, the character and intensity of appropriation in the vicinity and the patterning of such specific artifacts of settlement as fences, communications networks, houses and other structures.

The notion of 'generation', then, is an analytical concept which may, in the ecological context, guide our interpretation of 'surface' relations of various kinds. It is a historically specific process, which can only be examined *post hoc*. Generation may be defined as the process of inter-action between systemic variables which results in a specific set of 'surface' relationships at a given point in time. A 'cycle', on the other hand, is a systemic process in which the same chain of events repeats itself. Any social or ecological system consists of a number of inter-related cycles. The patterns which may be generated depend on the conjunction of different stages in different cycles at any one point in time. The number of possible combinations is often considerable, given the large number of cycles articulating to reproduce a social and ecological formation, and their complex internal differentiation. Any one system, therefore, can generate a range of possible patterns of surface relations. It is important to separate the notion of pattern from system. Pattern operates at the level of institutions, artifacts and sur-face relations; system operates at the functional level.

The notion of cycle implies repetition, but social and ecological systems are accumulative and constantly undergoing change, change which may arise from intrinsic factors, the working out of contradic-tions within the social formation and between the dynamics of an ecological system and that of a social system. It may, for example, arise from the articulation of contradictory cycles. These processes, whose overall dynamic is located in long-term productive and ecological forces, lead to system transformation.

CONCEPTUALIZING EVOLUTION AND HISTORY

Evolution has long been a concept employed in anthropology. Nineteenth-century writers had very specific assumptions about the directionality of the process. This notion of directionality was accom-panied by moral and ideological overtones, where the highest and most complex form was necessarily the most superior in adaptive terms. Historical time was divided into stages through which all cul-tures were bound to pass. The dominant idea was generally of uni-linear development. Moreover, cultural evolution was seen as being essentially simple in ecological terms: it was the process by which the carrying capacity of a particular environment was raised through tech-nological innovation to support an increased population.

The problem with this general, unilinear, progressivist concept of evolution is that evolutionary change in particular places for particular populations does not operate in this way. It is true that by collapsing and conflating all historical and archaeological evidence there is a statistical trend in human evolution from gathering, through simple domestication and cultivation to advanced agriculture and industrialism; from low-energy to high-energy transformation; from lower to higher levels of integration; from egalitarian bands, through kinship societies or chiefdoms to states; and from immediate- to delayed-consumption societies. But the existence of such general statistical trends does not help us to understand the forces of change in particular places at particular times. The direction of evolution is not universally the same, each phase does not have an invariable set of characteristics. The course of general evolution all depends upon the criteria used to measure success. The evolution of human populations has proceeded in different ways, and at different speeds, in different parts of the world. Local evolutionary sequences respond to different pressures, adapt in different ways, through different stages. Unilinear evolution is a gross abstraction. Indeed, those who have advocated unilineal sequences have often been aware that local adaptations to the environment were part of an evolutionary process, but they have been concerned with the grand general historical development of the human species, and with broad trends defined by single factors, such as greater energy production. They have tended to ignore specific trends in relation to local ecological conditions, and have become mere catalogues of the significant parts of the developmental process. For this reason, Steward (1955) advocated a concept of multilinear evolution. This acknowledges that evolution is a much more flexible mechanism than rigid typologies permit. Within a framework of general tendencies we can recognize specific sequences tied to particular environments, sets of conditions and combinations of variables. In this sense the !Kung or Hadza are not evolutionary failures, or frozen representatives of stages modern humanity passed through thousands of years ago, but specific solutions to particular environmental and social conditions over an indicated period of time, with a complex history of their own. Occasionally, within the broader framework of increasing complexity, societies have changed to apparently simpler forms. Quite apart from examples we might select from the dissolution of empires and the fragmentation of states, we find that, at the mundane level of subsistence, peoples have shifted from cultivation to gathering, or have been sustained in this latter mode of subsistence through external exchange. In such cases populations have simply adapted to current economic circumstances and have not 'reverted' at all. In Southeast Asia and India, where some of these groups occur, they are really specialist groups, part of a wider and more complex social formation and division of labour (e.g. Fox 1969, Peterson 1978).

The ideas of White and Steward have been elaborated and synthesized in the past two decades. Sahlins, Service and their collaborators

(1960) distinguish quite specifically between general and specific evolution, while the concept of specific evolution has been put to the test in a series of ethnographic case studies, examining changes in social organization under varying, but specific, ecological conditions (e.g. Sahlins 1958, 1961). But what are not adequately considered in this approach are the internal temporal dynamics of social systems and how these interact with ecological variables to give rise to change. In the cultural-ecological and cultural-materialist formulation, evolution arises from the mechanistic adaptation of cultural totalities to the environment; cultures respond to environmental pressure while their internal development is directly contingent upon technical advances in an environment which specifies what is possible. Put in Marxist terms, adaptive change thus arises from the forces rather than the social relations of production. But the motive force of cultural evolution is not outside the social system – as Steward, Service, the early Sahlins, White and Harris would maintain – but necessarily inherent within it (Faris 1975:237–9). If we then develop the discussion above on reproduction, cultural evolution becomes the product of the transformation of social systems through their inability to produce themselves in exactly the same form. Put differently, evolution occurs because no adaptation is permanent (Cohen 1971:3), and because all systems of social and ecological relations contain within them contractions which unfold and work themselves out over time. Laws of reproduction are also, necessarily, those of transformation.

There is some debate in the immediate post-war anthropological literature as to the relationship between history and evolution. For White (1945:238), the two concepts referred to two distinct levels of process. For Kroeber (1946), Murdock (1949:186) and Steward (1955) history was much the same as evolution. By evolution White understood a general process, and his critics a specific process. In fact, White's 'history' and Kroeber's 'evolution' were to some extent resolved by Sahlins and Service (1960) as 'specific evolution'. But, in many ways, this remains an inadequate conceptualization of the relationship between history and evolution.

Given the formulation worked out in earlier sections of this chapter, history becomes the temporal passage of successive social formations, their internal reproduction *and their various cultural representations*. In contrast, the evolution of systems of which culture and social formations are part, and the evolution of social formations themselves, finds its dynamic in (and is defined by) changes which arise in the articulation of social and ecological systems. These occur through adaptation, the consequences of adaptation, and the working out of systemic trends and contradictions. However, the more temporally distanced

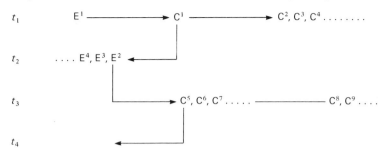

11.2 Cumulative changes resulting from the interaction of successive environmental conditions and cultural responses to them

historical and evolutionary processes become, the more difficult it is to distinguish clearly between them. The reason for this is that human history is, for the larger part, the history of environmental accommodation, the temporal succession of the ecological relations of past human societies and their habitats, and the accumulation of successive (and often contradictory) causations. But at any one point in time the effects of the environment (itself culturally constituted) are mediated by a historical legacy, also the product of environmental interactions. History therefore (in this sense) eventually dissolves into evolution,[2] although this is not to say that these respective phenomena can be understood through the application of a single theory.

Viewed from a systems angle no change is independent, each having ramifications throughout the matrix of social and ecological relations. Adaptive innovations may be responses to environmental perturbations, but themselves give rise to the need for adaptations to change the condition created by the first adaptation. Specific adaptations – say, the use of a plough to work heavy ground – not only have social repercussions for the organization of labour, but give rise to a new environmental condition to which the population must again adapt. Figure 11.2 illustrates in abstract terms how such cumulative changes might result from the interaction of successive environmental conditions and cultural responses to them. It is, of course, just a fragment of that vast network of interactions that must actually exist. Thus, environmental condition E^1 results in cultural response C^1. C^1 itself has further cultural consequences (C^2, C^3 . . .), but also results in further changes in environmental conditions (E^2, E^3, E^4). These, in turn, lead to further cultural consequences, and so on. An empirical example of this kind of process is provided by the consequences of swidden cultivation in parts of sub-Sahelian Africa (Netting 1968:19). In places, anthropogenic savannah grassland has replaced natural climax

261

vegetation through extensive burning and cultivation. The loss of tree cover has brought about changes in soil composition, ground temperatures, evaporation, wind and precipitation, which in turn have made formerly arable land less suitable for crops and better suited for herding. Consequently, local agriculturalists must either emphasize herding or give up their land to better-adapted pastoralists, all because of environmental changes which they themselves set in motion. A similar example is provided by developments in the New Guinea highlands (Sorenson 1972:350). Here the sweet potato (*Ipomoea batatas*) provided the opportunity to appropriate from new lands at higher altitudes, while egalitarian and group-segmenting social practices provided an appropriate context within which this could take place. However, expansion was finally limited by the very agricultural practices that originally made it possible.

But, while history may dissolve into evolution, human material modification of the environment brings nature increasingly under cultural control in objective terms as well as bringing it within the realm of cultural representations. The empirical evidence for this is provided in Chapters 1 and 2. Moreover, responses to environmental variables, or the actions made on environmental variables, to a large extent depend on how they are mediated by the structure of social relations. By this I mean that external causes become operational only through internal ones (Faris 1975:239). Human populations and sub-populations change and adapt, but social formations possess a quasi-independent dynamic of their own. Change is not simply anarchic; it takes place within populations *organized* through social relations: kinship relations, class relations, technical relations, relations of production, and so on. And so we come back to the axiom of Marx and its specific (though unappreciated) echo in Forde's 'middle term': that the environment acts *indirectly* through social relations and culture. The difference between the intellectual contexts in which both Marx and Forde were writing and the present is that we are now better placed (given the techniques and concepts of modern ecology) to examine precisely how it is that social relations filter environmental pressures, and how individuals entering into social relations cope with environmental variables through different flexible subsistence strategies and mechanisms of hazard protection.

Because social organization always pre-exists, populations faced with the same environmental pressure may adapt in different ways. While theoretically an underlying social structure may generate a number of different variants, the evolution of any one must be seen in a wider regional and ecological context. An example of this is found in the ethnography of the New Guinea highlands. Brookfield and Brown

(1963) have suggested that Chimbu respond to increased pressure on land by operating a more flexible lineage organization. This allows persons without land to attach themselves to clan hamlets which have more land, and is done by employing the morality of kinship. The Mae-Enga, on the other hand, studied by Mervyn Meggitt (1965), living in a similar area not far away and with a basically similar social structure, have responded in a completely opposite fashion. Because of pressure on land, their lineage organization appears to have rigidified. On the one hand, people have adapted to land shortage by making their kinship organization more flexible, perhaps under the pressure of kinship morality. On the other hand, that same morality has led to a closing of ranks, a narrower expression of kinship solidarity, which, too, has solved (at least for some clans) the problems of land pressure. Both populations have adapted to the same situation, but in opposite ways and with different consequences. In the Chimbu case, the practice leads to a more equitable spread of population over land, with reasonable and equal selective value for the many. The Mae-Enga solution leads to an inequitable distribution of people over land, with – other things being equal (which they seldom are) – greater selective advantage to some clans (those with a low population density) than others (Kelly 1968). Similarly, to argue that cognatic kinship groups are *generally* typical of low population densities, and tend to shift to unilineal patterns as pressure on resources increase (Harner 1970), is to ignore the evidence for viable cognatic arrangements in regions of high population density, such as Java. We should not worry about the inconsistency between Mandaya emphasis on lineality (Yengoyan 1973) and Sinhalese tendencies towards lineage decline (Leach 1961) in the face of a similar problem of land fragmentation. Consistency in this respect is no virtue and only represents a reversion to the naive correlative studies of an earlier generation.

THE RELATIONSHIP BETWEEN PHYLOGENETIC AND CULTURAL EVOLUTION

In most non-human species evolution proceeds through direct ecological pressure, on genetic material or the carriers of genetic material. Permanent genetic change is therefore brought about by natural selection. It is only in the higher primates that this ceases to be the sole significant source of trans-generational adaptations as culture begins to play an important role. Nevertheless, whatever degree of autonomy the body of cumulative cultural adaptations may attain, it remains dependent on the biological reproduction of populations and operates within the context of biological evolution. It is clear from Chapter 10 that phylogenetic, physiological, behavioural and cultural adaptations are closely interrelated through the evolution and history of human systems. Phylogenetic adaptation defines the range of possible environmental accommodations reached by the remaining three, but the scale of cultural adaptation in some human populations can redefine the conditions of biological existence for the species. For example, by creating a malaria-free environment, the sickling of red blood corpuscles no longer becomes adaptive and may be positively maladaptive for a population (Livingstone 1958). Similarly, by creating artificially oxygenated atmospheres it is possible to survive at altitudes and under planetary and interplanetary conditions beyond the limit of ordinary physiological accommodation, while cultural transmission obviates the process of much trial-and-error learning. In the long term cultural adaptation may actually reduce the rate and alter the direction of phylogenetic adaptation.

Human evolutionary processes are therefore a constant two-way interaction between biological adaptation and learned behaviour and the selective pressure on populations is the result of the conjunction of both ecological and social systems. One continually reinforces the other. This gradual change over time constitutes overall human evolution, but is the synthesis of two interdependent but recognizably separate processes. On the one hand there are genetic changes through the process of natural selection. These changes facilitate new kinds of learned behaviour. On the other hand learned behaviour (e.g. language) is changing much more rapidly as individuals learn from experience, communicate with each other and pass on information from one generation to the next. This process, as we have seen, is a more efficient means of adaptation than biological evolution when behaviour must adapt rapidly to changing or merely local conditions. It is a process we might conceptualize as cultural evolution when we stress its underlying structured, systemic, processual and adaptive aspects. As a succession of interrelated events and representations it becomes, in the sense that I have defined above, history.

Cultural evolution, then, is the process by which systemic changes occur through the accumulation of contradictions and by which human individuals and populations constantly adapt to new environmental pressures by learning. It may involve the invention of the plough to cultivate land more efficiently in the face of increasing population pressure or extraction of surplus labour; or the development of state institutions to enable a ruling group to control more effectively the flow of material and human resources. Much change in human populations has been of this kind, but occasionally the population–resource balance actually does reach a critical point where

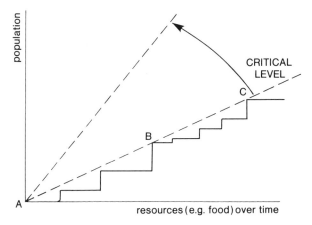

11.3 A schematic graph illustrating the relationship between cultural and genetic evolution. *Cultural evolution* (continuous line) follows a course within the critical constraints permitted by genetic adaptation. *Genetic evolution* can be traced through the points (A, B, C) where the continuous and broken lines meet

natural selection pressures begin to operate (Figure 11.3). This may sometimes be brought about by the existence of particular social formations, ideologies or cultural pressures: for example a taboo on contraception. In periods of critical food shortage, children who have more efficient means of food metabolism are more likely to survive than those who do not. In areas of malarial infestation, which in West Africa are inhabited by choice because of the absence of cattle-killing *Trypanosomiasis*, individuals with sickle-cell anaemia have a distinct selective advantage. On occasions, in critical conditions, certain genes have favoured (perhaps only in certain contexts) specific behaviours.[3] In this way behavioural evolution may have been subtly affected by natural selection. Natural selection, after all, only requires that a feature develop reliably in an environment where it is advantageous. But although it is parts of bodies which adapt, it is entire organisms which must survive. Consequently, humans no less than other animals must be seen as being composed of interrelated (and sometimes contradictory) adaptations, where natural selection and environmental adaptation take place within the constraints set by one another.

THE PROBLEM OF TRANSITION

Cultural evolution is not a regular, stable and incremental process. It is possible to divide evolutionary time into phases based on the

Environment, subsistence and system

occurrence of patterns of irregular events, phases which will vary depending on those events selected as being significant. Among the most crucial, observable and analysable discontinuites are those in which changes in many variables converge, becoming highly focussed in temporal terms. Such discontinuities take the form of a series of linked events and trends, often involving an imbalance between population and resources and sometimes spanning a very long period of time. They can be portrayed as transitions or transformations between two conditions which have recognizably systemic properties. On the other hand, the absence of such convergence and transition, and the accumulation of small changes within the system through internal differentiation, might be described as *involution*, following Geertz's (1963:80) embellishment of a concept originally suggested by Goldenweiser. The scale of transition may vary, from transitions in local social systems accompanied by only small perturbations in the wider ecological system to massive changes in the ecological system arising from the social system or from independent perturbations. In these terms transition applies to processes of varying magnitude depending upon how the boundaries of the system are drawn. But in each case a transition involves a transformation in a social formation, which leads to a corresponding shift in the ecological conditions of reproduction.

Anthropologists have devoted a good deal of attention to the discovery of the causes of such transitions. Among the most general of explanations are that population increase is the prime mover of subsistence change (population pressure models), that subsistence innovation determines the limits of population growth (Malthusian or Darwinian growth-limit models), or, more specifically, that the development of food production is a consequence of increasing mobilization of non-human effort (White 1959). Each of these explains the consequences of approaching carrying capacity in a different way. To all of them it is possible to find empirical exceptions, and these cannot be glossed over as being statistically unimportant. Because of the other-things-being-equal conditions of limiting factors, discussed in Chapter 2, and the variety of possible adaptive strategies, discussed in Chapters 6 and 7, it is impossible to formulate a single-factor theory of transitory process, let alone the entire course of evolution. It is possible to generalize *post facto* about such 'nomothetic' processes. This is what has been called 'general evolution' (Sahlins and Service 1960). But, although such measures may shed light on specific processes, represent a convenient summary of historical correlations and summarize general tendencies and the consequences of such changes, they can never explain them. Indeed, they may obscure basic functional relations. They bring us no nearer to understanding the functioning of specific social formations and ecological systems, while the search for testable explanations for general patterns is neither practicable nor necessary (Bronson 1975). In the real world changes occur in an open system and so involve *specific evolution*, a connected sequence of actual historical and systemic events. Such sequences may run contrary to general abstract trends. It is impossible to explain a specific empirical process in terms of an abstraction from a number of similar processes. While you can explain general evolution in terms of specific cases, the reverse is impossible. The problem here is that theory is confused with methodology. A general theory will not explain all specific cases, but a general methodology is essential if we are satisfactorily to begin to compare them. It is possible to reconstruct evolutionary pathways, but this cannot be done successfully by employing naive single-factor determinants. The ecological factors impinging on a particular population must be analysed broadly. To this end, the reconstruction of specific patterns of events and factors generating, for example, particular settlement patterns or procurement strategies is useful.

POPULATION, SUBSISTENCE CHANGE AND ENERGY OUTPUT

The difficulties encountered in single-factor and general explanations of transition and evolution are well illustrated by a discussion of the relationship of population growth to change. Population size is so easily measured and subjected to statistical manipulation and presentation, while its overall growth in historical time has been so dramatic, that it is no wonder that so much attention has been paid to it.

Discussions of cultural evolution have often revolved around the observation that the growth of human population has been exponential, rising only gradually between 10,000 B.P. and 2,000 B.P., but thereafter experiencing a steep upward swing (Deevey 1960). Population size is contingent upon the amount of energy available to an animal population, which in turn depends on its position in a food chain. *Homo sapiens* are unique in that within the space of 10,000 years they have been able to alter their position in food chains to manipulate and create feeding relations through cultural adaptations. Food chains have been simplified and shortened through the removal of competing organisms. Gross primary production has been raised (Figure 11.4) by removing physical limitations, such as water and nutrient shortage. Energy has been maximized by maintaining what are (in ecological terms) immature systems. The usefulness of species has been improved through genetic manipulation and husbandry. Technological modification of the surface of the earth, as in irrigation, has permitted

267

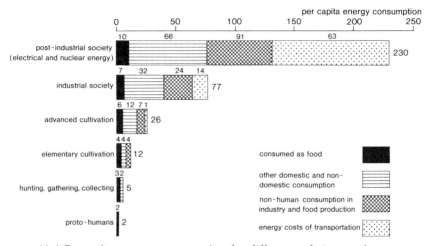

11.4 *Per capita* energy consumption for different subsistence forms measured in kcal 10³. Total *per capita* energy is shown at the end of each column, and fractions for each category of energy use are indicated (modified from data provided by Cook 1971)

expansion into previously unoccupied areas. In mentioning these things I am no more than re-stating and amplifying trends already noted in Chapter 2.

The demographic and technical trends mentioned in the previous paragraph are usually associated with the ability to capture and employ increasing amounts of energy, particularly those sources made available in the course of the industrial revolution. This point is illustrated clearly when population growth is plotted logarithmically (Deevey 1960). On such a scale, the graph shows jumps in population magnitude linked to transitions in ecological systems: hominization, domestication and industrialization. Energy consumption also rises exponentially. It was by observing that the increase of energy capture and transformation is characteristic of all life forms (Lotka 1922), and that the progressive ability among human populations (through technology) to capture an increasingly larger amount of energy from the environment is particularly impressive, that White (1949, 1959) and others came to develop energy as both a determinant and proxy of all cultural development. Such a mechanical approach to an understanding of the relationship between population and resources, however, ignores both the dramatic fluctuations in energy capture over time and space, and the fact that population growth and the appropriation of resources take place within a social as well as an ecological system.

It is true that relative energy efficiency can be used to measure the evolution of an aspect of human subsistence and ecological systems (e.g. Watson and Watson 1969:viii), while the relative cost of food has decreased overall in the course of cultural evolution. But although something approaching an exponential curve characterizes general use over the course of human evolution and history, curves of energy transformation of varying shapes characterize the adaptive pathways of specific historically delineated populations (Bennett 1976:47, Bronson 1972). Many populations have exhibited a remarkable stability in energy use, technology and population levels over time, others display curves of decline and collapse in patterns of resource utilization, returning to simpler ones. Exponential trends relate to *general* evolution only.

Moreover, the amount of energy available to a population can be increased through the political domination of occupied regions, through unequal trade, and exploitation in class relations. Such processes, therefore, necessarily involve an unequal distribution of resources. Also, social constraints often act to keep the population well below what is technically possible in a particular area. Put rather differently, technological innovation can be used in different ways: for increasing efficiency, for increasing population, or for increasing leisure. The particular option selected is the outcome of events in a system of social relations.

At this point, it makes some sense to focus on a particular example of transition in social and ecological systems: increasing dependence on plant cultivation. It has widely been accepted (Boserup 1965, Carneiro 1967, 1970, D. Harris 1977a:187–8, Wilkinson 1973, Cohen 1977) that agricultural origins and intensification, through the improvement of techniques in an effort to increase calories, can be explained as an adaptation triggered by demographic stress. Indeed, Harner (1970) has constructed a scale for the measurement of population pressure based on an inverse relation between the degree of dependence on hunting and gathering and the degree of population pressure. Fishing dependence is also predicted to show a positive correlation with an increase in the scarcity of land resources. When the scale is tested in relation to political complexity and social differentiation, very high correlations are found between the index of population growth and social evolution. But this is a defence of the stress model at the level of general evolution. It cannot be applied to specific cases and particular transitions, and fails to indicate the *cause* of population increase. White (1949) and others have argued that it is technological innovation which permits population increase, rather than population pressure encouraging innovation. But at the empirical level it is clear that population growth may be either the trigger *or* the consequence of agricultural

269

intensification. For example, a recent statistical analysis of data from 17 New Guinea highland groups (Brown and Podolefsky 1976:229) provides no evidence for a consistent uni-causal relationship between population density and agricultural intensity. Indeed, it is likely that, in every situation, subsistence change and population growth are interdependent and mutually reinforcing. Population is not an independent variable. Moreover, rate of growth must be distinguished from pressure on resources due to high density, and since density is often related to resources it does not automatically constitute a pressure (Bronson 1972:70). Population density may respond to many factors, not merely agricultural or technological ones, while new techniques and increased appropriation may be the outcome of intensification of a sedentary lifestyle, exchange, security, prestige, comfort and health as much as work efficiency (Bronson 1972:63, Polgar 1975:6). The specific proximate determinants are an outcome of a complex configuration of ecological and cultural conditions, and whether initially one or the other is important may not matter much. On the other hand, in some cases, one factor may become a key determinant through a process of system amplification. In certain cases overall human effort may become increasingly efficient through intensification and environmental modification. This is so, for example, with the introduction of animal traction or machinery powered by environmental rhythms or fossil fuel. But it is now very clear that intensification of food production may require more human energy rather than less (Table 6.3). So, while reduced subsistence yields are a major reason for altering techniques, White failed to associate such changes with declining productivity per man-hour as an economic condition of rising population pressure on resources (Netting 1974:24).

Intensification may well lead to greater overall inefficiency and expenditure of energy through human labour, but this conceals possible differences of structural importance within the population. In the process of class formation a small, increasingly non-productive group expends less labour and becomes increasingly inefficient in energetic terms, whereas subordinate groups of producers (slaves, peasants, industrial workers) may expend more labour and become more energetically efficient per unit produced, producing much more than they consume. The surpluses created in this way are mobilized to support the inefficient section of the population.

There has therefore been an overall increase in the *relative* efficiency of energy captured through technological complexity (Figure 11.4). However, *absolute* efficiency has decreased, since increasing technological complexity is linked to increasing energy, demands (human and non-human) to produce the same amount of food *pro rata*. Therefore the absolute energy cost of food production rises, and ecological efficiency declines. The theoretical basis and empirical evidence for this point have already been discussed in Chapter 6.

Boserup (1965) has calculated that swidden cultivators have low food yields but that each family works only about 1,000 hours each year. Intensive farming, with higher yields, is associated with 5,000 hours each year. But Boserup argues that, given a choice, a human group will always choose techniques which have the lowest absolute cost rather than the highest yield. Bronson (1972) and Sahlins (1972) have argued that this controversial statement suggests that we must consider the possibility that low cost is as advantageous as high yield under certain conditions. The maximization of food yields introduces other adaptive problems, the main one being that there is limited time available for all life-support activities. Maximization requires increasingly greater amounts of time (Lawton 1973). Boserup suggests that humans are time minimizers, and there is some evidence for this in the evolutionary importance of hunting as a subsistence strategy, since hunting takes a long time and increases the risk of predation (Hardesty 1977:61–2). Rapport and Turner (1975) argue that time minimization is associated with stable populations, while their increase raises the cost of foraging. This interpretation fits Boserup's data, as increasing food yield and cost are explained by population pressure. However, Waddell (1972:218–19) was unable to find that extensive systems were inherently more productive than intensive ones, noting that Boserup failed to include ecological and biological variables which might have some effect independent of technique. But Waddell's sample is small, and his results neither entirely prove nor disprove her thesis. Boserup is concerned with a much higher level of generality, with trend and tendency, and with peasant rather than tribal production (Bennett 1976:161).

THE EVOLUTION OF OPEN SYSTEMS

A high degree of system closure, which is a necessary condition of most of the hypothesis concerning transition discussed above, was probably a common feature of early human groups with very low population levels, as they migrated, became isolated and diversified. All existing human systems exhibit a much lower degree of closure, but it is possible that some still possess an extensive relative ecological autonomy.

The breakdown of local self-sufficiency marks a key ecological transition, while human evolution and history, overall, indicate a movement towards increasingly more inclusive and complex systems. There are a number of crucial processes associated with the increasing scale of human systems:

1. Demands, for matter or energy, on a local system by an external one may destabilize traditional organizations (including adaptive mechanisms) which have evolved over a long time span. If subsistence arrangements can no longer regulate the major articulation between the human population and the ecosystem, internal control may be lost, together with ecosystem stability (Nietschmann 1973:9). The loss of self-sufficiency, therefore, leads to loss of the possibility of regulatory autonomy, even if this has not been realized. The regulatory capacity found in smaller systems is not adequately replaced by increasingly remote centralized regulators responding to increasingly simplified variables.

2. As the scale of a system enlarges to incorporate other systems, its parts become more specialized in terms of economic production and social relations. The system generates new forms of organization to integrate and manage the wider differentiation of its parts each of which becomes more dependent upon the total enlarging system. The larger and more complex a population or social formation, and the more elaborate the artifacts it creates, the more it will create potential niches that become adopted, adapted to and differentiated by other organisms and populations (Audy 1971:308, Whyte 1977:70).

The process of subsistence (and therefore ecological) specialization is well illustrated by the intensification of cultivation. In some respects such a process represents a more significant change than that from reliance on non-domesticated resources to swiddening, since in the creation of a swidden plot the assemblage of cultigens is fulfilling a similar spatial and functional role as equivalent wild species (D. R. Harris 1969:6). With the shift to plots dominated by a single species, which may in some cases occupy the same space for periods from fifteen to seventy years without fallow, the structure and functional dynamics change considerably (Flannery 1965), reversing the usual process of ecological succession towards more mature systems. The pre-existing ecosystem is almost entirely destroyed and replaced with an artificial system with quite different properties and energy transfers (D. R. Harris 1973:393–4). To put it simply, the reduction of the species-diversity index may, although not necessarily, result in a weakened capacity to maximize the use of available solar energy. Cropping periods overlap less or do not overlap at all. This in turn means greater demands on land by the same population and possible changes in the overall pattern of settlement through expansion. Expansion of domestication in turn leads to a scarcity of non-domesticated resources (Harner 1970:71). In fact, entire regions undergoing crop specialization may lead to increasing environmental instability, with the inability of the fewer species that are found there to combat effectively the pressures of natural selection without seriously affecting the balance of the system. It has been suggested that monocrop plots are representative of the most fragile ecosystems of which there is knowledge (Rappaport 1977a; D. R. Harris 1973:393–4; Woodwell and Smith 1969).

3. Wider organizations facilitate the diffusion and generation of more innovations so that the potential rate of change is accelerated. This process is reflected historically.

4. Increased differentiation and rate of change generate more conflicts.

5. Greater scale and specialization reduce the diversity of local systems and hence the extent of flexible response.

6. Increased scale and specialization involve more energy expenditure on communication and organization. Consequently, overall efficiency declines. This we have already noted.

7. Greater organization and specialization lead to a more complex social and technical division of labour, the development of social institutions with sub-systemic properties, formal codification of acceptable cultural responses, and more extensive arrangements for social control.

I have already stressed the close functional relationship between social formations and ecological systems, while maintaining their analytic distinctiveness. Specific studies of the history and evolution of linked human social and ecological systems are few, and most remain speculative. Some, however, have specifically attempted to trace out evolutionary developments which hinge on the interaction of social formations and ecological systems. But studies in the evolution of systems – particularly regional systems – have been widely characterized by some of the same critical faults identified with systems approaches in general and negative feedback models. It has widely been assumed that the links in systems are stable and regular and that there is a general bias towards the location of slow irreversible adaptive change to higher systems (Adams 1974:242). It is clear, however, from the analysis of contemporary systems and well-documented historical sequences, that links fluctuate widely and that flows are often reversible. In general, the dynamics of increasingly open systems are much more complex and messy than has generally been recognized.

വവ

Ecology in anthropological method and theory

ON EMPIRICAL CONTRIBUTIONS AND TECHNIQUES

I have had two interrelated aims in writing this book. The first has been to indicate that there is much to be salvaged from contradictory and otherwise singularly inadequate theoretical styles in the analysis of human environmental relations. Different styles and emphasis have arisen as understandable responses to dissatisfaction with earlier approaches, or the ideological implications of those approaches. It is often difficult to separate ideology from theory in social science. We find a repetition (a re-cycling) of old debates and ideas. These, to a large degree, reflect ideology. But at the same time there is a cumulative growth in a body of knowledge and assumptions which prevents the formulation of old debates in precisely the same terms. This is science, and attempts to separate it from ideology mark some kind of movement towards the claim of a discipline to be scientific.

The second aim has been to show the ways in which particular techniques and concepts can be used to advantage in the analysis of human subsistence. At a purely empirical level, recent ecological research conducted in this field has furnished new and detailed data for the analysis of productive processes. In the first place, it has led to new ways of looking at the relations between different sets of information and the employment of different descriptive categories, giving rise to new and hitherto unperceived problems and relationships. As a result, things which were previously only of minor interest or neglected have assumed some significance and become subject to careful investigation: for example, the consequences of different technologies, subsistence strategies and other means by which human populations modify their environment; the effects of patterns of weed growth, long-term vegetational successions; the significance of soil conditions and their relation to cultivation practices; and the intensive study of particular plots and cropping patterns. In the second place, an ecological approach has meant greater accuracy and quantitative specificity in fieldwork methods. Carrying-capacity computations have become important (although not yet dependable); subsistence effort is measured in terms of the energy expenditure for various activities and localities; yield and consumption are specified by weight or in calories, with reference to individual food species, geographical source, social group and type of resource. The differential importance of particular resources, localities, groups and time periods is assessed through the calculation of unit-cost or yield ratios, while input–output indices provide some indication of overall efficiency for any one category based on such criteria. Intensive and detailed work of this kind has not only provided more accurate statements about the utilization of resources but has sometimes obtained results which a more cursory and conventional examination of subsistence might have missed. This necessarily gives rise to a more informed and accurate understanding of the structure and articulation of social relations and systems. The ecological analysis of subsistence techniques permits the identification, measurement and formulation of statements relating to those functional relationships associated with environmental interchanges.

It is no good deceiving ourselves about the ease of proper description – it remains a very real problem. Empirical work has indicated that ecological relations are complex and inadequately portrayed by simple correlations. There is still a scarcity of reliable measurements of subsistence productivity, yields, inputs and outputs of labour and effort, and time and distance factors. Such technical advances as discussed in Chapters 5, 6 and 7 may prove to be the most important and enduring contribution of ecological approaches in anthropology.

OF FRAMEWORKS AND THEORY

While stressing the practical contributions of particular techniques, I have tried to guard against theoretical reductionism. Ecology itself cannot answer all the questions we might wish to ask, it cannot even pose them. The assistance it can render in the formulation of problems is limited, and this is even more true when it comes to problem solving. Ecology has been seen as a frame of reference which anticipates theory, rather than theory itself (Cook 1973:27). It provides a framework which serves to delimit a problem for study, indicates ways in which problems might be approached, provides a focus for the convergence of similar interests in related disciplines, and integrates divergent research trends and ethnographic data.

The justification for the ecological approach offered in the previous paragraph is now commonplace, but attempts to construct some all-encompassing science can easily lead to diffuseness, incoherence and intellectual stagnation. Ecological approaches and data can only ever constitute *part* of a substantive analysis of a particular social formation, which must also be grounded in methodology and theory drawn from other than ecological precedent. It is particularly crucial to appreciate this since ecology is a realm in which amateurs are often found playing with professional tools. It is also all too easy for the anthropologist to become so enamoured of ecological jargon and the spurious science of counting calories for its own sake, that he does not note the cautiousness adopted by many biologists when making such measurements in their descriptions.

Ecological systems approaches supply not only data and a framework but also a methodological rubric. In saying this, I am distinguishing methodology in the strict sense from theory. Methodology can, and should, remain constant against certain kinds of theory, to enable the repeatability of the analysis. Theory, on the other hand, must be a response to particular sets of data and types of problem. For example, a theory to understand capitalism may look different from that required to understand feudalism, but if comparison is to be entertained then both must be grounded in a common methodology. Much of what is described as ecological theory is perhaps more accurately to be understood as methodology, in as much as in itself it does not (and does not claim to) offer explanations of phenomena, but instead offers procedures to facilitate explanation and exploration.

It is true that systems approaches encourage the logical hazard of infinite regress by insisting on the significance of indirect and increasingly more distant and diffuse variables (Mason and Langenheim 1957:339). Newcomer (1972:5) sees this as coming dangerously close to providing no explanation at all. But although direct factors are the only ones to which a causal response can (in the end) be confirmed, it seems to me that he is being needlessly polemical. Seeking causation in a social system is an essentially empirical pursuit, although theory may help to locate causes. The location of causes cannot be determined theoretically, except in theoretical terms. It is fruitless to generalize about how proximate the calculus of determination might be.

Human ecology can make sense only if we bring social structure and social systems back in, and cease to regard social artifacts and variables as atomized and unconnected points in an ecological system. Theoretically, this can be avoided in part by shifting the emphasis from eco-systems to systems, by emphasizing the open-endedness of such systems and the flexibility of human populations in them. Human ecology, therefore, ultimately dissolves into a general theory of human society. It must inevitably do so, and in the end the distinctive and useful aspects of the ecological approach must be incorporated into a general anthropology. Dialectical materialism and systems approaches must extend outwards to ecological systems, and not confine themselves to social formations. In the same way as it is ultimately necessary to understand wider solar chemistry in order to explain the biological system of Earth, so to understand social systems we must ultimately seek some answers in the ecosphere.

RESISTING A DISCOURSE OF OPPOSITIONS AND IMMANENCE

It is the grappling with empirical reality over successive generations and the conceptual inadequacies of successive formulations of objective concepts of 'environment' and 'nature' in anthropological discourse which has led, through systems approaches, to a position in which the acknowledged dialectical relationship between the concepts threatens their existence as useful objective categories. *Homo sapiens* and nature are not two independent entities; society is not the negation of nature. It is now clear that humans are paradoxically a part of nature and apart from it; constrained by it, but transforming it. But this is no simple relationship, since every social action and idea, every rule, every category, is mediated by several million years of human and proto-human history and evolution. It is a self-amplifying process of continual re-interpretation and re-transformation, such that to pose simple questions regarding whether a particular trait is naturally or socially determined becomes meaningless.

The relationship between the terms of another key conceptual antithesis is rather different. For as long as the terms ecology and economy have been etymologically distinguishable they have been used interchangeably in certain circumstances, such that it was obvious for Haeckel (1911:793) to define his neologism as 'the economy of nature'. The semantic similarity between the two concepts has sustained a widespread belief that economic analysis (and therefore economic anthropology) would eventually be subordinated to ecology (Wells, Huxley and Wells 1934:962, Bates 1953, J. G. D. Clark 1954:2). This notion has been reworked in the new anthropological systems ecology (Vayda 1967, Anderson 1973:183). Such a position is not only unhelpful but fundamentally mistaken, not least because it encourages the blurring of distinct formal languages, concepts, models and data for ideological reasons. The main objection, however, has already been set out in the first section of Chapter 11 – that economic relations are grounded in a concept of value. From a formal, theoretical and systemic point of view, ecological and economic relations have much in common (Cook 1973:42). Indeed, economic relations are necessarily also ecological ones. Both emphasize the circularity of process, the cyclical nature of transactions and flows, negative and positive feedback rather than manifest and latent function, and tend towards optimal states of equilibrium but never achieve it.

Economic systems, like their ecological counterpart, can be interpreted in terms of the cycles of material and energy necessary to reproduce them, where the various phases of production and consumption reflect two aspects of a single reality (cf. Lawton 1973:table 1; Marx 1971:195–6). An energy-flow approach stresses the fact that every social system has a theoretically measurable and objective energy cost of reproduction, in addition to a rate of potential surplus determined by available technology (Friedman 1974:446). The energetic approach gives quantitative form to key theoretical concepts such that total energy costs and allocations can be traced over time. Ecological energetics and the environmental systems approach offer a sound material basis for the descriptive ethnography of production, for an ecology of the means of production and its articulation with other components of society, and for the theory of economic anthropology.[1]

However, material relationships between humans (those we describe as economic) are predicated by a notion of value, and value which is not reducible to matter can affect material transactions. Furthermore, it is based on a cultural division of tasks (Lee 1969:73) and on exchange between individuals of the same species, rather than between species. Based on value, the economic may become increasingly differentiated from the ecological, and as – through exchange – economic relations become increasingly separate from other status relations in local social formations, so economic institutions and the economy as a separate phenomenal form emerge.

In view of this, it might seem somewhat paradoxical to suggest that the central problem of economic anthropology increasingly has to do with the character of the differentiation and articulation of economy and ecosystem, of how environmental, ecological and technical processes relate to economically productive social activities (those involving labour and energy expenditure), together with flows of material resources and information in events of appropriation, transformation, transfer and utilization which are both calculated and planned (Cook 1973:41). The focus on production brings together both ecological and economic approaches, and emphasizes their essential complementarity rather than their antagonism. The kind of empirical data referred to above and the ecological approach in general, with its attention to the structure and energy cost of the food-gathering process and the reproduction of social structures and species, have gone some way in endorsing the importance of production in the analysis of economic systems in general, somewhat neglected under the influence of neo-classical and exchange models of economic behaviour (Meillassoux 1972, Dupré and Rey 1969). Godelier has argued for the primacy of production on materialist grounds (1972:263–8), while others have stressed its adaptive role, the effective productive use of environmental resources (e.g. Sahlins and Service 1960). Because of its necessary association with technology, the productive process integrates the ecological with the economic, while, through its link with the organization of work and ideology, production connects both ecology and economy with the wider social system. Finally, the relationship of individuals to the process of production through participation or control of resources determines their relative portion of the total social product and the social relationships between them (Cook 1973:39).

One matter is clear beyond doubt: the relationship between *Homo sapiens* and the environment cannot be reduced to essences or imperatives – not environmentalism, sociologism nor ecologism. Ecology as *human* ecology cannot ever be an autonomous discipline, except in the limited sense of an understanding of the dynamics of human populations in their ecological context. Any attempt at a rational division of intellectual labour which, because of the specialized technical skills involved, is always tempting, is to be avoided. Ecology is best represented as a problematic – a discursive practice – rather than a discipline. It brings into focus the articulation of several fields of knowledge, skills and disciplines. The conditions for its legitimate existence as a discipline are additionally questionable because – as has been shown – this would deny the (undoubted) specificity and distinctive character of human social systems. Science requires that a system of data shall be sufficiently autonomous for certain internal theoretical concepts to be developed at a given level. Given the relative interconnectedness of 'data' and theoretical systems it is doubtful that 'subjects' can ever be 'disciplines' in the strict sense, and most remain either ideological categories or convenient means of dividing up research interests. What we call 'ecology' has to be saved from both its critics and its more enthusiastic and naive practitioners, for it provides one possible route out of an errant anthropology which has been criticized for having lost its way and become an arbitrary combination of disciplines. Ecology (whatever else it may or may not do) does stress integration (Forde 1948, 1970). The intellectual unity provided by evolutionism until its demise can only be recaptured through a theoretical emphasis on system, history, evolution and cultural adaptation. And, as we have seen, it is precisely the ecological problematic which squarely faces these issues together.

Notes

vwvwvwvwvwvwvwvwvwvwvwvwvwvwvwvwvwvwvwvwvwvwvwvwvwvwvwvwvwvwvwvwvwvwvwvwvwvwvw

Preface

1 Formal definitions of 'ecology' vary. It is widely held as the study of the relations of plants and animals, particularly plant and animal communities, to their surroundings, animate and inanimate. It has also been seen as 'the study of adaptations' (Bates 1960:547–68), or the study of any 'property that has a measurable direct influence on the fecundity, longevity, speed of development, or spatial position of an organism' (Maelzer 1965:160).

1. Environmental determinism and causal correlation

1 Hippocrates, whose views on environmental determinism were influential until the nineteenth century, regarded climate as responsible for establishing that balance of the four humours which accounted for all differences in geography, personality and physical form (Glacken 1967:80–115).

2 In this respect it is of some interest to observe developments in interstitial areas of the natural and social sciences. Thus, explanations of behaviour differences in terms of contrasting environment, both between species and within them, are current in studies of animal behaviour (Crook and Gartlan 1966, Crook 1970, Denham 1971, Eisenberg *et al.* 1972). Other studies have questioned the validity of specific analyses and have suggested a much more complex relationship between environment and evolution in primate social patterns (Struhsacker 1969, Hladick 1975). Whatever the case may be, it is worth noting that non-human animals (even primates) participate in environmental interactions which are enormously simplified by comparison with *Homo sapiens*. This is in large part due to the absence of complex cultural traditions and values mediating between the use of resources and adaptive mechanisms.

3 A more general and theoretical treatment of the way in which social factors intervene to determine environmental relations long before the environment itself compels such action is found in the recent critical literature on cultural adaptation (Friedman 1974).

4 This is well illustrated by the apparently conflicting accounts in the New Guinea highlands literature on the relationship between demographic pressure and flexibility in lineage membership. See Chapter 11.

280

5 For a formal demonstration of the logic entailed in this proposition see Chapter 11, note 2.

2. *Possibilism and limiting factors*

1 For Marx and Engels human manipulation of the landscape was important because it was frequently a condition for the development of certain kinds of production, for example hydraulic engineering and the institution of effective agriculture in the Netherlands. Neither developed the theme at any length, and their influence on the shaping of environmental possibilism has been negligible. It has been left to later commentators to embellish their remarks. However, the widespread characterization of their work as crude environmentalism is a palpable falsehood.

2 Despite his insistence (1934:464) that 'broad general classifications of climatic and vegetational regions are quite inadequate for the analysis of cultural possibilities', Forde certainly over-emphasized the homogeneity of the three vegetation zones of West Africa in his analysis of the development of states in that region (1953; cf. Morton-Williams 1969:80).

3 Weiner (1972:405–6) has argued that carrying capacity computations should also take into account the extent to which an individual is biologically able to work, a capacity affected by adequacy of diet, intensity of effort, heat load and disease.

3. *Cultural ecology and the explanatory imperative*

1 Although this term is sometimes used more widely to refer to analyses of the relationship between culture, social organization and the environment (e.g. D. R. Harris 1978), it is less misleading, more accurate and useful to restrict it to the work of Steward and those most directly influenced by him (cf. Vayda and Rappaport 1968). The idea that 'cultural ecology' is a substantive field is particularly confusing when applied to contemporary work influenced by explicitly biological concepts, since Steward was adamant in rejecting the idea that human ecology should be a kind of animal ecology, and upheld the strict analytical independence of the 'superorganic' (Ellen 1978a:122).

2 I have restricted myself here to examples firmly within the Stewardian tradition. However, dissatisfaction with existing theory and an interest in environmental adaptation as an explanatory device has given rise to other analyses, less explicitly part of this movement. Some of the correlative studies discussed in the previous chapter incline towards this position. A notable case is the suggestion by Yengoyan (1968) that Australian genealogical sections function to regulate not only marriage but also resource appropriation by increasing the number of sections (and therefore resource-bearing social relations) in poor areas of low population density.

3 A similar argument has been propounded by Goldschmidt (1965) for East African pastoralist societies. Segmentary lineages, and kinship relations more generally, are seen as being important where movement is essential

and spatially based social units therefore impracticable. Military organization is encouraged by the vulnerability of herds.

4 Harris is not entirely satisfied with the Stewardian formulation, however, and is particularly critical of the concept of 'cultural core'. Whereas the components of Marx's 'base' are seen as being explicit, those of the core vary; whereas the residual features of social organization external to the base are still, however tenuously, related to it, Steward's 'secondary features' may be in no causal relation to the core at all.

5 For Mauss (1979 (1906):80), and for Durkheim, social morphology comprised those features – the mass, density, form and composition of groups – which closely reflect environmental rhythms, and upon which the institutions of social life are *dependent*.

6 This point is developed more fully in Chapter 4.

7 Cf. the distinction between a specialized and generalized ecosystem (see pp. 86–9). A generalized ecosystem permits a wider range of subsistence modifications, and therefore of technical relations of production. In this sense it might be regarded as *permissive*. For its employment in this sense see Burnham (1979).

8 More recently Steward seems to have conceded the theoretical point about feedback and has emphasized more generally the way in which social and cultural relations at different levels of integration affect the interaction of biological, cultural and environmental factors (Steward 1968:341, 338).

9 The matter is discussed further in Chapters 4 and 7.

4. Human ecology and the biological model

1 The publication of Warming's *Plantesamfund* (1895) is usually taken as marking the beginning of systematic plant ecology. The first textbook devoted to the study of animal ecology was C. C. Adams's *Guide* (1913), while a study by Victor Shelford published in the same year (*Animal communities in temperate America*) represents the first comprehensive contribution to the subject. Although these signify the beginnings of modern ecological studies, Buffon, in 1749, had seriously attempted to systematize knowledge concerning the relations between animals and their environments, while I have noted the pioneer thinking of Haeckel. For a more detailed examination of the development of ecology as a biological science see Allee *et al.* (1949) and Pearse (1939:1–3).

2 For example: Adams (1935), Allee (1931, 1951), Bews (1935), Darling (1951), Dice (1955), E. P. Odum (1953), H. T. Odum (1971).

3 The definition of an ecosystem provided by Tansley (1946:206) refers to organisms as 'naturally living together as a sociological unit'. Consider also the uses and abuses of 'community', 'society', 'culture', 'caste', and 'currency' (e.g. H. T. Odum 1971).

4 Arising from (and in part related to) such work was an interest in food habits as an adjunct to nutritional research. The relationship is particularly clear from Richards's (1939) study of the Bemba, and is specifically exemplified in the writings of Mead (e.g. 1945) and Bennett (1946; see also Bennett

1976:241). This literature has been orientated largely towards policy recommendations, and developed for the most part quite separately from that ethnography and theory explicitly concerned with environmental relations. It has, however, served to familiarize certain anthropologists with the concepts of nutrition and energetics (but see also McArthur 1960).

5 These remarks apply to developments in social and cultural anthropology. The growth of ecological sophistication in the biological study of human populations has proceeded rather differently. Curiously, though, students of primate ethology have only recently recognized the importance of the detailed examination of environmental data (Glander 1975), and often statements concerning social behaviour have been related to generalized descriptions of a particular habitat. There is some evidence to suggest (Denham 1971) that current anthropological approaches have led to conceptual innovation and empirical rigour in the ecological work of primatologists.

6 In fact, Barth had noted the usefulness of the niche concept much earlier (1950:338). However, this interest had been primarily archaeological.

7 For recent discussion of the properties of ecosystems see H. T. Odum (1971), E. P. Odum (1963), Phillipson (1966), and Stoddart (1969).

8 In a rather different (and more specific) context, Leach (1961:304–5) was making much the same point in criticizing those British functionalists who had tended to contrast 'society' and 'material environment' in the analysis of kinship.

9 It has been suggested that while it may be necessary to refer to non-cultural variables, the anthropologist is not in a position to deal with them as such. This view is enshrined as methodological dogma by Gluckman (1964). But, while there are practical and technical reasons for treating boundaries with other disciplines warily and with respect, they should never impede the direction of analysis.

10 For an interesting and early exception see Wissler (1926:216–17).

11 Interaction between ideological and scientific ecology has given rise to certain popular theoretical illusions, for example the notion that the biosphere and surface of the earth constitute not only a giant system, but a single organism (Lovelock and Epton 1975). Its existence is predicated on two propositions: (a) that life exists only because material conditions on earth happen to be just right for its existence, and (b) that life defines the material conditions needed for its survival and ensures that they remain.

12 Others concerned with the development of a human ecology relevant to questions of public policy have made a more balanced appraisal of the situation and adopted a more rational and realistic posture (e.g. Bennett 1976).

6. Ecosystems and subsistence patterns I

1 For an earlier, and slightly different, attempt to specify theoretically the range of variables crucial for a full and accurate description of subsistence strategies see Greenfield (1965).

7. Ecosystems and subsistence patterns II

1 Sahlins (1972:104–5, and *passim*) has also made use of the production data collected by Pospisil and Scudder on the Kapauku and Valley Tonga respectively. But these well-known types of statistic are not necessarily a direct product of ecological approaches or particularly unique to ecological investigations.

2 This issue has been of growing concern in archaeology with the development of site-catchment analysis (e.g. Higgs 1972, 1975).

3 See Morren (1977:308) on the particular case of the New Guinea highlands. More generally, Beals (1964) has drawn attention to the inadequacies of the categories of subsistence employed in the *Ethnographic atlas* (Murdock 1967), by Hobhouse, Wheeler and Ginsberg (1915) and by Forde (1934), emphasizing the way in which they separate strategies which have much in common while grouping those which possess only a superficial technical similarity. The problem was one which Lowie (1938) had long ago identified.

8. Systems and their regulation

1 My concern here is with those who use systems theory as an extension of biological ecology. Some writers (e.g. Emery 1973) have used the term 'social ecology' to refer to any systems approach, but specifically to studies of post-industrialism, futurology and planning, influenced by general systems theory and the cybernetics of such writers as Ackoff, Ashby and K. Lewin.

9. Information and the manipulation of the environment

1 This would include data on species diversity within the geographical limits of a population studied, and for different ecological niches. It is necessary to understand the behaviour, population biology and ecology of the various species, and the patterned nature of plant and animal communities. The ecological grid determines a high degree of discontinuity between forms perceived and the notice man takes of his environment to ensure his own survival (Bulmer 1975:9, 11–13.).

2 There is evidence that biological ecology is anticipating or paralleling ethnoecology in this respect. Birds, for example, are no longer treated as single fixed behavioural repertoires. Rather, ecologists now attempt to model the feeding strategies of individuals of species involved in ecological systems (Hunn 1977).

3 For example, Bulmer (1967) informs us that the Kalam divide their environment vertically into *aerial, arboreal, low vegetation, terrestrial* and *subterranean;* and concentric-horizontally into *homesteads, garden, open country* and *forest*.

10. Adaptation: a summary and reconsideration

1 Modified from Kummer (1971:12–13), but comparable distinctions are made widely in the literature (Bateson 1963, Slobodkin 1968).

2 More recently Alland (and McCay 1973:171) has acknowledged that, while much cultural evolution might be the outcome of random behaviour fixed through environmental rewards, theory construction may also increase the spread of adaptation.

3 Alland and McCay's endorsement of this view seems to contradict a statement elsewhere in the same essay (1973:171).

4 See, however, M. Harris 1971:152.

11. The reproduction and evolution of social and ecological systems

1 My own presentation differs somewhat from that of Ruyle. In particular, I find his biological analogies and discussion in terms of thermodynamics unhelpful. It is difficult to see how his concept of *ethnoenergetics* furthers our understanding of the processes involved in social and ecological systems. It is misleading in that it conveys the impression that all significant material flow is to be measured in calories. As we have seen in Chapters 5 and 10 this is plainly not so. It also confuses and mystifies, not least in its conflation of objective surplus materials and surplus value. It is important that these two concepts be kept analytically separate.

2 The crude mathematical logic of this argument might be represented as follows. At t_1 the social organization of a given population can be understood as the sum of both environmental and social-historical forces, which for the purposes of the illustration are regarded as of equal value $(e_1 + h_1)$. Therefore if at t_1 $s = (e_1 + h_1)$ then the value of s may be seen to alter as follows through time thus:

$$t_2 \quad e_2 + h_2, \text{ where } h_2 = (e_1 + h_1)$$
$$t_3 \quad e_3 + h_3, \text{ where } h_3 = (e_2 + h_2)$$

and so on. Therefore, as we approach t_n the determinant significance of h_1 becomes increasingly negligible.

3 On the role of social barriers separating gene pools see, for example, Hiernaux 1966. Neel and Salzano (1966) provide a striking example of differential social selection among the Brazilian Xavante, where a tribal chief is responsible, through polygamy, for the genetic endowment of nearly one-third of the next generation. The work on genetic adaptations to different subsistence patterns is scattered but interesting. Although only some 400 breeding generations have elapsed since the earliest forms of domestication, the possibility of genetic adaptations to diets containing domesticated produce cannot be ruled out, although for some (e.g. Weiner 1973) it is doubtful. Simons (1978) has suggested that the introduction of dairying in certain populations around 6,000–7,000 B.P. led to selection for an ability to secrete large quantities of lactase in adulthood. High frequencies of this trait are found only in populations descended from early dairying populations. Simons has also suggested that an inherited sensitivity to gluten in wheat and some other cereals (coeliac disease) may have been strongly selected against in traditionally wheat-eating populations, as it appears to be most

prevalent on the eastern and western margins of wheat cultivation. Ho *et al.* (1971) suggest that the very low serum cholesterol levels among Masai pastoralists are linked to a diet of blood and milk. Hipsley (1976) and Oomen and Corden (1970) have both suggested the existence of genetic adaptations in Papua New Guinea. More generally on the question of genetic-cultural interactions, see Bennett, Osborne and Miller (1975).

12. Ecology in anthropological method and theory

1 Both ecology and materialist dialectics arose in response to nineteenth-century developments in science and society (Parsons 1977). It is perhaps not entirely surprising, therefore, that there should be certain parallels between Marxism and systems approaches, and that it is these which have aided the recent theoretical *rapprochement* of ecology and economy (e.g. Cook 1973, Friedman 1974, Ingold 1980, Klejn 1973).

Bibliography

vvvvvvvvvvvvvvvvvvvvvvvvvvvvvvvvvvvvvvvvvvvvvvvvvvvvvvvvvvvvvvvvvvvvvvvvvvvvvvvvvv

Note: Wherever possible I have referred to and indicated first editions, and first dates of publication where papers have subsequently been reprinted. Where this has not been possible, date of first publication appears in brackets.

Abbott, Joan M. W. 1970 Cultural anthropology and the man–environment relationship: an historical discussion. *Kroeber Anthropological Society Papers* 43, 10–31

Adams, C. C. 1913 *Guide to the study of animal ecology*. New York: Macmillan
1935 The relation of general ecology to human ecology. *Ecology* 16, 316–35

Adams, Robert McC. 1974 Anthropological perspectives on ancient trade. *Current Anthropology* 15, 239–58

Ahrens, R. 1927 *Wirtschaftsformen und Landschaft*. Hamburg: Abhandlungen aus dem Gebiet der Auslandskunde

Alexander, R. D. 1974 The evolution of social behaviour. *Annual Review of Ecology and Systematics* 5, 325–83

Alihan, M. A. 1938 *Social ecology: a critical analysis*. New York: Columbia University Press

Alkire, W. H. 1965 *Lamotrek atoll and inter-island socio-economic ties*. Urbana: University of Illinois Press

Allan, W. 1949 *Studies in African land use in Northern Rhodesia* (Rhodes–Livingstone Papers 15). London: Oxford University Press
1965 *The African husbandman*. Edinburgh: Oliver and Boyd

Alland, A. 1970 *Adaptation in cultural evolution: an approach to medical anthropology*. New York: Columbia University Press

Alland, A. and B. McCay 1973 The concept of adaptation in biological and cultural evolution. In *Handbook of social and cultural anthropology*, J. J. Honingmann (ed.). Chicago: Rand McNally

Allee, W. C. 1931 *Animal aggregations: a study in general sociology*. Chicago: University of Chicago Press
1943 Where angels fear to tread: a contribution from general sociology to human ethics. *Science* 97, 517–25
1951 *Cooperation among animals, with human implications*. New York: Schuman

Allee, W. C., Alfred E. Emerson, Orlando Park, Thomas Park and Karl P. Schmidt 1949 *Principles of animal ecology*. Philadelphia, London: Saunders

Bibliography

Anderson, E. N. Jr 1972 The life and culture of ecotopia. In *Reinventing anthropology*, D. Hymes (ed.). New York: Random House

Anderson, J. N. 1973 Ecological anthropology and anthropological ecology. In *Handbook of social and cultural anthropology*, J. J. Honingmann (ed.). Chicago: Rand McNally

Ashby, W. R. 1958 General systems theory as a new discipline. *General Systems Yearbook* 3, 1–6

Audy, J. R. 1971 The ipsefact: in ecology, ethology, parasitology, sociology and anthropology. In *Behaviour and environment*, A. H. Esser (ed.). New York: Plenum Press

Baker, P. T. 1962 The application of ecological theory to anthropology. *American Anthropologist* 64, 15–21

Barrau, J. (ed.) 1960 *Plants and the migrations of Pacific peoples*. Honolulu: Bernice P. Bishop Museum

1965 L'humide et le sec: an essay on ethnobiological adaptation to contrasted environments in the Indo-Pacific area. *Journal of the Polynesian Society* 74, 329–46

n.d. *An ethnobotanical guide for anthropological research in Malayo-Oceania* (Preliminary Draft). Jakarta: UNESCO science cooperation office for Southeast Asia

Barrows, H. H. 1923 Geography as human ecology. *Annals of the Association of American Geographers* 13, 1–14

Barth, F. 1950 Ecologic adaptation and cultural change in archaeology. *American antiquity* 15, 338–9

1956 Ecological relationships of ethnic groups in Swat, North Pakistan. *American Anthropologist* 58, 1079–89

Basso, K. H., 1972 Ice and travel among the Fort Norman Slave: folk taxonomies and cultural rules. *Language in Society* 1, 31–49

Bates, M. 1953 Human ecology. In *Anthropology today*, A. L. Kroeber (ed.). Chicago: University of Chicago Press

1960 Ecology and evolution. In *Evolution after Darwin* 1, Sol Tax (ed.). Chicago: University of Chicago Press

Bateson, G. 1963 The role of somatic change in evolution. *Evolution* 17, 529–39

Baumhoff, M. A. 1963 *Ecological determinants of aboriginal California populations*. University of California Publications in American Archaeology and Ethnology 49 (2). Berkeley: University of California Press

Bayliss-Smith, T. P. 1977 Human ecology and island populations: the problem of change. In *Subsistence and survival: rural ecology in the Pacific*, T. P. Bayliss-Smith and R. G. A. Feachem (eds.). London: Academic Press

1977a Energy use and economic development in Pacific communities. In *Subsistence and survival: rural ecology in the Pacific*, T. P. Bayliss-Smith and R. G. A. Feachem (eds.). London: Academic Press

1978 Maximum populations and standard populations: the carrying capacity question. In *Social organisation and settlement*, D. Green, C. Haselgrove and M. Spriggs (eds.). British Archaeological Reports International Series (Supplementary) 47 (i)

Beals, Alan R. 1964 Food is to eat: the nature of subsistence activity. *American Anthropologist* 66, 134–6

Bibliography

Bennett, J. W. 1946 An interpretation of the scope and implications of social scientific research in human subsistence. *American Anthropologist* 48, 553–73

1976 *The ecological transition: cultural anthropology and human adaptation.* New York: Pergamon Press

Bennett, K. A., R. H. Osborne and R. J. Miller 1975 Biocultural ecology. In *Annual review of anthropology*, B. J. Siegel, A. R. Beals and S. A. Tyler (eds.). Palo Alto, Calif.: Annual Reviews Inc

Berlin, B., D. Breedlove and P. Raven 1974 *Principles of Tzeltal plant classification: an introduction to the botanical ethnography of a Mayan-speaking people of the highland Chiapas.* New York: Academic Press

Berreman, G. 1966 Anemic and emetic analysis in social anthroplogy. *American Anthropologist* 68, 346–54

Berrien, F. K. 1968 *General and social systems.* New Brunswick: Rutgers University Press

Bertalanffy, L. von 1968 *General systems theory.* New York: Braziller

Bews, J. W. 1935 *Human ecology.* London: Oxford University Press

Birdsell, J. B. 1953 Some environmental and cultural factors influencing the structuring of Australian aboriginal populations. *American Naturalist* 87, 171–207

1973 A basic demographic unit. *Current Anthropology*, 14 (4), 337–50

Bloch, M. 1973 The long term and the short term: the economic and political significance of the morality of kinship. In *The character of kinship*, J. Goody (ed.). Cambridge: Cambridge University Press

Blurton-Jones, N. 1975 Ethology, anthropology, and childhood. In *Biosocial anthropology*, R. Fox (ed.). London: Malaby

Boas, F. 1888 *The central Eskimo.* Report of the Bureau of Ethnology 1884–5. Washington: Smithsonian Institution (reprinted 1964 University of Nebraska: Lincoln, with introduction by H. B. Collins)

1896 The limitations of the comparative method of anthropology. *Science* (N.S.) 4, 901–8

Boehm, C. 1978 Rational preselection from hamadryas to *Homo sapiens*: the place of decisions in adaptive process. *American Anthropologist* 80 (2), 265–96

Bonte, P. 1979 Pastoral production, territorial organisation and kinship in segmentary lineages. In *Social and ecological systems*, P. Burnham and R. F. Ellen (eds.) (Association of Social Anthropologists Monograph 18). London: Academic Press

Boserup, Ester 1965 *The conditions of agricultural growth; the economics of agrarian change under population pressure.* London: Allen and Unwin

Boulding, K. D. 1978 *Ecodynamics: a new theory of social evolution* London, Beverly Hills: Sage

Bourdieu, P. 1977 *Outline of a theory of practice.* Cambridge: Cambridge University Press

Bradfield, M. 1971 *The changing pattern of Hopi agriculture.* Occasional Paper of the Royal Anthropological Institute 30, London

Bronson, B. 1966 Roots and the subsistence of the ancient Maya. *Southwestern Journal of Anthropology* 22, 251–79

Bibliography

1972 Farm labour and the evolution of food production. In *Population growth*, Brian Spooner (ed.). Cambridge, Mass.: MIT Press

1975 The earliest farming; demography as cause and consequence. In *Population, ecology and social evolution*, S. Polgar (ed.). The Hague, Paris: Mouton

Brookfield, H. C. 1968 New directions in the study of agricultural systems in tropical areas. In *Evolution and environment: a symposium presented on the occasion of the one hundredth anniversary of the foundation of Peabody Museum of natural history at Yale University*, Ellen T. Drake (ed.). New Haven and London: Yale University Press

1969 On the environment as perceived. *Progress in Geography: International Review of Current Research* 1, 51–80

1972 Intensification and distintensification in Pacific agriculture: a theoretical approach. *Pacific Viewpoint* 13, 30–48

Brookfield, H. C. and P. Brown 1963. *Struggle for land: agriculture and group territories among the Chimbu of the New Guinea highlands*. Melbourne: Oxford University Press

Brookfield, H. C. and D. Hart 1971 *Melanesia: a geographical interpretation of an island world*. London: Methuen

Brown, Lester R. 1970 Human food production as a process in the biosphere. In *The biosphere (Scientific American)*. San Francisco: W. H. Freeman

Brown, P. and A. Podolefsky 1976 Population density, agricultural intensity, land tenure, and group size in the New Guinea highlands. *Ethnology* 15, 211–38

Brush, S. B. 1975 The concept of carrying capacity for systems of shifting cultivation. *American Anthropologist* 77, 799–811

Buchbinder, Georgeda 1977 Nutritional stress and postcontact population decline among the Maring of New Guinea. In *Malnutrition, behaviour and social organization*, L. S. Greene (ed.). London: Academic Press

Buckley, W. 1967 *Sociology and modern systems theory*. Englewood Cliffs, N. J.: Prentice-Hall

Bulmer, R. 1965 Beliefs concerning the propagation of new varieties of sweet potato in two New Guinea highlands' societies. *Journal of the Polynesian Society* 74, 237–9

1967 Why is the cassowary not a bird? A problem of zoological taxonomy among the Karam of the New Guinea highlands. *Man* (N.s.) 2, 5–25

1968 The strategies of hunting in New Guinea. *Oceania* 38, 302–18

1975 Folk biology in the New Guinea highlands. *Social Science Information* 13, 9–28

Bulmer, R. and J. Menzies 1972–3 Karam classification of marsupials and rodents. *Journal of the Polynesian Society* 81, 472–99; 82, 86–107

Bulmer, R., J. Menzies and F. Parker 1975 Kalam classification of reptiles and fishes. *Journal of the Polynesian Society* 84, 267–308

Bulmer, R. and M. Tyler 1968 Karam classification of frogs. *Journal of the Polynesian Society* 77, 335–85

Burch, E. S. Jr 1971 The non-empirical environment of the Arctic Alaskan Eskimos. *Southwestern Journal of Anthropology* 27, 148–65

Bibliography

Burling, R. 1964 Cognition and componential analysis: God's truth or hocus-pocus? *American Anthropologist* 66, 20–8

Burnham, P. 1973 The explanatory value of the concept of adaptation in studies of culture change. In *Explanation of culture*, C. Renfrew (ed.). London: Duckworth

1979 Permissive ecology and structural conservatism in Gbaya society. In *Social and ecological systems*, P. Burnham and R. F. Ellen (eds.) (Association of Social Anthropologists Monograph 18). London: Academic Press

Carneiro, Robert L. 1960 Slash and burn agriculture: a closer look at its implications for settlement patterns. In *Men and cultures: selected papers of the fifth international congress of anthropological and ethnological sciences, 1956*, A. F. C. Wallace (ed.). Philadelphia: University of Pennsylvania Press

1964 Shifting agriculture among the Amahuaca of eastern Peru. *Völkerkundliche Abhandlungen* 1, 9–18

1967 On the relationship between size of population and complexity of social organisation. *Southwestern Journal of Anthropology* 23, 234–43

1970 A theory of the origin of the state. *Science* 169, 733–8

Childe, Vere G. 1951 *Social evolution*. London: Watts

Chisholm, M. 1962 *Rural settlement and land use*. London: Hutchinson

Chorley, R. J. 1973 Geography as human ecology. In *Directions in geography*, R. J. Chorley (ed.). London: Methuen

Clark, C. and M. Haswell 1971 *The economics of subsistence agriculture*. London: Macmillan

Clark, J. G. D. 1954 *The study of prehistory: an inaugural lecture*. London: Cambridge University Press

Clarke, D. L. 1968 *Analytical archaeology*. London: Methuen

1972 Models and paradigms in contemporary archaeology. In *Models in archaeology*, D. L. Clarke (ed.). London: Methuen

Clarke, W. C. 1966 From extensive to intensive shifting cultivation: a succession from New Guinea. *Ethnology* 5, 347–59

1971 *Place and people: an ecology of a New Guinean community*. Berkeley, Los Angeles: University of California Press

1977 The structure of permanence: the relevance of self-subsistence communities for world ecosystem management. In *Subsistence and survival: rural ecology in the Pacific*, T. P. Bayliss-Smith and R. G. Feachem (eds.). London: Academic Press

Clarke, W. C. and S. Street 1967 Soil fertility and cultivation practices. *Journal of Tropical Geography* 24, 7–11

Coe, M. D. and K. Flannery 1964 Microenvironments and Mesoamerican prehistory. *Science* 143, 650–4

Cohen, M. N. 1977 *The food crisis in prehistory: overpopulation and the origins of agriculture*. New Haven: Yale University Press

Cohen, Y. A. 1971 (ed.) *Man in adaptation: the institutional framework*. Chicago, New York: Aldine, Atherton

Cole, L. 1958 The ecosphere. *Scientific American* 198 (4), 83–92

Coles, J. 1973 *Archaeology by experiment*. New York: Charles Scribner's Sons

Bibliography

Collins, P. W. 1965 Functional analyses in the symposium: man, culture and animals. In *Man, culture and animals*, A. Leeds and A. P. Vayda (eds.). Washington D. C.: American Association for the Advancement of Science

Conklin, H. C. 1954 *The relation of Hanunoo culture to the plant world*. Ph.D. dissertation in anthropology, Yale University, New Haven. Published (1967) by University Microfilms, Ann Arbor, Michigan (No. 67–4119)

1954a An ethnoecological approach to shifting agriculture *Transactions of the New York Academy of Sciences* 17, 133–42. Reprinted 1969 in *Environment and cultural behaviour: ecological studies in cultural anthropology*, A. P. Vayda (ed.). New York: The Natural History Press

1957 *Hanunoo agriculture, a report on an integral system of shifting cultivation in the Philippines* (Forestry Development Paper 12). Rome: Food and Agricultural Organization of the United Nations.

1961 The study of shifting cultivation. *Current Anthropology* 2, 27–61. Also published 1963, Pan American Union Studies and Monographs 6, Washington

1967 Ifugao ethnobotany, 1905–1965: the 1911 Beyer–Merill Report in perspective. In *Studies in Philippine anthropology: in honour of H. Otley Beyer*, M. Zamora (ed.). Quezon City: Alemar-Phoenix

1968 Some aspects of ethnographic research in Ifugao. *Transactions of the New York Academy of Sciences* (ser. II) 30, 99–121

(ed.) 1972 *Folk classification: a topically-arranged bibliography*. New Haven, Conn.: Department of Anthropology, Yale University

1976 Ethnographic semantic analysis of Ifugao land-form categories. In *Environmental knowing: theories, research and methods*, G. T. Moore (ed.). Stroudsburg, Pa.: Dowden, Hutchinson and Ross

Cook, E. 1971 The energy flow in an industrial society. *Scientific American* 225 (September), 134–44

Cook, S. 1973 Production, ecology and economic anthropology: notes towards an integrated frame of reference. *Social Science Information* 12 (1), 25–52

Cotgrove, S. 1976 Environmentalism and utopia. *Sociological Review* (N.S.) 24, 23–42

Cottrell, Fred 1970 *Energy and society: the relation between energy, social change and economic development*. Westport, Conn.: Greenwood Press

Cowgill, V. 1966 The season of birth in Man. *Man* (N.S.) 1(2), 232–40.

Crook, J. H. 1970 Social organization and the environment: aspects of contemporary social ethology. *Animal Behaviour* 18, 197–209

Crook, J. H. and J. S. Gartlan, 1966 Evolution of primate societies. *Nature* (London) 210, 1200–3

Cummins, K. W. and J. C. Wuycheck 1971 Caloric equivalents for investigations in ecological energetics. *Mitteilungen der Internationalen Vereinigun für theoretische und angewandte Limnologie* 18, 1–158

Damas, D. 1969 Environment, history and central Eskimo society. In *Contributions to anthropology: ecological essays*, D. Damas (ed.) National Museum of Canada Bulletin, 230. Anthropological Series 86. Ottawa: Queen's Printers for Canada

Bibliography

Darling, F. F. 1951 The ecological approach to the social sciences. *American Scientist* 39, 244–54

Darlington, P. J. 1957 *Zoogeography: the geographical distribution of animals*. New York: Wiley

Dawkins, R. 1978 *The selfish gene*. London: Granada

Day, Gordon 1953 The Indian as an ecological factor in the northeastern forest. *Ecology* 34, 329–46

Deevey, E. S. 1960 The human population. *Scientific American* 203 (September), 195–204

Denevan, William M. 1966 A cultural-ecological view of former aboriginal settlement in the Amazon basin. *The Professional Geographer* 18, 346–51

Denham, W. W. 1971 Energy relations and some basic properties of primate social organization. *American Anthropologist* 73, 77–95

Deshler, W. W. 1965 Native cattle keeping in eastern Africa. In *Man, culture and animals*, A. Leeds and A. P. Vayda (eds.). Washington: American Association for the Advancement of Science, Publication 78

Diamond, J. 1966 Zoological classification system of a primitive people. *Science* 151 (3714), 1102–4

Dice, Lee R. 1955 *Man's nature and nature's man: the ecology of human communities*. Westport, Conn.: Greenwood Press

Diener, P., D. Nonini and E. E. Robkin 1980 Ecology and evolution in cultural anthropology. *Man* (N.s.) 15 (1), 1–31

Digby, A. 1949 Techniques and time factor in relation to economic organization. *Man* 49, 16–18

Dornstreich, M. 1977 The ecological description and analysis of tropical subsistence patterns: an example from New Guinea. In *Subsistence and survival: rural ecology in the Pacific*, T. Bayliss-Smith and R. G. Feachem (eds.). London: Academic Press

Douglas, M. 1966 Population control in primitive groups. *British Journal of sociology* 17 (3), 263–73

1972 Environments at risk. In *Ecology in theory and practice*, J. Benthall (ed.). New York: Viking Press

1972a Symbolic orders in the use of domestic space. In *Man, settlement and urbanism*, P. J. Ucko, R. Tringham and G. W. Dimbleby (eds.). London: Duckworth

Dow, James 1976 Systems models of cultural ecology. *Social Science Information* 15 (6), 953–76

Dumond, D. E. 1961 Swidden agriculture and the rise of Maya civilization. *Southwestern Journal of Anthropology* 17, 301–16

Dunn, F. L. 1975 *Rainforest collectors and traders: a study of resource utilization in modern and ancient Malaya*. Monographs of the Malaysian Branch of the Royal Asiatic Society 5

Dupré, G. and P. P. Rey 1969 Réflexions sur la pertinence d'une théorie de l'histoire des échanges. *Cahiers Internationaux de Sociologie* 46, 133–62

Durkheim, E. 1900 Review of Ratzel, 'Anthropogéographie, vol. I', *L'Année Sociologique* 1898–9 3, 550–8

Bibliography

Durnin, J. V. G. A. and R. Passmore 1967 *Energy, work and leisure*. London: Heinemann Educational Books

Dwyer, P. D. 1974 The price of protein: five-hundred hours of hunting in the New Guinea highlands. *Oceania* 44 (4), 278–93

1976 Beetles, butterflies and bats: species transformation in a New Guinea folk classification. *Oceania* 46, 188–205

Dyson-Hudson, N. 1966 *Karimojong politics*. Oxford: Clarendon Press

Dyson-Hudson, R. and N. Dyson-Hudson 1970 The food production system of a semi-nomadic society: the Karimojong, Uganda. In *African food production systems*, P. F. M. McLoughlin (ed.). Baltimore: Johns Hopkins Press

Edholm F., K. Young and O. Harris 1977 Conceptualising women. *Critique of Anthropology* 3 (9–10), 101–30

Eisenberg, J. F., N. A. Muckenhirn and R. Rudran 1972 The relation between ecology and social structure in primates. *Science* 175, 863–74

Ellen, Roy F. 1973 Nuaulu settlement and ecology: an approach to the environmental relations of an eastern Indonesian community. Unpublished thesis presented for the degree of Doctor of Philosophy in the University of London

1975 Non-domesticated resources in Nuaulu ecological relations. *Social Science Information* 14, 127–50

1976 Comment on an evolutionary approach to the Southeast Asian cultural sequence. *Current Anthropology* 17 (2), 231

1977 Resource and commodity: problems in the analysis of the social relations of Nuaulu land use. *Journal of Anthropological Research* 33 (1), 50–72

1978 *Nuaulu settlement and ecology: an approach to the environmental relations of an eastern Indonesian community* (Verhandelingen van het Koninklijk Instituut voor Taal-, Land en Volkenkunde 83). The Hague: Martinus Nijhoff

1978a Ecological perspectives on social behaviour. In *Social organisation and settlement*. D. Green, C. Haselgrove and M. Spriggs (eds.). Oxford: British Archaeological Reports International Series (Supplementary) 47 (i)

1978b Restricted faunas and ethno-zoological inventories in Wallacea. In *Nature and man in Southeast Asia*, P. H. Stott (ed.). London: School of Oriental and African Studies

1979 Sago subsistence and the trade in spices: a provisional model of ecological succession and imbalance in Moluccan history. In *Social and ecological systems*, P. Burnham and R. F. Ellen (eds.) (Association of Social Anthropologists Monograph 18). London: Academic Press

1979a Introductory essay. In *Classifications in their social context*, R. Ellen and D. Reason (eds.). London: Academic Press

Ellen, R. and D. Reason (eds.) 1979 *Classifications in their social context*. London: Academic Press

Ellen, R., A. Stimson and J. Menzies 1976 Structure and inconsistency in Nuaulu categories for amphibians. *Journal d'Agriculture Tropicale et Botanique Appliquée* 23, 125–38

Elton, C. 1927 *Animal ecology*. London: Sidgwick and Jackson

Emery, F. E. 1973 *Towards a social ecology: contextual appreciations of the future in the present*. London and New York: Plenum

Bibliography

Engels, F. 1954 (1876) *Dialectics of nature*, Moscow: Foreign Languages Publishing House

Evans-Pritchard, E. 1940 *The Nuer*. Oxford: Clarendon Press

Eyre, S. R. 1964 Determinism and the ecological approach to geography. *Geography* 49, 369–76

Eyre, S. R. and G. Jones (eds.) 1966 *Geography as human ecology: methodology by example*. London: Arnold

Faris, J. C. 1975 Social evolution, population and production. In *Population, ecology and social evolution*, S. Polgar (ed.). The Hague, Paris: Mouton

Feachem, R. G. A. 1973 A clarification of carrying-capacity formulae. *Australian Geographical Studies* 11, 234–6

1977 The human ecologist as superman. In *Subsistence and survival: rural ecology in the Pacific*, T. P. Bayliss-Smith and R. G. A. Feachem (eds.). London: Academic Press

Febvre, L. 1925 (1922) *A geographical introduction to history* (trans. E. G. Mountford and J. H. Paxton). London: Kegan Paul, Trench, Trubner

Fei Hsiao-t'ung and Chang Chih-i 1945 *Earthbound China: a study of rural economy in Yunnan*. Chicago: University of Chicago Press

Feldman, Douglas A. 1975 The history of the relationship between environment and culture in ethnological thought: an overview. *Journal of the History of the Behavioural Sciences* 11 (1), 67–81

Flannery, K. 1965 The ecology of early food production in Mesopotamia. *Science* 147, 1247–56. Reprinted (1969) in *Environment and cultural behaviour*, A. P. Vayda (ed.). New York: The Natural History Press

1968 Archaeological systems theory and early Mesoamerica. In *Anthropological archaeology in the Americas*, B. Meggers (ed.). Reprinted (1971) in *Prehistoric agriculture*, S. Struever (ed.). New York: The Natural History Press

1972 The cultural evolution of civilizations. *Annual Review of Ecology and Systematics* 3, 399–425

Foley, R. 1977 Space and energy: a method for analysing habitat value and utilisation in relation to archaeological sites. In *Spatial Archaeology*, D. L. Clarke (ed.). London: Academic Press

Forde, C. D. 1934 *Habitat, economy and society*, London: Methuen

1948 The integration of anthropological studies. *Journal of the Royal Anthropological Institute* 78, 1–10

1953 The cultural map of West Africa, successive adaptations to tropical forests and grasslands. *Transactions of the New York Academy of Sciences* (ser. II) 15, 206–19

1970 Ecology and social structure. *Proceedings of the Royal Anthropological Institute of Great Britain and Ireland for 1970*, 15–29

Forman, S. 1967 Cognition and the catch: the location of fishing spots in a Brazilian coastal village. *Ethnology* 6, 417–26

Fortes, M. 1976 Cyril Daryll Forde 1902–1973 *Proceedings of the British Academy* 62, 459–83

Fosberg, F. R. (ed.). 1963 *Man's place in the island ecosystem*. Honolulu: Bernice P. Bishop Museum

Bibliography

Foucault, Michel 1970 *The order of things: an archaeology of the human sciences.* London: Tavistock Publications

Fox, J. J. 1979 Translator's Foreword. In *Seasonal variations of the Eskimo: a study in social morphology*, M. Mauss, in collaboration with H. Beuchat. London: Routledge and Kegan Paul

Fox, R. G. 1969 'Professional primitives': hunters and gatherers of nuclear south Asia. *Man in India* 49, 139–60

Fox, R. H. 1953 A study of energy expenditure of Africans engaged in various rural activities. University of London: unpublished Ph.D. thesis

Frake, C. O. 1962 Cultural ecology and ethnography. *American Anthropologist* 64, 53–9

Frankenberg, R. 1967 Economic anthropology: one anthropologist's view. In *Themes in economic anthropology*, R. Firth (ed.). London: Tavistock

Freeman, D. 1955 *Iban agriculture* (Colonial Research Studies 18). London: H.M.S.O.

1970 *Report on the Iban* (London School of Economics Monographs on Social Anthropology 41). London: Athlone

Freilich, Morris 1963 The natural experiment, ecology and culture. *South-western Journal of Anthropology* 19 (1), 21–39

Friedman, J. 1974 Marxism, structuralism and vulgar materialism. *Man* (N.S.) 9 (3), 444–69

1976 Marxist theory and systems of total reproduction. Part I: negative. *Critique of Anthropology* 2 (7), 3–16

1979 Hegelian ecology: between Rousseau and the world spirit. In *Social and ecological systems*, P. Burnham and R. F. Ellen (eds.) (Association of social Anthropologists Monograph 18). London: Academic Press

Friedman, J. and M. Rowlands 1977 Notes toward an epigenetic model of the evolution of 'civilization'. In *The evolution of social systems*, J. Friedman and M. Rowlands (eds.). London: Duckworth

Geddes, W. R. 1954 *The Land Dayaks of Sarawak.* London: H.M.S.O.

Geertz, C. 1963 *Agricultural involution, the process of ecological change in Indonesia.* Berkeley and Los Angeles: University of California Press

Gellner, E. 1958 Time and theory in social anthropology. *Mind* 67 (266), 182–202

1963 Nature and society in social anthropology. *Philosophy of Science* 30, 236–51

1970 Concepts and society. In *Rationality*, B. Wilson (ed.). Oxford: Blackwell

Gerlach, L. P. 1965 Nutrition in its sociocultural matrix: food getting and using along the east African coast. In *ecology and economic development in tropical Africa*, D. Brokensha (ed.). Berkeley: Institute of International Studies, University of California

Glacken, C. J. 1967 *Traces on the Rhodian shore: nature and culture in Western thought from ancient times to the end of the eighteenth century.* Berkeley: University of California Press

Glander, K. E. 1975 Habitat description and resource utilization: a preliminary report on mantled howling monkey ecology. In *Socioecology and psychology of primates*, R. H. Tuttle (ed.). The Hague, Paris: Mouton

Bibliography

Gluckman, M. 1945 How the Bemba make their living: an appreciation of Richards' *Land, Labour and diet in Northern Rhodesia*. *Journal of the Rhodes Livingstone Institute* (June), 55–75

(ed.) 1964 *Closed systems and open minds*. Edinburgh: Oliver and Boyd

Godelier, M. 1972 *Rationality and irrationality in economics* (trans. Brian Pearce). London: New Left Review Editions

1977 *Perspectives in Marxist anthropology* (trans. R. Brain). Cambridge: Cambridge University Press

Godelier, M. and J. Garanger 1973 Outils de pierre, outils d'acier chez les Baruya de Nouvelle-Guinée: quelques données ethnographiques et quantitatives. *L'Homme* 13 (3), 187–220

Goldschmidt, W. 1965 Theory and strategy in the study of cultural adaptability. *American Anthropologist* 67, 402–7

Goodey, B. 1971 *Perception of the environment: an introduction to the literature* (Occasional Paper 17). Birmingham: University Centre for Urban and Regional Studies

Goodman, D. 1975 The theory of diversity: stability relationships in ecology *The Quarterly Review of Biology* 50, 237–66

Goody, J. (ed.) 1958 *The developmental cycle in domestic groups* (Cambridge Papers in Social Anthropology 1). Cambridge: Cambridge University Press

Gould, R. C., D. D. Fowler and C. S. Fowler 1972 Diggers and doggers: parallel failures in economic acculturation. *Southwestern Journal of Anthropology* 28, 265–81

Gray, R. F. 1964 Introduction. In *The family estate in Africa*, R. F. Gray and P. H. Gulliver (eds.). London: Routledge and Kegan Paul

Greene, L. S. (ed.) 1977 *Malnutrition, behaviour and social organization*. London: Academic Press

1977a Hyperdemic goitre, cretinism, and social organization in highland Ecuador. In *Malnutrition, behaviour and social organization*, L. S. Greene (ed.). London: Academic Press

Greenfield, Sydney 1965 More on the study of subsistence activities. *American Anthropologist* 67, 737–44

Gross, D. R. and B. A. Underwood 1971 Technological change and caloric costs: sisal agriculture in northeastern Brazil. *American Anthropologist* 73, 725–40

Gulliver, P. H. 1955 *The family herds: a study of two pastoral tribes in east Africa, the Jie and Turkana*. London: Routledge and Kegan Paul

Haeckel, E. 1911 (1868) *Natürliche Schöpfungsgeschichte*. Berlin: Georg Reimer

Hagen, E. E. 1961 Analytical models in the study of social systems. *The American Journal of Sociology* 67, 144–51

Hamburg, D. A., G. V. Coelho and J. E Adams 1974 Coping and adaptation: steps toward a synthesis of biological and social perspectives. In *Coping and adaptation*, G. V. Coelho, D. A. Hamburg and J. E. Adams (eds.). New York: Basic Books

Hames, R. B. 1979 A comparison of the efficiencies of the shotgun and the bow in neotropical forest hunting. *Human Ecology* 7 (3), 219–52

Bibliography

Hardesty, D. L. 1975 The niche concept: suggestions for its use in studies of human ecology. *Human Ecology* 3, 71–85

1977 *Ecological Anthropology*. New York: Wiley and Sons

Harner, M. J. 1970 Population pressure and the social evolution of agriculturalists. *Southwestern Journal of Anthropology* 26, 67–86

Harpending, H. and H. Davis 1977 Some implications for hunter-gatherer ecology derived from the spatial structure of resources. *World Archaeology* 8, 275–86

Harris, D. R. 1969 Agricultural systems, ecosystems and the origins of agriculture. In *The domestication and exploitation of plants and animals*, P. J. Ucko and G. W. Dimbleby (eds.). London: Duckworth

1972 Swidden systems and settlement. In *Man, settlement and urbanism*, P. J. Ucko, R. Tringham and G. W. Dimbleby (eds.). London: Duckworth

1973 The prehistory of tropical agriculture: an ethnoecological model. In *Explanation of culture*, C. Renfrew (ed.), London: Duckworth

1977 Settling down: an evolutionary model for the transformation of mobile bands into sedentary communities. In *The evolution of social systems*, J. Friedman and M. J. Rowlands (eds.). London: Duckworth

1977a Alternative pathways towards agriculture. In *The origins of agriculture*, C. A. Reed (ed.). New York: Mouton

1978 Group territories or terrritorial groups? Comments on an interdisciplinary problem in cultural ecology. In *Social organisation and settlement*, D. Green, C. Haselgrove and M. Spriggs (eds.). Oxford: British Archaeological Reports International Series (Supplementary) 47 (i)

Harris, M. 1960 Adaptation in biological and cultural science. *Transactions of the New York Academy of Sciences* (ser. II) 23, 59–65

1965 The myth of the sacred cow. In *Man, culture and animals: the role of animals in human ecological adjustments*, A. Leeds and A. P. Vayda (eds.). Washington: American Association for the Advancement of Science, Publication 78

1968 *The rise of anthropological theory*. London: Routledge and Kegan Paul

1971 *Culture, man and nature: an introduction to general anthropology*. New York: Crowell

1974 Why a perfect knowledge of all the rules one must know to act like a native cannot lead to a knowledge of how natives act. *Journal of Anthropological Research* 30, 242–51.

Harvey, D. 1969 *Explanation in geography*. London: Edward Arnold

Haswell, M. R. 1953 *Economics of agriculture in a savannah village: report on three years' study in Genieri village* (Colonial Research Studies 8). London: H.M.S.O.

Hawley, A. H. 1950 *Human ecology: a theory of community structure*. New York: Ronald Press

Hayden, B. 1975 The carrying-capacity dilemma. In *Population studies in archaeology and biological anthropology: a symposium*, A. C. Swedlund (ed.), Society for American Archaeology, Memoir 30

Hays, T. 1974 *Mauna: explorations in Ndumba ethnobotany*. Ph.D. dissertation. Seattle: University of Washington

Bibliography

Helm, J. 1962 The ecological approach in anthropology. *American Journal of Sociology* 67, 630–9

Heston, A. 1971 An approach to the sacred cow of India. *Current Anthropology* 12 (2), 191–210

Hiatt, L. 1962 Local organization among the Australian aborigines. Oceania 32, 267–86

  1968 Ownership and use of land among the Australian aborigines. In *Man the hunter*, R. Lee and I. DeVore (eds.). Chicago: Aldine

Hiernaux, J. 1966 Human biological diversity in central Africa. *Man* (N.S.) 1, 287–306

Higgs, E. S. (ed.) 1972 *Papers in economic prehistory*. Cambridge: Cambridge University Press

  1975 *Palaeo-economy*. Cambridge: Cambridge University Press

Hipsley, E. H. 1976 Concerning the adaptation of Papua New Guineans to low-protein diets. *Food Nutrition Notes Review* 33, 37–43

Hipsley, E. H. and F. W. Clements 1947 *Report of the New Guinea nutrition survey expedition*. Canberra: Department of External Territories

Hipsley, E. H. and Nancy Kirk 1965 *Studies of dietary intake and expenditure of energy by New Guineas* (South Pacific Commission Technical Paper 147). Noumea: South Pacific Commission

Hladick, C. M. 1975 Ecology, diet and social patterning in old and new world primates. In *Socioecology and psychology of primates*, R. H. Tuttle (ed.). The Hague, Paris: Mouton

Ho, K. J., K. Biss, B. Mikkelson, L. A. Lewis and C. B. Taylor 1971 The Masai of East Africa: some unique biological characteristics. *Archives of Pathology* 91, 387–410

Hobhouse, L. T., G. C. Wheeler and M. Ginsberg 1915 *The material culture and social institutions of the simpler peoples: an essay in correlation*. University of London Monographs of Sociology 3. London: Chapman-Hall

Holling, C. S. 1973 Resilience and stability of ecological systems. *Annual Review of Ecology and Systematics* 4, 1–23

Hollingshead, A. B. 1940 Human ecology and human society. *Ecological Monograph* 10, 354–66

Holmes, G. 1919 *Handbook of aboriginal American antiquities*. Smithsonian Institution, Bureau of American Ethnology, Bulletin 60, Part 1, Washington D. C.

Holmes, W. H. 1914 Areas of American culture characterization tentatively outlined as an aid in the study of antiquities. *American Anthropologist* 16, 423–6

Hornabrook, R. W. 1977 Human ecology and biomedical research: a critical review of the International Biological Programme in New Guinea. In *Subsistence and survival: rural ecology in the Pacific*, T. P. Bayliss-Smith and R. G. A. Feachem (eds.). London: Academic Press

Hunn, E. 1977 Does cultural ecology need ethnoecology? *Folk Classification Bulletin* 1, 2–4

Huntington, E. 1924 (1915) *Civilization and climate*. New Haven: Yale University Press; London: Humphrey Milford, Oxford University Press

Bibliography

Hutterer, K. L. 1976 An evolutionary approach to the Southeast Asian cultural sequence. *Current Anthropology* 17 (2), 221–7

Ingold, T. 1979 The social and ecological relations of culture-bearing organisms: an essay in evolutionary dynamics. In *Social and ecological systems*, P. Burnham and R. Ellen (eds.). London: Academic Press

1980 *Hunters, pastoralists and ranchers.* Cambridge Studies in Social Anthropology 28. Cambridge: Cambridge University Press

Izikowitz, K. G. 1951 *Lamet, hill peasants in French Indochina* (Etnologiska Studier 17). Göteborg: Etnografiska Museet

Janzen, D. H. 1973 Tropical agroecosystems. *Science* 182, 1212–19

Johnson, A. 1974 Ethnoecology and planting practices in a swidden agricultural system. *American Ethnologist* 1, 87–101

1975 The allocation of time in a Machiguenga community. *Ethnology* 14, 301–10

Judd, L. C. 1964 *Dry-rice agriculture in northern Thailand.* Data paper number 52, Southeast Asia Program, Department of Asian Studies, Cornell University, New York: Ithaca

Kaplan, D. and R. Manners 1972 *Culture theory.* Englewood Cliffs, N.J.: Prentice-Hall

Keesing, R. M. 1972 Paradigms lost: the new ethnography and the new linguistics. *Southwestern Journal of Anthropology* 28, 299–332

1973 Kwara?ae ethnoglottochronology: procedures used by Malaita cannibals for determining percentages of shared cognates. *American Anthropologist* 75, 1282–9

Kelly, R. C. 1968 Demographic pressure and descent-group structure in the New Guinea highlands. *Oceania* 39, 36–63

Kemp, W. B. 1971 The flow of energy in a hunting society. *Scientific American* 225 (3), 105–15

Klejn, L. S. 1973 Marxism, the systemic approach, and archaeology. In *The explanation of culture change: models in prehistory.* C. Renfrew (ed.). London: Duckworth

Krader, L. 1955 Ecology of central Asian pastoralism. *Southwestern Journal of Anthropology* 11, 301–26

Krantz, G. S. 1970 Human activities and megafaunal extinctions. *American Scientist* 58 (2), 164–70

Kroeber, A. L. 1917 The superorganic. *American Anthropologist* 19, 163–213

1923 *Anthropology.* London: Harrap

1939 *Cultural and natural areas of native north America* University of California Publications in American Archaeology and Ethnology 38. Berkeley: University of California Press

1946 History and evolution. *Southwestern Journal of Anthropology* 2 (1), 1–15

Kula, N. 1968 On the typology of economic systems. In *The social sciences: problems and orientations*, UNESCO. The Hague: Mouton

Kummer, H. 1971 *Primate societies: group techniques of ecological adaptation.* Chicago: Aldine

Kunstadter, Peter 1972 Demography, ecology, social structure, and settlement patterns. In *The structure of human populations*, G. A. Harrison and J. A. Boyce (eds.). Oxford: Clarendon Press

Langton, J. 1973 Potentialities and problems of adopting a systems approach to the study of change in human geography. *Progress in Geography: International Review of Current Research* 4, 125–79

Lathrap, D. W. 1968 The 'hunting' economies of the tropical forest zone of South America: an attempt at historical perspective. In *Man the hunter*, R. B. Lee and I. DeVore (eds.). Chicago: Aldine

Lawton, J. H. 1973 The energy cost of 'food-gathering'. In *Resources and population*, B. Benjamin, P. R. Cox and J. Peel (eds.). London: Academic Press

Lea, D. A. M. 1964 Abelam land and sustenance: swidden horticulture in an area of high population density, Maprik, New Guinea. Thesis submitted for the degree of Doctor of Philosophy in the Australian National University (mimeographed), Canberra

Leach, E. R. 1954 *Political systems of highland Burma*. London: Bell
1959 Some economic advantages of shifting cultivation. *Proceedings of the ninth Pacific Science Congress*, Bangkok 1957. 7, 64–6
1961 *Pul Eliya; a village in Ceylon: a study of land tenure and kinship*. Cambridge: Cambridge University Press

Leach, G. 1976 *Energy and food production*. Guildford: IPC Science and Technology Press

Lee, R. B. 1969 !Kung Bushman subsistence: an input-output analysis. In *Contributions to anthropology: ecological essays*, D. Damas (ed.) National Museums of Canada Bulletin 3–94, 230, Anthropological series 86. Ottowa: Queen's Printers for Canada
1972 !Kung spatial organization: an ecological and historical perspective. *Human Ecology* 1 (2), 125–48

Lee, R. B. and I. DeVore (eds.) 1968 *Man the hunter*. Chicago: Aldine

Leeds, A. 1961 Yaruro incipient tropical forest horticulture: possibilities and limits. In *The evolution of horticultural systems in native South America: causes and consquences*, J. Wilbert (ed.). *Antropologica*, Supplement Publication 2. Caracas: Sociedad de Ciencias Naturales la Salle

Leeds, A. and A. P. Vayda (eds.) 1965 *Man, culture and animals: the role of animals in human ecological adjustments*. Washington: American Association for the Advancement of Science, Publication 78

Le Roy Ladurie, E. 1972 *Times of feast, times of famine: a history of climate since the year 1000* (trans. Barbara Bray). London: Allen and Unwin

Lévi-Strauss, C. 1962 *La pensée sauvage*. Paris: Plon

Levins, R. 1968 *Evolution in changing environments: some theoretical explorations* (Monographs in Population Biology 2). Princeton, N.J.: Princeton University Press

Lewis, I. 1965 Problems in the comparative study of unilineal descent. In *The relevance of models for social anthropology*, M. Banton (ed.) (Association of Social Anthropologists Monograph 1). London: Tavistock

Lewis, O. 1963 (1951) *Life in a Mexican village: Tepoztlán restudied*. Urbana: University of Illinois Press

Bibliography

Leynseele, P. van 1979 Ecological stability and intensive fish production: the case of the Libinza people of the middle Ngiri (Zaire). In *Social and ecological systems*, R. Ellen and P. Burnham (eds.) (Association of Social Anthropologists Monograph 18). London: Academic Press

Lienhardt, G. 1964 *Social anthropology.* Oxford: Oxford University Press

Lindeman, R. L. 1942 The trophic-dynamic aspect of ecology. *Ecology* 23, 399–418

Little, M. A. and G. E. B. Morren 1977 *Ecology, energetics and human variability.* Duburque: William Brown

Livingstone, Frank B. 1958 Anthropological implications of sickle-cell gene distribution in West Africa, *American Anthropologist* 60, 533–62

Llobera, J. R. 1979 Techno-economic determinism and the work of Marx on pre-capitalist societies. *Man* (N.s.) 14 (2), 249–70

Löffler, Lorenz G. 1960 Bodenbedarf und Ertragsfaktor in Brandrodungsbau. *Tribus* 9, 39–43

Lotka, A. J. 1922 Contribution to the energetics of evolution. *Proceedings of the National Academy of Science* 8, 147–51

Lovelock, J. and S. Epton 1975 The quest for Gaia. *New Scientist* 6 (February), 304–6

Lowie, R. 1937 *History of ethnological theory*, New York: Farrar and Rinehart
1938 Subsistence. In *General anthropology*, F. Boas (ed.). Boston: Heath

Lowman-Vayda, C. 1971 Maring Big Men. In *Politics in New Guinea*, R. M. Berndt and P. Lawrence (eds.). Nedlands: University of Western Australia Press

Lukacs, G. 1971 *History and class consciousness.* London: Merlin Press

McArthur, M. 1960 Food consumption and dietary levels of groups of aborigines living on naturally occurring foods. *Records of the Australian–American scientific expedition to Arnhem Land vol. 2: anthropology and nutrition*, C. P. Mountford (ed.). Melbourne: Melbourne University Press
1977 Nutritional research in Melanesia: a second look at the Tsembaga. In *Subsistence and survival: rural ecology in the Pacific*, T. Bayliss-Smith and R. G. Feachem (eds.). London: Academic Press

McCarthy, F. D. and M. McArthur 1960 The food quest and the time factor in aboriginal economic life. In *Records of the Australian–American scientific expedition to Arnhem Land vol. 2: anthropology and nutrition*, C. P. Mountford (ed.). Melbourne: Melbourne University Press

Mackenzie, R. D. 1968 *On human ecology: selected writings*, A. H. Hawley (ed.). Chicago: Chicago University Press

McLellan, D. 1971 *The thought of Karl Marx: an introduction.* London: Macmillan

McNeill, S. and J. H. Lawton 1970 Annual production and respiration in animal populations. *Nature* (London) 225, 472–4

Maelzer, D. A. 1965 A discussion of components of environment in ecology. *Journal of Theoretical Biology* 8, 141–62

Mair, L. P. 1972 *An introduction to social anthropology.* London: Oxford University Press

Manner, H. I. 1977 Biomass: its determination and implications in tropical agro-ecosystems: an example from montane New Guinea. In *Subsistence*

Bibliography

and survival: rural ecology in the Pacific, T. P. Bayliss-Smith and R. G. A. Feachem (eds.). London: Academic Press

Marett, R. R. 1912 Anthropology. London: Thornton Butterworth

Margalef, Ramon 1968 Perspectives in ecological theory. Chicago, London: University of Chicago Press

Marsh, G. P. 1965 (1864) Man and nature, D. Lowenthal (ed.). Cambridge: Belknap-Harvard

Marshall, G. 1974–5 Durkheim and British social anthropology: critique of a methodological tradition. Sociological Analysis and Theory 4 (3), 3–45; 5 (1), 3–52

Marshall, L. 1960 !Kung Bushman bands. Africa 30, 325–55

Maruyama, M. 1963 The second cybernetics: deviation-amplifying mutual causal processes. American Scientist 51, 164–79

Marx, K. 1964 Pre-capitalist economic formations (trans. Jack Cohen). London: Lawrence and Wishart

    1970 Capital 1 (trans. S. Moore and E. Aveling 1887). London: Lawrence and Wishart

    1971 A contribution to the critique of political economy (trans. S. W. Ryazanskaya). London: Lawrence and Wishart

    1975 Economic and philosophical manuscripts. In Karl Marx: early writings, Lucio Colletti (ed.). London: Penguin and New Left Review

Mason, H. L. and J. H. Langenheim 1957 Language analysis and the concept environment Ecology 38, 325–40

Mason, L. 1962 Habitat, man and culture. Pacific Viewpoint 3, 3–11

Mason, O. 1895 Influence of environment upon human industries and arts. Annual Report of the Smithsonian Institution, 639–65

Matley, Ian M. 1972 The Marxist approach to the geographical environment. In The conceptual revolution in geography, K. Wayne and D. Davies (eds.). London: University of London Press

Mauss, M. (in collaboration with H. Beuchat) 1906 Variations saisonnières des sociétés Eskimos: étude de morphologie sociale. L'Année Sociologique (ser. I) (1905–6), 39–132. Trans. (1979) J. Fox as Seasonal variations of the Eskimo: a study in social morphology. London: Routledge and Kegan Paul

May, Robert, M. 1973 Stability and complexity in model ecosystems. Princeton, N.J.: Princeton University Press

    1974 Ecosystem patterns in randomly fluctuating environments. Progress in Theoretical Biology 3, 1–50

Mayr, E. 1949 Speciation and selection. Proceedings of the American Philosophical Society 18, 514–19

Mazess, R. B. 1975 Biological adaptation: aptitudes and acclimatization. In Biosocial interrelations in population adaptation, E. S. Watts, F. E. Johnston and G. W. Lasker (eds.). The Hague, Paris: Mouton

Mead, Margaret (ed.) 1945 Manual for the study of food habits. Bulletin 111. Washington, D.C.: Committee on Food Habits, National Research Council

Meggers, B. J. 1954 Environmental limitations on the development of culture. American Anthropologist 56, 801–23

Bibliography

Meggitt, M. J. 1965 *The lineage system of the Mae Enga of New Guinea*. Edinburgh and London: Oliver and Boyd
1965a The association between Australian aborigines and dingoes. In *Man, culture and animals: the role of animals in human ecological adjustments*, A. Leeds, A. P. Vayda (eds.). Washington: American Association for the Advancement of Science, Publication 78

Meighan, C. *et al*. 1958 Ecological interpretation in archaeology. *American Antiquity* 24, 1–23; 131–50

Meillassoux, C. 1972 From reproduction to production. *Economy and Society* 1 (1), 93–105

Mikesell, M. 1967 Geographical perspectives in anthropology. *Annals of the Association of American Geographers* 57, 617–34

Millar, J. G. 1965 Living systems: basic concepts. *Behavioural Science* 10, 193–237

Moore, O. K. 1965 Divination – a new perspective. *American Anthropologist* 59, 69–74

Morren, G. E. B. 1977 From hunting to herding: pigs and the control of energy in montane New Guinea. In *Subsistence and survival: rural ecology in the Pacific*, T. P. Bayliss-Smith and R. G. Feachem (eds.). London: Academic Press

Morrill, W. 1967 Ethnoicthyology of the Cha-Cha. *Ethnology* 6, 405–16

Morris, B. 1976 Whither the savage mind? Notes on the natural taxonomies of a hunting and gathering people. *Man* (N.S.) 11, 542–57

Morton-Williams, P. 1969 The influence of habitat and trade on the politics of Oyo and Ashanti. In *Man in Africa*, P. Kaberry and M. Douglas (eds.). London: Tavistock

Moscovici, S. 1976 *Society against nature*. London: Harvester Press

Murdock, G. P. 1949 *Social structure*. New York: Macmillan
1967 *Ethnographic atlas*: a summary. *Ethnology* 6, 109–236
1969 Correlations of exploitative and settlement patterns. In *Contributions to anthropology: ecological essays*, D. Damas (ed.) National Museums of Canada Bulletin 230. Anthropological Series 86. Ottawa: Queen's Printers for Canada

Murphy, R. F. 1970 Basin ethnography and ecological theory. In *Languages and cultures of western North America*, E. H. Swanson (ed.). Pocatello: Idaho State University Press

Murphy, R. F. and J. H. Steward 1956 Tappers and trappers: parallel processes in acculturation. *Economic development and cultural change* 4, 335–53. Reprinted (1977) in *Evolution and ecology, essays on social transformation by Julian H. Steward*, J. C. Steward and R. F. Murphy (eds.). Urbana: University of Illinois Press

Nagel, E. 1956 A formalization of functionalism. In *Logic without metaphysics*. New York: Free Press

Neel, J. V. and F. M. Salzano 1966 A prospectus for genetic studies on the American Indians. In *The biology of human adaptability*, P. T. Baker and J. S. Weiner (eds.). Oxford: Clarendon Press

Netting, R. McC. 1968 *Hill farmers of Nigeria: cultural ecology of the Kofyar of the Jos Plateau*. Seattle and London: University of Washington Press

Bibliography

1971 *The ecological approach in cultural study*. Addison-Wesley Modular Publications 15259

1974 Agrarian ecology. In *Annual review of anthropology*, B. J. Siegal, A. R. Beals and S. A. Tyler (eds.). Palo Alto: Annual Reviews Inc.

Newcomer, P. J. 1972 The Nuer are Dinka: an essay on origins and environmental determinism. *Man* (N.S.) 7, 5–11

Nietschmann, B. 1973 *Between land and water*. New York: Seminar Press

Norgan, N. G., A. Ferro-Luzzi and J. V. G. A. Durnin 1974 The energy and nutrient intake and the energy expenditure of 204 New Guinean adults. *Philosophical Transactions of the Royal Society of London* B 268, 309–48

Nye, P. H. and D. J. Greenland 1960 *The soil under shifting cultivation*. Technical Communication 51. Commonwealth Agricultural Bureaux: Farnham Royal Commonwealth Bureau of Soils

Odum, E. P. 1953 *Fundamentals of ecology*. London: W. B. Saunders

1963 *Ecology*. New York: Holt, Rinehart and Winston

Odum, H. T. 1971 *Environment, power and society*. New York, London: Wiley-Interscience

Ohtsuka, Ryutaro 1977 Time–space use of the Papuans depending on sago and game. In *Human activity system: its spatiotemporal structure*, H. Watanabe (ed.). Tokyo: University Press

Oliver, S. C. 1962 *Ecology and cultural continuity as contributing factors in the social organization of the plains Indians*. University of California Publications in American Archaeology and Ethnology 48. Berkeley: University of California Press

Ollier, C. D., D. P. Drover and M. Godelier 1971 Soil knowledge amongst the Baruya of Wonerara, New Guinea. *Oceania* 42 (1), 33–41

Oomen, H. Q. P. C. and M. W. Corden 1970 Metabolic studies in New Guinea: nitrogen metabolism in sweet-potato eaters. *South Pacific Commission Technical Paper* 163. Noumea

Park, R. E. and E. W. Burgess 1924 (1921) *Introduction to the science of sociology*. Chicago: Chicago University Press

Parrack, D. W. 1969 An approach to the bioenergetics of rural West Bengal. In *Environment and cultural behaviour: ecological studies in cultural anthropology*, Vayda, A. P. (ed.). New York: The Natural History Press

Parsons, H. L. (ed.) 1977 *Marx and Engels on ecology*. Westport, Conn.: Greenwood Press

Pearse, A. S. 1939 *Animal ecology*. New York, London: McGraw-Hill

Peterson, J. 1978 Hunter-gatherer/farmer exchange. *American Anthropologist* 80, 335–51

Peterson, N. 1979 Territorial adaptations among desert hunter-gatherers: the !Kung and Australians compared. In *Social and ecological systems*, P. Burnham and R. Ellen (eds.) (Association of Social Anthropologists, Monograph 18). London: Academic Press

Phillipson, J. 1966 *Ecological energetics*. London: Edward Arnold

1973 The biological efficiency of protein production by grazing and other land-based systems. In *The biological efficiency of protein production*, J. G. W. Jones (ed.). Cambridge: Cambridge University Press

Bibliography

Piddocke, S. 1965 The potlatch system of the southern Kwakiutl: a new perspective. *Southwestern Journal of Anthropology* 21, 244–64

Pimentel, D. 1966 Complexity of ecological systems and problems in their study and management. In *Systems analysis in ecology*, K. E. F. Watt (ed.). London: Academic Press

Pimentel, D. and M. Pimentel 1979 *Food, energy and society*. London: Edward Arnold

Polgar, S. 1975 Population, evolution and theoretical paradigms. In *Population, ecology and social evolution*, S. Polgar (ed.). The Hague: Mouton

Porter, Philip W. 1965 Environmental potentials and economic opportunities: a background for cultural adaptation. *American Anthropologist* 67, 409–20

Pospisil, L. 1963 *Kapauku Papuan economy*. Yale University Publications in Anthropology 67

Rappaport, Roy A. 1963 Aspects of man's influence on island ecosystems: alteration and control. In *Man's place in the island ecosystem* F. R. Fosberg (ed.). Honolulu: Bernice P. Bishop Museum

1968 *Pigs for the ancestors: ritual in the ecology of a New Guinea people*. New Haven and London: Yale University Press

1969 Some suggestions concerning concept and method in ecological anthropology. In *Contributions to anthropology: ecological essays*, D. Damas (ed.). National Museums of Canada Bulletin 230, Anthropological Series 86. Ottawa: Queen's Printer for Canada

1971 The flow of energy in an agricultural society. *Scientific American* 225, 117–32

1971a Nature, culture and ecological anthropology. In *Man, culture and society*, H. Shapiro (ed.). London: Oxford University Press

1971b Ritual, sanctity and cybernetics. *American Anthropologist* 73 (1), 59–76

1971c The sacred in human evolution. *Annual Review of Ecology and Systematics* 2, 23–44

1977 Ecology, adaptation and the ills of functionalism (being, among other things, a response to Jonathan Friedman). *Michigan Discussions in Anthropology* 2, 138–90

1977a Maladaptation in social systems. In *The evolution of social systems*, J. Friedman and M. Rowlands (eds.). London: Duckworth

Rapport, D. J. and J. E. Turner 1975 Feeding rates and population growth. *Ecology* 56, 942–9

Ratzel, F. 1889 (1882) *Anthropo-Geographie, oder Grundzüge der Anwendung der Erdkunde auf die Geschichte*. Stuttgart: J. Engelhorn

1896 (1885–8) *The history of mankind* (trans. A. J. Butler). London: Macmillan

Redfield, R. 1960 *'The little community' and 'Peasant society and culture'*. Chicago: University of Chicago Press

Reynolds, V. 1976 *The biology of human action*. Reading and San Francisco: Freeman

Richards, A. I. 1932 *Hunger and work in a savage tribe*. London: Routledge and Kegan Paul

1939 *Land, labour and diet in Northern Rhodesia*. London: Oxford University Press

Bibliography

Richards, P. 1978 Ethno-ecological studies and the control of the variegated grasshopper (*Zonocerus variegatus* L.) in West Africa. Unpublished paper

Rogers, E. S. 1972 The Mistassini Cree. In *Hunters and gatherers today*, M. G. Bicchieri (ed.). New York: Holt, Rinehart and Winston

Royal Anthropological Institute 1951 *Notes and queries on anthropology* London: Routledge and Kegan Paul

Ruyle, E. E. 1973 Genetic and cultural pools: some suggestions for a unified theory of biocultural evolution. *Human Ecology* 1 (3), 201–16

    1973a Slavery, surplus and stratification on the north-west coast: the ethnoenergetics of an incipient stratification system. *Current Anthropology* 14 (5), 603–31

Sahlins, M. 1958 *Social stratification in Polynesia*. American Ethnological Society, Monograph 29. Seattle: Washington University Press

    1961 The segmentary lineage: an organization for predatory expansion. *American Anthropologist* 63, 322–45

    1964 Culture and environment: the study of cultural ecology. In *Horizons in anthropology*, S. Tax (ed.). Chicago: Aldine

    1969 Economic anthropology and anthropological economics. *Social Science Information* 8, 13–33

    1971 The intensity of domestic production: social inflections of the Chayanov slope. In *Studies in Economic anthropology*, G. Dalton (ed.). Washington: American Anthropological Association

    1972 *Stone Age economies*. Chicago: Aldine, Atherton

Sahlins, M. and E. Service (eds.) 1960 *Evolution and culture*. Ann Arbor: University of Michigan Press

Salisbury, R. F. 1962 *From stone to steel*. Cambridge: Cambridge University Press

Sangster, R. P. 1971 *Ecology: a selected bibliography*. Monticello, Ill. Council of Planning Librarians Exchange Bibliography

Sauer, C. 1925 The morphology of landscape. *University of California Publications in Geography* II, 19–54. Reprinted (1963) in *Land and life*, John Leighly (ed.). Berkeley and Los Angeles: Unversity of California Press

    1934 Ellen Churchill Semple. In E. R. A. Seligman (ed.) *Encyclopedia of the Social Sciences*. New York: Macmillan 13, 661–2

    1941 Foreword to historical geography. *Annals of the Association of American Geographers* 31, 1–24. Reprinted (1963) in *Land and life*, John Leighly (ed.). Berkeley and Los Angeles: University of California Press

Schlippe, P. de 1956 *Shifting cultivation in Africa: the Zande system of agriculture*. London: Routledge and Kegan Paul

Schmidt, A. 1971 *The concept of nature in Marx*. London: New Left Review Books

Schwartz, D. W. 1959 Culture area and time depth: the four worlds of the Havasupai. *American Anthropologist* 61, 1060–70

Scudder, T. 1962 *The ecology of the Gwembe Tonga*. Kariba Studies, Vol. II. Manchester. Manchester University Press

    1971 *Gathering among African woodland savannah cultivators. A case study: the*

Bibliography

Gwembe Tonga. Zambian papers. University of Zambia Institute for African Studies

Sebeok, T. 1970 Is a comparative semiotics possible? In *Échanges et communications: Mélanges offerts à Claude Lévi-Strauss à l'occasion de son 60ème anniversaire*, J. P. Pouillon and P. Maranda (es.). Paris: Mouton

Semple, E. C. 1911 *Influences of geographic environment: on the basis of Ratzel's system of authropogeography*. New York: Holt

Service, E. 1971 *Cultural evolutionism, theory in practice*. New York: Holt, Rinehard and Winston

Shawcross, W. 1972 Energy and ecology: thermodynamic models in archaeology. In *Models in archaeology*, D. Clarke (ed.). London: Methuen

Shelford, V. E. 1913 *Animal communities in temperate America as illustrated in the Chicago region*. Geographic Society of Chicago, Bulletin 5. Chicago: University of Chicago Press

Simmons, I. G. 1969 Evidence for vegetation changes associated with mesolithic man in Britain. In *The domestication and exploitation of plants and animals*, P. J. Ucko and G. W. Dimbleby (eds.). London: Duckworth

Simons, F. J. 1978 Traditional use and avoidance of foods of animal origin. *Bioscience* 28, 178–84

Slobodkin, L. B. 1961 *Growth and regulation of animal populations*. New York: Holt, Rinehart and Winston

1968 Toward a predictive theory of evolution. In *Population biology and evolution*, R. C. Lewontin (ed.). Syracuse: University Press

1972 On the inconstancy of ecological efficiency and the form of ecological theories. *Transactions of the Connecticut Academy of Sciences* 44, 293–305

Smith, E. A. 1979 Human adaptation and energetic efficiency. *Human Ecology* 7 (1), 53–74

Smith, J. M. B. 1977 Man's impact upon some New Guinea mountain ecosystems. In *Subsistence and survival: rural ecology in the Pacific*, T. P. Bayliss-Smith and R. G. A. Feachem (eds.). London: Academic Press

Sorenson, E. R. 1972 Socio-ecological change among the Fore of New Guinea. *Current Anthropology* 13 (3–4), 359–72

Sorre, M. 1948 La notion de genre de vie et sa valeur actuelle. *Annales de Géographie* 62, 97–108, 193–204

Spate, O. H. K. 1968 Environmentalism. In *International Encyclopedia of the Social Sciences* 5, 93–7

Spencer, J. E. 1966 *Shifting cultivation in southeastern Asia* (University of California Publications in Geography, 19) Berkeley and Los Angeles: University of California Press

Stauder, Jack 1971 *The Majangir, ecology and society of a southwest Ethiopian people* Cambridge Studies in Social Anthropology 5. Cambridge: Cambridge University Press

Stenning, D. J. 1957 Transhumance, migratory drift, migration. *Journal of the Royal Anthropological Institute* 87, 57–73

Steward, J. 1936 The economic and social basis of primitive bands. In *Essays on anthropology in honor of Alfred Louis Kroeber*, R. H. Lowie (ed.). Berkeley: University of California Press

Bibliography

1938 *Basin – plateau aboriginal sociopolitical groups*. Smithsonian Institution, Bureau of American Ethnology, Bulletin 120

1955 *The theory of culture change*. Urbana: University of Illinois Press

1968 Cultural ecology. *International Encyclopedia of the Social Sciences* 4, 337–44

Stocking, G. W. Jr 1968 *Race, culture and evolution*. New York: Free Press

Stoddart, D. R. 1965 Geography and the ecological approach; the ecosystem as a geographic principle and method, *Geography* 50, 242–51. Reprinted 1972 in *The conceptual revolution in geography* K. Wayne and D. Davies (eds.). London: University of London Press

1969 Organism and ecosystem as geographical models. In *Integrated models in geography*, R. J. Chorley and P. Haggett (eds.), London: Methuen

Street, John M. 1969 An evaluation of the concept of carrying capacity. *The Professional Geographer* 21 (2), 104–7

Struhsacker, T. T. 1969 Correlates of ecology and social organization among African cercopithecines. *Folia Primatologica* 11, 80–118

Sturtevant, W. C. 1964 Studies in ethnoscience. In *Transcultural studies in cognition*, A. K. Romney and R. G. D'Andrade (eds.) American Anthropologist Special Publication 66.3 (part 2): Menasha

Sweet, L. 1969 Camel pastoralism in north Arabia and the minimal camping unit. In *Environment and cultural behaviour: ecological studies in cultural anthropology*, A. P. Vayda (ed.). New York: The Natural History Press. First published 1965 in *Man, culture and animals: the role of animals in human ecological adjustments*, A. Leeds and A. P. Vayda (eds.) Washington: American Association for the Advancement of Science, Publication 78

Tansley, A. G. 1946 *Introduction to plant ecology*. London: George Allen and Unwin

Taylor, P. 1979 Review of *Social and ecological systems*, P. Burnham and R. Ellen (eds.). *Journal of the Anthropological Society of Oxford* 10 (3), 180–1

Teal, J. M. 1962 Energy flow in the salt-marsh ecosystem of Georgia. *Ecology* 43, 614–24

Thomas, F. 1925 *The environmental basis of society: a study in the history of sociological theory*. New York: Century

Thomas, R. B. 1973 *Human adaptation to a high Andean energy-flow system*. (*Occasional Papers in Anthropology* 7) University Park: Pennyslvania State University Department of Anthropology

1976 Energy flow at high altitude. In *Man in the Andes: a multidisciplinary study of high-altitude Quechua*, P. T. Baker and M. A. Little (eds.). Stroudsburg, Pa.: Dowden, Hutchinson and Ross

Thomas, W. L. et al. (eds.) 1956 *Man's role in changing the face of the earth*. Chicago: University of Chicago Press

Thompson, L. 1949 The relations of man, animals and plants in an island community (Fiji). *American Anthropologist* 51, 253–67

Thomson, D. F. 1939 The seasonal factor in human culture illustrated from the life of a contemporary nomadic group. *Proceedings of the Prehistoric Society* 5, 209–21

Thorpe, W. H. 1963 *Learning and instinct in animals*. London: Methuen

Bibliography

Townsend, W. H. 1969 Stone and steel tool use in a New Guinea society. *Ethnology* 8, 199–205

Tyler, S. A. 1969 *Cognitive anthropology*. New York: Holt, Rinehart and Winston

Ucko, P. J. and G. W. Dimbleby (eds.) 1969 *The domestication and exploitation of plants and animals*. London: Duckworth

Vayda, A. P. 1965 Anthropologists and ecological problems. In *Man, culture and animals*, A. Leeds and A. P. Vayda (eds.). Washington: American Association for the Advancement of Science, Publication 78

1967 On the anthropological study of economics. *Journal of Economic Issues* 1, 86–90

1969 An ecological approach in cultural anthropology. *Bucknell Review* 17, 112–19

1970 Maoris and muskets in New Zealand: disruption of a war system. *Political Science Quarterly* 85, 560–84

1974 Warfare in ecological perspective. *Annual Review of Ecology and Systematics* 5, 183–93

Vayda, A. P. and B. J. McCay 1975 New directions in ecology and ecological anthropology. In *Annual review of anthropology*, B. J. Siegal, A. R. Beals and S. A. Tyler (eds.). Palo Alto, Calif.: Annual Reviews Inc.

1977 Problems in the identification of environmental problems. In *Subsistence and survival: rural ecology in the Pacific*, T. P. Bayliss-Smith and R. G. Feachem (eds.). London: Academic Press

Vayda, A. P., A. Leeds and D. Smith (eds.) 1961 The place of pigs in Melanesian subsistence. *Proceedings of the 1961 Annual Spring Meeting of the American Ethnological Society*. Seattle: University of Washington Press

Vayda, A. P. and Roy A. Rappaport 1968 Ecology, cultural and non-cultural. In *Introduction to cultural anthropology: essays in the scope and methods of the science of man*, J. A. Clifton (ed.). Boston: Houghton Mifflin

Vidal de la Blache, P. 1902 Les conditions géographiques des faits sociaux. *Annales de Géographie* 11, 13–23

1911 Les genres de vie dans la géographie humaine. *Annales de Géographie* 20, 193–212, 289–304

Vogt, E. Z. (ed.) 1974 *Aerial photography in anthropological field research*. Cambridge, Mass.: Harvard University Press

Waddell, E. 1972 *The mound builders: agricultural practices, environment and society in the central highlands of New Guinea* (American Ethnological Society Monograph 53). Seattle and London: University of Washington Press

1975 How the Enga cope with frost: responses to climatic perturbations in the central highlands of New Guinea. *Human Ecology* 3 (4), 249–273

Waddington, C. H. 1970 *Towards a theoretical biology*, 1. Edinburgh: Edinburgh University Press

Wagley, C. 1951 Cultural influences on population: a comparison of two Tupi tribes. *Revista do Museu Paulista* (N.S.) 5, 95–104

Wanklyn, H. 1961 *Friedrich Ratzel: a biographical memoir and bibliography*. Cambridge: Cambridge University Press

Warming, J. E. B. 1895 *Plantesamfund: Grundtroek af den økologiske plantegeographi*. Copenhagen: P. B. Philipsen

Bibliography

Watanabe, Hitoshi (ed.) 1977 *Human activity system: its spatio-temporal structure*. Tokyo: University Press

Watson, R. A. and P. J. Watson 1969 *Man and nature: an anthropological essay in human ecology*. New York: Harcourt, Brace and World

Watt, Kenneth E. F. 1966 The nature of systems analysis. In *Systems analysis in ecology*. New York, London: Academic Press

Weber, M. 1949 *The methodology of the social sciences* (trans. E. Shils and H. Finch). New York: Free Press

Weiner, J. S. 1964 Human ecology. In *Human biology*, G. A. Harrison, J. S. Weiner, J. Tanner and N. Barnicot (eds.). Oxford: Clarendon Press

1964a The biology of social man. *Journal of the Royal Anthropological Institute* 94, 230–40

1972 Tropical ecology and population structure. In *The structure of human populations*, G. A. Harrison and J. A. Boyce (eds.). Oxford: Clarendon Press

1973 Man the hunter. *Proceedings of the Royal Society of Medicine* 66, 89–93

Wells, H. G., J. S. Huxley and G. P. Wells 1934 *Science of life* vol. 1. London: Cassell

Wells, P. V. 1970 Postglacial vegetational history of the Great Plains. *Science* 167, 1574–82

White, B. 1975 The economic importance of children in a Javanese village. In *Population and social organisation*, Moni Nag (ed.). The Hague, Paris: Mouton

White, L. A. 1945 History, evolutionism and funtionalism: three types of interpretation of culture. *Southwestern Journal of Anthropology* 1, 221–48

1949 *The science of culture: a study of man and civilization*. Grove Press: New York

1959 *The evolution of culture*. New York: McGraw-Hill

Whiting, J. W. M. 1964 Effects of climate on certain cultural practices. In *Explorations in cultural anthropology*, W. H. Goodenough (ed.), New York: McGraw-Hill. Reprinted 1969 in *Environment and cultural behaviour: ecological studies in cultural anthropology*, A. P. Vayda (ed.). New York: The Natural History Press

Whittlesey, Derwent 1937 Shifting cultivation. *Economic Geography* 13 (1) 35–52

Whyte, A. 1977 Systems as perceived: a discussion of 'Maladaptation in social systems'. In *the evolution of social systems*, J. Friedman and M. Rowlands (eds.). London: Duckworth

Wiesenfeld, Stephen L. 1967 Sickle-cell trait in human biological and cultural evolution. *Science* 157, 1134–40

Wilden, A. 1972 *System and structure: essays in communication and exchange*. London: Tavistock

Wilkinson, R. G. 1973 *Poverty and progress: an ecological model of economic development*. London: Methuen

Williams, B. J. 1974 *A model of band society*. Memoirs of the Society for American Archaeology 29. Washington D.C.

Bibliography

Williams, G. C. 1966 *Adaptation and natural selection: a critique of some evolutionary thought*. Princeton, N. J.: Princeton University Press

1971 *Group selection*. Chicago: Aldine, Atherton

Winterhalder, B. 1980 Environmental analysis in human evolution and adaptation research. *Human Ecology* 8 (2), 135–70

Winterhalder, B., R. Larsen and R. B. Thomas 1974 Dung as an essential resource in a highland Peruvian community. *Human Ecology* 2, 89–104

Wissler, C. 1917 *The American Indian: an introduction to the anthropology of the New World*. New York: McMurtie

1926 *The relation of nature to man in aboriginal America*. New York: Oxford University Press

1929 *An introduction to social anthropology*. New York: Holt

Woodburn, J. 1968 An introduction to Hadza ecology. In *Man the hunter*, R. B. Lee and I. DeVore (eds) Chicago: Aldine

1972 Ecology, nomadic movement and the composition of the local group among hunters and gatherers: an East African example and its implications. In *Man, settlement and urbanism*, P. J. Ucko, R. Tringham and G. W. Dimbleby (eds.). London: Duckworth

Woodwell, G. M. 1970 The energy cycle of the biosphere. In *The biosphere* (*Scientific American*). San Francisco: W. H. Freeman

Woodwell, G. M. and H. H. Smith (eds.) 1969 *Diversity and stability in ecological systems*. Brookhaven Symposia in Biology 22. Brookhaven: National Laboratory, Biology Department

Worsley, P. 1956 The kinship system of the Tallensi: a re-evaluation. *Journal of the Royal Anthropological Institute* 86, 37–77

Wynne-Edwards, V. C. 1962 *Animal dispersion in relation to animal behaviour*. Edinburgh: Oliver and Boyd

Yellen, J. E. and H. Harpending 1972 Hunter-gatherer populations and archaeological inference. *World Archaeology* 4, 244–53

Yengoyan, A. A. 1968 Demographic and ecological influences on aboriginal Australian marriage sections. In *Man the hunter*, R. B. Lee and I. DeVore (eds.). Chicago: Aldine

1973 Kindreds and task groups in Mandaya social organization. *Ethnology* 12, 163–77

Name Index

vwvwvwvwvwvwvwvwvwvwvwvwvwvwvwvwvwvwvwvwvwvwvwvwvwvwvwvwvwvwvwvwvwvwvwvwvwvwvwvwvwvwvwvwvwvwvwvwvwvwvwvwv

Abbott, Joan M. W., 4, 92
Ackoff, R., 284n
Adams, C. C., 67, 282n
Adams, J. E., 243
Adams, Robert McC., 273
Ahrens, R., 27
Alexander, R. D., 245
Alihan, M. A., 67
Alkire, W. H., 108, 127
Allan, W., 37, 38, 41, 42
Alland, A., 24, 238, 242, 243, 245, 250, 285n
Allee, W. C., 282n
Anderson, E. N. Jr, 92
Anderson, J. N., 4, 92, 93, 99, 184, 196, 277
Arbuthnot, John, 2
Aristotle, 1, 2, 66
Ashby, W. R., 89, 284n
Audy, J. R., 272

Bacon, F., 22
Baker, P. T., 49, 58
Barrau, J., 137, 207, 218
Barrows, H. H., 68
Barth, F., 9, 74, 82–3, 283n
Basso, K. H., 214, 218
Bates, M., 68, 70, 73, 277, 280n
Bateson, G., 93, 284n
Baumhoff, M. A., 29
Bayliss-Smith, T. P., 43, 45, 79, 120, 127, 133, 135, 150, 151, 201
Beals, Alan R., 284n
Bennett, J. W., 25, 35, 60, 62, 67, 73, 83, 86, 107, 185, 192, 193, 201, 249, 269, 271, 282n, 283n
Bennett, K. A., 286n
Berlin, B., 86, 208, 211, 233
Berreman, G., 209
Berrien, F. K., 248

Bertalanffy, L. von, 177
Beuchat, H., 24, 30, 154
Bews, J. W., 91, 282n
Birdsell, J. B., 11–12, 19, 34–5, 50, 155
Bloch, M., 249
Blurton-Jones, N., 251
Boas, F., 9, 24, 27, 28, 29, 30, 91
Bodin, Jean, 2
Boehm, C., 237
Bonte, P., 31, 59
Boserup, Ester, 40, 137, 269, 271
Boulding, K. D., 15
Bourdieu, P., 253
Bradfield, M., 69
Breedlove, D., 86
Bronson, B., 40, 267, 269, 270, 271
Brookfield, M. C., 36, 44, 48, 70, 118, 171, 184, 206, 208, 234, 262
Brown, Lester R., 23
Brown, P., 36, 44, 70, 262, 270
Brush, S. B., 41, 44
Buchbinder, Georgeda, 158, 184
Buckley, W., 179
Buffon, Comte de, 22, 282n
Bulmer, R., 206, 207, 208, 211, 218, 284n
Burch, E. S. Jr, 217
Burgess, E. W., 67
Burling, R., 209, 216
Burnham, P., 191, 239, 282n

Carneiro, Robert L., 37, 38, 39, 40, 41, 43, 141, 269
Chang Chih-i, 127
Childe, Vere G., 28
Chisholm, M., 162
Chorley, R. J., 68
Clark, C., 45, 168
Clark, J. G. D., 23, 28, 68, 277
Clarke, D. L., 69, 177

Name Index

Clarke, W. C., 37, 38, 40, 44, 126, 127, 195
Clements, Frederick, 67, 95
Clements, F. W., 107
Coe, M. D., 83
Coelho, G. V., 243
Cohen, M. N., 269
Cohen, Y. A., 260
Cole, L., 79
Coles, J., 149, 150
Collins, P. W., 242
Comte, A., 26
Conklin, H. C., 7, 15, 38, 39, 43, 69, 70, 71–2, 86, 126, 147, 206, 207, 211, 214, 216, 218, 219, 220, 233
Cook, E., 268
Cook, S., 91, 118, 226, 275, 278, 279, 286n
Corden, M. W., 286n
Cotgrove, S., 93
Cottrell, Fred, 102
Cousin, Victor, 2
Cowgill, V., 13
Crook, J. H., 280n
Cummins, K. W., 114

Damas, D., 154
Darling, F. F., 282n
Darlington, P. J., 10
Darwin, C., 1
Davis, H., 88
Dawkins, R., 245
Day, Gordon, 23
Deevey, E. S., 267, 268
Demolins, M., 26
Denevan, William M., 40
Denham, W. W., 280n, 283n
Deshler, W. W., 126
DeVore, I., 56, 57
Diamond, J., 211
Dice, Lee R., 68, 187, 282n
Diener, P., 234
Digby, A., 143
Dimbleby, G. W., 23
Dornstreich, M., 48, 137, 140, 141, 152, 164, 166, 169, 171, 172, 173, 175
Douglas, M., 15, 24, 194, 206, 208
Dow, James, 106, 117, 118, 224
Drover, D. P., 214
Dumond, D. E., 40
Dunn, F. L., 141
Dupré, G., 279
Durkheim, E., 16, 27, 30, 91, 208, 282n
Durnin, J. V. G. A., 111, 143
Dwyer, P. D., 137, 152, 155, 211
Dyson-Hudson, N., 31, 173
Dyson-Hudson, R., 173

Edholm, F., 169
Eisenberg, J. F., 280n
Ellen, Roy F., 19, 37, 38, 43, 44, 46, 70, 86, 111, 116, 126, 141, 150, 154, 159, 162, 164, 165, 169, 175, 196, 198, 200, 206, 208, 209, 214, 215, 216, 219, 221, 222, 227, 230, 231, 232, 235, 281n
Elton, C., 81, 95
Emery, F. E., 284n
Engels, F., 3, 22, 59, 281n
Epton, S., 283n
Evans-Pritchard, E., 30, 31, 58, 126
Eyre, S. R., 68

Fagen, R. E., 177
Faris, J. C., 253, 260, 262
Feachem, R. G. A., 41, 90
Febvre, L., 27
Fei Hsiao-t'ung, 127
Feldman, Douglas A., xii, 14
Ferguson, A., 26
Ferro-Luzzi, A., 111
Flannery, K., 83, 177, 189, 196, 226, 272
Foley, R., 99, 102–3, 131, 160, 162, 163
Forde, C. D., 27–8, 31–2, 51, 52, 64, 177, 180, 234, 262, 279, 281n, 284n
Forman, S., 218
Fortes, M., 28, 30
Fosberg, F. R., 74, 79, 97
Foucauit, Michel, 1
Fowler, C. S., 55
Fowler, D. D., 55
Fox, J. J., 24, 30
Fox, R. G., 259
Fox, R. H., 110, 156
Frake, C. O., 224, 225
Frankenberg, R., 61
Freeman, D., 37, 43, 58, 69, 127, 159
Freilich, Morris, 63–4
Friedman, J., 62, 73, 93, 180, 190, 193, 196, 202, 246, 255, 256, 278, 280n, 286n

Garanger, J., 149
Gartlan, J. S., 280n
Geertz, C., 4, 75, 76, 88, 101, 188, 202, 266
Gellner, E., 49, 180
Gerlach, L. P., 110
Ginsberg, M., 284n
Glacken, C. J., 22, 66, 280n
Glander, K. E., 283n
Gluckman, M., 27, 71, 283n
Godelier, M., 60, 62, 91, 149, 214, 257, 279
Goldenweiser, A. A., 266

Name Index

Goldschmidt, W., 58, 72, 281n
Goodey, B., 208
Goodman, D., 189
Goody, J., 254
Gould, R. C., 55
Gray, R. F., 27, 29, 76
Green, R. C., 43
Greene, L. S., 170
Greenfield, Sydney, 283n
Greenland, D. J., 36, 44
Gross, D. R., 113, 170
Gulliver, P. H., 31, 172

Haeckel, E., 1, 66, 277, 282n
Hagen, E. E., 179
Hall, A. D., 177
Hamburg, D. A., 243
Hames, R. B., 149
Hardesty, D. L., 80, 82, 83, 84, 85, 101,
   136, 189, 242, 243, 271
Harner, M. J., 14, 263, 269, 272
Harpending, H., 88–9
Harris, Alfred, 28
Harris, D. R., 19, 35, 37, 39, 88, 124,
   188, 196, 207, 269, 272, 273, 281n
Harris, M., xii, 2, 29, 45, 53, 54, 59–63,
   73, 127, 134, 135, 174, 182, 196, 208,
   209, 216, 242, 247, 256, 260, 282n,
   285n
Harris, O., 169
Hart, D., 48, 171, 234
Harvey, D., 178
Haswell, M. R., 45, 127, 168
Hawley, A. H., 67
Hayden, B., 44
Hays, T., 216
Hegel, G. W. F., 60
Helm, J., 76
Helvetius, C-A., 2
Herodotus, 2
Heston, A., 196
Hiatt, L., 11, 55
Hiernaux, J., 285n
Higgs, E. S., 284n
Hippocrates, 2
Hipsley, E. H., 104, 107, 149, 151, 286n
Hladick, C. M., 280n
Ho, K. J., 285n
Hobhouse, L. T., 284n
Holbach, Baron P. H. T. d', 2
Holling, C. S., 187, 188, 242
Hollingshead, A. B., 64
Holmes, G., 3
Holmes, W. H., 8
Hornabrook, R. W., 111
Hume, David, 26
Hunn, E., 215, 284n

Huntington, E., 1, 2, 6
Hutterer, K. L., 150
Huxley, J. S., 277

Ibn Kaldun, 2
Ingold, T., 75, 83, 128, 130, 171, 175,
   176, 286n
Isidore of Seville, 2
Izikowitz, K. G., 43

Janzen, D. H., 36
Johnson, A., 159, 174, 220
Jones, G., 68
Judd, L. C., 38, 43

Kaplan, D., 76, 180
Keesing, R. M., 208, 209
Kelly, R. C., 263
Kemp, W. B., 104, 126, 132, 153
Kirk, Nancy, 104, 149, 151
Kirkby, A. V. T., 43
Klejn, L. S., 286n
Krader, L., 214
Krantz, G. S., 22
Kroeber, A. L., 9, 10, 24–5, 27, 28, 30,
   52, 53, 68, 73, 91, 260
Kula, N., 206
Kummer, H., 237, 284n
Kunstadter, Peter, 255

Langenheim, J. H., 276
Langton, J., 178, 179, 186, 195, 199, 201,
   202, 204, 230
Larsen, R., 119
Lathrap, D. W., 41
Lawton, J. H., 99, 101, 107, 111, 115,
   138, 145, 150, 271, 278
Lea, D. A. M., 44, 70, 211, 215
Leach, E. R., 5, 15, 30, 39, 43, 50, 127,
   159, 263, 283n
Leach, G., 45
Lee, R. B., 11, 56, 57, 126, 132, 134, 141,
   143, 153, 162, 169, 196, 278
Leeds, A., 14, 42, 43, 72, 126, 182
Le Play, F., 26
Le Roy Ladurie, E., 1
Levins, R., 84
Lévi-Strauss, C., 215, 233
Lewin, K., 284n
Lewis, I., 59
Lewis, O., 127, 147, 149
Leynseele, P. van, 218
Liebig, Justus, 34–5, 48
Lienhardt, G., 30
Lindeman, R. L., 95, 118
Little, M. A., 48, 108, 117, 123, 126, 133,
   135, 150, 171

315

Name Index

Livingstone, Frank B., 264
Llobera, J. R., 60
Locke, John, 2
Löffler, Lorenz G., 43
Lotka, A. J., 268
Lovelock, J., 283n
Lowie, R., 24, 26, 28, 284n
Lowman-Vayda, C., 184

McArthur, M., 69, 84, 110, 115–16, 126,
   143, 150, 159, 184, 185, 283n
McCarthy, F. D., 69, 126, 142, 150, 159
McCay, B., 24, 48, 118, 171, 188, 193,
   194, 196, 238, 242, 243, 245, 248,
   250, 285n
Mackenzie, R. D., 91
McLellan, D., 3
McNeill, S., 115
Maelzor, D. A., 280n
Mair, L. P., 30
Malthus, T., 124, 192, 266
Manner, H. I., 23, 114
Manners, R., 76, 180
Marett, R. R., 26
Margalef, Ramon, 79, 88
Marsh, G. P., 22
Marshall, G., 16
Marshall, L., 56
Maruyama, M., 195
Marx, K., 3, 15, 22, 59, 60, 252, 254, 262,
   278, 281n, 282n
Mason, H. L., 276
Mason, L., 70
Mason, O., 3, 8
Matley, Ian M., 1, 3, 8, 21
Mauss, M., 24, 30, 60, 61, 154, 282n
May, Robert M., 188, 189
Mayr, E., 243
Mazess, R. B., 242, 243
Mead, Margaret, 107, 282n
Mechnikov, Lev, 1
Meggers, B. J., 25–6, 40
Meggitt, M. J., 75, 263
Meighan, C., 68
Meillassoux, C., 279
Menzies, J., 214
Mikesell, M., 29
Millar, J. G., 178, 180
Miller, R. J., 286n
Montesquieu, Charles Louis de, 2, 26
Moore, O. K., 193, 217
Morgan, L. H., 26
Morren, G. E. B., 48, 98, 104, 108, 116,
   117, 120, 123, 126, 127, 132, 133,
   135, 137, 143, 150, 171, 174, 175,
   284n
Morrill, W., 217

Morris, B., 215
Morton-Williams, P., 281n
Moscovici, S., 15, 204
Murdock, G. P., 125, 260, 284n
Murphy, R. F., 54, 190

Nagel, E., 180
Neel, J. V., 285n
Netting, R. McC., 27, 36, 41, 46, 58, 59,
   64, 70, 71, 72, 113, 127, 189, 217,
   261, 270
Newcomer, P. J., 276
Nietschmann, B., 43, 44, 79, 80, 81, 86,
   101, 102, 120, 127, 137, 147, 150,
   154, 157, 158, 159, 162, 163, 168,
   169, 173, 174, 208, 214, 217, 272
Nonini, D., 234
Norgan, N. G., 111, 116
Nye, P. H., 36, 44

Odum, E. P., 34, 100, 282n, 283n
Odum, H. T., 92, 96, 98, 108, 118, 127,
   282n, 283n
Ohtsuka, Ryutaro, 159, 162, 163, 164
Oliver, S. C., 29, 56
Ollier, C. D., 214
Oomen, H. Q. P. C., 286n
Osborne, R. H., 286n

Park, R. E., 67
Parrack, D. W., 97, 103, 143
Parsons, H. L., 3, 286n
Parsons, T., 190
Passmore, R., 143
Pearse, A. S., 282n
Peterson, J., 259
Peterson, N., 57
Phillipson, J., 103, 136, 283n
Piddocke, S., 190, 246
Pimentel, D., 87, 89, 126, 127, 137, 138,
   149, 168
Pimentel, M., 126, 127, 137, 138, 149,
   168
Plato, 2
Plekhanov, G. V., 3, 8
Podolefsky, A., 270
Polgar, S., 270
Pollio, Marcus Vitruvius, 2
Polybius, 2
Popper, K., 203
Porter, Phillip W., 72
Pospisil, L., 69, 284n

Radcliffe-Brown, A. R., 27
Rappaport, Roy A., 8, 9, 20, 28, 32, 38,
   42, 43, 44, 45, 47, 63, 64, 72, 75, 76,

316

77, 78, 88, 93, 102, 104–6, 111, 112,
115–16, 126, 132, 143, 149, 150, 151,
152, 169, 177, 178, 181, 182–6, 188,
190, 191, 192, 193, 195, 196, 206,
210, 214, 217, 226, 227, 228, 234,
241, 245, 250, 273, 281n
Rapport, D. J., 271
Ratzel, F., 2–3, 8, 26, 29, 30, 208, 256
Raven, P., 86
Reason, D., 208
Redfield, Robert, 73
Rey, P. P., 279
Reynolds, V., 32
Richards, A. I., 29, 49, 70–1, 107, 111,
218, 282n
Richards, P., 217
Robkin, E. E., 234
Rogers, E. S., 85, 154
Romer, A. S., 241
Rousseau, J. J., 14, 22, 39, 218
Rowlands, M., 256
Royal Anthropological Institute, 29
Ruyle, E. E., 168, 246, 252, 254, 255,
285n

Sahlins, M., 46, 56, 57, 58–9, 73, 89, 159,
170, 174, 185, 191, 194, 242, 259,
260, 266, 271, 279, 284n
Salisbury, R. F., 137, 149
Salzano, F. M., 285n
Sangster, R. P., 23
Sauer, C., 2, 22, 73
Schlippé, P. de, 207
Schmidt, A., 3, 15, 22
Schwartz, D. W., 10
Scudder, T., 69, 142, 284n
Sebeok, T., 205
Semple, E. C., 2
Service, E., 55, 57, 89, 239, 242, 260,
266, 279
Shawcross, W., 103, 120
Shelford, V. E., 48, 95, 282n
Simmons, I. G., 22
Simons, F. J., 285n
Slobodkin, L. B., 118, 201, 238, 243,
284n
Smith, D., 72, 182
Smith, E. A., 119
Smith, H. H., 114, 273
Sorenson, E. R., 69, 262
Sorre, M., 208
Spate, O. H. K., 2
Spencer, Herbert, 26
Spencer, J. E., 39, 71
Stauder, Jack, 18
Stenning, D. J., 13, 50, 172
Steward, J. H., 10, 29, 52–7, 58, 59, 60,

61–5, 70, 78, 91, 180, 185, 256, 259,
260, 281n, 282n
Stimson, A., 214
Stocking, G. W. Jr, 26, 29
Stoddart, D., 177, 283n
Street, John M., 39, 44
Struhsacker, T. T., 280n
Sturtevant, W. C., 207
Sweet, L, 9, 14, 57, 58

Tansley, A. G., 74, 282n
Taylor, P., xiv
Teal, J. M., 97
Thomas, F., 2, 26
Thomas, R. B., 104, 108, 111, 116, 119,
127, 132, 169
Thomas, W. L., 14, 23
Thompson, D. F., 154
Thompson, L., 79, 92
Thorpe, W. H., 237
Thünen, J. H. von, 162
Townsend, W. H., 149
Turgot, A-R-J., 14
Turner, J. E., 271
Tyler, S. A., 208

Ucko, P. J., 23
Underwood, B. A., 113, 170

Vayda, A. P., 4, 5, 8, 9, 14, 20, 28, 32,
48, 63, 64, 72, 75, 76, 77, 118, 171,
182, 188, 193, 194, 196, 210, 234,
238, 248, 250, 277, 281n
Vidal de la Blache, P., 21, 27, 208
Vogt, E. Z., 69

Waddell, E., 46, 127, 184, 248, 271
Waddington, C. H., 195, 256
Wagley, C., 238
Wanklyn, H., 3
Warming, J. E. B., 282n
Watanabe, Hitoshi, 159
Watson, P. J., 49, 147, 186, 203, 269
Watson, R. A., 49, 147, 186, 203, 269
Watt, Kenneth E. F., 90, 114, 178, 179
Weber, M., 236
Weiner, J. S., 13, 77, 126, 155, 156, 237,
281n, 285n
Wells, G. P., 277
Wells, H. G., 277
Wells, P. V., 22
Wheeler, G. C., 284n
White, B., 169
White, L. A., 47, 102, 117, 130, 143, 242,
259, 260, 266, 268, 269, 270
Whiting, J. W. M., 13
Whittlesey, Derwent, 39

Name Index

Whyte, A., 272
Wiesenfeld, Stephen L., 237
Wilden, A., 187, 195, 205
Wilkinson, R. G., 269
Williams, B. J., 57
Williams, G. C., 240, 242, 243, 244, 245, 247
Winterhalder, B., 81, 119, 243, 244
Wissler, C., 8–9, 10, 19, 21, 25, 52, 53, 68, 283n

Woodburn, J., 4, 5, 56, 126, 141, 194
Woodwell, G. M., 89, 114, 273
Worsley, P., 30
Wuycheck, J. C., 114
Wynne-Edwards, V. C., 182, 194, 244

Yellen, J. E., 89
Yengoyan, A. A., 263, 281n
Young, K., 169

Subject Index

vwvwvwvwvwvwvwvwvwvwvwvwvwvwvwvwvwvwvwvwvwvwvwvwvwvwvwvwvwvwvwvwvwvwvwvwvwvwvwvw

Abelam (Papua New Guinea), 215
adaptation
    concept of, 24, 61, 64, 67, 68, 70, 72,
        73, 74, 77, 83, 117–19, 136, 172, 190,
        191, 194, 215, 227, 236–51, 257, 258,
        260, 261, 269, 272, 273, 280, 281,
        284, 285
    and context, 249–50
    contradictions in, 249–50
    defined, 240–3
    group, 194–5, 244–5, 246
    levels of, 244–7
    measurement of, 240–3
    phylogenetic, 236, 237, 241, 264, 285
    and temporal context, 247–9
    see also evolution, cultural
affiliation, bilateral, 57
age-area hypothesis, 10
agriculture, *see* cultivation
Algonkian (Canada), 54, 55
altitude, 32, 42, 46, 166, 167
Amahuaca (Peru), 37
America
    pre-Columbian, 9, 25, 52
    United States of, 21, 24, 28, 52, 95,
        127, 131, 133, 138
Amerindians, plains, 22, 56, 171
anthropogeography, 2
Arabia, 9, 13
archaeology, 25, 27, 52, 68–9, 83, 86, 90,
    103, 177, 207, 258, 283, 284
Australians, aboriginal, 11–12, 19, 32, 34,
    50, 55, 57, 75, 126, 281
    Arnhemlanders, 144, 150, 159
autoecology, 93, 130, 135

Bali (Indonesia), 88
Baruya (Papua New Guinea), 214
Batainabura (Papua New Guinea), 38
Bedouin, 32, 33, 57, 172

Bemba (Zambia), 29, 33, 71, 107, 282
bioenergetics, *see* energetics
biogeography, 9, 10, 14, 68, 70, 79
biologisms, 91
biology, 1, 52, 73, 76, 78, 81, 85, 89–93,
    118, 177, 182, 187, 188, 194, 201,
    242, 244, 245, 276
biome, 74
biotope, 80–1, 83, 84, 89, 163, 164, 168,
    186
birth, incidence of, 13
'black box' concept, 89, 201, 204, 225
Bomagai Angoiong Maring, 126, 131, 133
    see also Maring
Brassica oleracea, 86, 87
Brazil, 170, 220
Britain, 2, 52, 95, 138
    see also social anthropology, British
bushmen (Kalahari), 55, 57
    see also !Kung San

Californian indians, 25, 33
calorimetry, 102, 114
capitalism, 16–17, 73, 199, 276
carrying capacity, 41-6, 70, 84, 191, 244,
    266, 275, 281
    see also limiting factors
causality, 48, 53, 76, 94, 202, 276
    reciprocal, 180, 182, 193
    see also correlations, environmental
Ceylon, *see* Sri Lanka
Chicago School of Urban Sociology, 67,
    73, 91
Chimbu (Papua New Guinea), 36, 70,
    104, 184, 263
circumcision, 11
class, social, 16–17, 91, 246, 262, 269,
    270
classifications, folk, 207–11, 214, 218–23,
    224, 233, 234, 235, 253

climate, 11–13, 15, 17, 25, 26, 31, 32, 76, 81, 155–9, 213, 281
cline, 78
cognitive models, 206–7, 209, 210, 217, 227, 230, 234, 235
commensalism, 75
control hierarchy, 190
Cordyline, 182
correlations, environmental, 30, 32, 53, 61, 63
  and causality, 17–20
  and scale, 5–8, 9, 16–17
  types of, 11–14
cultivation, 6, 7, 23, 25, 31, 35, 70, 72, 82, 125, 199, 259, 262, 268, 270, 281
  intensification of, 40, 269–70
  selection of sites for, 19, 46–7, 230–1, 232
  see also rice, swidden cultivation
cultural adaptation, 53, 82, 236–51, 264, 279, 280
  mechanisms of, 238–40
  see also adaptation
cultural climax, 25, 68
cultural core, 54, 61, 63, 64, 282
cultural ecology, xii, 52–65, 66, 69, 73, 74, 75, 76, 94, 117, 260, 281
  critique of, 61–5
culture, 10, 15, 24–5, 62, 64, 66, 76, 130
  -area concept, 8–11, 21, 25, 28, 53, 78, 82
  types, 53, 54, 55, 56, 58, 62, 63
Cuna (Panama), 84
cybernetics, 93, 180, 191, 227, 241, 284

Darwinism, 66, 236, 241, 266
  see also Darwin
decision making, 192, 209, 210, 216, 219, 223–6, 230, 231, 233, 234, 240
deme, 77
demography, *see* population
determinism, 50–1, 61, 63, 64
  environmental, *see* environmentalism
  'techno-environmental', 60, 62
development, economic, 73, 88, 136
diet, 70, 107–10, 111, 113, 158, 281
  see also nutrition
diffusionism, 26, 27, 53
Dinka (Sudan), 171
divination, 193
division of labour
  technical 169, 273
  sexual, 169
  social, 128, 134, 199, 273
Dodo (Uganda), 108, 126

East Africa, 72
ecological movement, the, 22, 92

ecology
  and anthropology, xi–xiv, 1, 26, 52, 61, 64, 90, 95, 97, 274–9, 286
  and biology, xi, xii, xiii, 1, 66, 97, 114, 282, 284
  defined, 280
  and economy 277–8, 279, 286
  see also human ecology
economic anthropology, 102, 277, 278
economy, *see* ecology
ecosystem
  boundaries, 78–9
  concept, xii, 13, 73–8, 89, 92–4, 102, 283
  defined, 74, 282
  diversity, 86–9, 95, 123, 128, 282
  and social formations, 254–7, 266, 273
  types of, 123–8
ecotypes, 124
empiricism, 3–4, 27, 28, 49, 52, 67, 73, 117, 119, 202
  see also factualism
end-states, ecological 226–33
energetics, xii, xiii, 102–4, 110, 283
  see also energy
energy, and its flow, 47–8, 56, 74, 77, 95–122, 184, 201, 204, 205, 214, 223, 252, 259, 267, 272, 275, 278
  evolution in use of, 267–71
  exchange between populations, 141–3
  primary production, 102–3, 267
  reductionism, 118
  see also energy efficiency, energy input, energy output
energy (ecological) efficiency, 103, 104, 118, 119, 120, 129, 130, 135–7, 270
  patterned, 150–3
  population fraction, 168–70
  spatial distribution, 160–8
  temporal distribution, 154–61
energy input (expenditure), 110–13, 131
  total, 130, 134–5
  according to activity, 143–50
  population fraction, 168–70
  distributed spatially, 160–8
  distributed temporally, 154–61
energy output (production), 107–10, 131, 267–71
  total, 130–4, 267–71
  population fraction, 168–70
  distributed spatially, 160–8
  according to technique, 137–43
  distributed temporally, 154–61
Enga (Papua New Guinea), 248
  see also Gadio Enga, Mae-Enga, Raiapu Enga
England, *see* Britain

Subject Index

enlightenment, 2, 26

environment
  human modification of, 14–15, 21, 22–3
  perception of, 204, 206, 208, 210, 214, 218, 223, 225, 227, 234, 284

environmentalism, xii, 1–20, 21, 22, 24, 26, 27, 30, 32, 49, 53, 60, 62, 66, 68, 76, 90, 94, 256, 279, 280, 281
  defined, 1–2
  some inadequacies of, 3–5

epidemiology, xiii, 91

equilibrium models, 186–9, 190, 195, 196, 278

Eskimo, 24, 29, 30, 33, 56, 126, 131, 132, 133, 139, 142, 144, 154, 156, 170, 214, 217

ethnobiology (including ethnobotany, ethnozoology), 206, 207, 211, 214, 231

ethnoecology, 206, 207, 210, 211–18, 219, 224, 233, 234, 235, 284

ethnoenergetics, 285

ethnohistory, 25, 207

ethnoscience, 207, 210, 224, 225

Europe, 22, 23, 162, 196, 197

evolution, 53, 62, 66, 77, 120, 193, 195, 201, 241, 242, 243, 247, 252–73, 277, 279, 280, 285
  cultural, 49, 53, 136, 258, 263–5, 285
  multilinear, 53, 54, 259
  phylogenetic (biological), 263–5
  of systems, 50, 74, 79, 225
  of open systems, 271–3
  unilinear, 53, 258, 259

evolutionism, 1, 26, 49, 56

exchange, economic, 45, 77, 91, 99, 119, 132, 141, 142, 143, 151, 169, 184, 197, 198, 199, 216, 259, 269

factualism, 16–17
  see also empiricism

fallow, 6, 35, 36, 37, 38, 39, 40, 41, 42, 72

fatalism, geographical, 1
  see also environmentalism

feedback, 191, 192, 195, 202
  negative, 180–1, 190, 191, 196, 205, 241, 273
  positive, 184, 195–9, 278

feudalism, 276

fieldwork, ethnographic, 21, 28–9, 30, 49, 65, 69, 70, 90, 107

fire, 6, 22–3, 35, 71

folk models, see cognitive models

food chains, 95–6, 110, 132, 137, 215, 218, 267

food-collecting mode of
  subsistence, 14, 32, 34, 88, 125, 143, 168, 247

Fulani (Nigeria), 13, 33, 50, 172

functionalism, sociological, 21, 24–30, 39, 52, 57, 64, 67, 73, 91, 93, 180, 182, 190, 193, 196, 283
  ecological, 73, 186, 190–2

fungi, hallucinogenic, 13

Gadio Enga (Papua New Guinea), 48, 137, 140, 164, 166, 169, 170

Galla (Ethiopia), 58

Gambia, 154, 156

Gbaya (Cameroon), 191

generative analysis, 226–33, 257, 258

Genieri (Gambia), 127, 131, 133

genital mutilation, 13
  see also circumcision, subincision

genres de vie, 208

geographical determinism, see environmentalism

geography, 1, 13, 22, 27, 32, 52, 68, 69, 70, 76, 78, 101, 177, 207, 208, 211, 280

geology, 13

geomorphology, 12–13, 68

Germany, 21

Ghana, 36, 217

Greece, 2

Guatamala, 83, 138

Gujars (Pakistan), 82

habitat, concept of, 2, 8, 13, 54, 74, 91, 164

Hadza (Tanzania), 4, 5, 33, 56, 126, 141, 170, 172, 259

Hanunoo (Philippines), 38, 39, 43, 71, 72, 126, 170, 218

history, 51, 53, 54, 61, 62, 252, 258–65, 269, 271, 273, 277, 279, 285

homeostasis, 180–1, 182, 191, 192, 194, 195, 196, 227, 241, 245

Hopi (American southwest), 25

human ecology and biology, 66–94
  see also ecology

humanism, liberal, 22

humidity, 12, 26

hunting, 18–19, 20, 54, 75, 125, 128, 129, 140, 141, 144, 145, 146, 148, 152, 155, 156, 157, 158, 162, 164, 165, 166, 167, 171, 173, 176, 181, 193, 217, 269, 271
  and gathering, 23, 29, 55–7, 137, 159, 170, 171
  see also food-collecting

hypercoherence, 189

Iban (Sarawak), 37, 43, 58, 127, 133, 138, 159, 169, 170
Ifugao (Philippines), 211, 219, 220, 222, 223
Imperata, 23, 39, 46, 47, 71, 220
Incas (Peru), 62
India, 259
  sacred cows in, 182, 196
Indonesia, 88
inductivism, 5, 49, 67
involution, 266
irrigation, 23, 83, 124, 267
  see also rice

Java, 88, 197, 263
Jie, 31–2

Kachin (Burma), 31, 39, 43
Kalam (Papua New Guinea), 211, 284
Kapauku (Indonesian New Guinea), 284
Karimojong (Uganda), 31–2, 173
Kauwasi Maring, 184
Kazak, 15
kinship, 55, 57, 59, 61, 77, 169, 246, 248, 249, 257, 259, 263, 281, 283
  see also patrilineal descent, segmentary lineages
Kofyar (Nigeria), 58, 127, 189
Kohistanis (Pakistan), 82
Komonku-Siane (Papua New Guinea), 137, 152, 155
Kompiai (Papua New Guinea), 37, 38
Kuikuru (Brazil), 33, 37, 38, 43
!Kung San (Botswana), 11, 32, 33, 56, 88, 121, 126, 131, 133, 134, 139, 141, 142, 144, 162, 172, 259
Kwakiutl (Canada), 246, 254

Lamet (Vietnam), 43
Lamotrek atoll (Micronesia), 108, 127, 131, 133
Lapps, 33
learning, 237, 241, 264
limiting factors, 21, 24, 32, 44, 46–51, 101, 134, 183, 194
  see also carrying capacity
Lomatium, 216
Luts'un (China), 127, 131, 133

Maasai, 171, 286
Madura (Indonesia), 88
Mae-Enga (Papua New Guinea), 263
Majanger (Ethiopia), 18
Malaria, 14, 237, 264, 265

Malaya, 141
malnutrition, 170
Mambwe (Zambia), 37
Mandaya (Philippines), 263
maps, 13, 69
Mapuche (Chile), 33
Maring (New Guinea), 48, 158, 171, 184, 195
Marxism, 27, 49, 59–61, 91, 94, 246, 253, 260, 286
  and environmentalism, 3
  see also Marx
materialism, 1, 27, 49, 53, 94, 277, 279, 286
  cultural, 59–61, 73, 122, 260
  historical, 24
Maya (Yucatan), 26, 40
Mbuti (Zaïre), 33, 88
measurement, 69
Meru (Kenya), 46
Mesoamerica, 83
Mesolithic, European, 22, 33
Mesopotamia, 83
Metroxylon palm, 13, 16, 17, 18, 19, 20, 121, 132, 140, 145, 146, 147, 148, 150, 164, 165, 166, 167, 172, 180, 181, 189, 196–9, 200, 219, 221, 232
Mexico, 25, 138, 147, 149
micro-environment, concept of, 15, 50, 79–81, 83
minimum, law of, 34–5, 48
Miskito (Nicaragua), 33, 43, 79, 80–1, 84, 101, 127, 131, 133, 150, 151, 154, 156, 157, 158, 159, 162, 168, 173, 174, 217
Mistassini Cree (United States of America), 85
Miyanmin (Papua New Guinea), 108, 126, 131, 133, 139, 141, 142, 144, 146, 150, 171, 193
Moluccas, 189, 196–9, 200
Mongols, 1, 33, 171, 214
Montagnais (Canada), 54
Mru (Vietnam), 43
Mundurucu (Brazil), 54
mutualism, symbiotic, 75, 81–6

Nacamaki (Fiji), 127, 131, 133, 139, 142, 143
Nasaqalau (Fiji), 127, 131, 133, 139, 142, 143
Naskapi (Canada), 33, 193, 217
natural history, 1, 22, 66, 252
natural regions, concept of, 10, 14, 79
natural selection, 194, 239, 247, 263, 265, 273
nature, concept of, 4, 14–15, 277

Subject Index

Navaho (American southwest), 25
Nduimba (Papua New Guinea), 37, 38
Ndumba (Papua New Guinea), 216
Neolithic, 83, 149
Netherlands, the, 281
New Guinea, 22–3, 40, 46, 48, 72, 79,
   111, 114, 116, 132, 149, 152, 170,
   182, 184, 262, 270, 280, 284, 286
niche, concept of ecological, 13, 74,
   82–6, 173, 217, 283
Nigeria, 138, 217
nomadism, 82, 124
   see also pastoralism
Nuaulu (Seram, eastern Indonesia), 6,
   16, 17, 19, 38, 43, 46, 111, 121, 126,
   131, 133, 139, 141, 142, 143, 144,
   145, 146, 147, 148, 150, 151, 152,
   153, 154, 155, 159, 162, 163, 164,
   165, 167, 169, 170, 172, 173, 175,
   180–1, 210, 214, 219, 220, 221, 222,
   223, 225, 226, 230, 231, 232, 250
Nuer (Sudan), 30, 31, 58, 59, 126
nutrient flows, 36, 95–7, 98, 100–2,
   106–7, 134, 140, 141, 267
nutrition, xiii, 69, 102, 107, 110, 113,
   114, 115, 131, 159, 172, 173, 184,
   185, 253, 282, 283

Oaxaca (Mexico), 43
Occam's razor, 18
Ontong Java (Solomon Islands), 43, 127,
   131, 133, 139, 142, 143, 144, 150,
   151, 152
Oriomo (Papua New Guinea), 159, 163,
   164

Pakistan, 9
palaeoenvironments, 162
particularism, cultural and historical, 9,
   21, 24–30, 52, 53
pastoralism, 13–14, 15, 30, 31, 50, 58, 72,
   75, 125, 171, 175, 248, 262, 281, 286
   carnivorous, 75, 171
   milch, 75, 171
Pathans (Pakistan), 82
patrilineal descent, 55, 58, 59
patrilocal band, 55–7
Pawnee (United States of America), 33
photography, aerial, 13, 69
physiological modification, 236, 237, 241
Pleistocene megafauna, 22
political organization, 11, 40, 82, 83
Polynesia, 57
population, xiii, 14, 19, 25, 31, 40, 41,
   45, 52, 55, 56, 57, 91, 181, 182, 184,
   196, 267–71, 280, 281
   control, 123–4, 186, 192

fractions, 168–70
   see also carrying capacity
populations, as analytic units, 77–8
positivism, sociological, 3, 16
possibilism, xii, 21–51, 52, 53, 66, 69, 75,
   76, 94, 204, 281
potlatch, 190, 194, 246
pressure, barometric, 1, 32
primitivism, 39, 73
production
   ecological, 130, 255; *see also* energy
   economic, 62, 63, 130, 252
   relations of (technical and social), 62,
      83, 119, 128, 158, 196, 256
protein, 20, 40, 48, 56, 72, 84, 85, 100,
   101, 102, 132, 134, 135, 156, 158,
   168, 169, 172, 184, 193, 205, 214, 244
   deficiency of, 170
Pueblos, 25
Pul Eliya (Sri Lanka), 127
   see also Sri Lanka, Sinhalese
purposive behaviour, 192–3

Quechua (Peru), 108, 116, 119, 127, 131,
   132, 133, 139, 142, 144, 150, 238

racism, 26
Raiapu Enga (Papua New Guinea), 127,
   131, 133, 139, 142, 143, 144, 146, 150
rainfall, 1, 6, 11, 12, 16, 17, 19, 20, 25,
   26, 34, 69, 72, 154, 155, 225
rain forest, 17, 26, 33, 36, 40, 79, 80, 88,
   141, 166, 168
regulation, 91, 94, 177–203, 205, 227,
   272, 284
religion, 2, 61, 62, 118, 257
reproduction
   biological, 123, 124, 263
   ecological, 252–73, 285
   social, 123, 252–73, 285
rice, irrigated cultivation of, 15, 122,
   158, 159, 219, 220, 223
Ricinodendron, 56, 121, 162
ritual, 116, 182, 183, 184, 190, 191, 192,
   193, 226–9, 244, 257
   see also religion
romanticism, 26
Russia, 1, 3, 21

sago, *see Metroxylon* palm
Sahaptin (United States of America),
   216
scheduling, 223–6, 230, 231, 233, 235
Schistosomiasis, 23
scientism, 3
seasonality, 13, 31, 154, 155, 156, 158,
   159

segmentary lineages, 58–9, 281
shifting cultivation, *see* swidden
  cultivation
Shoshoni (United States of America), 56,
  57
Siberia, 15, 79
Sinhalese (Sri Lanka), 263
site-catchment analysis, 284
social anthropology, British, xiii, 26–7,
  28, 29, 30, 31, 69, 190
social formation, concept of, 10, 254,
  255, 277
soil, character and fertility of, 6, 7, 13,
  16, 17, 23, 26, 34, 36, 37, 42, 44, 46,
  47, 69, 70, 72, 76, 81, 101, 162, 210,
  211, 212, 214, 215, 217, 219, 220,
  230, 262, 274
spices, trade in, 189, 196–9, 200
Sri Lanka, 40, 159
Stalinism, 21
Subanan (Philippines), 224, 230
subincision, 11
subsistence
  change, 267–71
  concept of, 29
  description of, 170–6, 283
  modes and techniques, 128–30
  patterns, 13, 123–76, 257
succession, concept of, 67, 91
superorganic, concept of, 24, 27, 62, 64,
  65, 73, 281
surplus, 39, 40, 45, 48, 169, 254, 264,
  270, 278, 285
swidden cultivation, 6, 26, 30, 35–41, 50,
  70–2, 88, 101, 104–6, 122, 125, 129,
  134, 141, 148, 158, 159, 162, 167,
  170, 171, 172, 173, 189, 218, 220,
  221, 223, 224, 225, 271, 272
symbiosis, *see* mutualism
synecology, 93, 130
systems
  approaches, xiii, 28, 69, 186, 196,
    199–203, 204, 256, 277, 284, 286
  closure, 179–80, 185–6, 194, 224, 271
  definition of, 177–8
  ecological, *see* ecosystem
  open, 179, 192–3, 271–3, 276
  theory, xii, 68, 83, 177–8, 195, 199,
    201, 202, 284
  see also ecosystem

Tallensi (Ghana), 30
Tapirapé (Brazil), 238–9
Tasaday (Philippines), 33, 170

technology, 53, 56, 60, 62, 63, 136–7,
  147–50, 256, 267, 268, 269, 270
Tehuacan Valley (Mexico), 83
Tehuelche (Argentina), 33
temperature, 7, 12, 13, 32, 34, 98, 108,
  237, 238, 250, 262
Tenetehara (Brazil), 238–9
Tepozoztlan (Mexico), 127, 133
Thailand, northern, 38, 43
time-and-motion studies, 104, 111, 112,
  143
Tiv (Nigeria), 58
Tonga (Zambia)
  Gwembe, 142
  Valley, 284
Tongatapu (Tonga), 43
topography, 13, 15, 46, 47, 50, 66, 124,
  164, 211, 218–23, 230
totems, 215
trade, *see* exchange
transhumance, 13, 31, 82
transition, concept of, 265–7
Trinidad, 63
Trypanosomiasis, 50, 72, 265
Tsembaga (Papua New Guinea), 38, 43,
  102, 104–6, 111, 112, 115–16, 126,
  131, 133, 138, 139, 141, 142, 143,
  144, 146, 147, 149, 150, 182, 183–5,
  186, 190, 191, 192, 193, 210, 226–9, 240
tsetse fly, 13, 50
Tuareg (Sahara), 32, 33
Tungus (Soviet Union), 33
Turkana (Kenya, northern Uganda),
  31–2
Tzeltal (Mexico), 211

ungulates, 18–19, 83, 196
United Kingdom, *see* Britain
Ute (United States of America), 56
utopianism, ecological, 93, 218

value 234, 252–4, 278
Virgin Islands, 217

warfare, 58, 182, 184, 193, 257
wind movement, 2, 5, 7, 12, 32, 155,
  213, 262

Xavante (Brazil), 285

Yaruro (Venezuela), 43, 126, 133

Zebu cattle, 13
Zonocerus, 217